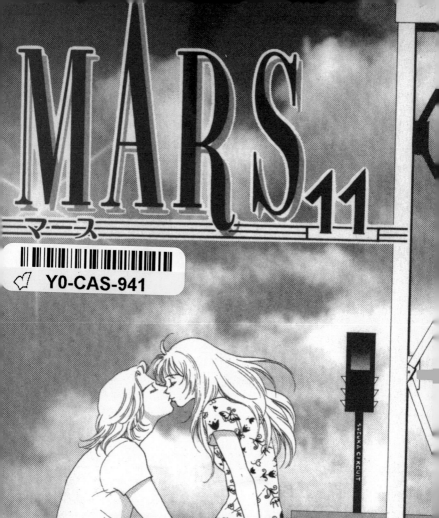

MARS

マース

11

namco

SUZUKA CIRCUIT

惣領冬実

ALSO AVAILABLE FROM TOKYOPOP®

Volume 11
By Fuyumi Soryo

LOS ANGELES • TOKYO • LONDON

Translator - Shirley Kubo
English Adaptation - Elizabeth Hurchalla
Contributing Editor - Jodi Bryson
Retouch and Lettering - Sean Chang
Cover Layout - Anna Kernbaum

Editor - Julie Taylor
Managing Editor - Jill Freshney
Production Coordinator - Antonio DePietro
Production Manager - Jennifer Miller
Art Director - Matthew Alford
Director of Editorial - Jeremy Ross
VP of Production & Manufacturing - Ron Klamert
President & C.O.O. - John Parker
Publisher & C.E.O. - Stuart Levy

Email: editor@TOKYOPOP.com
Come visit us online at www.TOKYOPOP.com

A **TOKYOPOP** Manga
TOKYOPOP® is an imprint of Mixx Entertainment, Inc.
5900 Wilshire Blvd. Suite 2000, Los Angeles, CA 90036

ISBN: 1-59182-130-4

First TOKYOPOP® printing: June 2003

10 9 8 7 6 5 4 3 2 1
Printed in the USA

MARS

LEGEND OF MARS
レジェンド　オブ　マース

THE STORY UNTIL NOW:

KIRA FALLS FOR REI WHEN SHE SEES HIM KISSING A STATUE OF MARS IN THE ART STUDIO, AND SOON THEY START GOING OUT. BUT WHEN KIRA AND HER MOM MOVE BACK IN WITH THE MAN WHO RAPED HER DURING JUNIOR HIGH, REI AND KIRA'S RELATIONSHIP IS TORN APART. HOWEVER, THEY SOON FIND THEY CAN'T STAY AWAY FROM EACH OTHER AND GET BACK TOGETHER. WHEN KIRA'S STEP-FATHER STARTS GRILLING HER ABOUT HER RELATIONSHIP WITH REI, SHE HAS FLASHBACKS OF HER HORRIBLE PAST AND FEELS SUCH HATRED TOWARD HER STEPFATHER THAT SHE ENDS UP SERIOUSLY INJURING HIM. AFTERWARD, SHE MOVES IN WITH REI AND DECIDES TO OFFER ALL OF HERSELF TO HIM. MEANWHILE, REI RESOLVES TO PROTECT KIRA AND ASKS HER TO MARRY HIM. HE DROPS OUT OF SCHOOL AND TRIES TO BECOME A PRO MOTORCYCLE RACER...

REI KASHINO:
A HIGH SCHOOL STU-DENT WHO RACES MOTORCYCLES AND IS ENGAGED TO KIRA. HIS TWIN BROTHER SEI IS DEAD.

KIRA'S STEPFATHER:
THE MAN WHO RAPED KIRA AND IS MARRIED TO KIRA'S MOTHER.

KIRA ASO:
REI'S GIRLFRIEND. SHE JUST MOVED IN WITH REI AND THEY'VE DECIDED TO GET MARRIED. SHE WAS RAPED BY HER STEP-FATHER DURING JUNIOR HIGH.

HARUMI SUGIHARA:
KIRA'S BEST FRIEND. SHE AND KIRA WORK TOGETHER.

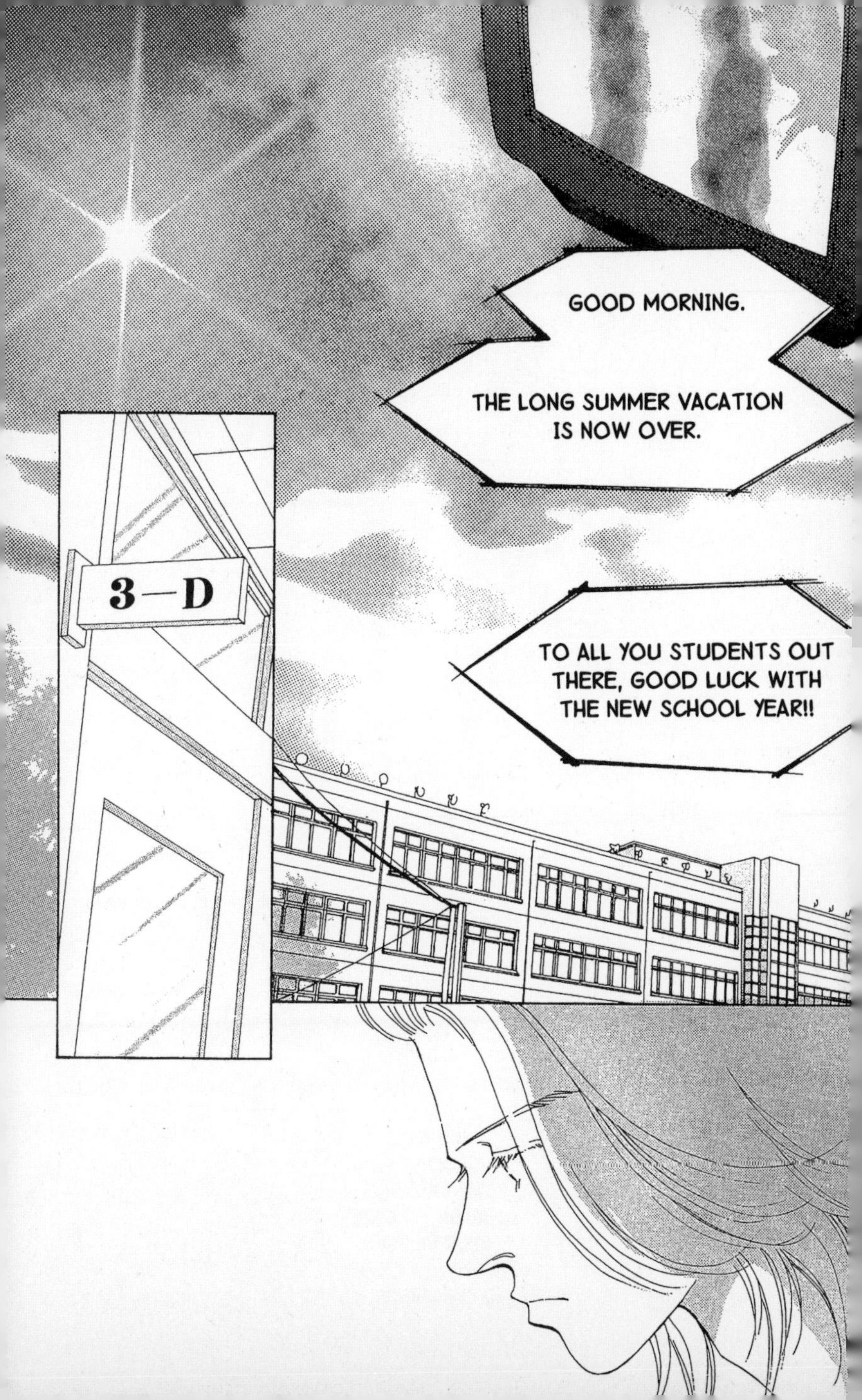
GOOD MORNING.
THE LONG SUMMER VACATION IS NOW OVER.
3—D
TO ALL YOU STUDENTS OUT THERE, GOOD LUCK WITH THE NEW SCHOOL YEAR!!

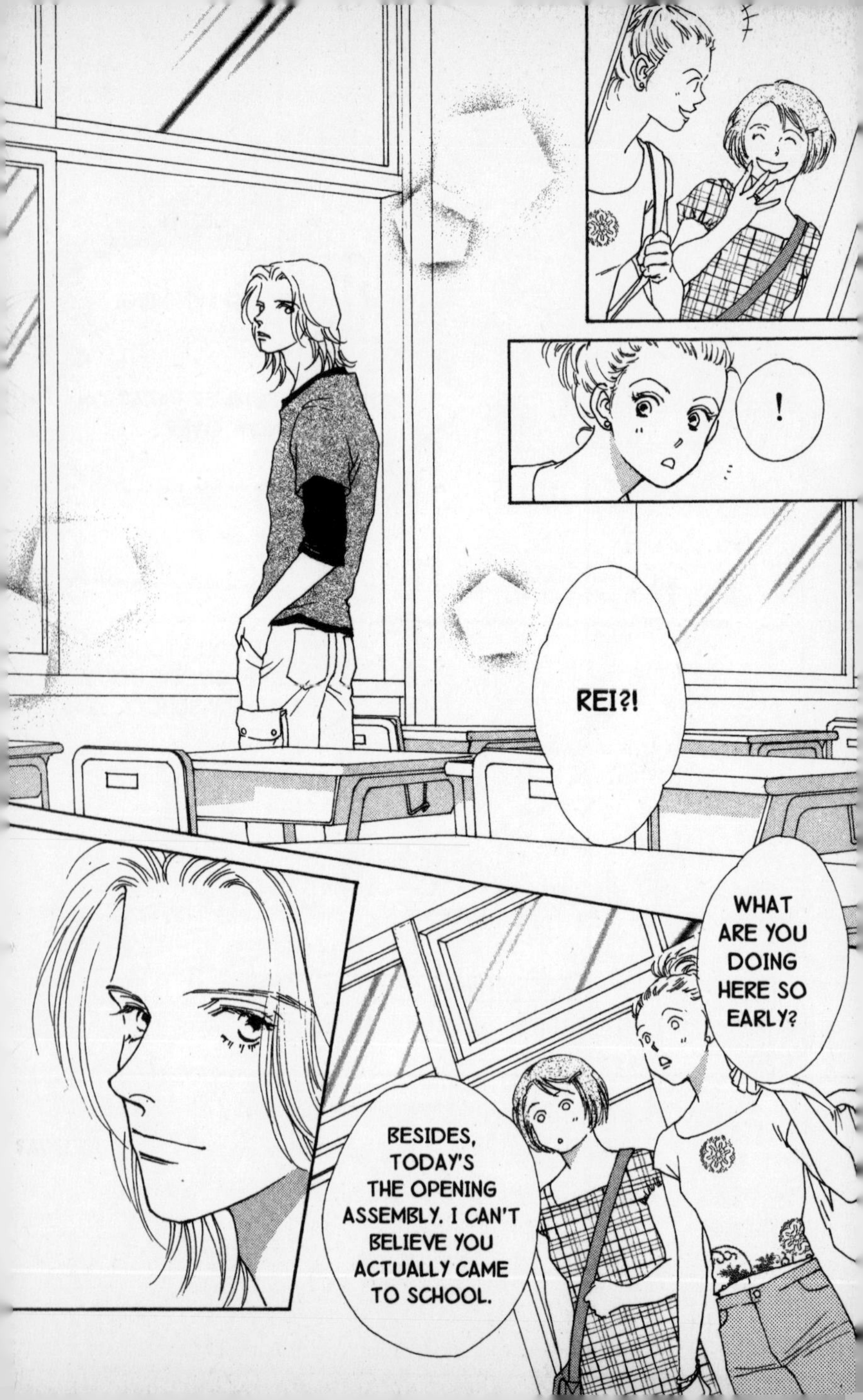
!
REI?!
WHAT ARE YOU DOING HERE SO EARLY?
BESIDES, TODAY'S THE OPENING ASSEMBLY. I CAN'T BELIEVE YOU ACTUALLY CAME TO SCHOOL.

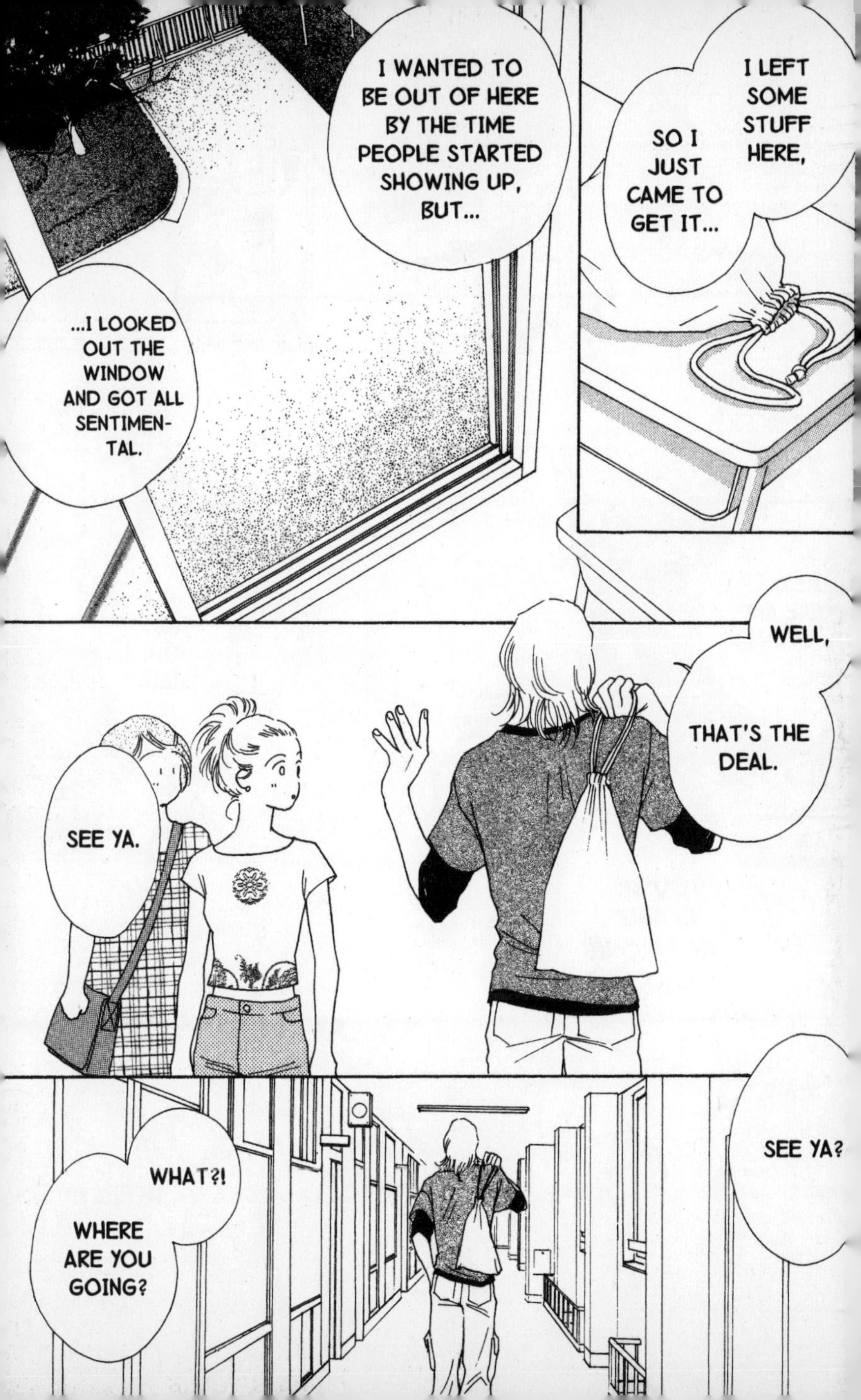
I LEFT SOME STUFF HERE,
SO I JUST CAME TO GET IT...
I WANTED TO BE OUT OF HERE BY THE TIME PEOPLE STARTED SHOWING UP, BUT...
...I LOOKED OUT THE WINDOW AND GOT ALL SENTIMEN-TAL.
WELL,
THAT'S THE DEAL.
SEE YA.
SEE YA?
WHAT?!
WHERE ARE YOU GOING?

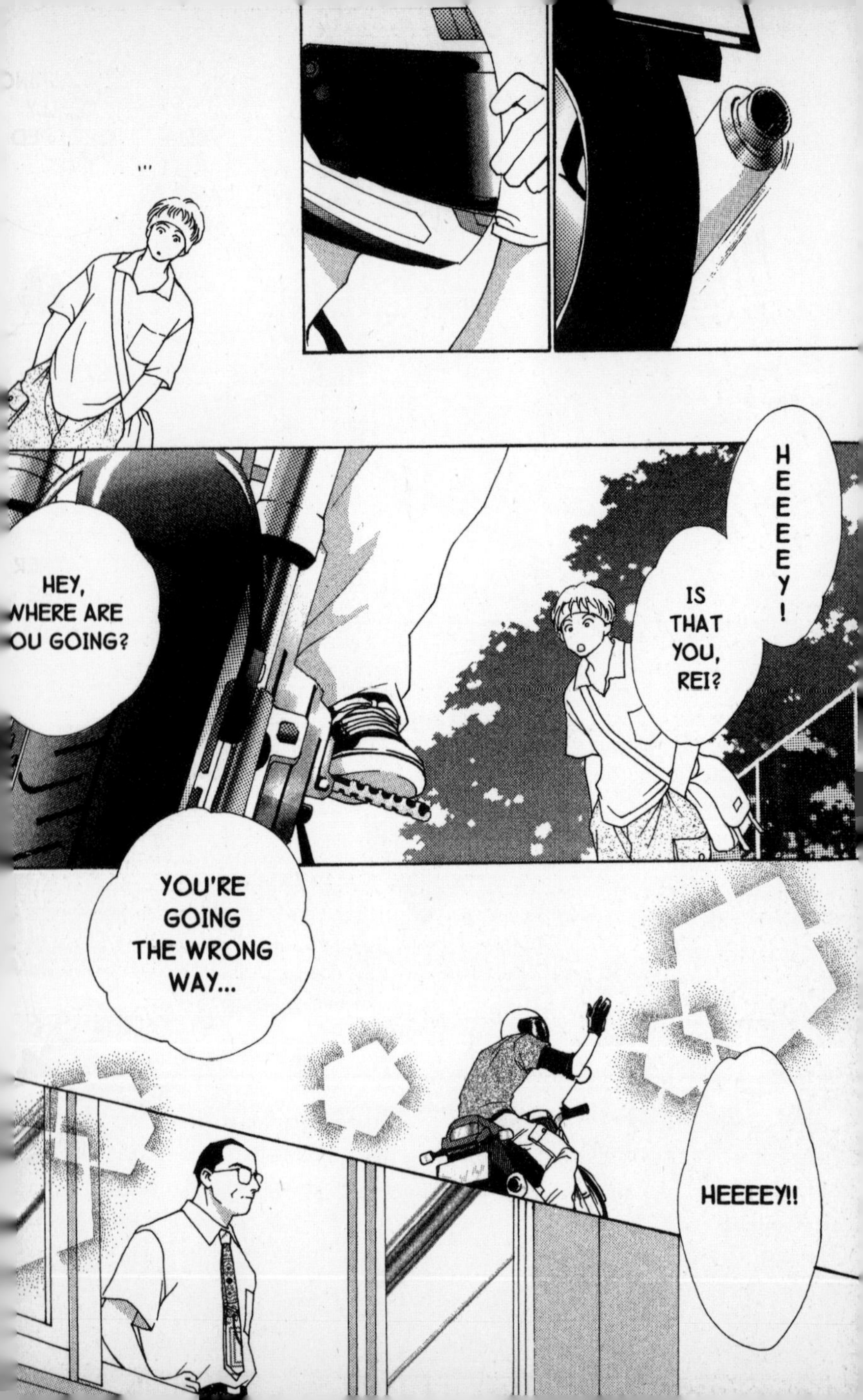
...
HEEEEY!
IS THAT YOU, REI?
HEY, WHERE ARE OU GOING?
HEEEEY!!
YOU'RE GOING THE WRONG WAY...

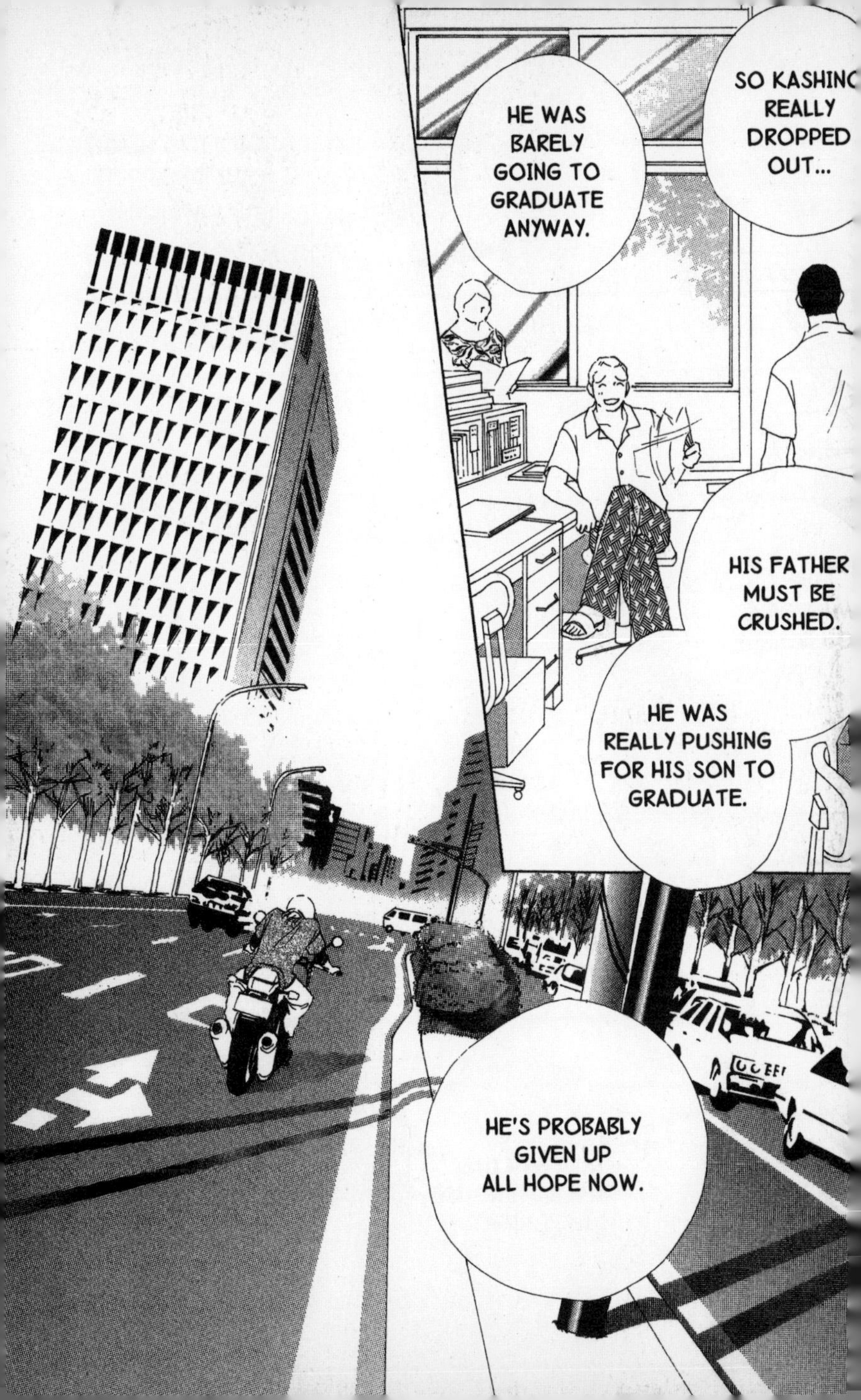
SO KASHING REALLY DROPPED OUT...
HE WAS BARELY GOING TO GRADUATE ANYWAY.
HIS FATHER MUST BE CRUSHED.
HE WAS REALLY PUSHING FOR HIS SON TO GRADUATE.
HE'S PROBABLY GIVEN UP ALL HOPE NOW.

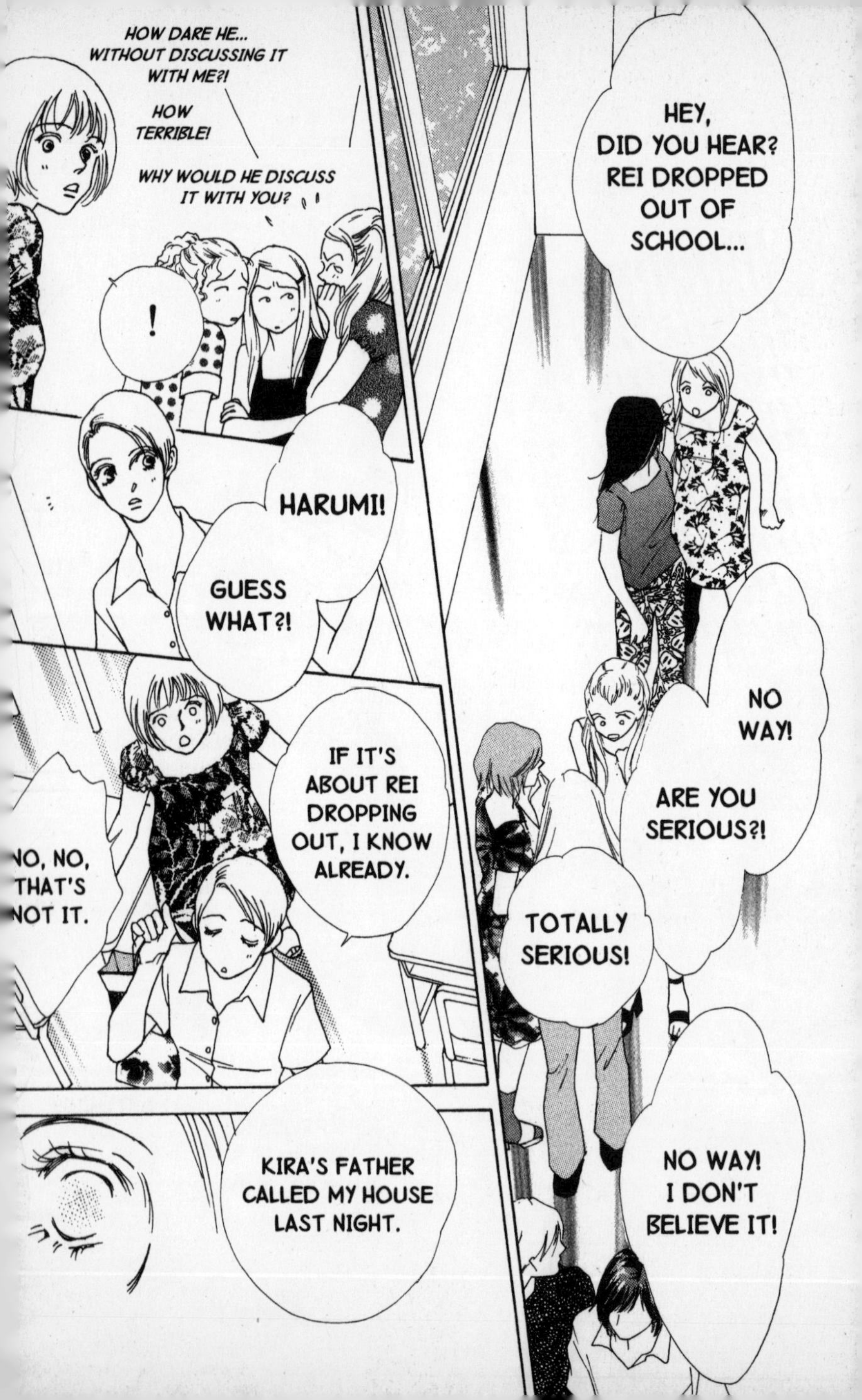
HEY, DID YOU HEAR? REI DROPPED OUT OF SCHOOL...
NO WAY!
ARE YOU SERIOUS?!
TOTALLY SERIOUS!
NO WAY! I DON'T BELIEVE IT!
HOW DARE HE... WITHOUT DISCUSSING IT WITH ME?!
HOW TERRIBLE!
WHY WOULD HE DISCUSS IT WITH YOU?
!
HARUMI!
GUESS WHAT?!
IF IT'S ABOUT REI DROPPING OUT, I KNOW ALREADY.
NO, NO, THAT'S NOT IT.
KIRA'S FATHER CALLED MY HOUSE LAST NIGHT.

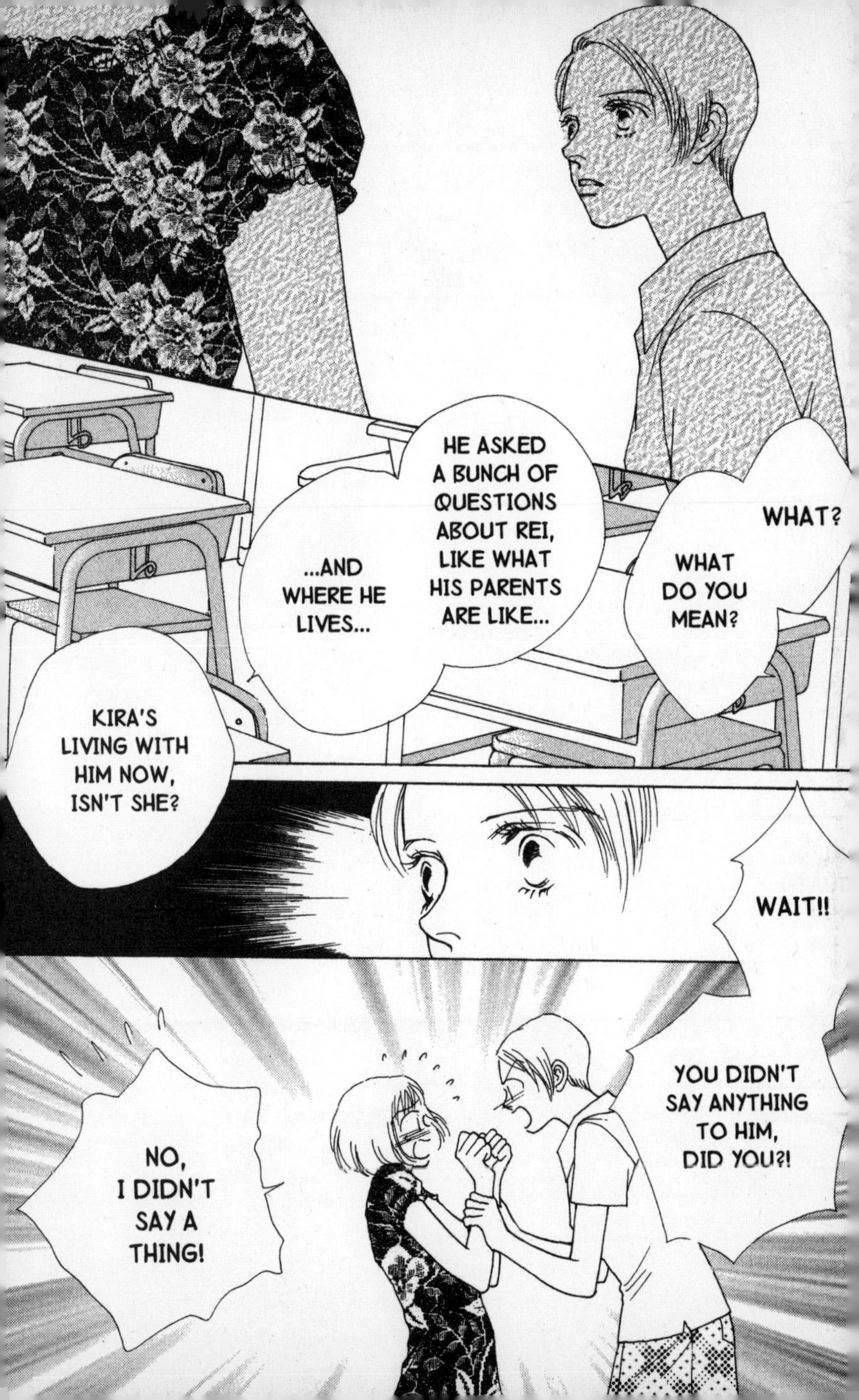
WHAT?
WHAT DO YOU MEAN?
HE ASKED A BUNCH OF QUESTIONS ABOUT REI, LIKE WHAT HIS PARENTS ARE LIKE...
...AND WHERE HE LIVES...
KIRA'S LIVING WITH HIM NOW, ISN'T SHE?
WAIT!!
YOU DIDN'T SAY ANYTHING TO HIM, DID YOU?!
NO, I DIDN'T SAY A THING!

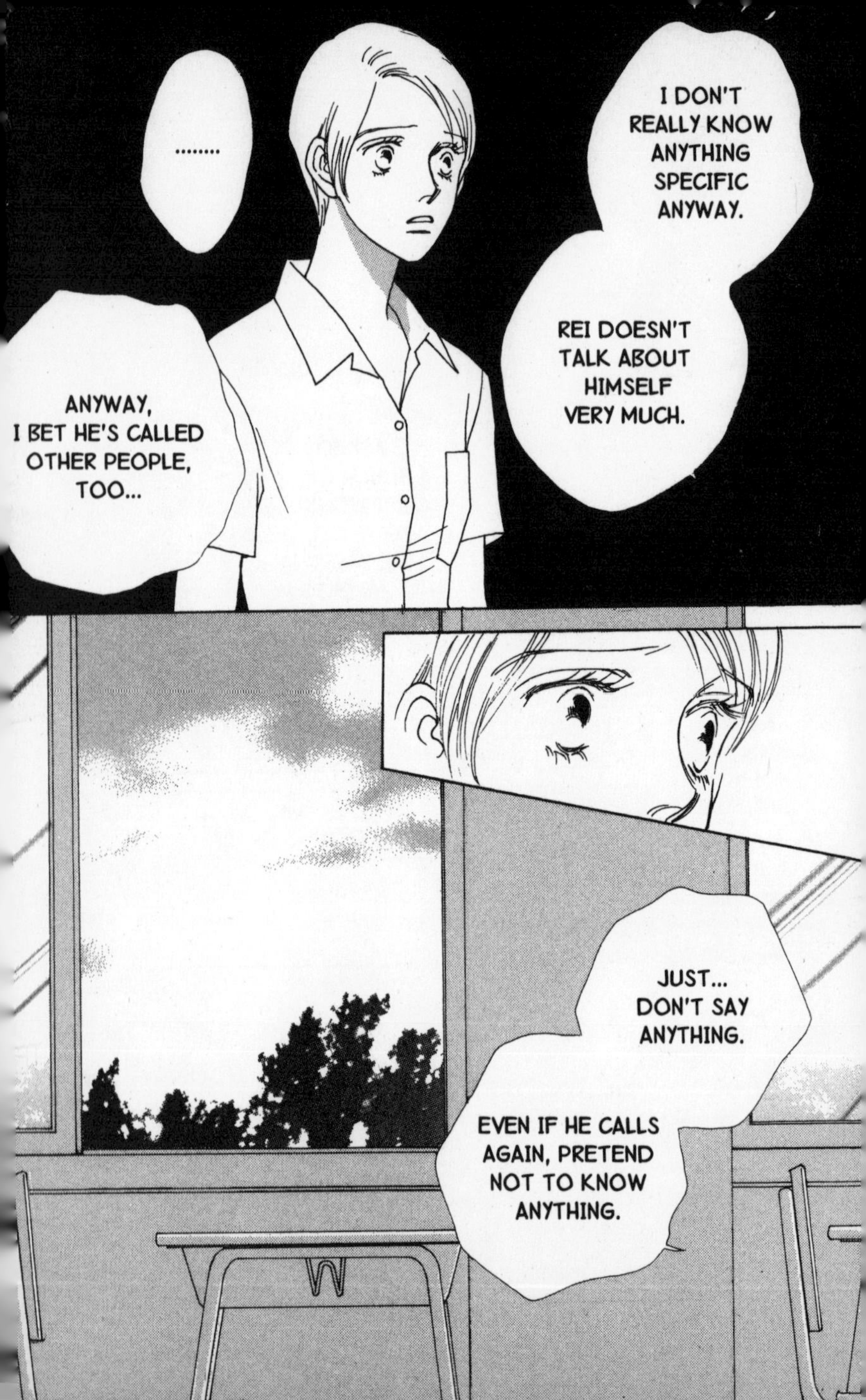
I DON'T REALLY KNOW ANYTHING SPECIFIC ANYWAY.
REI DOESN'T TALK ABOUT HIMSELF VERY MUCH.
....
ANYWAY, I BET HE'S CALLED OTHER PEOPLE, TOO...
JUST... DON'T SAY ANYTHING.
EVEN IF HE CALLS AGAIN, PRETEND NOT TO KNOW ANYTHING.

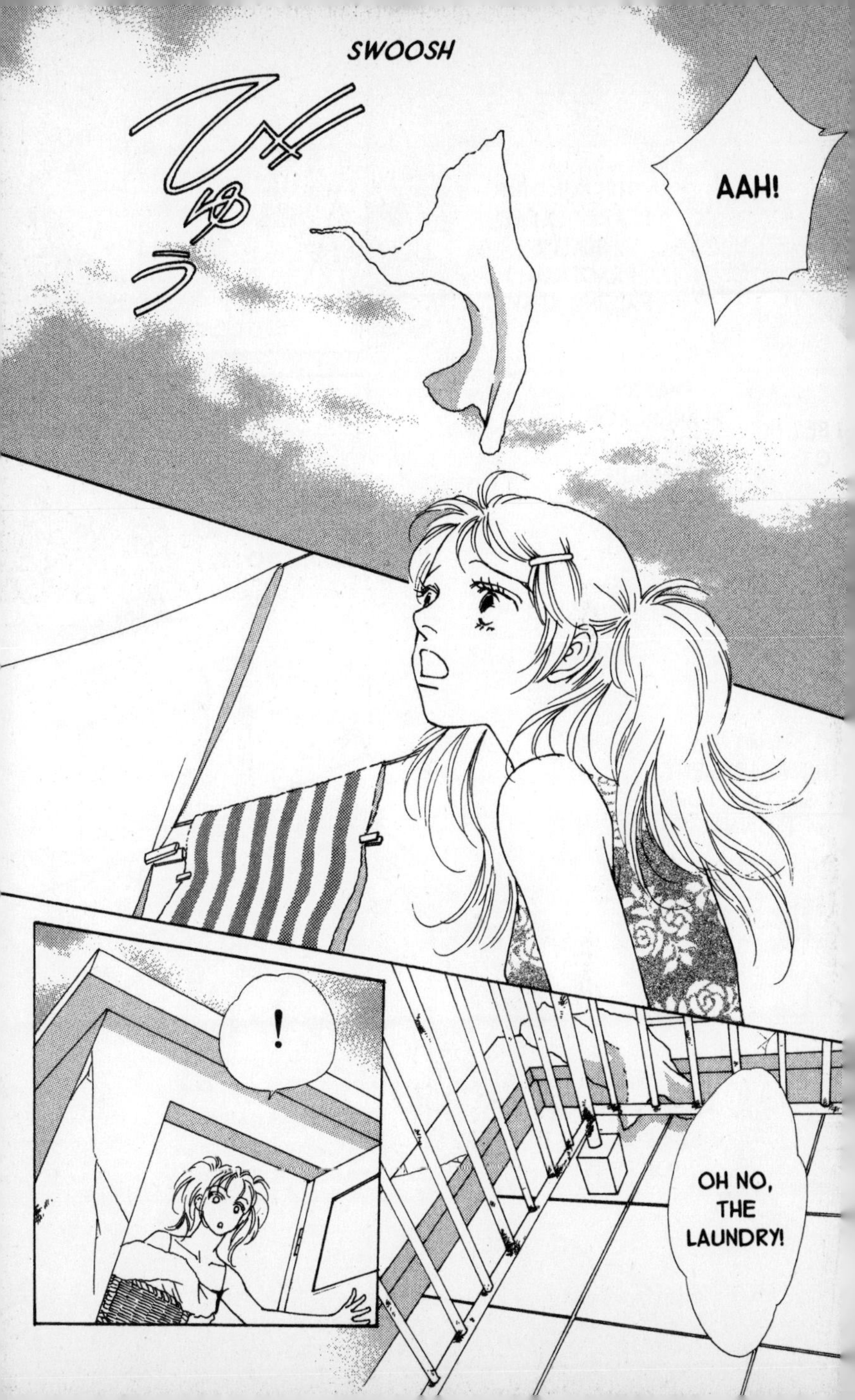
SWOOSH
ひゅう
AAH!
OH NO, THE LAUNDRY!
!

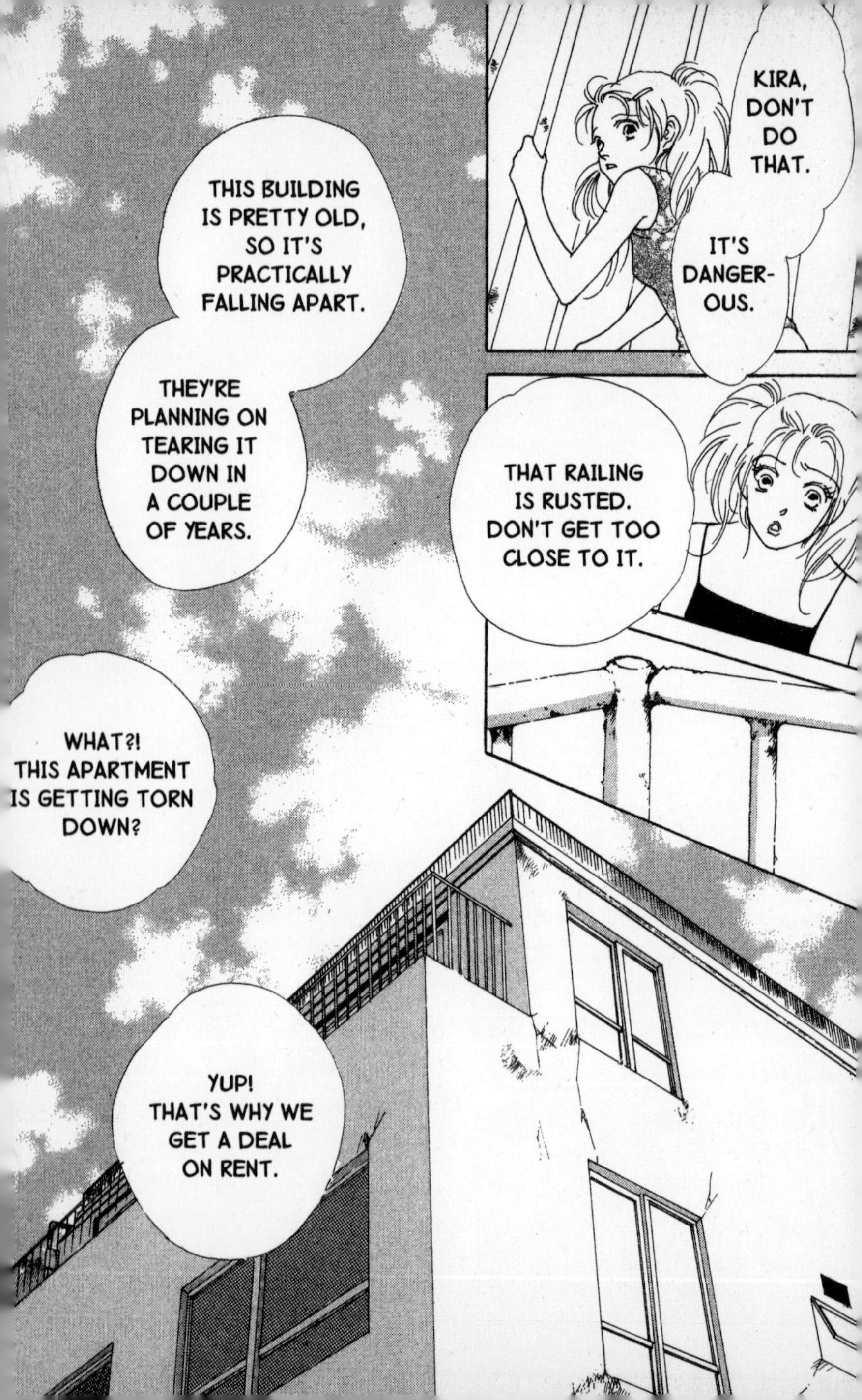
KIRA, DON'T DO THAT.
IT'S DANGER-OUS.
THAT RAILING IS RUSTED. DON'T GET TOO CLOSE TO IT.
THIS BUILDING IS PRETTY OLD, SO IT'S PRACTICALLY FALLING APART.
THEY'RE PLANNING ON TEARING IT DOWN IN A COUPLE OF YEARS.
WHAT?! THIS APARTMENT IS GETTING TORN DOWN?
YUP! THAT'S WHY WE GET A DEAL ON RENT.

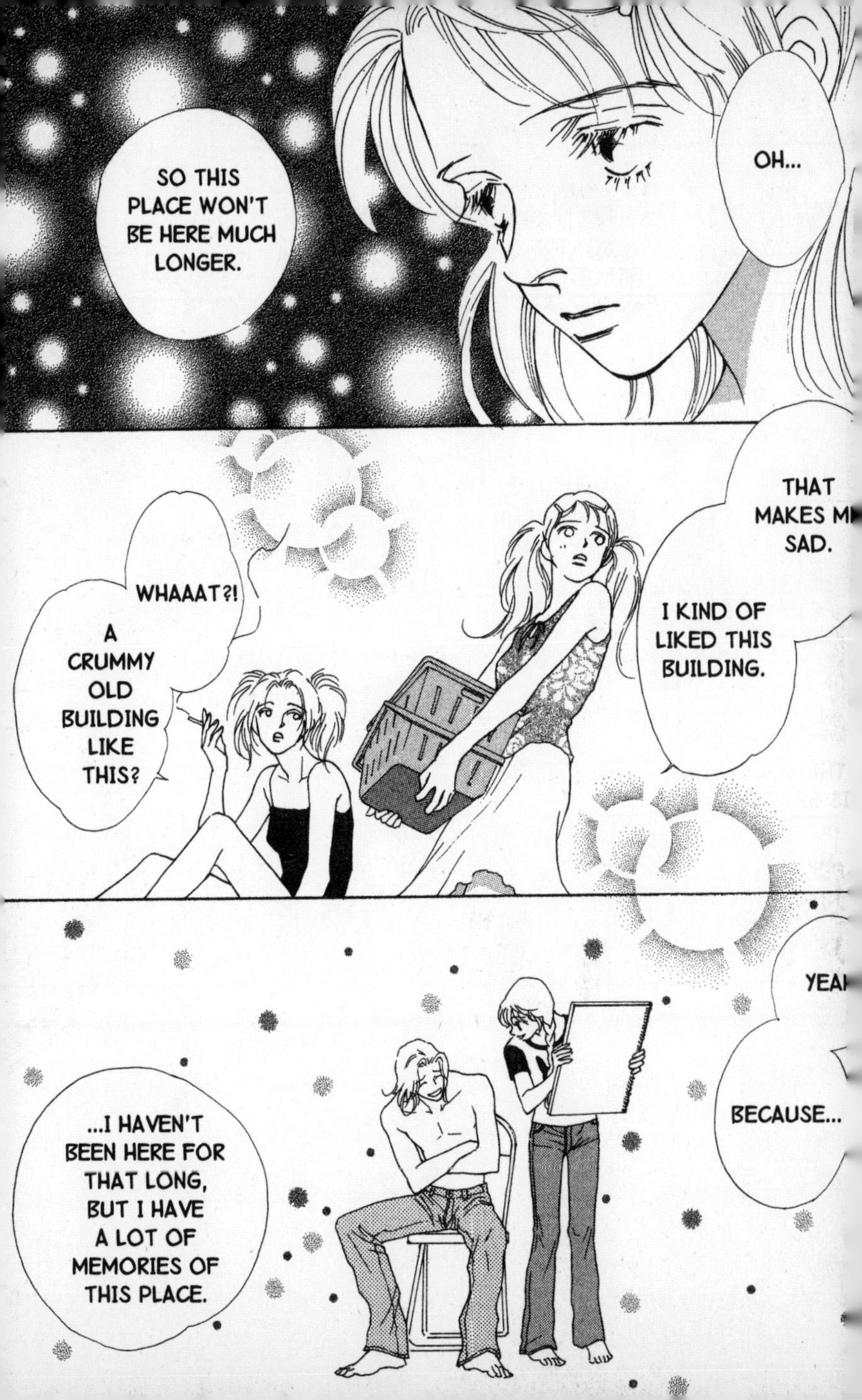
OH...
SO THIS PLACE WON'T BE HERE MUCH LONGER.
THAT MAKES M SAD.
I KIND OF LIKED THIS BUILDING.
WHAAAT?!
A CRUMMY OLD BUILDING LIKE THIS?
YEA
BECAUSE...
...I HAVEN'T BEEN HERE FOR THAT LONG, BUT I HAVE A LOT OF MEMORIES OF THIS PLACE.

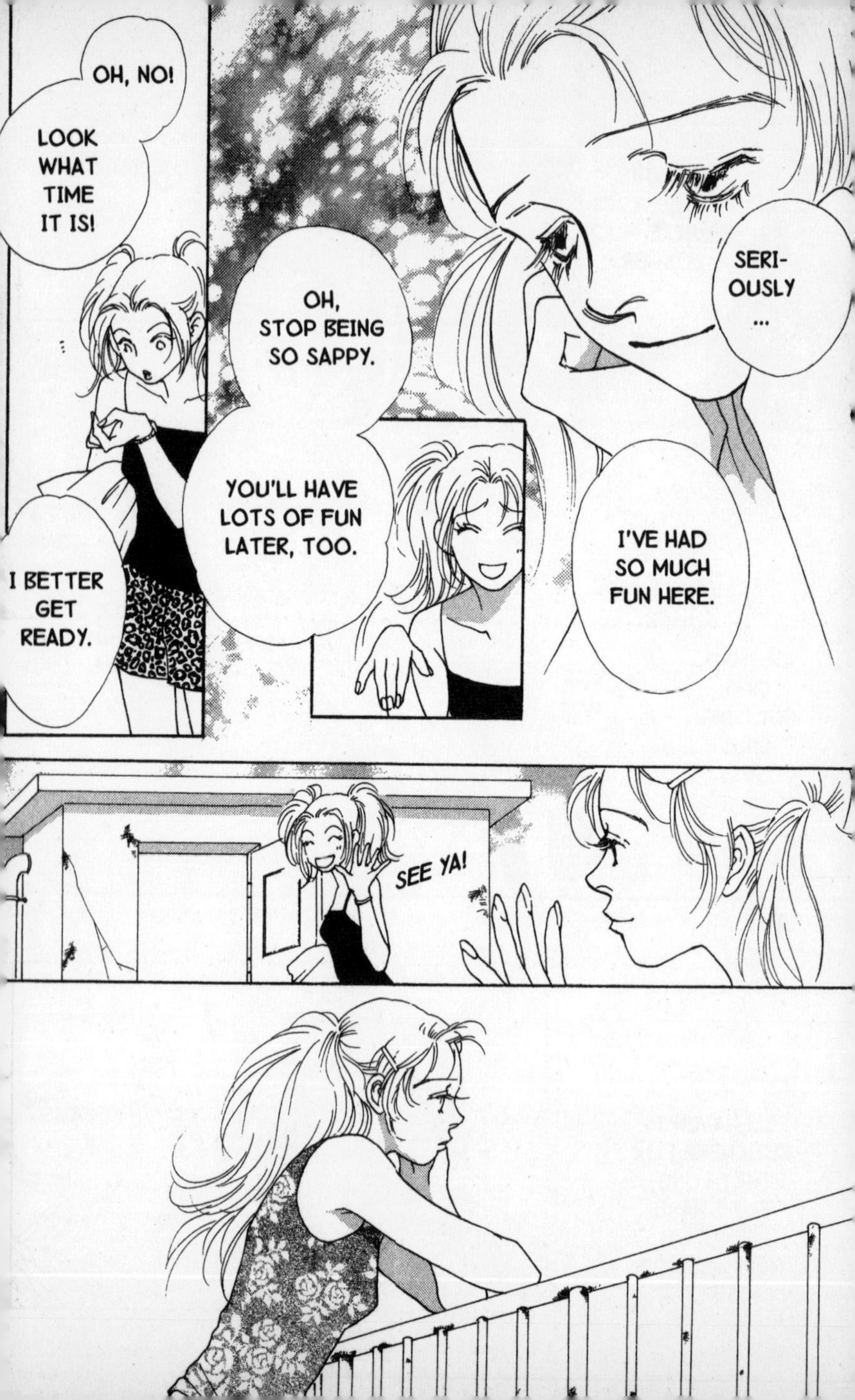
SERI-OUSLY...
I'VE HAD SO MUCH FUN HERE.
OH, STOP BEING SO SAPPY.
YOU'LL HAVE LOTS OF FUN LATER, TOO.
OH, NO!
LOOK WHAT TIME IT IS!
I BETTER GET READY.
SEE YA!

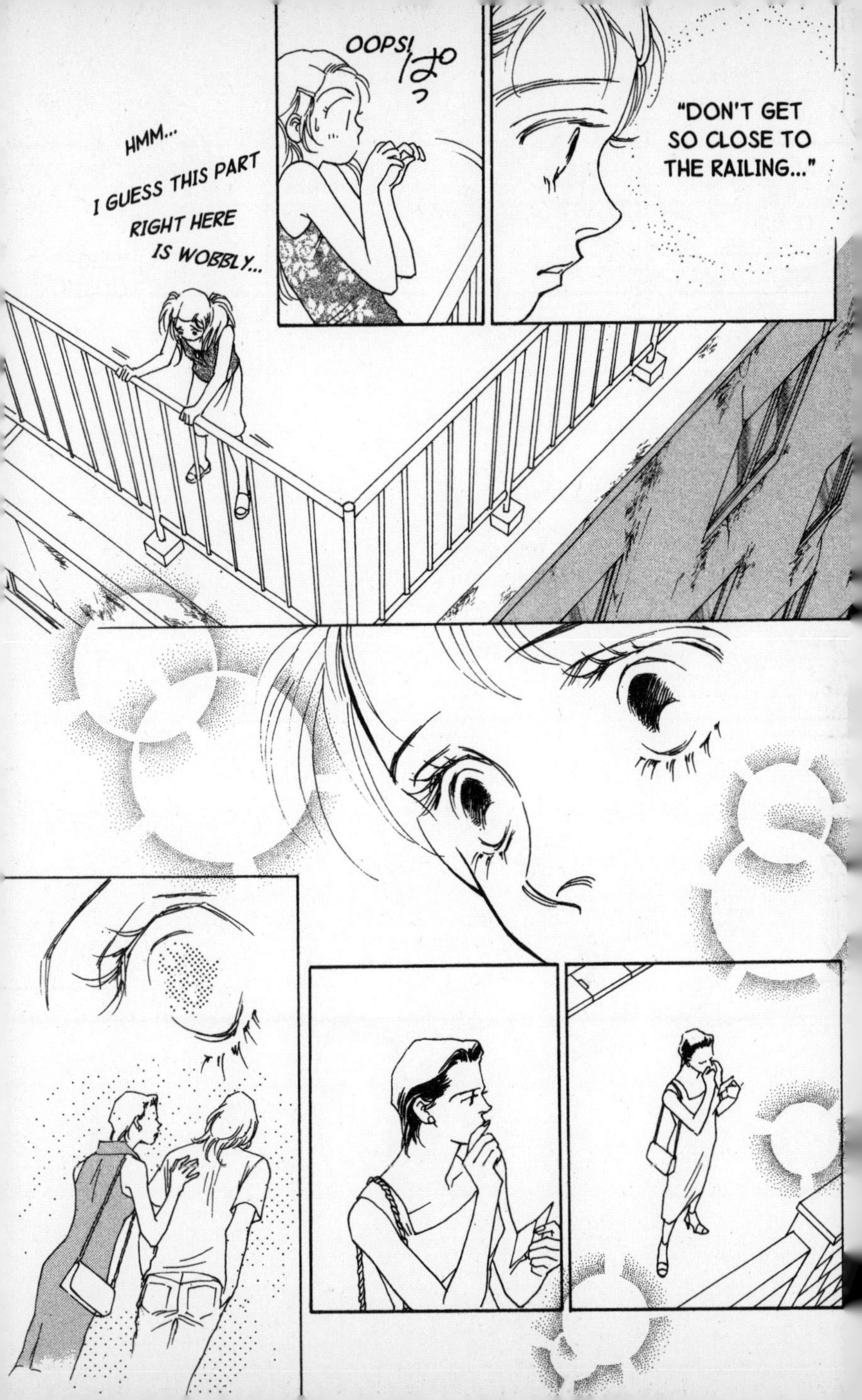
"DON'T GET SO CLOSE TO THE RAILING..."
OOPS!
ぱっ
HMM... I GUESS THIS PART RIGHT HERE IS WOBBLY...

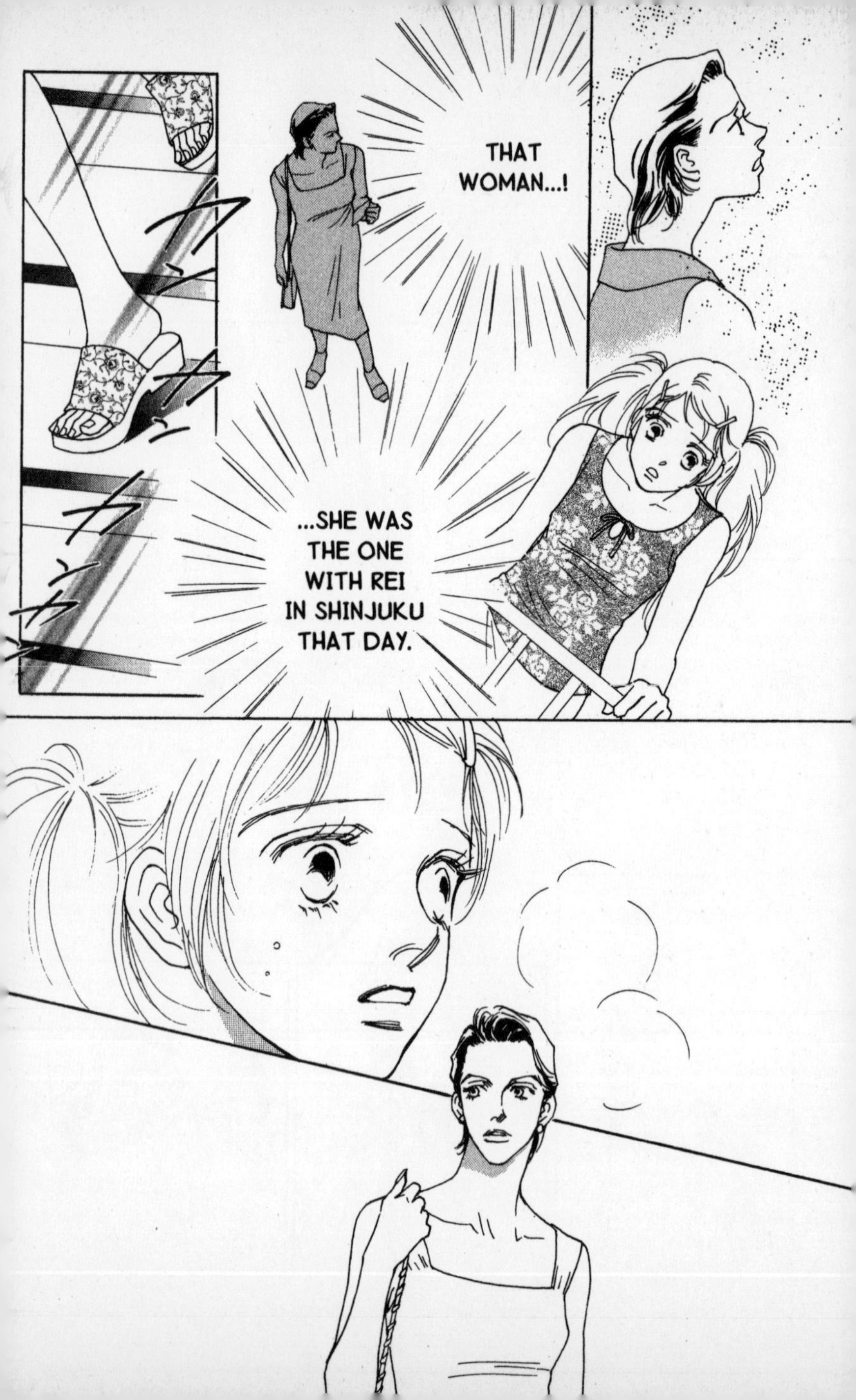
THAT WOMAN...!
...SHE WAS THE ONE WITH REI IN SHINJUKU THAT DAY.

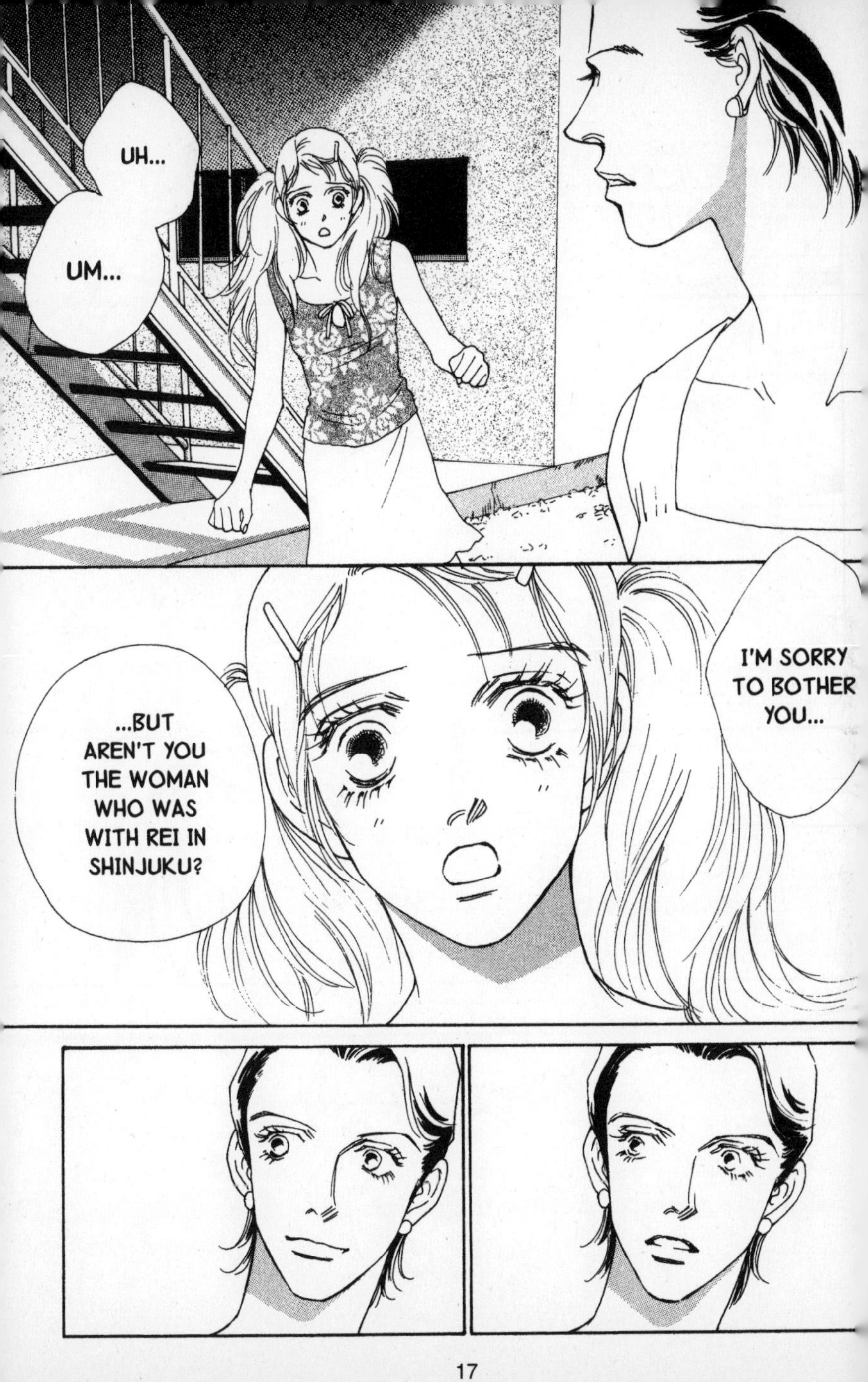
UH...
UM...
I'M SORRY TO BOTHER YOU...
...BUT AREN'T YOU THE WOMAN WHO WAS WITH REI IN SHINJUKU?

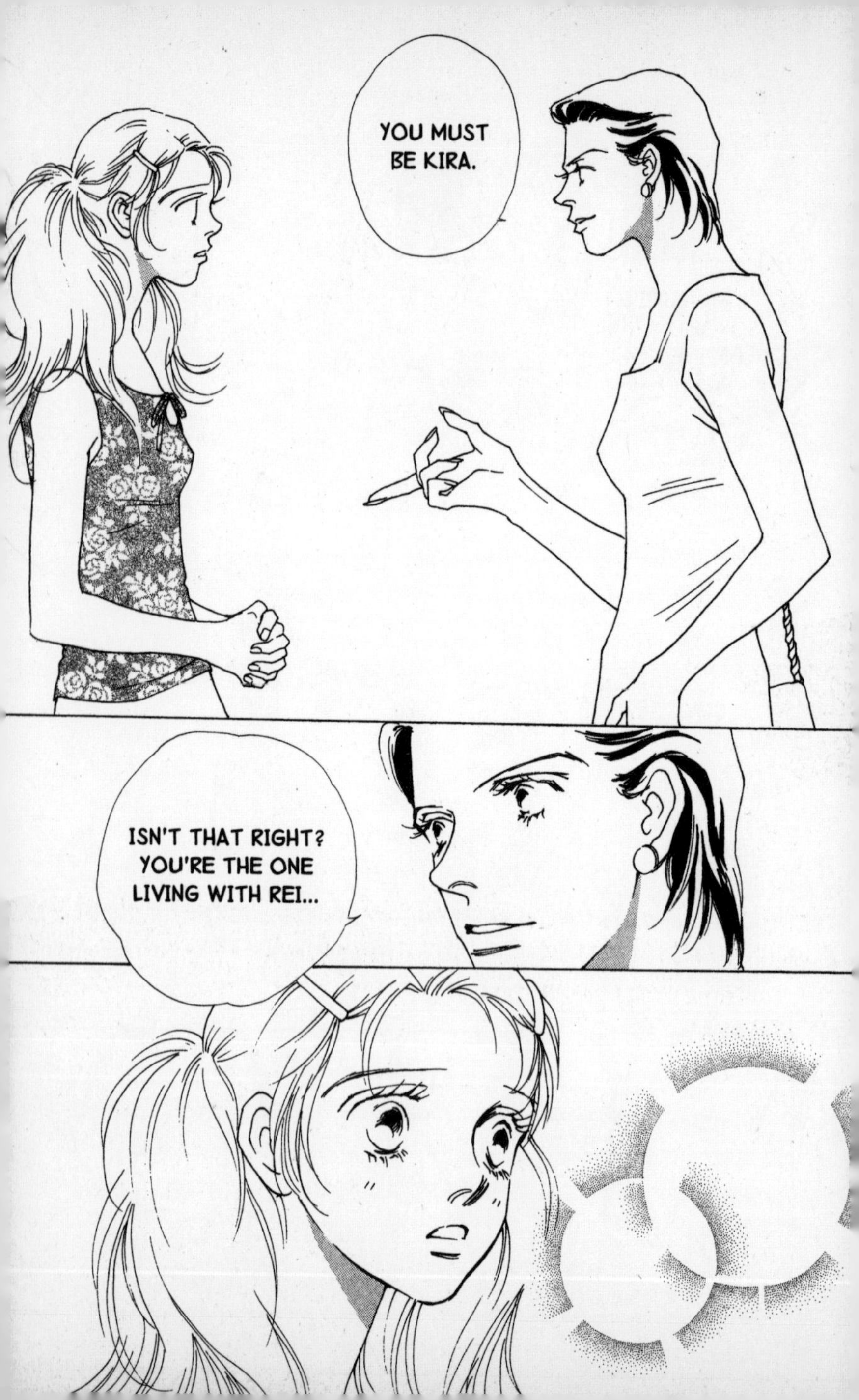
YOU MUST BE KIRA.
ISN'T THAT RIGHT? YOU'RE THE ONE LIVING WITH REI...

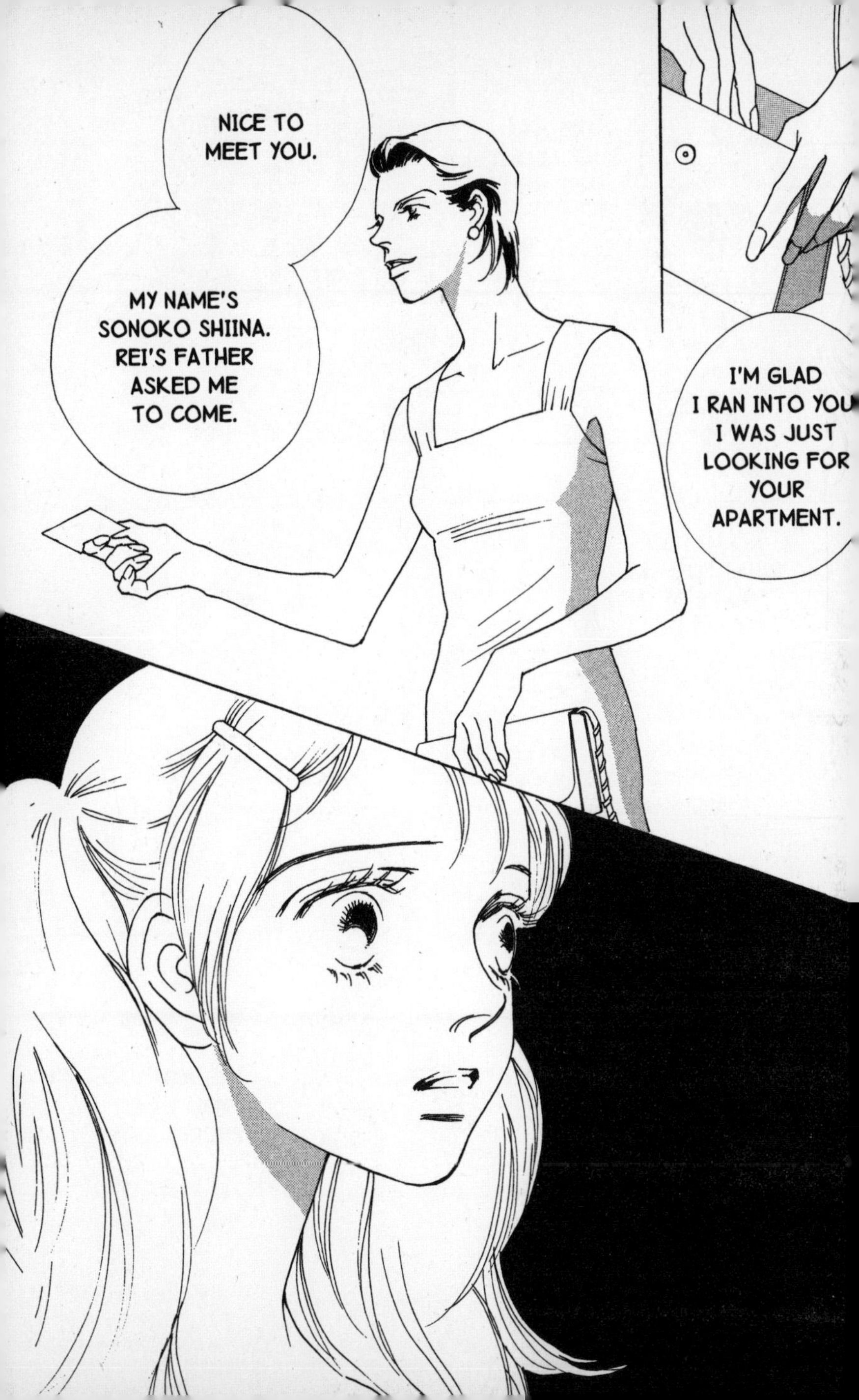
I'M GLAD I RAN INTO YOU I WAS JUST LOOKING FOR YOUR APARTMENT.
NICE TO MEET YOU.
MY NAME'S SONOKO SHIINA. REI'S FATHER ASKED ME TO COME.

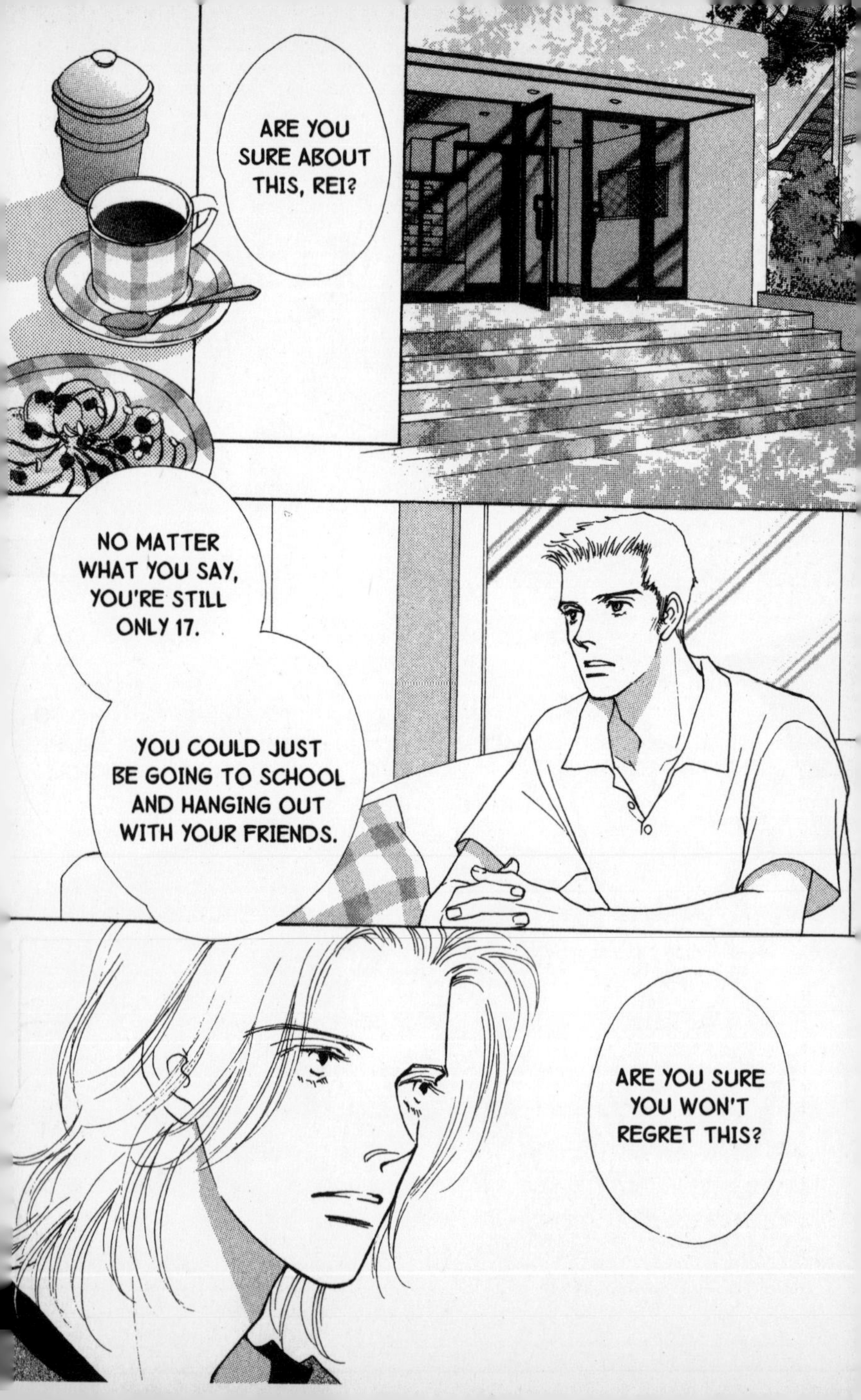
ARE YOU SURE ABOUT THIS, REI?
NO MATTER WHAT YOU SAY, YOU'RE STILL ONLY 17.
YOU COULD JUST BE GOING TO SCHOOL AND HANGING OUT WITH YOUR FRIENDS.
ARE YOU SURE YOU WON'T REGRET THIS?

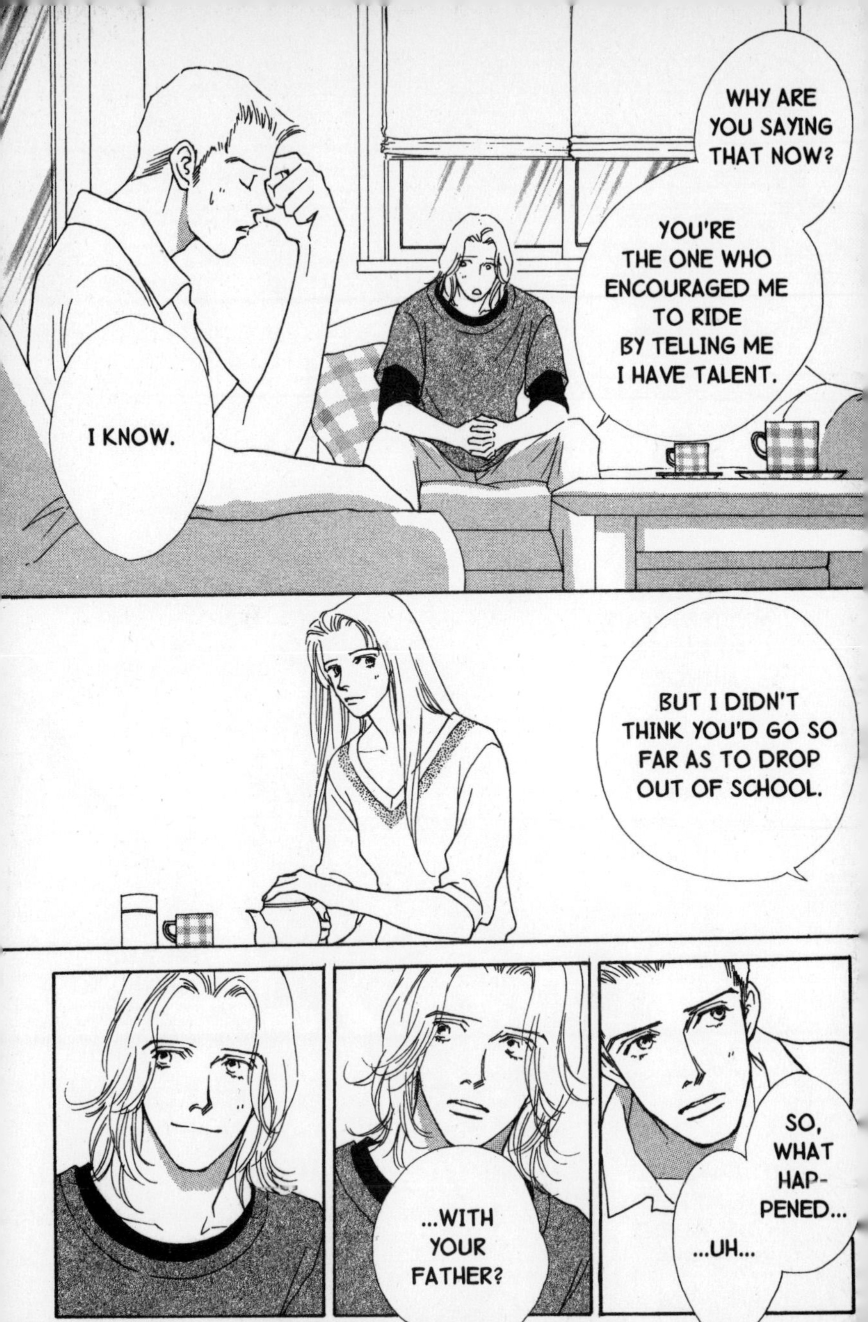
WHY ARE YOU SAYING THAT NOW?
YOU'RE THE ONE WHO ENCOURAGED ME TO RIDE BY TELLING ME I HAVE TALENT.
I KNOW.
BUT I DIDN'T THINK YOU'D GO SO FAR AS TO DROP OUT OF SCHOOL.
SO, WHAT HAP-PENED...
...UH...
...WITH YOUR FATHER?

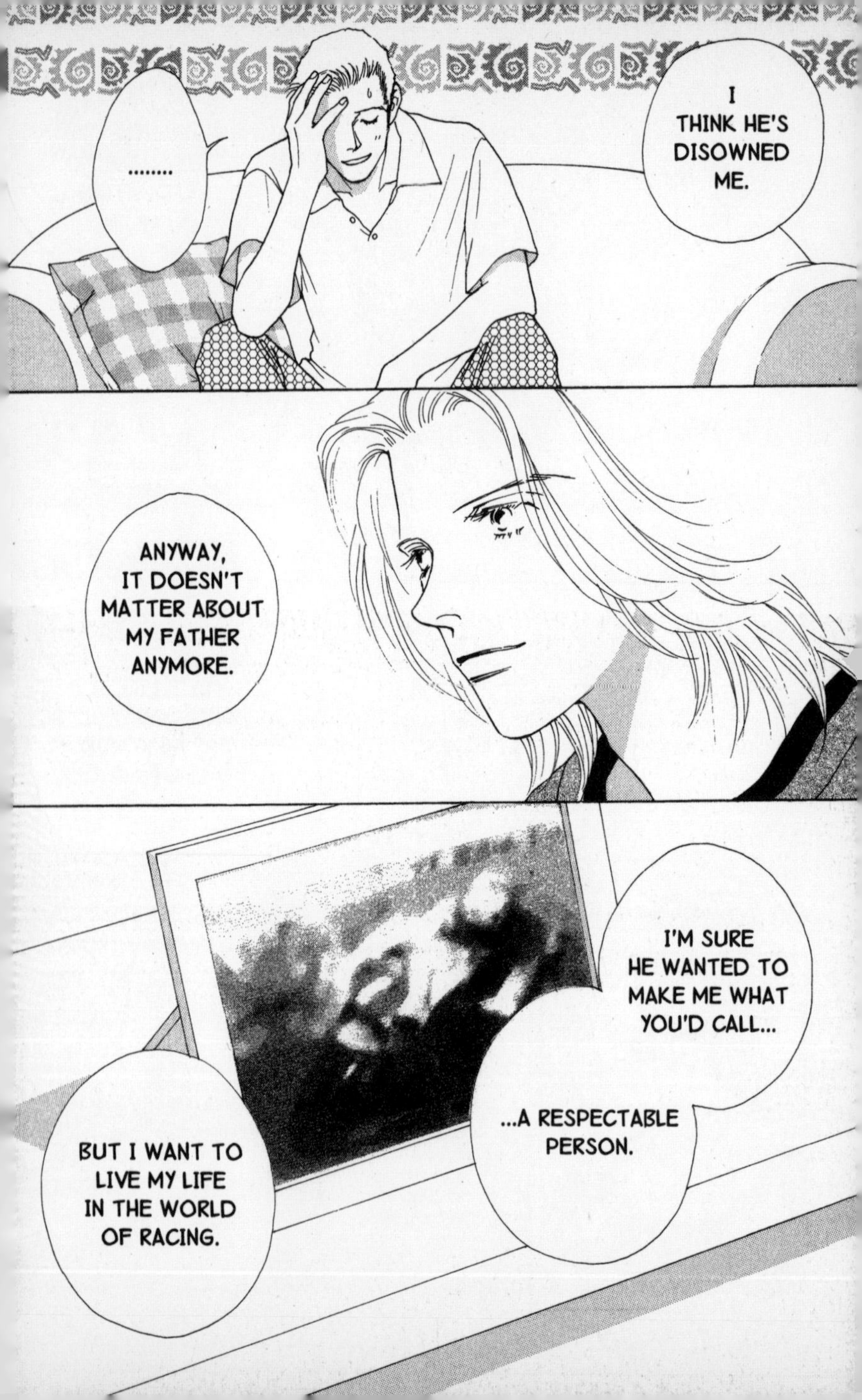
I THINK HE'S DISOWNED ME.
....
ANYWAY, IT DOESN'T MATTER ABOUT MY FATHER ANYMORE.
I'M SURE HE WANTED TO MAKE ME WHAT YOU'D CALL...
...A RESPECTABLE PERSON.
BUT I WANT TO LIVE MY LIFE IN THE WORLD OF RACING.

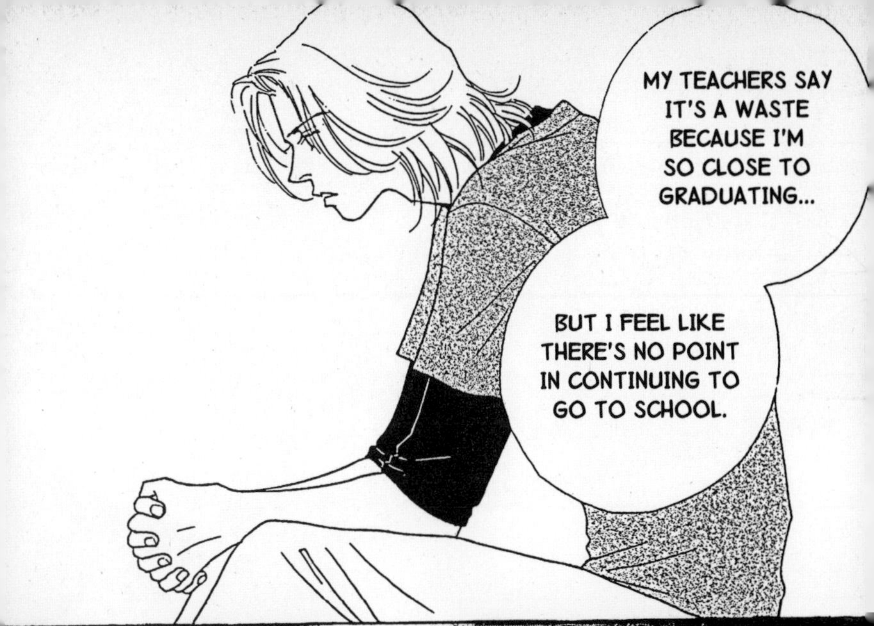
MY TEACHERS SAY IT'S A WASTE BECAUSE I'M SO CLOSE TO GRADUATING...
BUT I FEEL LIKE THERE'S NO POINT IN CONTINUING TO GO TO SCHOOL.
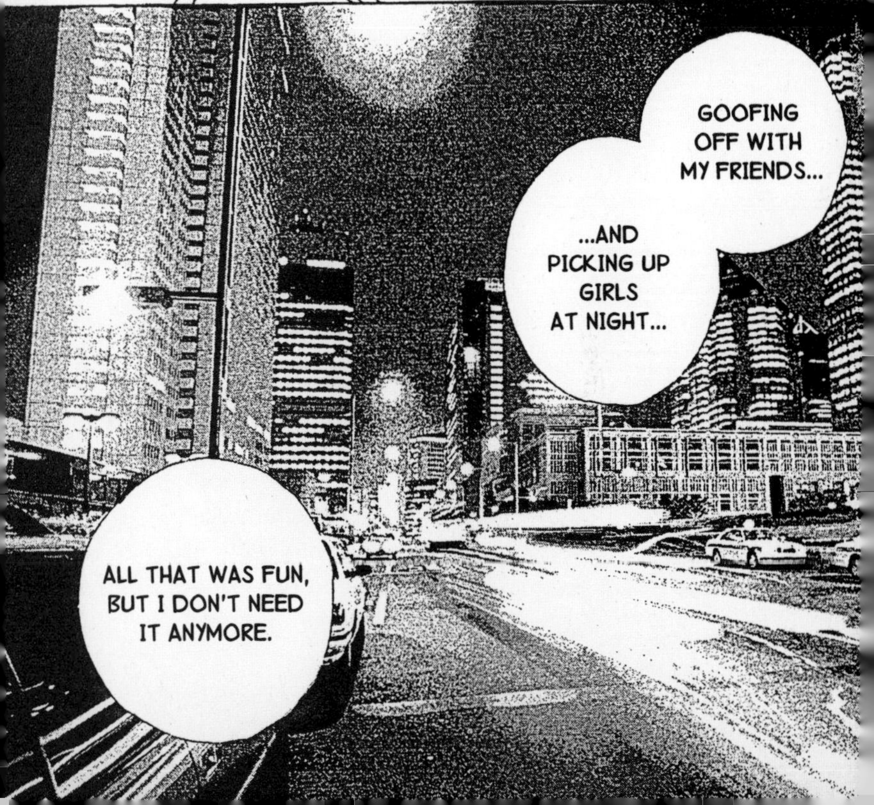
GOOFING OFF WITH MY FRIENDS...
...AND PICKING UP GIRLS AT NIGHT...
ALL THAT WAS FUN, BUT I DON'T NEED IT ANYMORE.

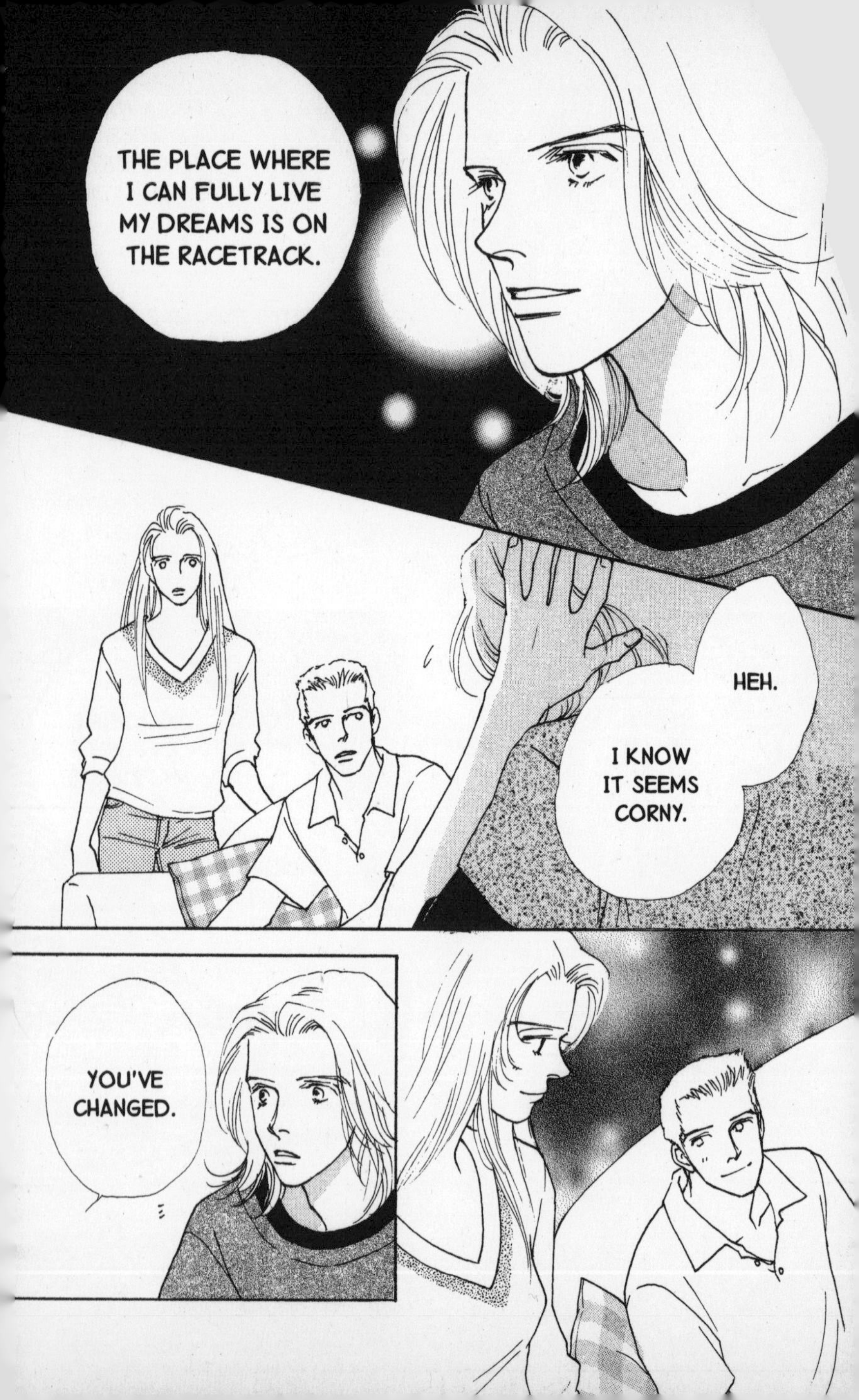
THE PLACE WHERE I CAN FULLY LIVE MY DREAMS IS ON THE RACETRACK.
HEH.
I KNOW IT SEEMS CORNY.
YOU'VE CHANGED.

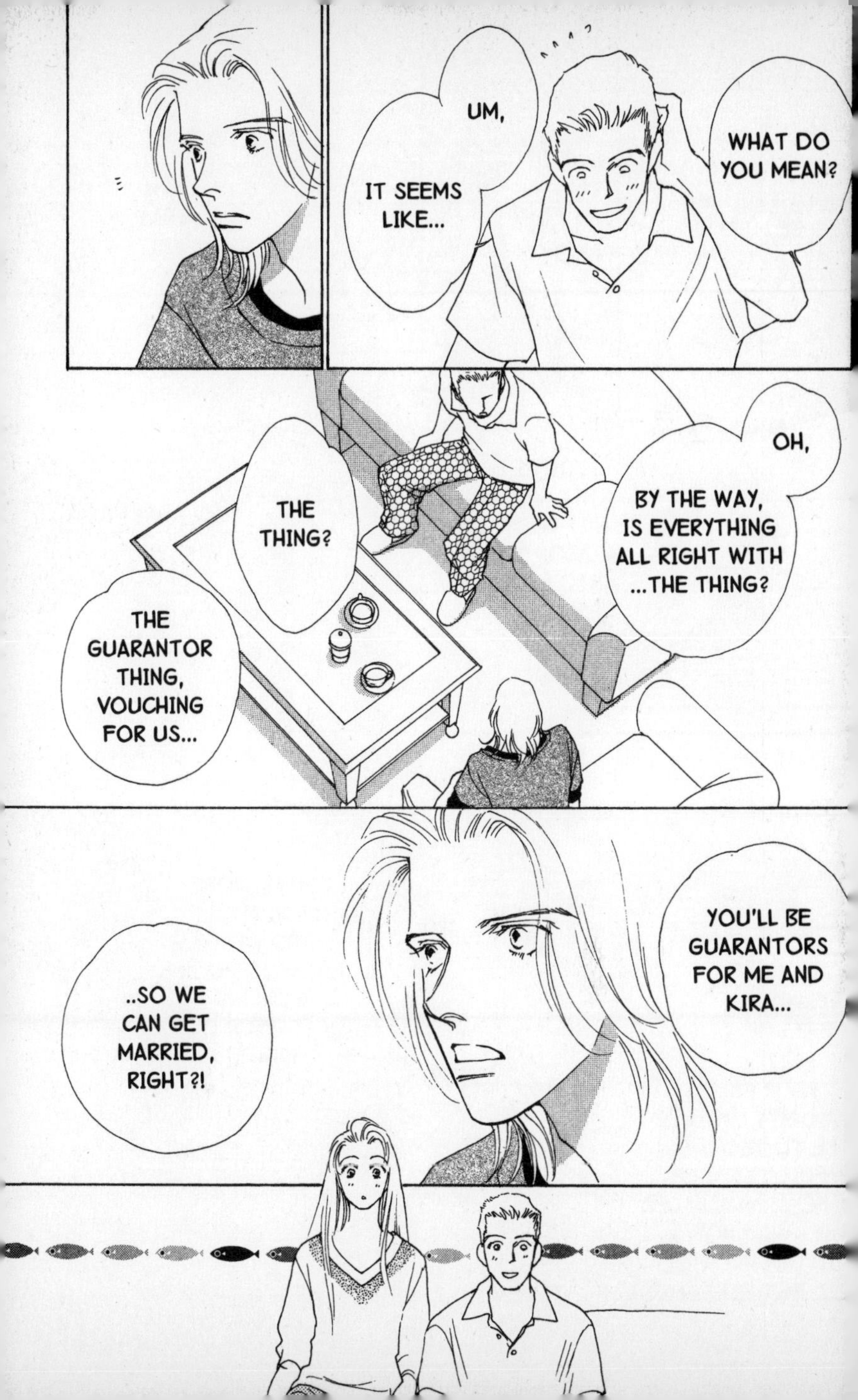
WHAT DO YOU MEAN?
UM, IT SEEMS LIKE...
OH, BY THE WAY, IS EVERYTHING ALL RIGHT WITH ...THE THING?
THE THING?
THE GUARANTOR THING, VOUCHING FOR US...
YOU'LL BE GUARANTORS FOR ME AND KIRA...
..SO WE CAN GET MARRIED, RIGHT?!

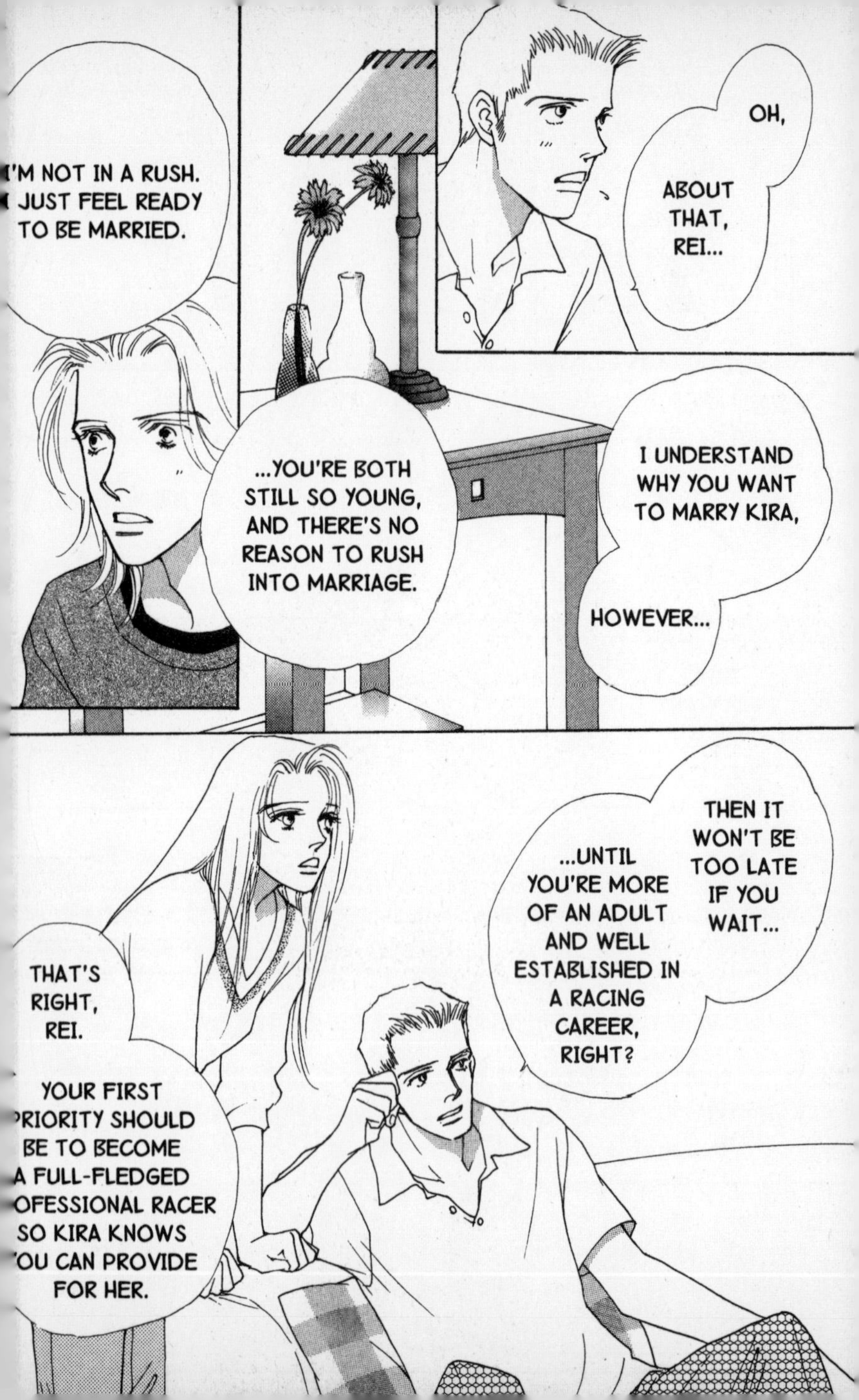
OH,
ABOUT THAT, REI...
I UNDERSTAND WHY YOU WANT TO MARRY KIRA,
HOWEVER...
...YOU'RE BOTH STILL SO YOUNG, AND THERE'S NO REASON TO RUSH INTO MARRIAGE.
I'M NOT IN A RUSH. JUST FEEL READY TO BE MARRIED.
THEN IT WON'T BE TOO LATE IF YOU WAIT...
...UNTIL YOU'RE MORE OF AN ADULT AND WELL ESTABLISHED IN A RACING CAREER, RIGHT?
THAT'S RIGHT, REI.
YOUR FIRST RIORITY SHOULD BE TO BECOME A FULL-FLEDGED OFESSIONAL RACER SO KIRA KNOWS OU CAN PROVIDE FOR HER.

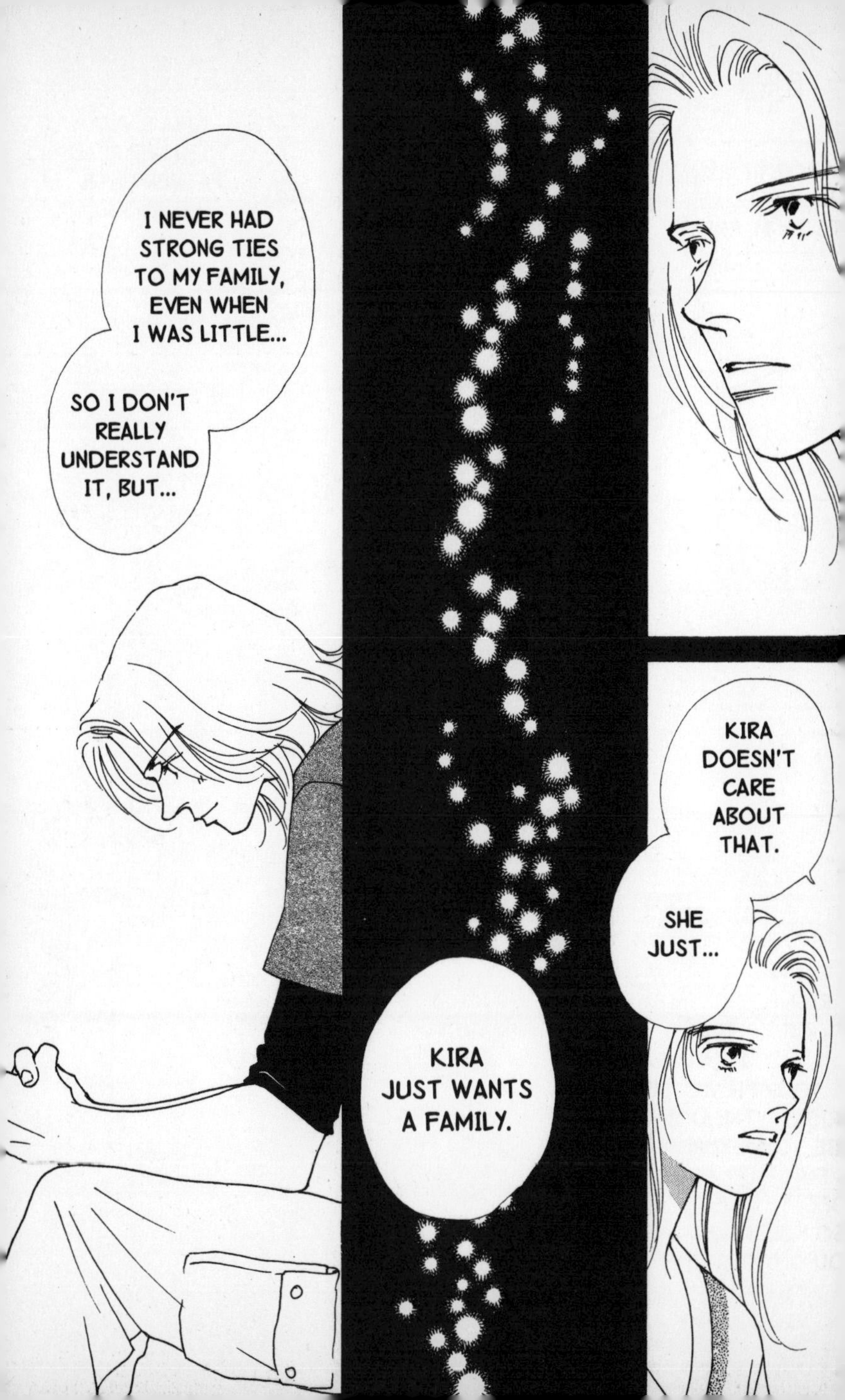
KIRA DOESN'T CARE ABOUT THAT.
SHE JUST...
KIRA JUST WANTS A FAMILY.
I NEVER HAD STRONG TIES TO MY FAMILY, EVEN WHEN I WAS LITTLE...
SO I DON'T REALLY UNDERSTAND IT, BUT...

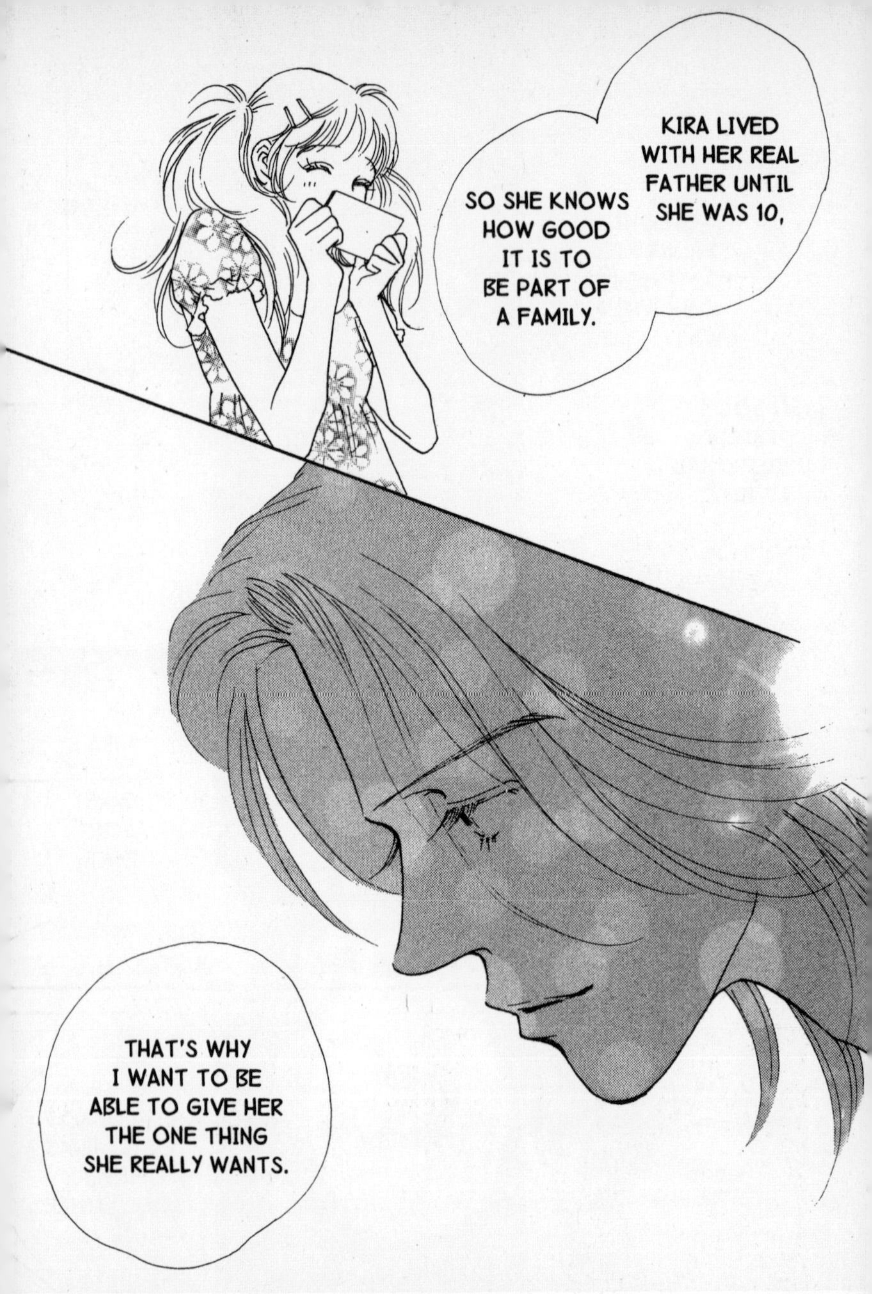
KIRA LIVED WITH HER REAL FATHER UNTIL SHE WAS 10,
SO SHE KNOWS HOW GOOD IT IS TO BE PART OF A FAMILY.
THAT'S WHY I WANT TO BE ABLE TO GIVE HER THE ONE THING SHE REALLY WANTS.

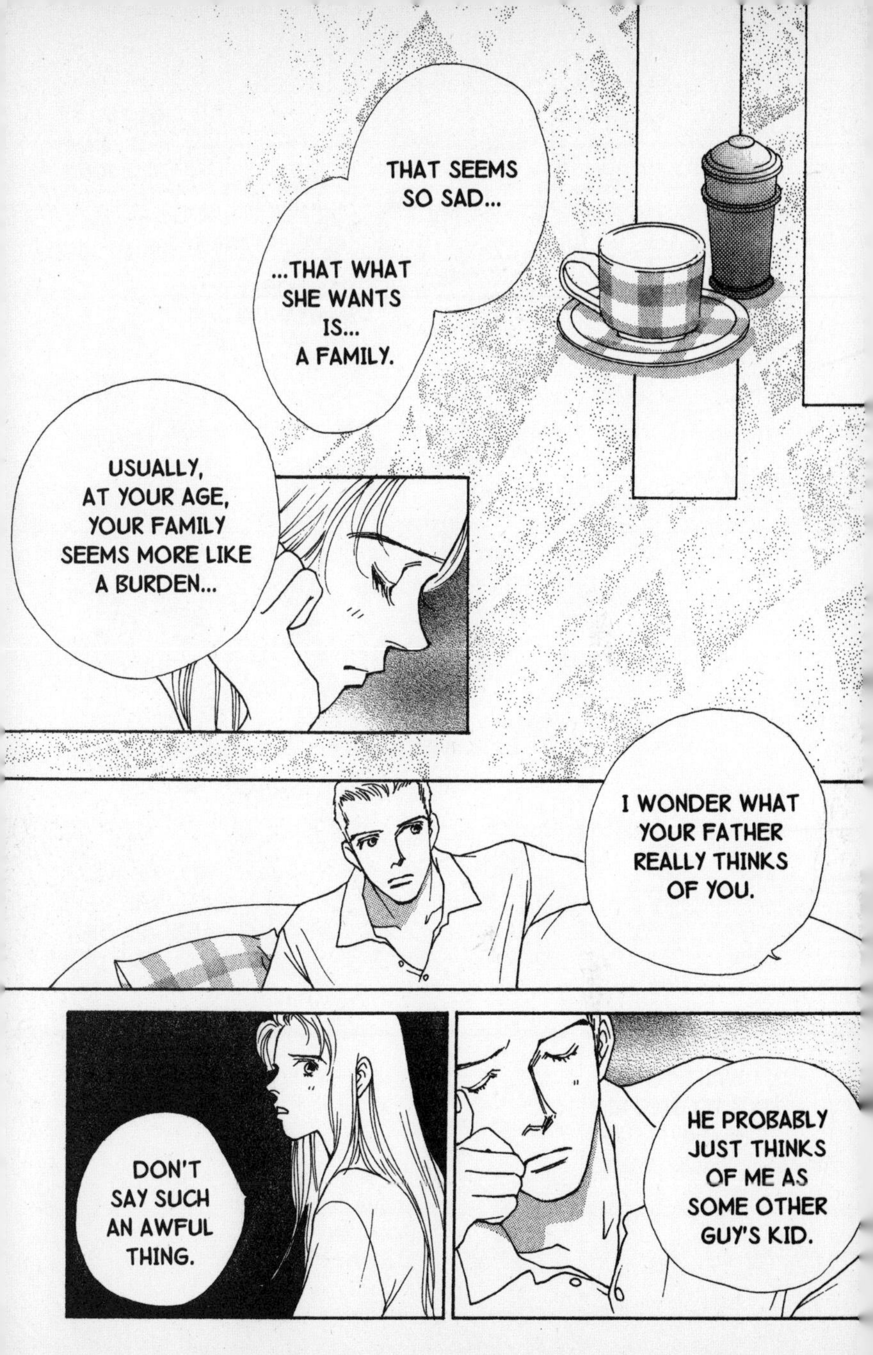
THAT SEEMS SO SAD...
...THAT WHAT SHE WANTS IS... A FAMILY.
USUALLY, AT YOUR AGE, YOUR FAMILY SEEMS MORE LIKE A BURDEN...
I WONDER WHAT YOUR FATHER REALLY THINKS OF YOU.
HE PROBABLY JUST THINKS OF ME AS SOME OTHER GUY'S KID.
DON'T SAY SUCH AN AWFUL THING.

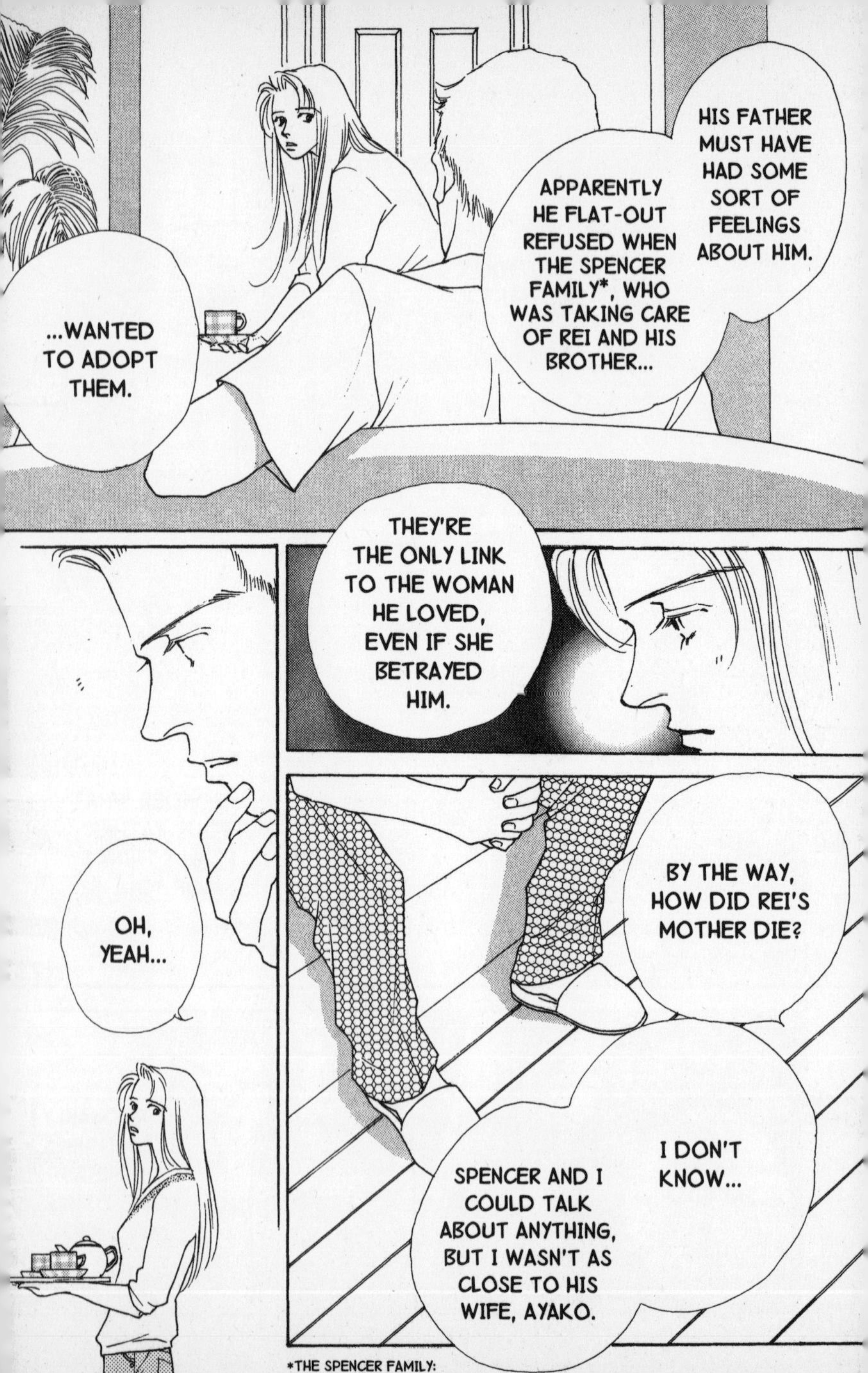
HIS FATHER MUST HAVE HAD SOME SORT OF FEELINGS ABOUT HIM.
APPARENTLY HE FLAT-OUT REFUSED WHEN THE SPENCER FAMILY*, WHO WAS TAKING CARE OF REI AND HIS BROTHER...
...WANTED TO ADOPT THEM.
THEY'RE THE ONLY LINK TO THE WOMAN HE LOVED, EVEN IF SHE BETRAYED HIM.
BY THE WAY, HOW DID REI'S MOTHER DIE?
I DON'T KNOW...
SPENCER AND I COULD TALK ABOUT ANYTHING, BUT I WASN'T AS CLOSE TO HIS WIFE, AYAKO.
OH, YEAH...

*THE SPENCER FAMILY:
THE FAMILY WHO LOOKED AFTER REI AND SEI WHEN THEY LIVED IN L.A.

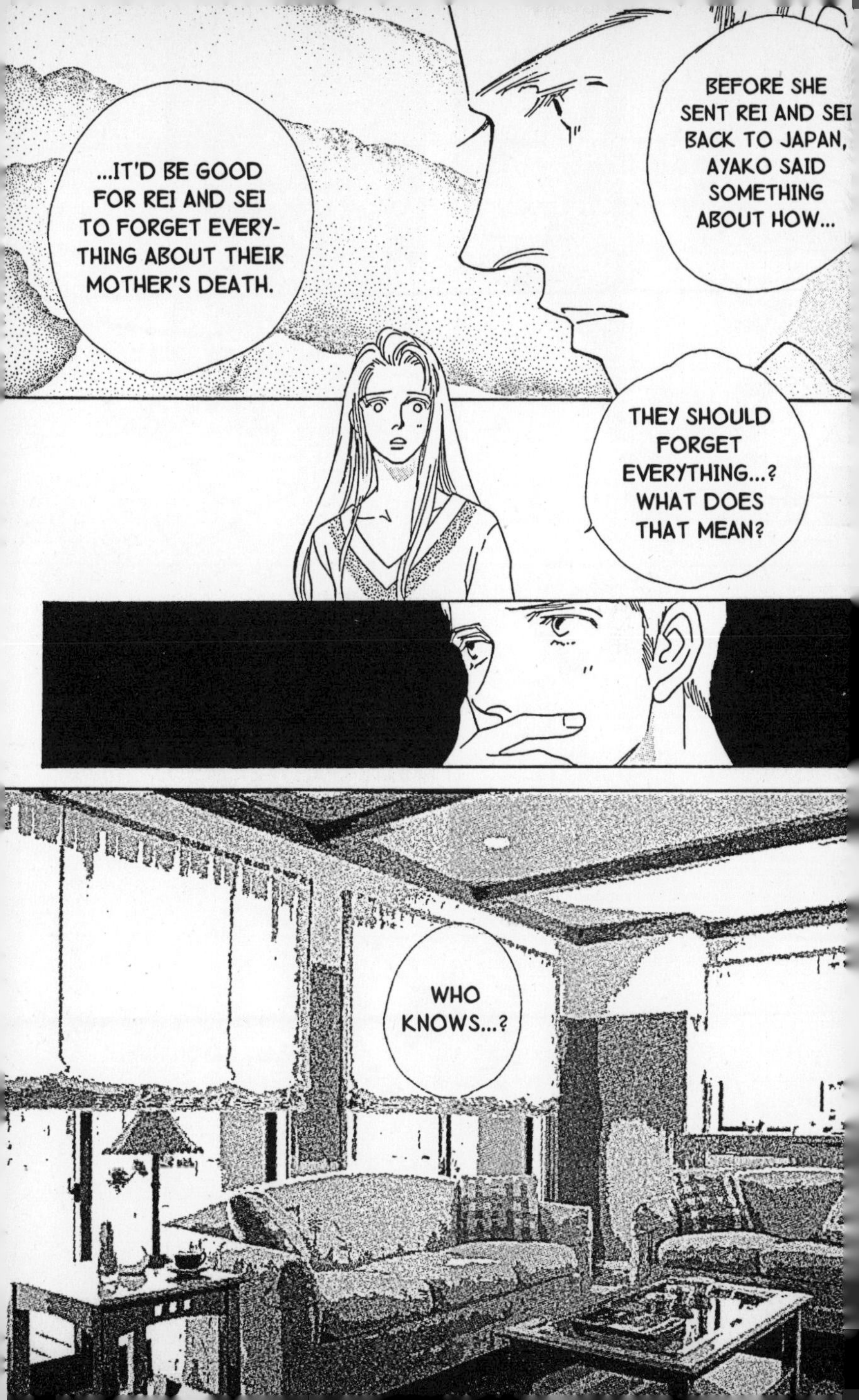
BEFORE SHE SENT REI AND SEI BACK TO JAPAN, AYAKO SAID SOMETHING ABOUT HOW...
...IT'D BE GOOD FOR REI AND SEI TO FORGET EVERYTHING ABOUT THEIR MOTHER'S DEATH.
THEY SHOULD FORGET EVERYTHING...? WHAT DOES THAT MEAN?
WHO KNOWS...?

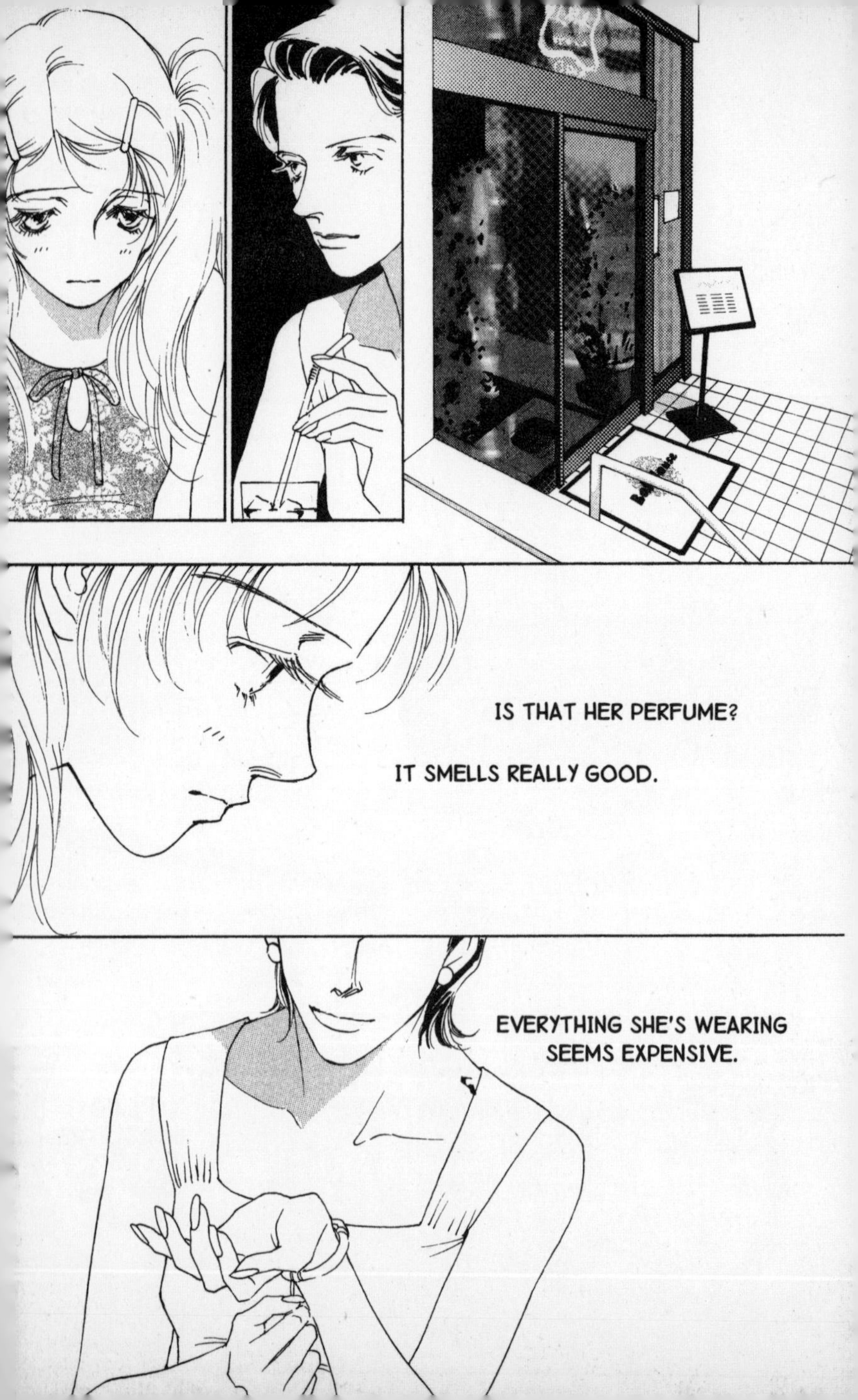
IS THAT HER PERFUME?
IT SMELLS REALLY GOOD.
EVERYTHING SHE'S WEARING SEEMS EXPENSIVE.

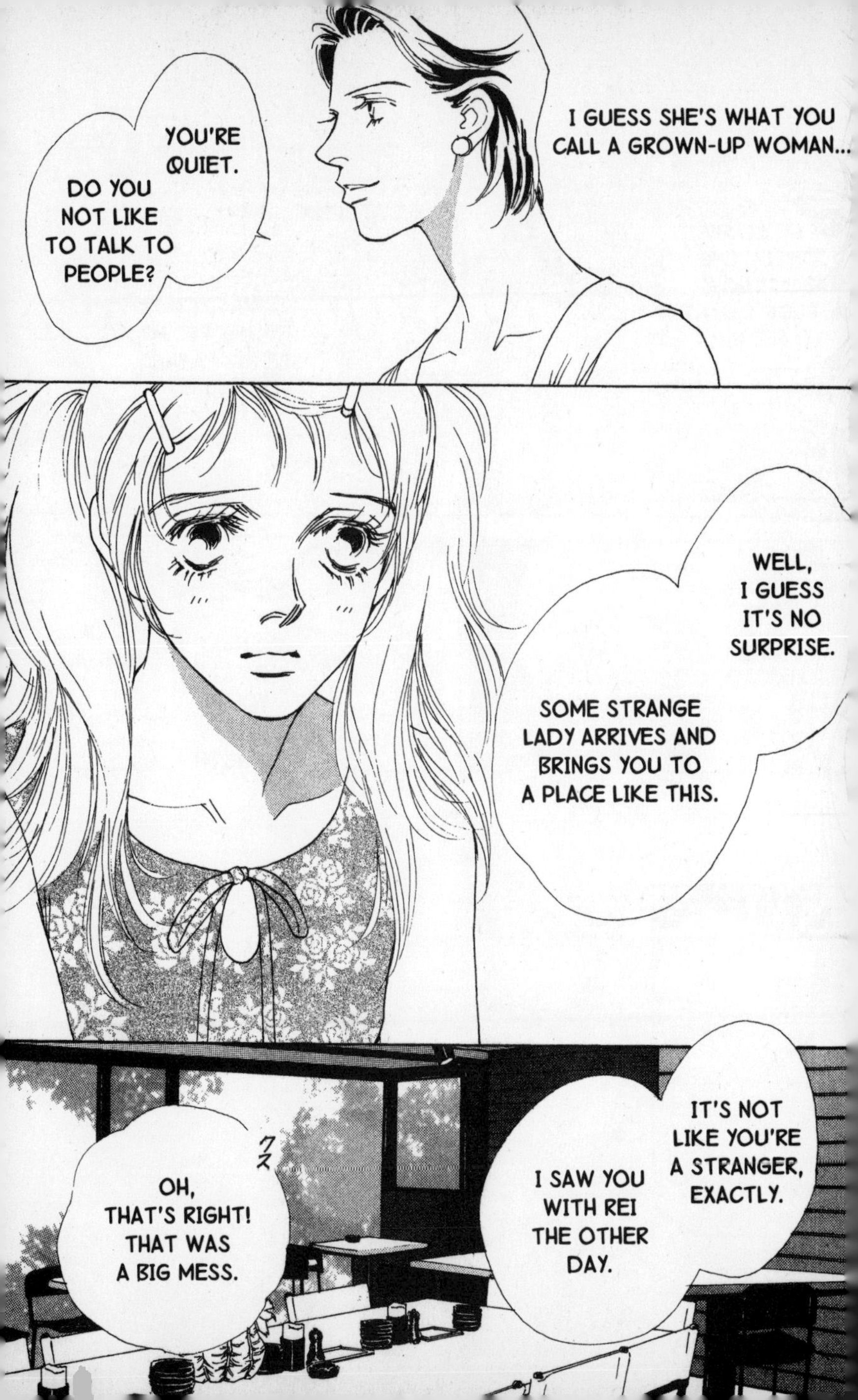
I GUESS SHE'S WHAT YOU CALL A GROWN-UP WOMAN...
YOU'RE QUIET. DO YOU NOT LIKE TO TALK TO PEOPLE?
WELL, I GUESS IT'S NO SURPRISE.
SOME STRANGE LADY ARRIVES AND BRINGS YOU TO A PLACE LIKE THIS.
IT'S NOT LIKE YOU'RE A STRANGER, EXACTLY.
I SAW YOU WITH REI THE OTHER DAY.
クス
OH, THAT'S RIGHT! THAT WAS A BIG MESS.

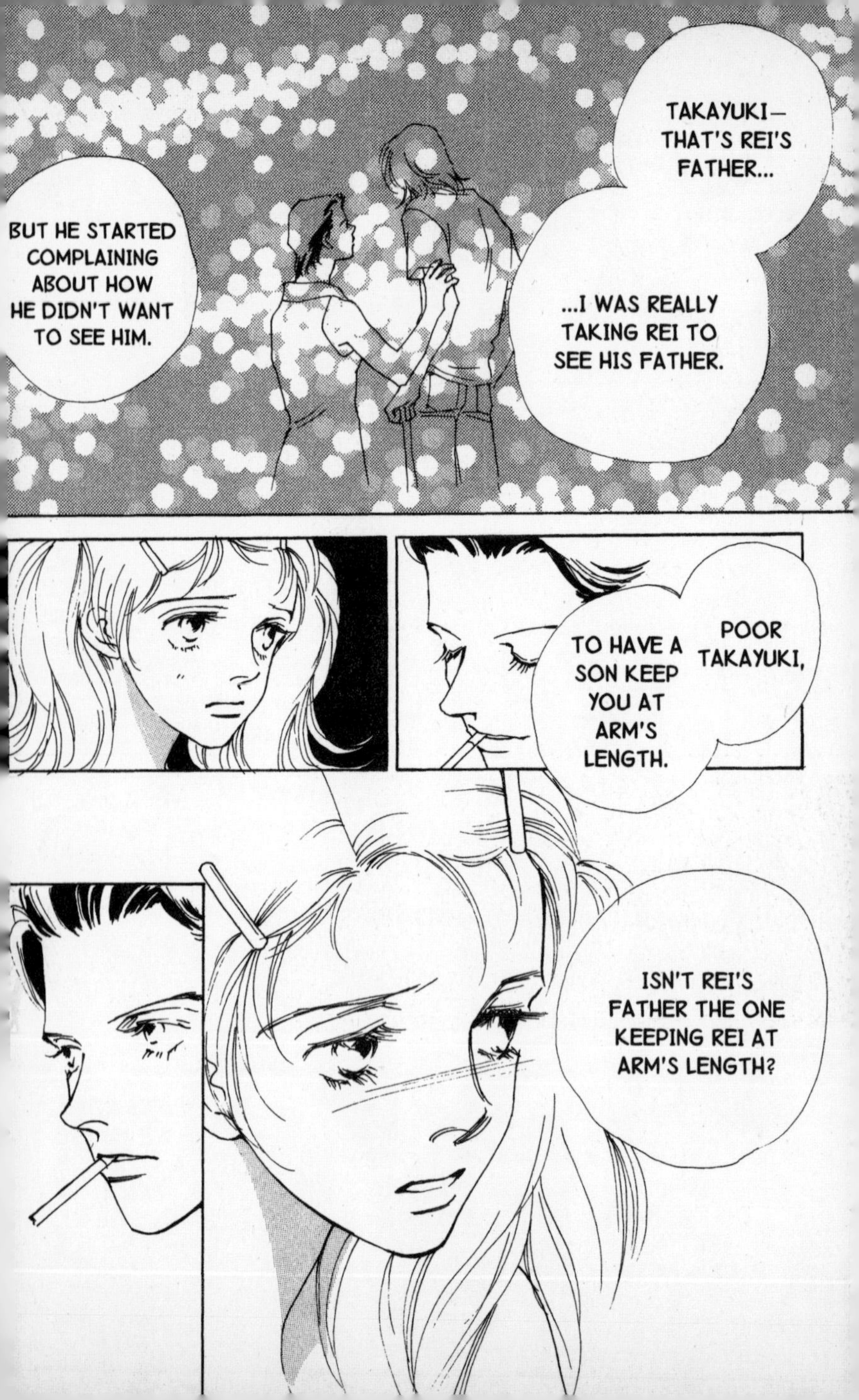
TAKAYUKI— THAT'S REI'S FATHER...
...I WAS REALLY TAKING REI TO SEE HIS FATHER.
BUT HE STARTED COMPLAINING ABOUT HOW HE DIDN'T WANT TO SEE HIM.
POOR TAKAYUKI,
TO HAVE A SON KEEP YOU AT ARM'S LENGTH.
ISN'T REI'S FATHER THE ONE KEEPING REI AT ARM'S LENGTH?

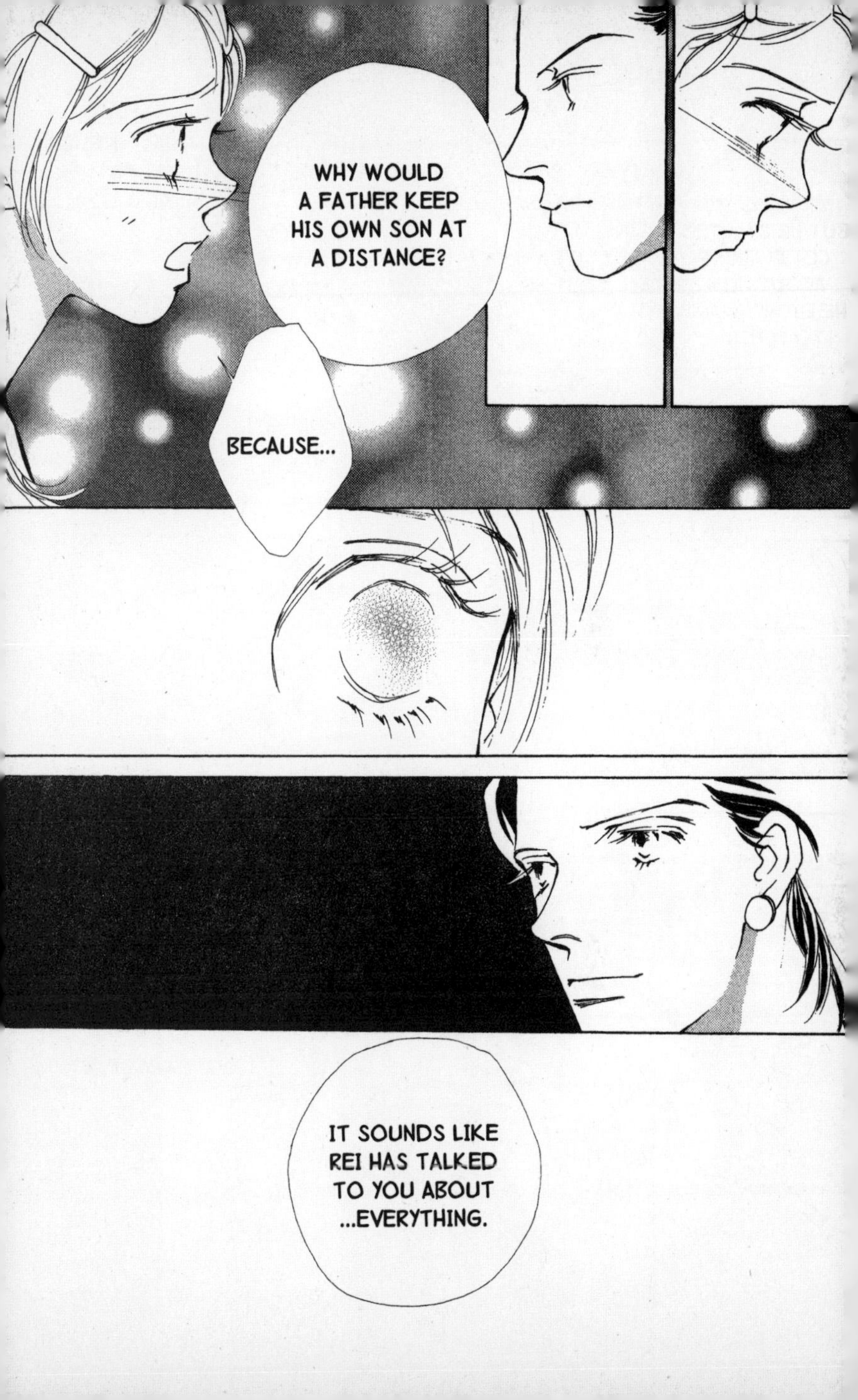
WHY WOULD A FATHER KEEP HIS OWN SON AT A DISTANCE?
BECAUSE...
IT SOUNDS LIKE REI HAS TALKED TO YOU ABOUT ...EVERYTHING.

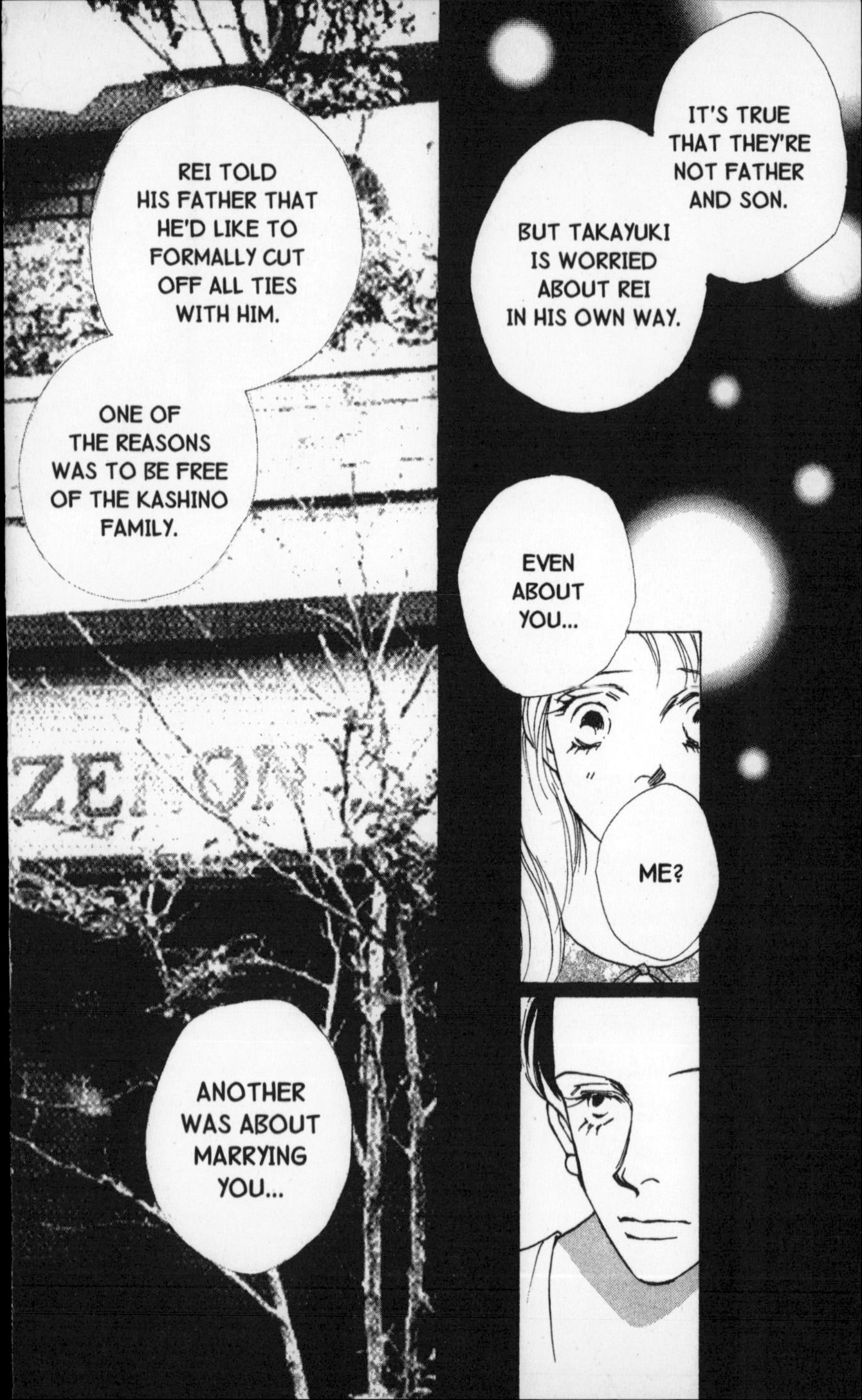
REI TOLD HIS FATHER THAT HE'D LIKE TO FORMALLY CUT OFF ALL TIES WITH HIM.
ONE OF THE REASONS WAS TO BE FREE OF THE KASHINO FAMILY.
ANOTHER WAS ABOUT MARRYING YOU...
IT'S TRUE THAT THEY'RE NOT FATHER AND SON.
BUT TAKAYUKI IS WORRIED ABOUT REI IN HIS OWN WAY.
EVEN ABOUT YOU...
ME?

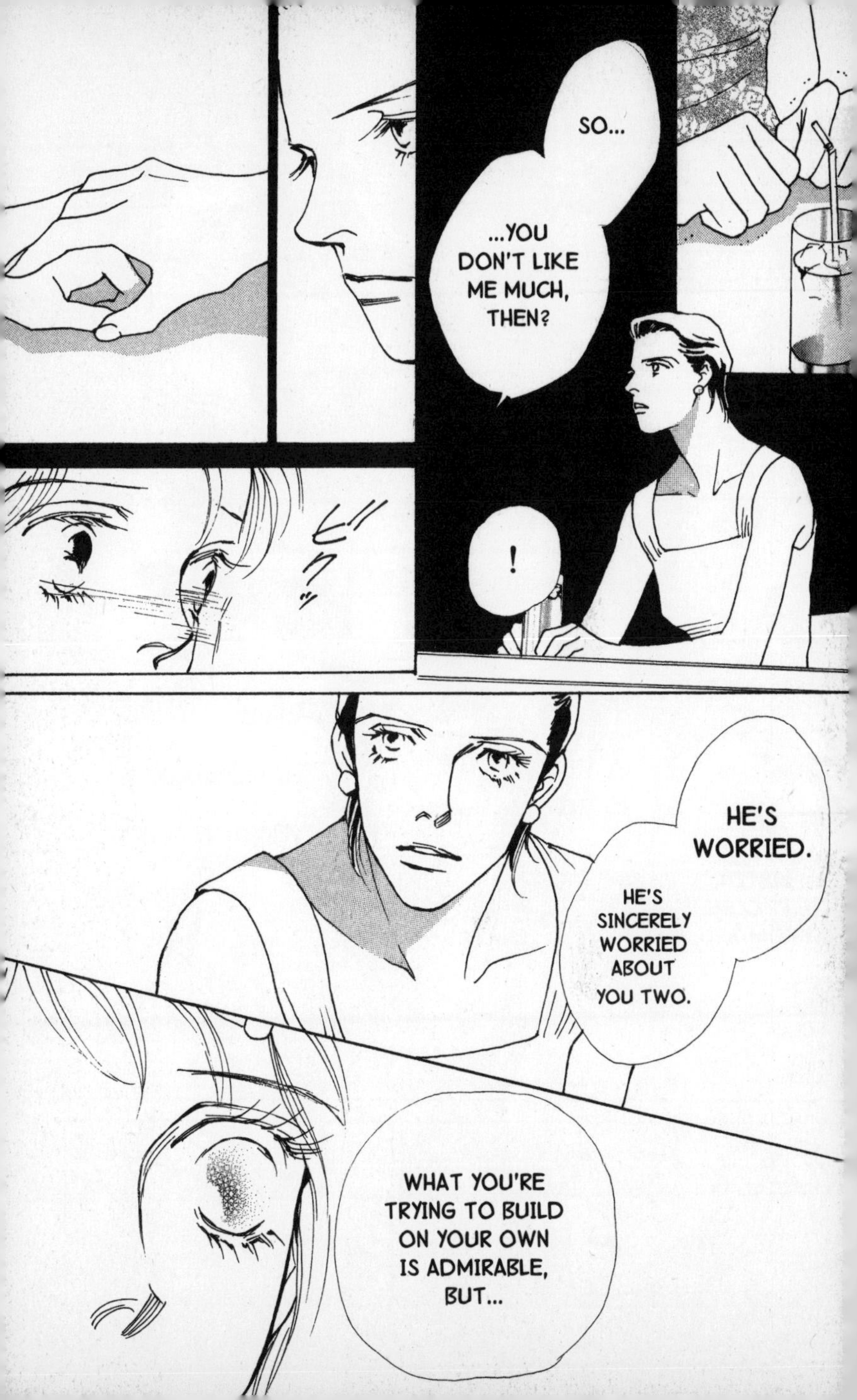
SO...
...YOU DON'T LIKE ME MUCH, THEN?
!
ビクッ
HE'S WORRIED.
HE'S SINCERELY WORRIED ABOUT YOU TWO.
WHAT YOU'RE TRYING TO BUILD ON YOUR OWN IS ADMIRABLE, BUT...

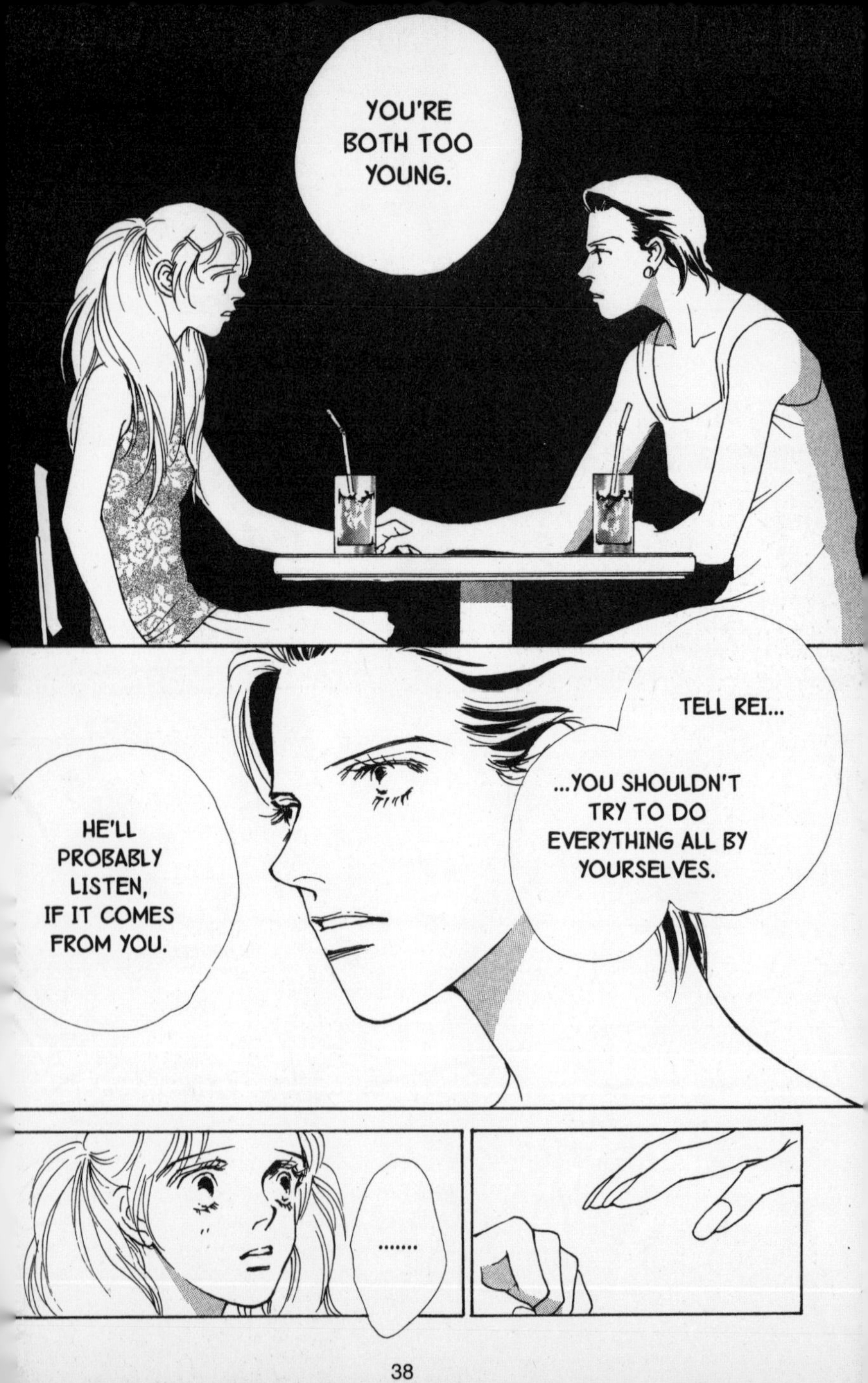
YOU'RE BOTH TOO YOUNG.
TELL REI...
...YOU SHOULDN'T TRY TO DO EVERYTHING ALL BY YOURSELVES.
HE'LL PROBABLY LISTEN, IF IT COMES FROM YOU.
....

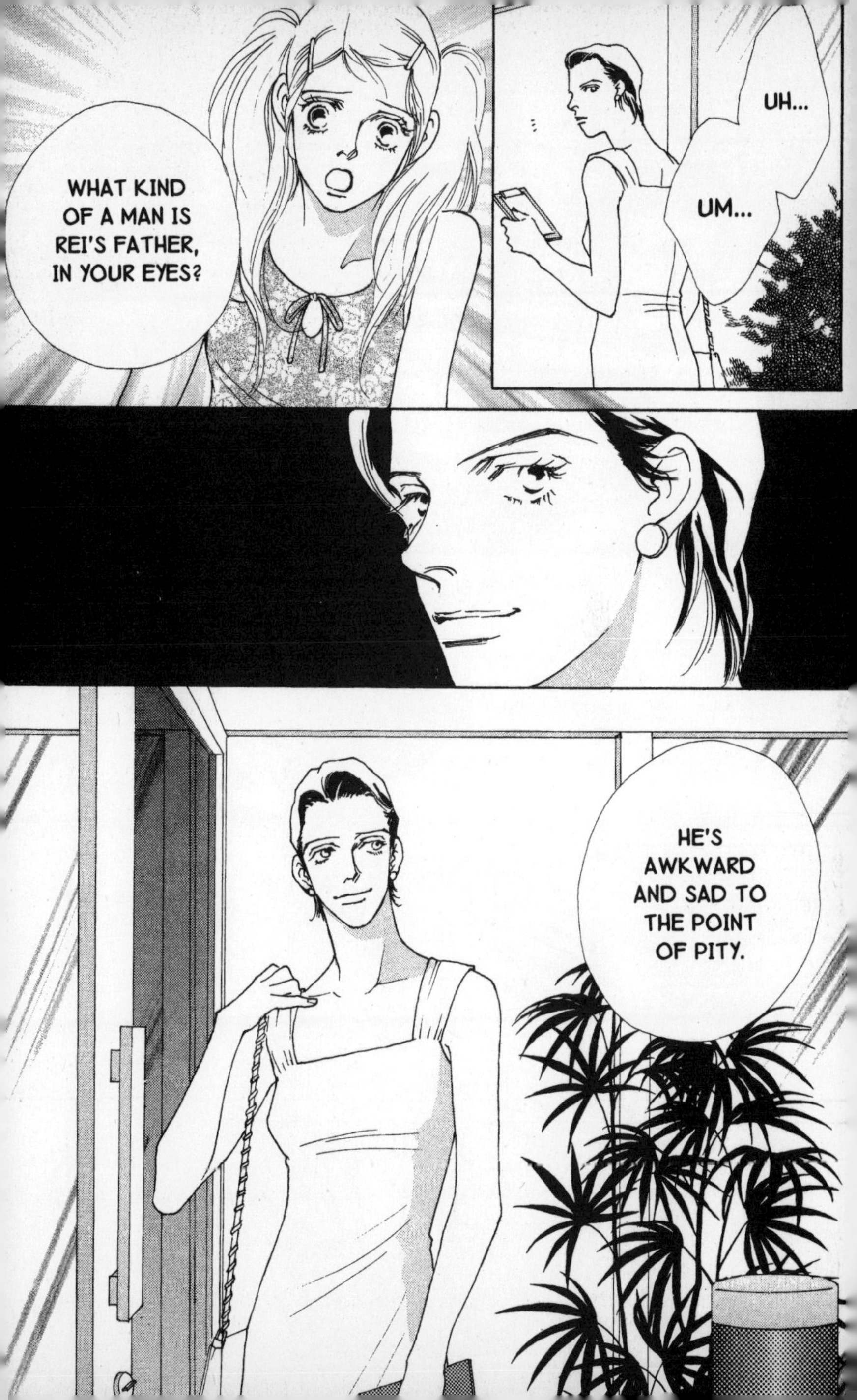
UH...
UM...
WHAT KIND OF A MAN IS REI'S FATHER, IN YOUR EYES?
HE'S AWKWARD AND SAD TO THE POINT OF PITY.

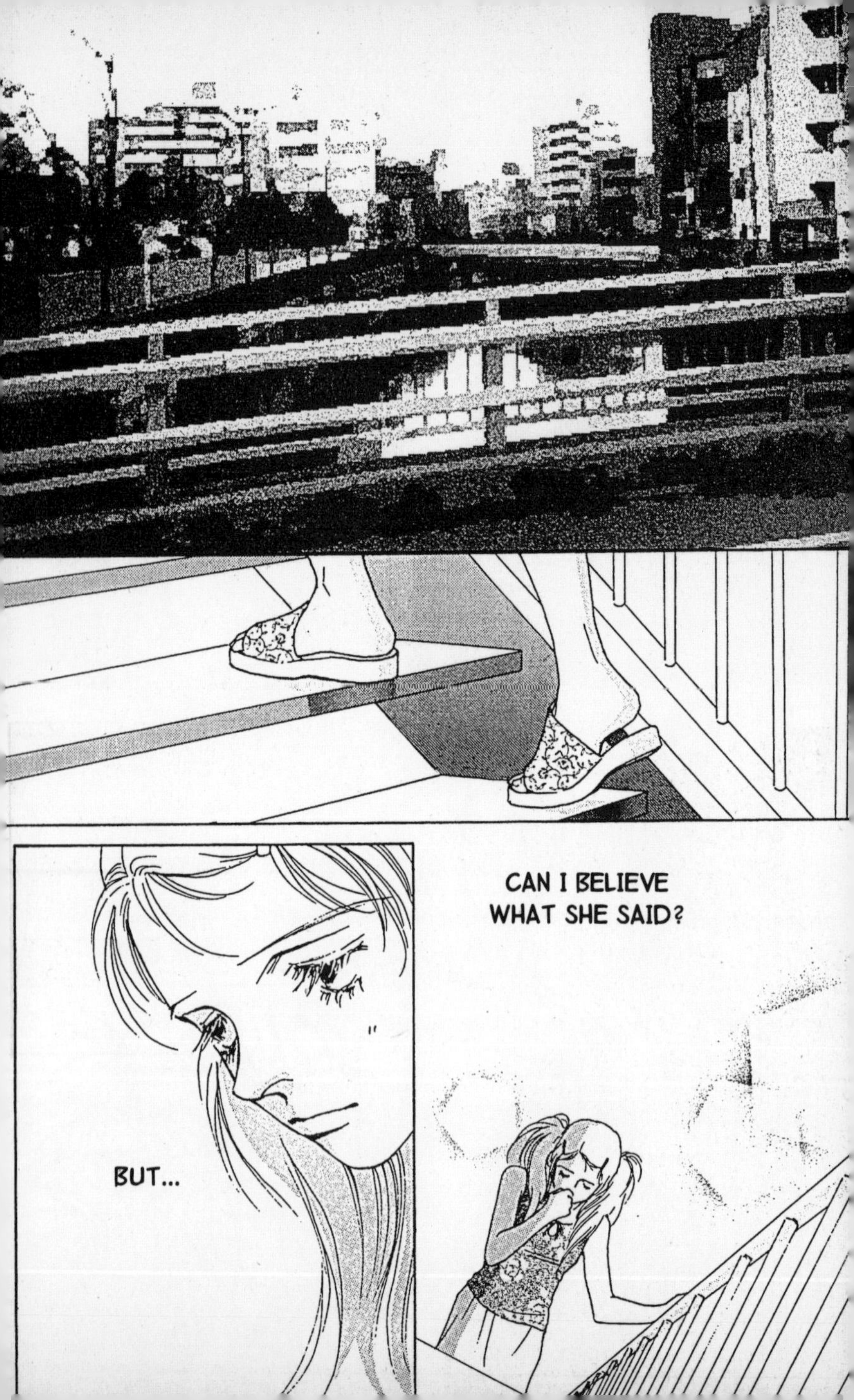
CAN I BELIEVE
WHAT SHE SAID?
BUT...

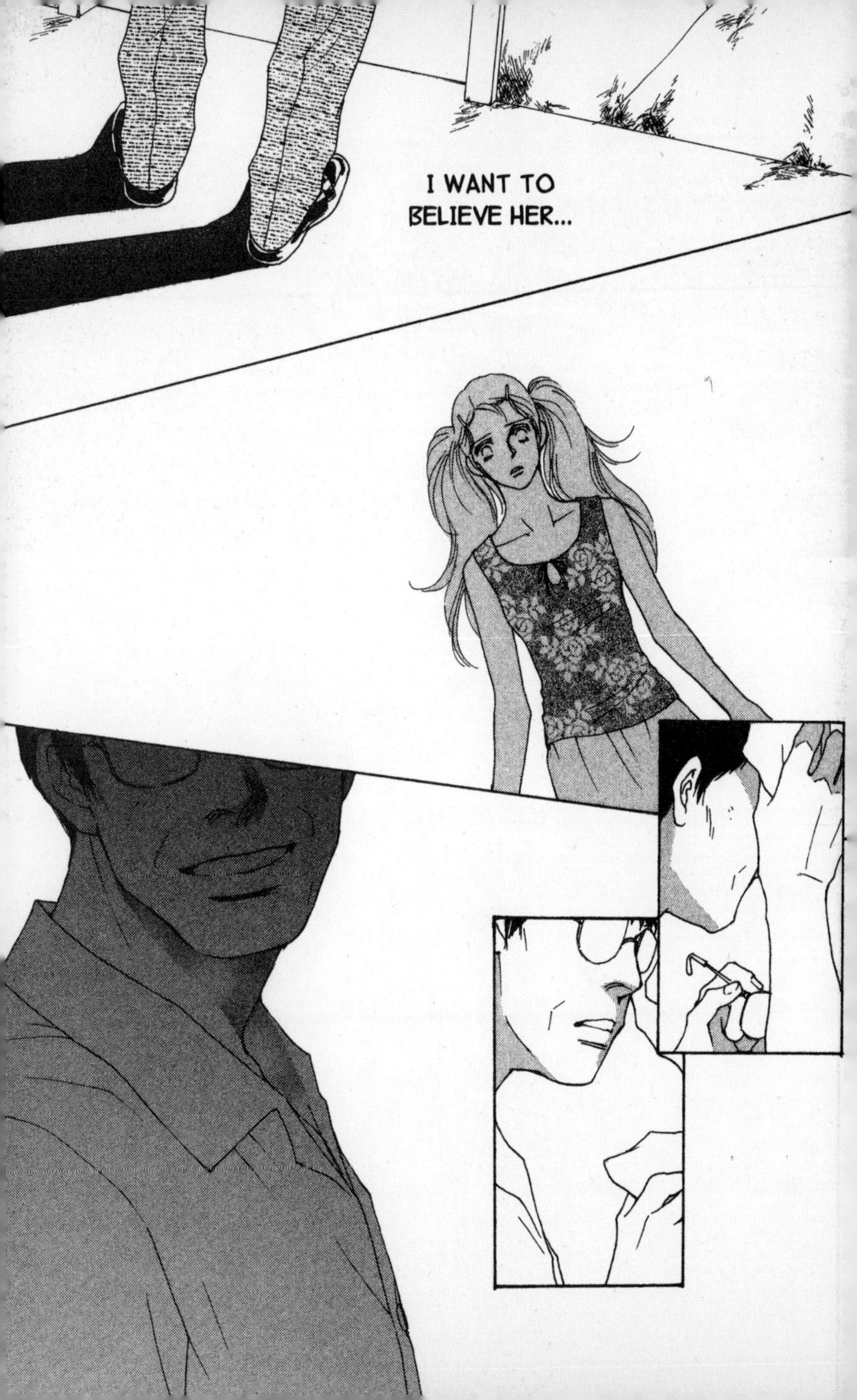
I WANT TO
BELIEVE HER...

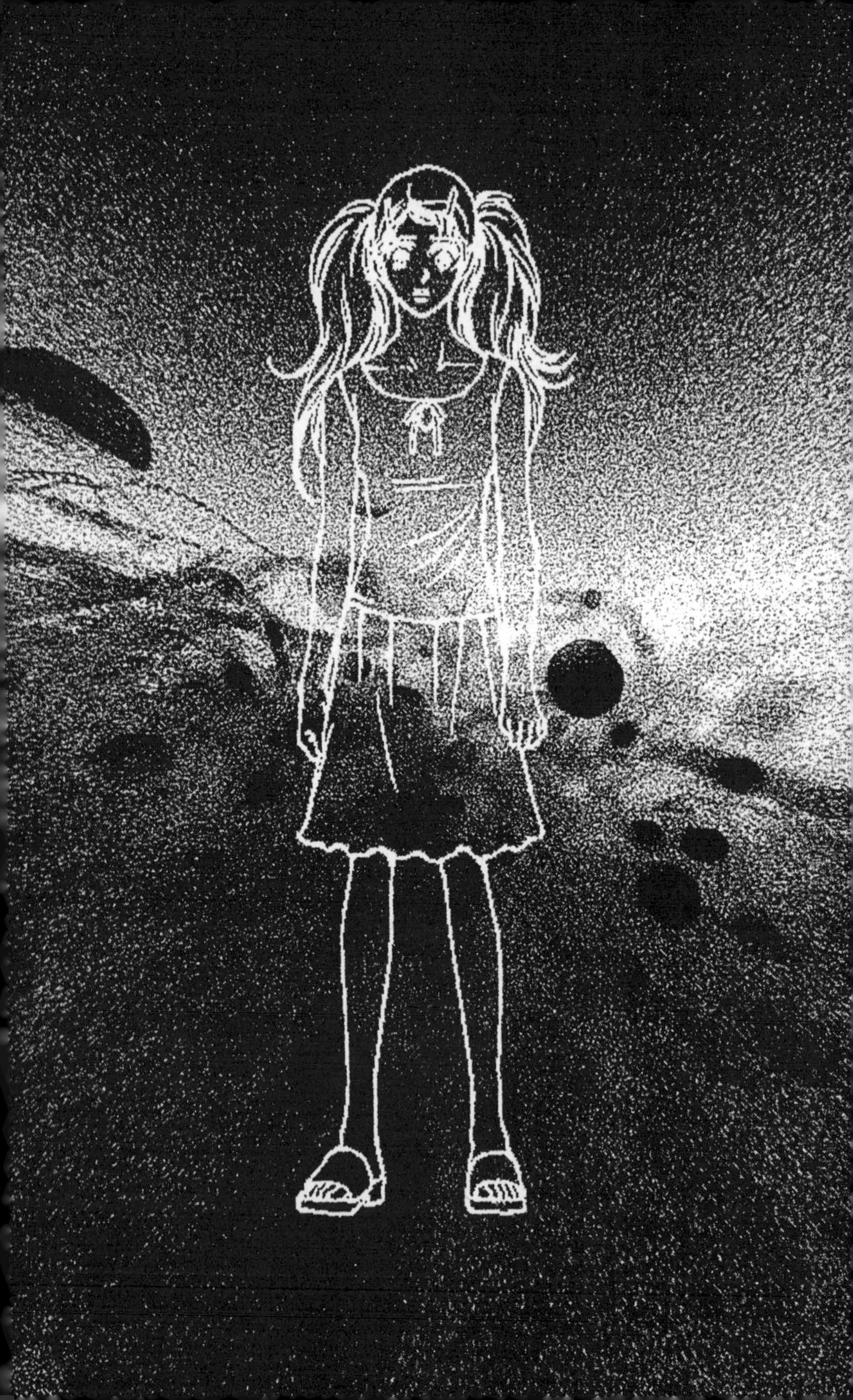

MARS

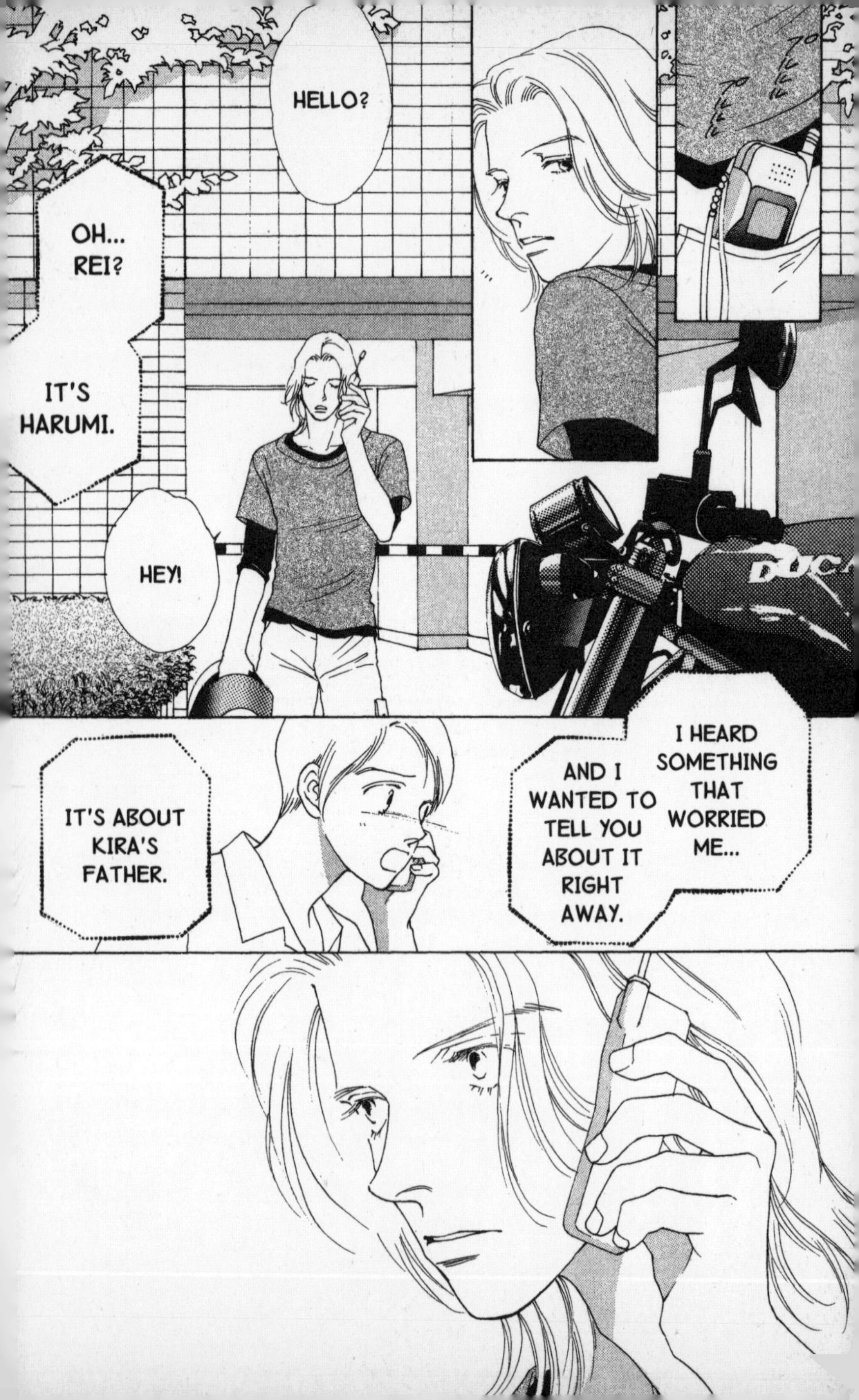
HELLO?
OH... REI?
IT'S HARUMI.
HEY!
I HEARD SOMETHING THAT WORRIED ME...
AND I WANTED TO TELL YOU ABOUT IT RIGHT AWAY.
IT'S ABOUT KIRA'S FATHER.

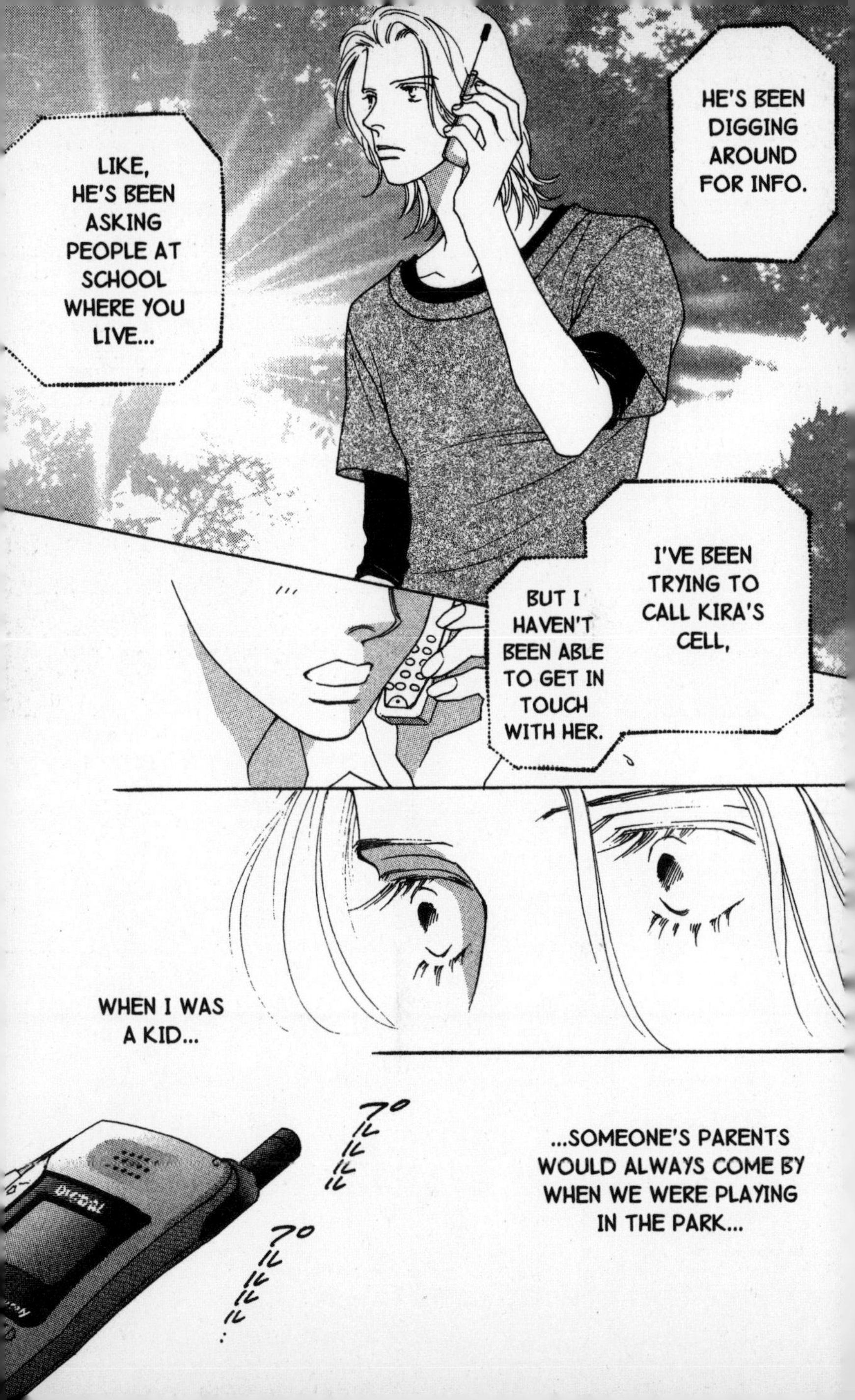
HE'S BEEN DIGGING AROUND FOR INFO.
LIKE, HE'S BEEN ASKING PEOPLE AT SCHOOL WHERE YOU LIVE...
I'VE BEEN TRYING TO CALL KIRA'S CELL,
BUT I HAVEN'T BEEN ABLE TO GET IN TOUCH WITH HER.
WHEN I WAS A KID...
...SOMEONE'S PARENTS WOULD ALWAYS COME BY WHEN WE WERE PLAYING IN THE PARK...
プルルル
プルルル

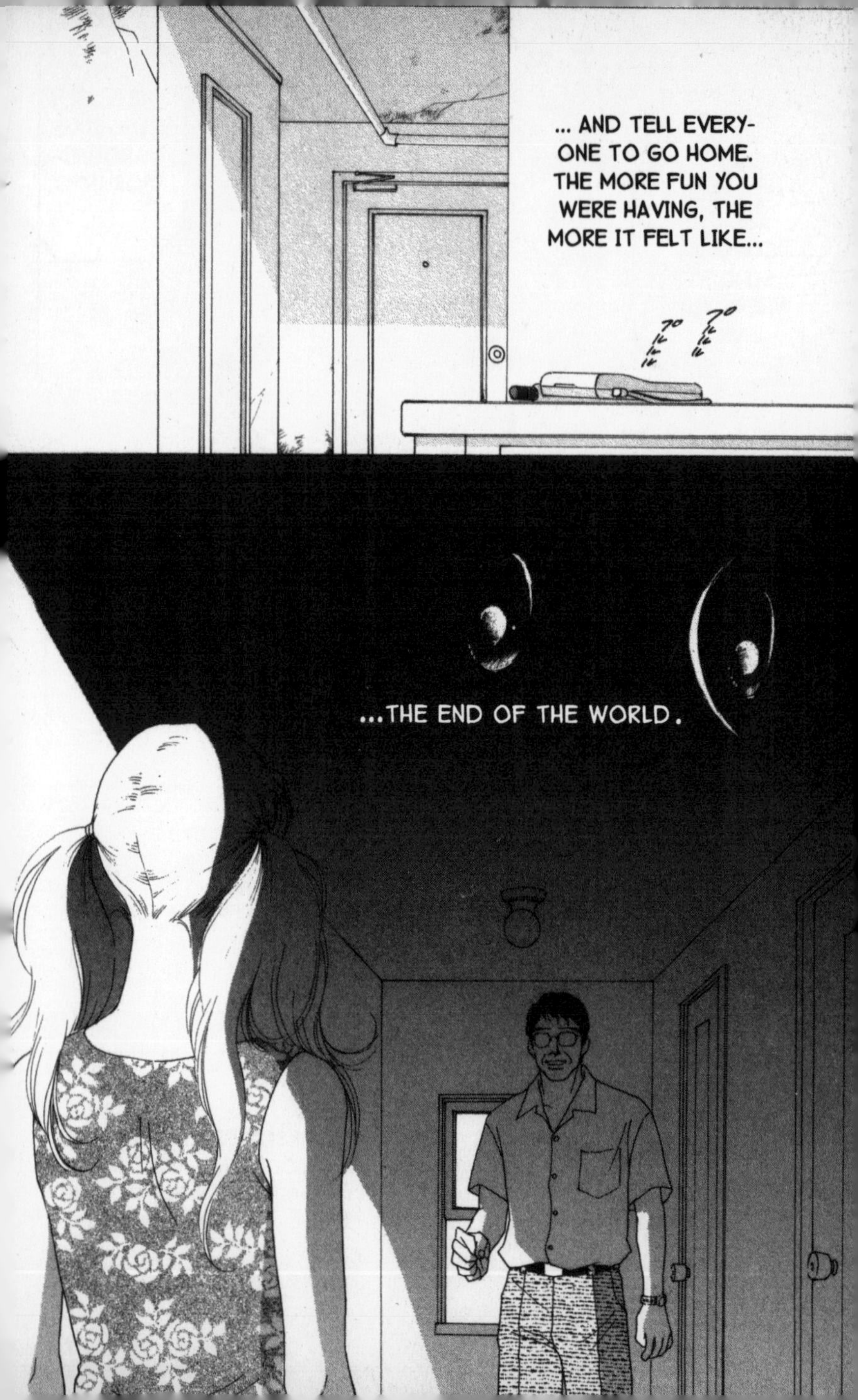
... AND TELL EVERY-ONE TO GO HOME. THE MORE FUN YOU WERE HAVING, THE MORE IT FELT LIKE...
...THE END OF THE WORLD.

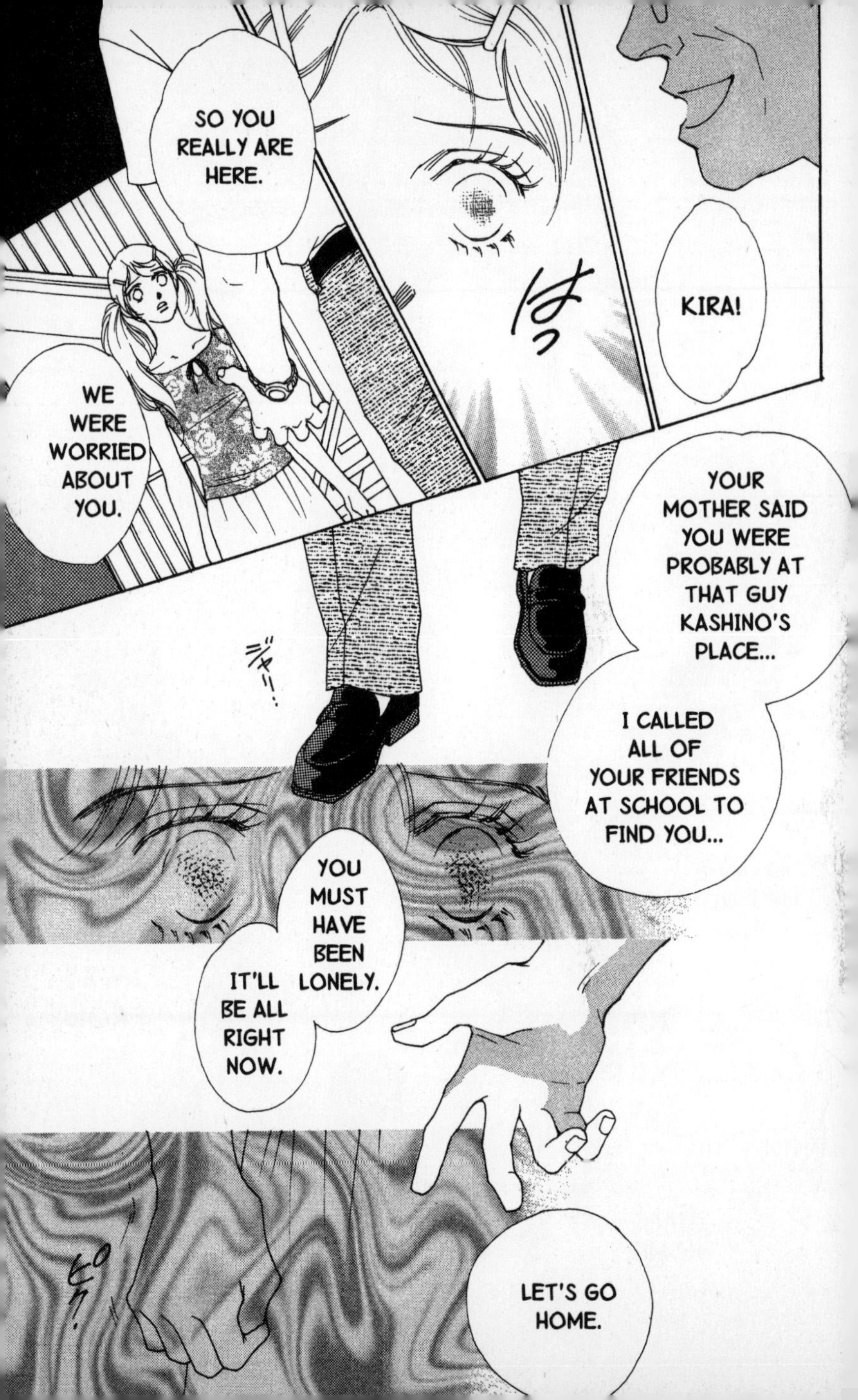
KIRA!
はっ
SO YOU REALLY ARE HERE.
WE WERE WORRIED ABOUT YOU.
YOUR MOTHER SAID YOU WERE PROBABLY AT THAT GUY KASHINO'S PLACE...
I CALLED ALL OF YOUR FRIENDS AT SCHOOL TO FIND YOU...
ジャ…
YOU MUST HAVE BEEN LONELY.
IT'LL BE ALL RIGHT NOW.
LET'S GO HOME.
ピク

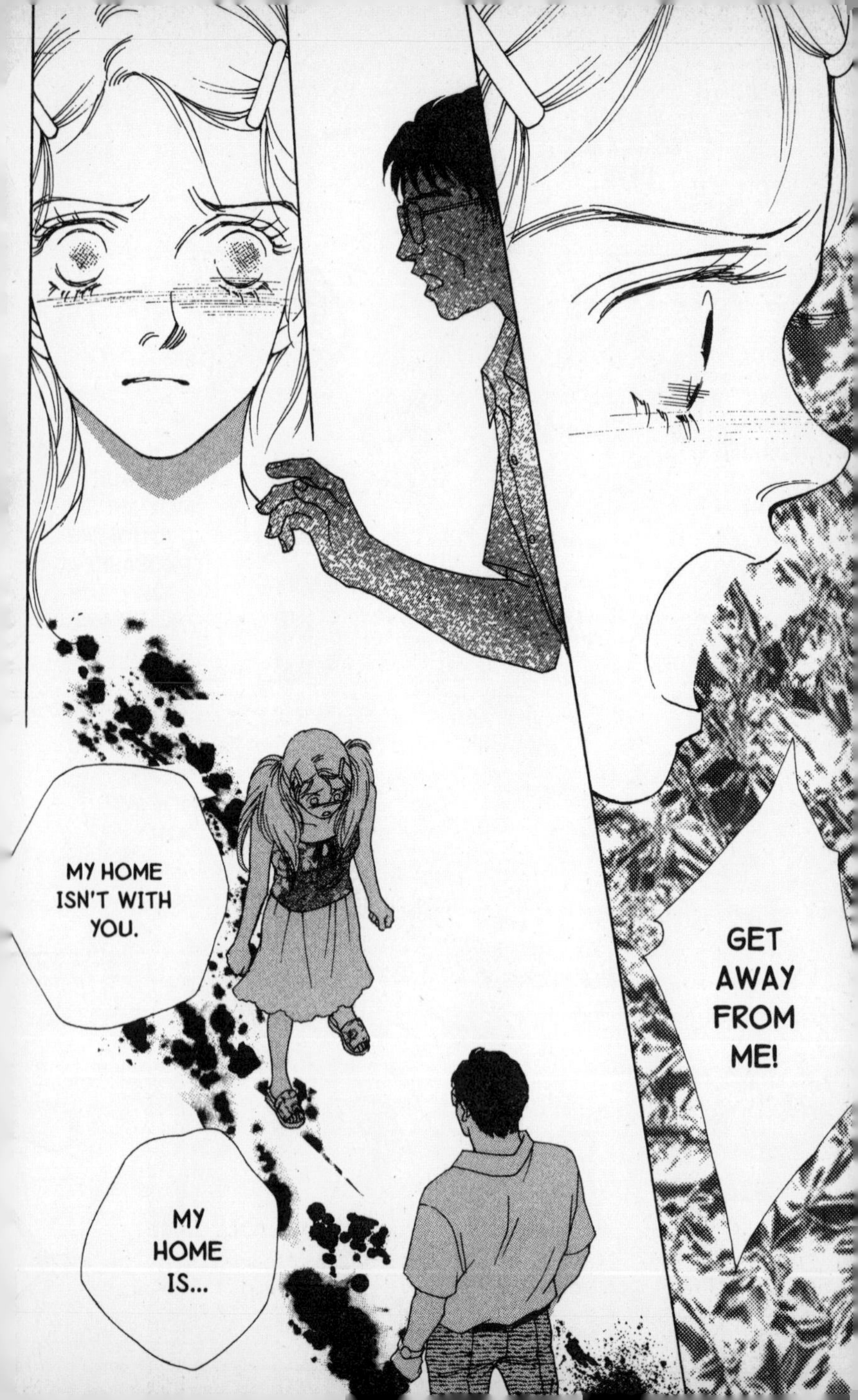
GET AWAY FROM ME!
MY HOME ISN'T WITH YOU.
MY HOME IS...

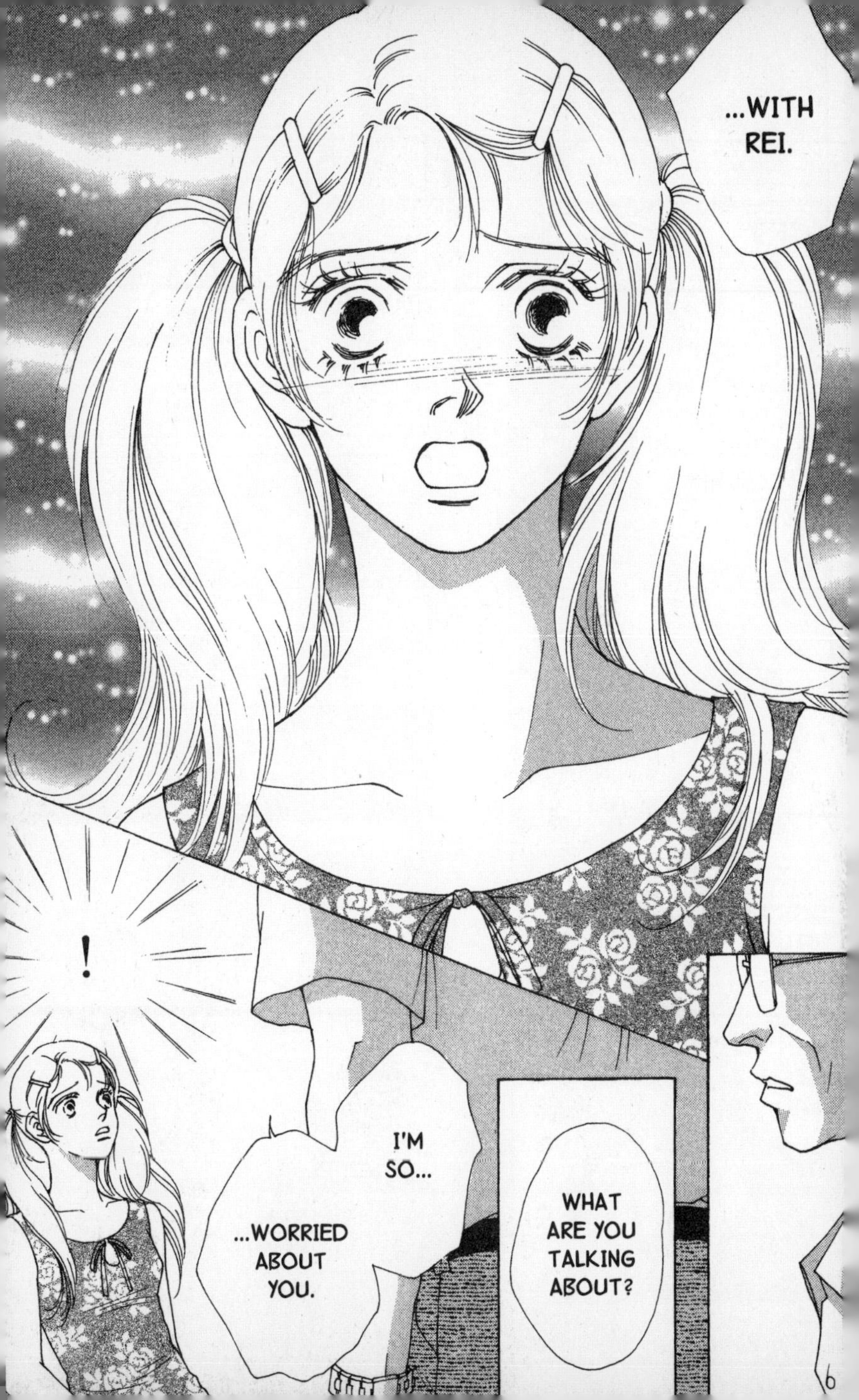
...WITH REI.
WHAT ARE YOU TALKING ABOUT?
!
I'M SO...
...WORRIED ABOUT YOU.

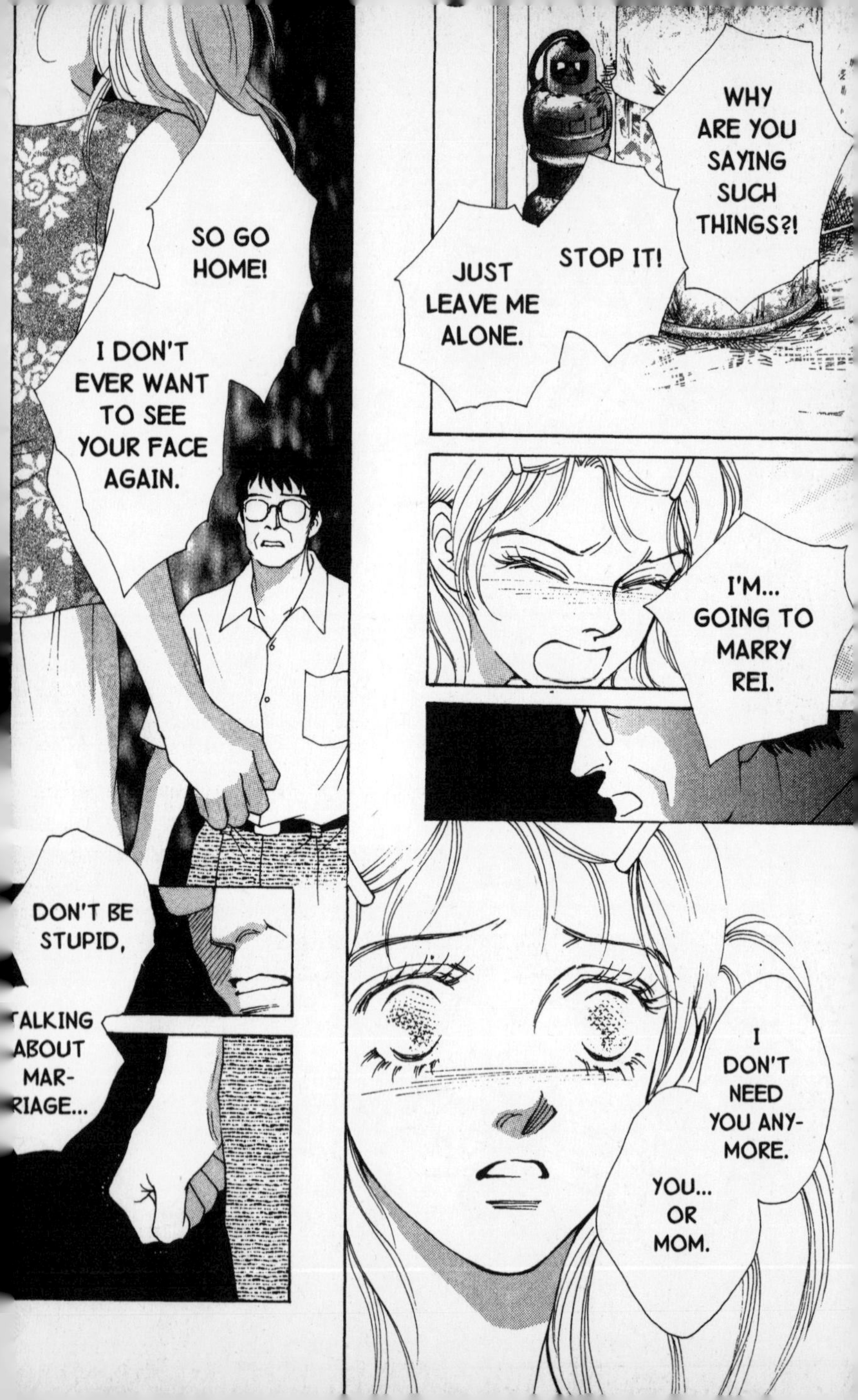
WHY ARE YOU SAYING SUCH THINGS?!
STOP IT!
JUST LEAVE ME ALONE.
I'M... GOING TO MARRY REI.
I DON'T NEED YOU ANY-MORE.
YOU... OR MOM.
SO GO HOME!
I DON'T EVER WANT TO SEE YOUR FACE AGAIN.
DON'T BE STUPID,
TALKING ABOUT MAR-RIAGE...

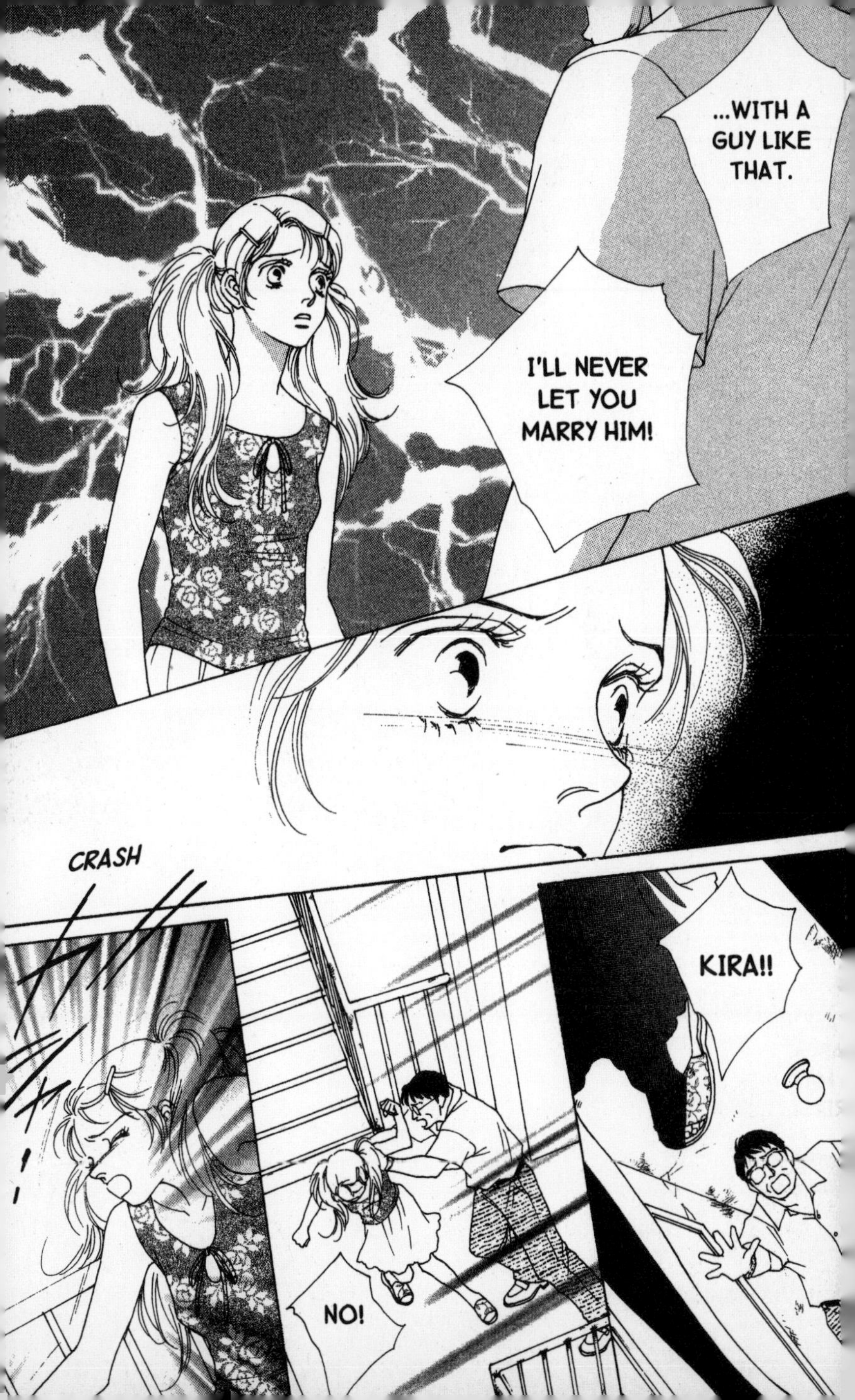
...WITH A GUY LIKE THAT.
I'LL NEVER LET YOU MARRY HIM!
KIRA!!
NO!
CRASH

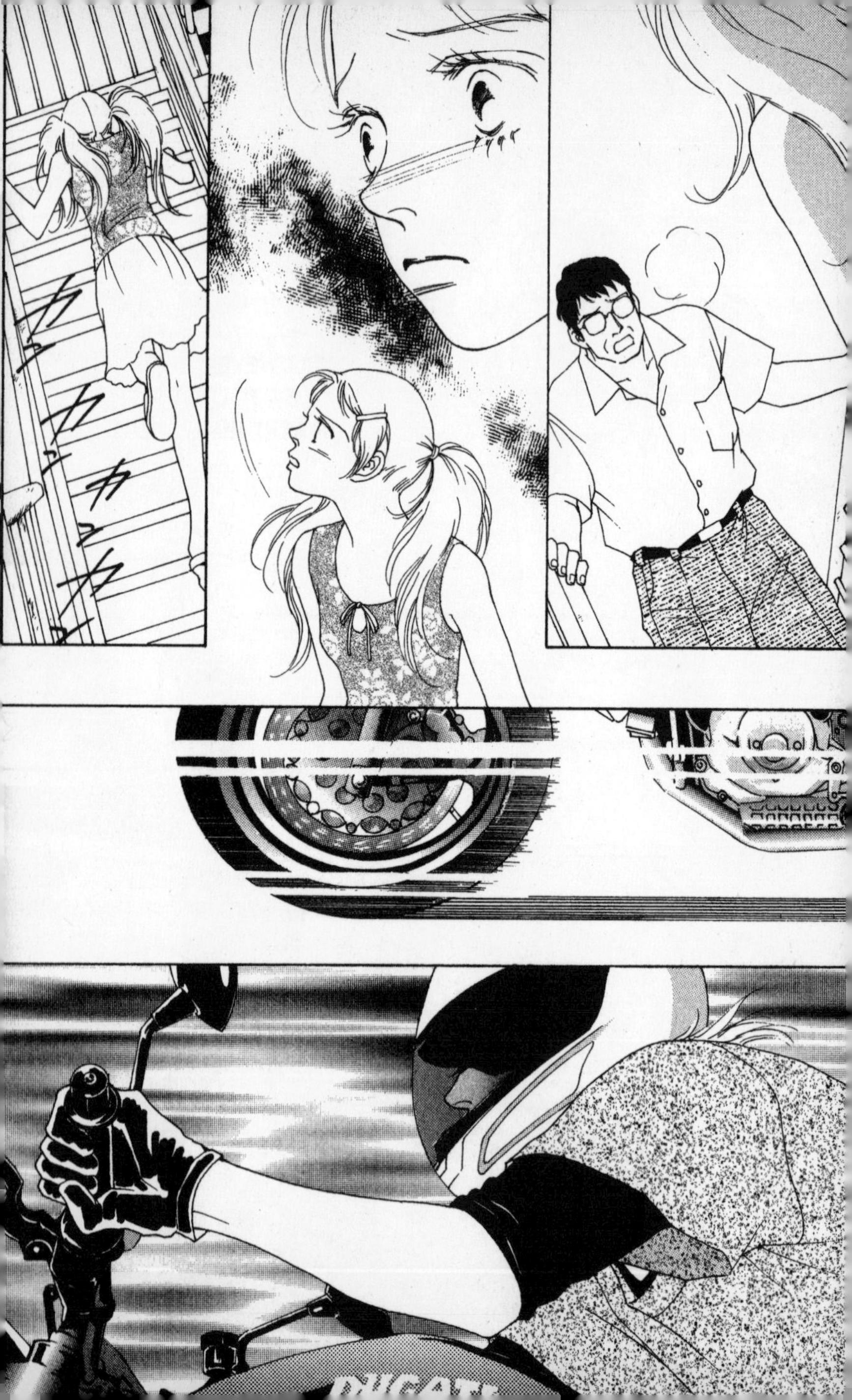

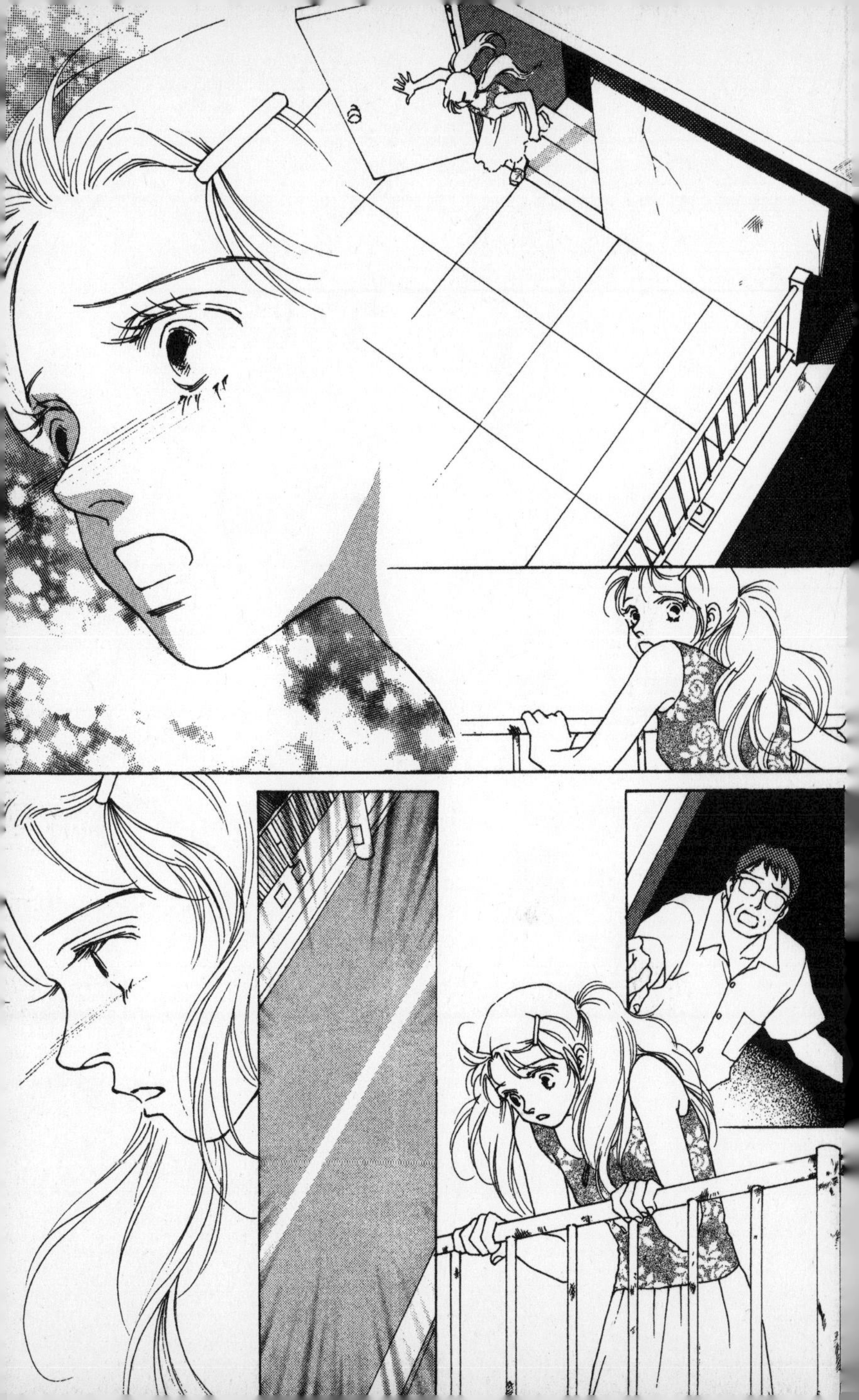

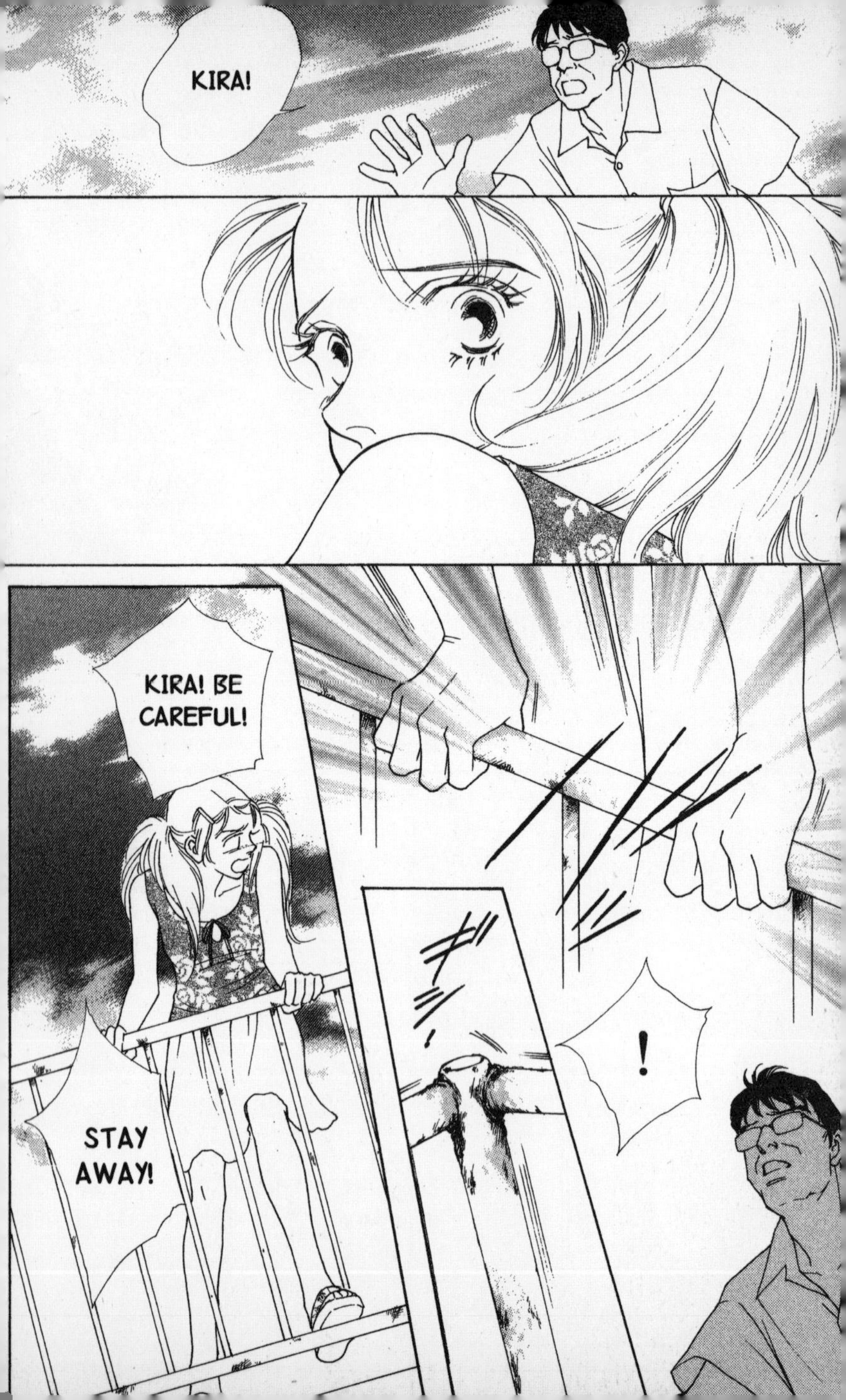
KIRA!
KIRA! BE CAREFUL!
STAY AWAY!
!

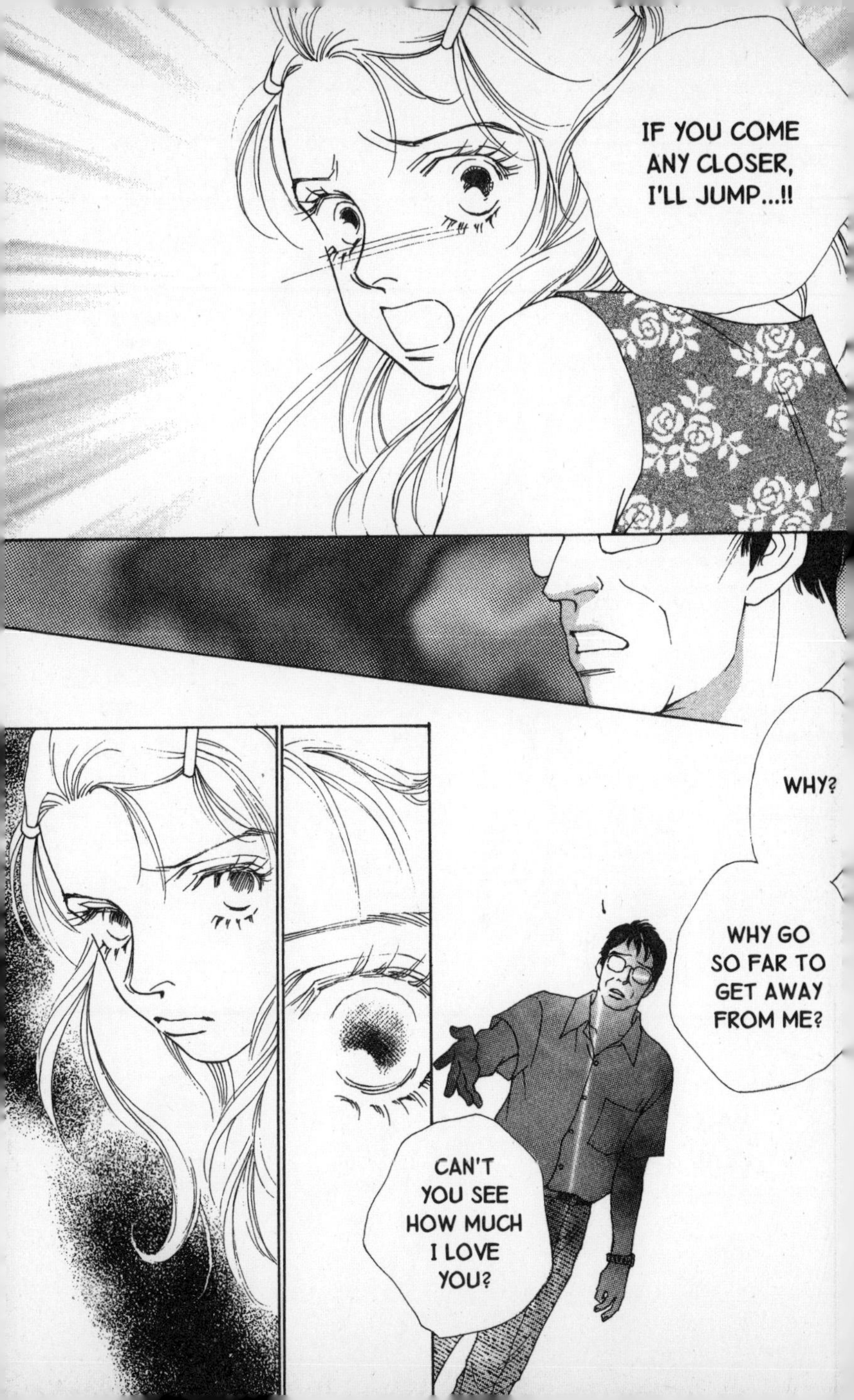
IF YOU COME ANY CLOSER, I'LL JUMP...!!
WHY?
WHY GO SO FAR TO GET AWAY FROM ME?
CAN'T YOU SEE HOW MUCH I LOVE YOU?

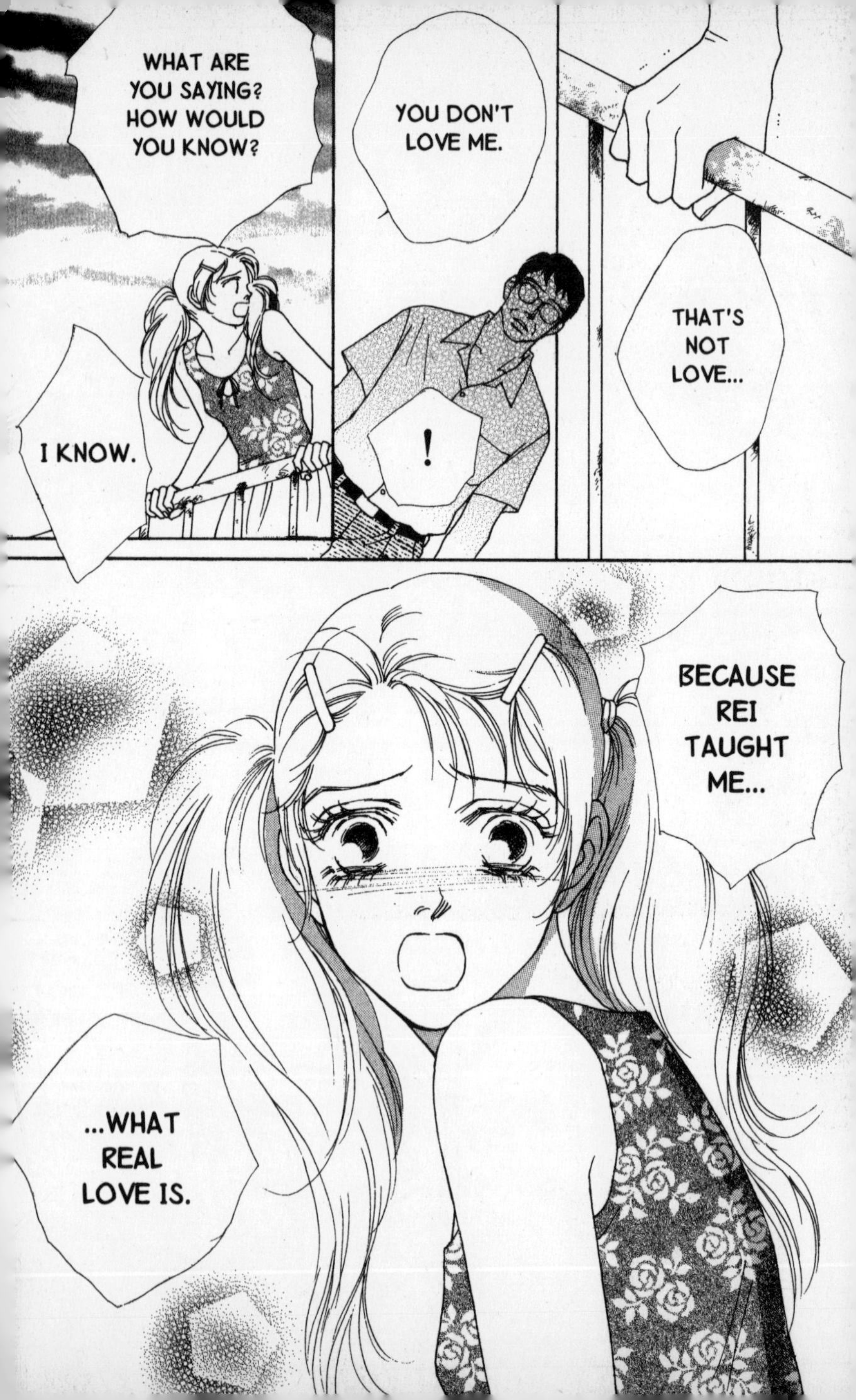
THAT'S NOT LOVE...
YOU DON'T LOVE ME.
!
WHAT ARE YOU SAYING? HOW WOULD YOU KNOW?
I KNOW.
BECAUSE REI TAUGHT ME...
...WHAT REAL LOVE IS.

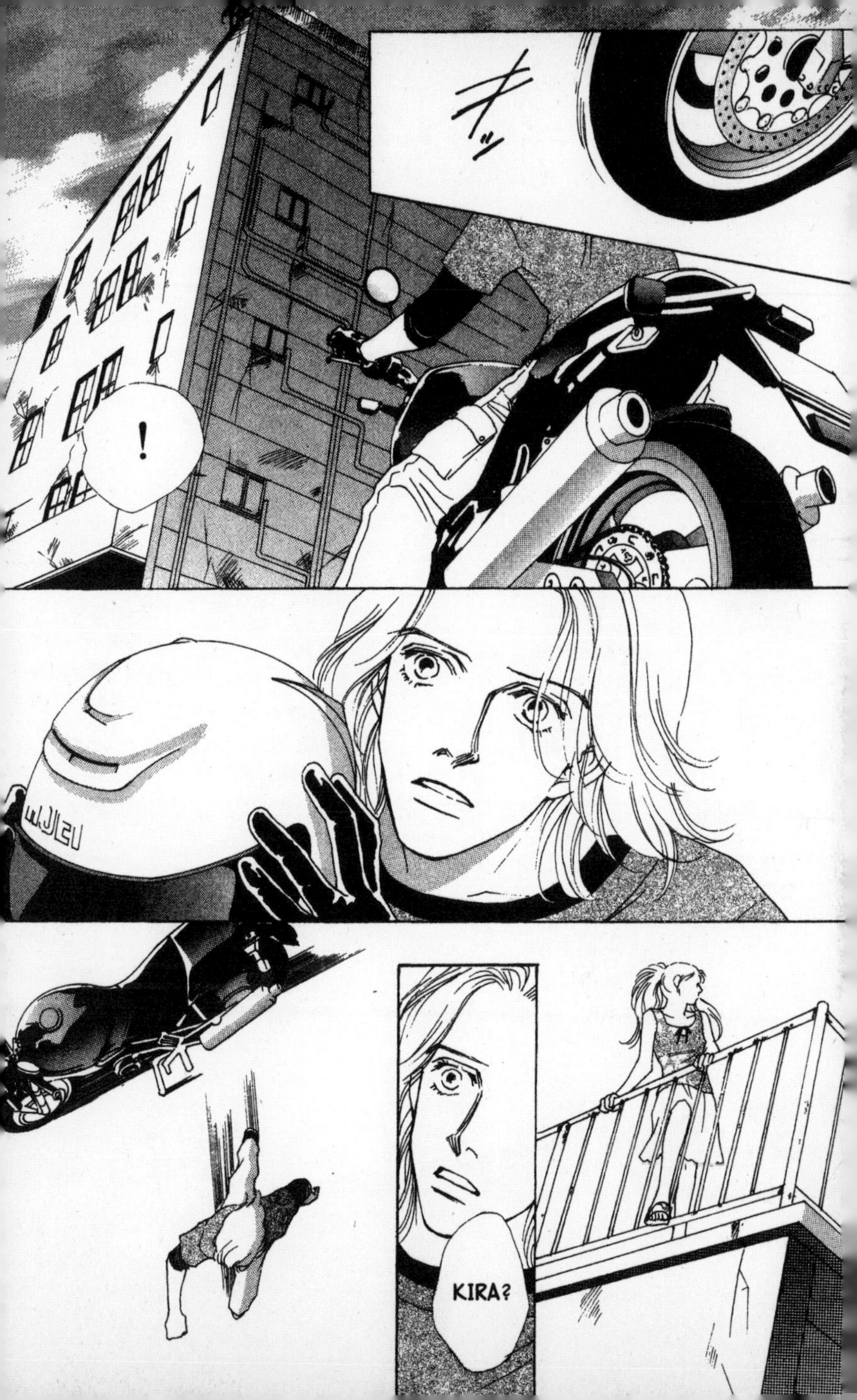
!
KIRA?

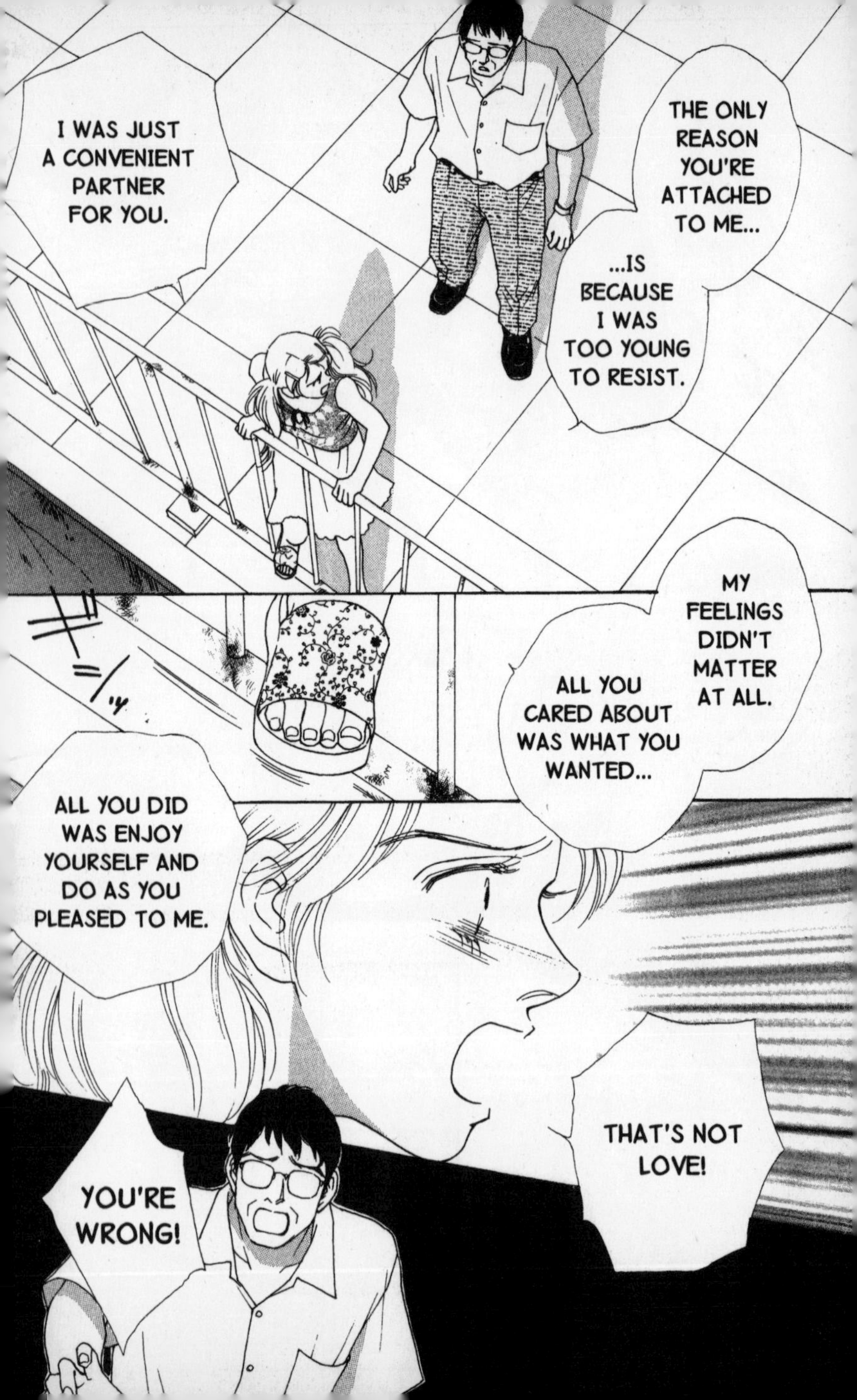
THE ONLY REASON YOU'RE ATTACHED TO ME...
...IS BECAUSE I WAS TOO YOUNG TO RESIST.
I WAS JUST A CONVENIENT PARTNER FOR YOU.
MY FEELINGS DIDN'T MATTER AT ALL.
ALL YOU CARED ABOUT WAS WHAT YOU WANTED...
ALL YOU DID WAS ENJOY YOURSELF AND DO AS YOU PLEASED TO ME.
THAT'S NOT LOVE!
YOU'RE WRONG!

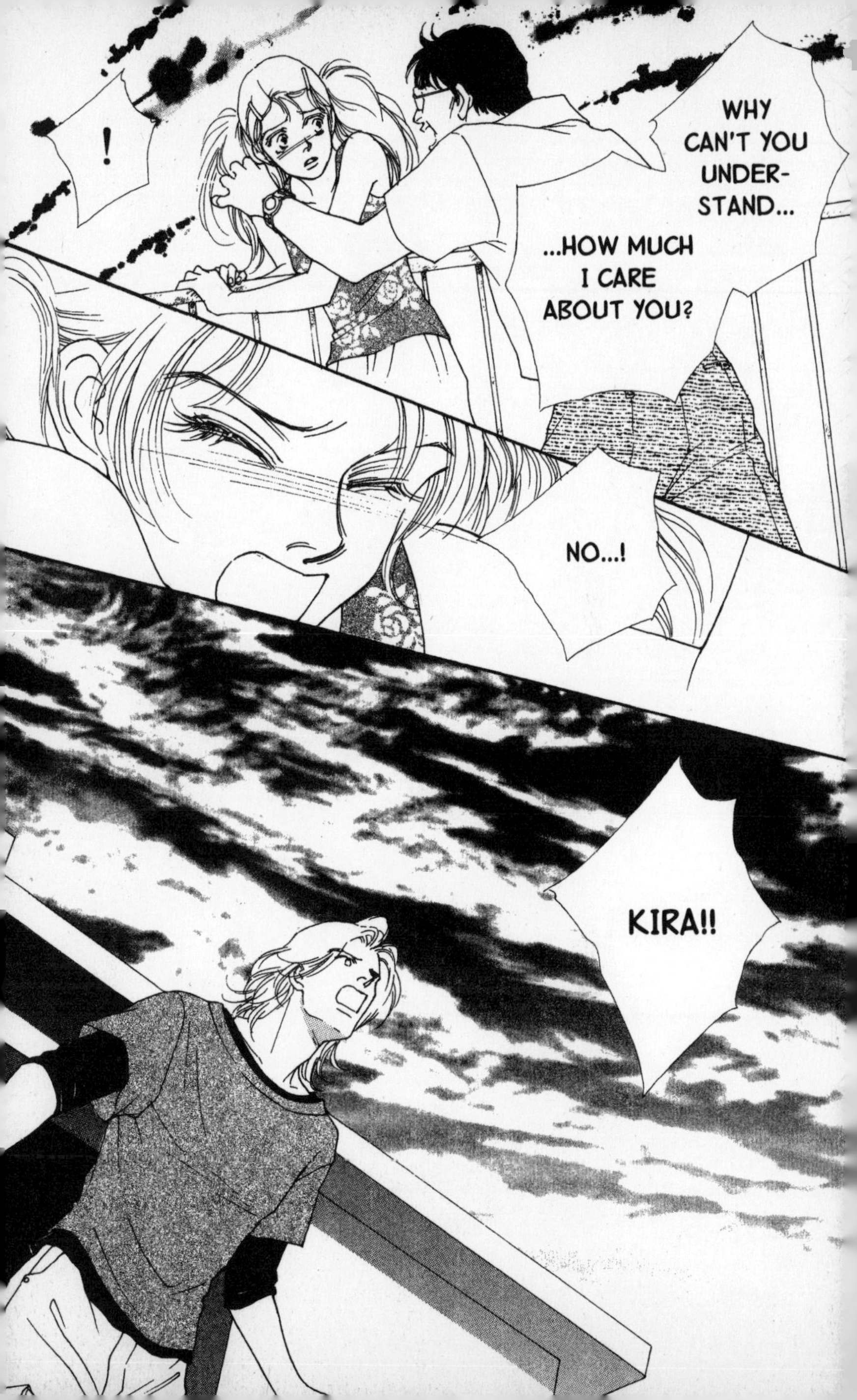
WHY CAN'T YOU UNDER-STAND...
...HOW MUCH I CARE ABOUT YOU?
!
NO...!
KIRA!!

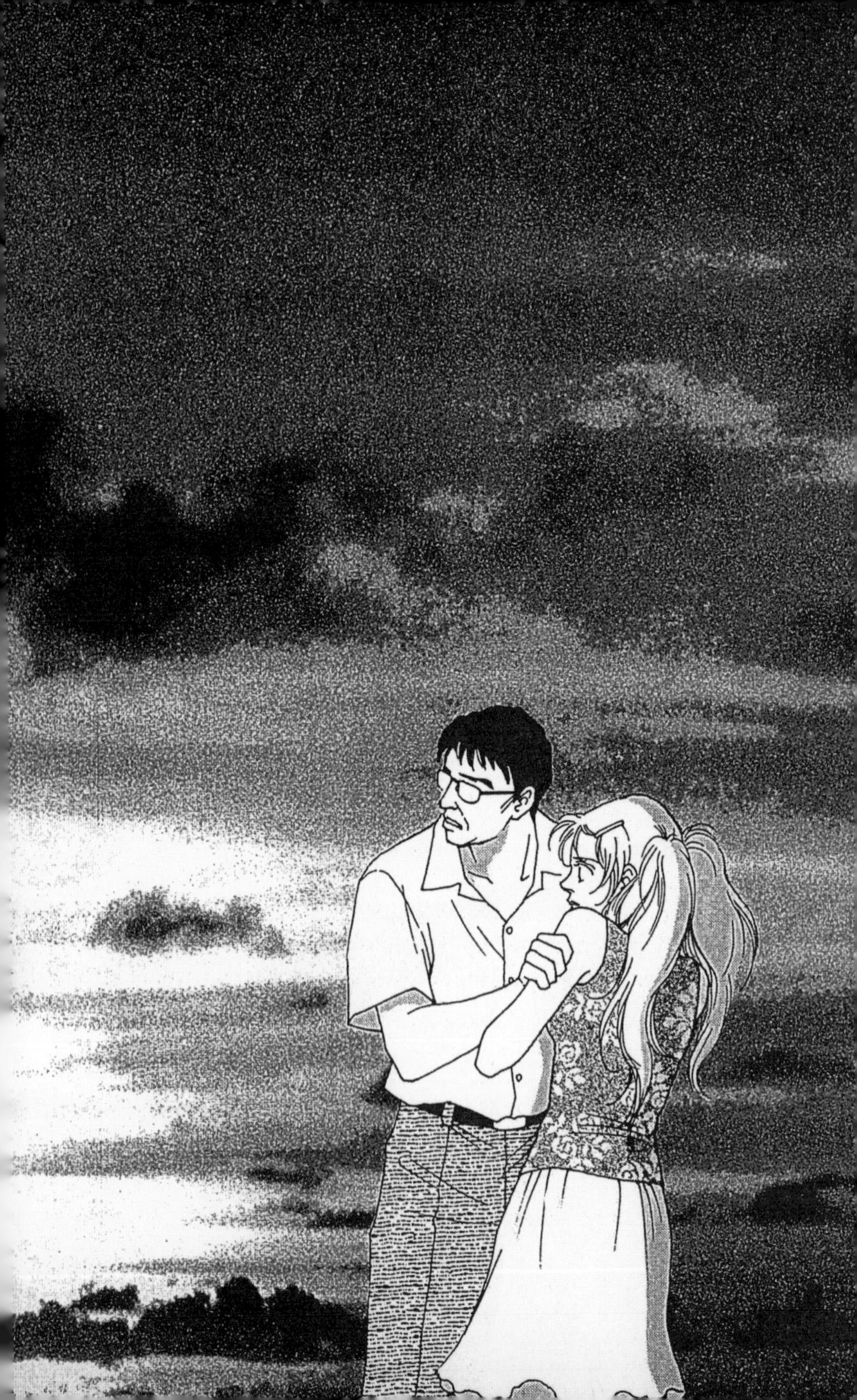

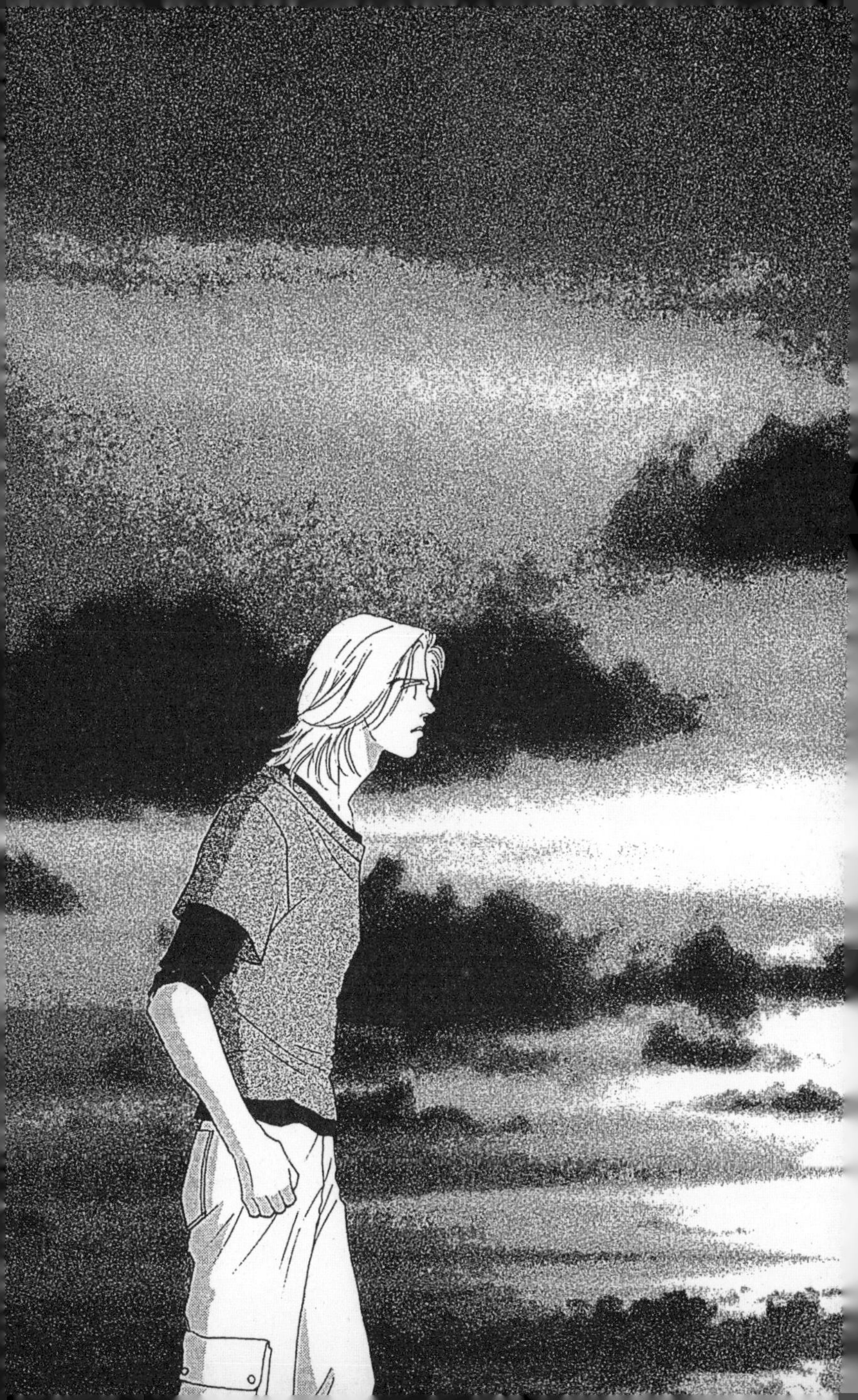

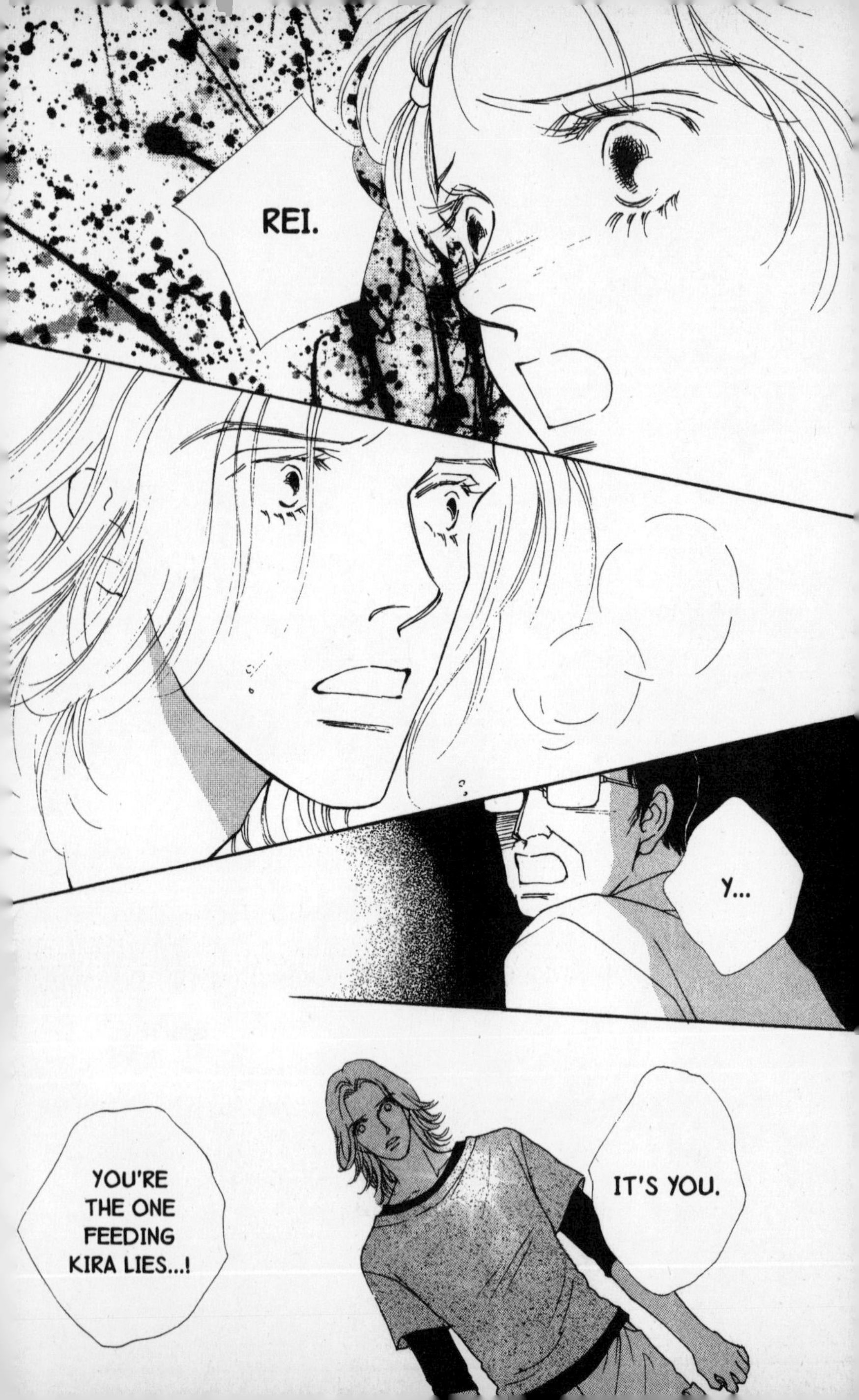
REI.
Y...
IT'S YOU.
YOU'RE THE ONE FEEDING KIRA LIES...!

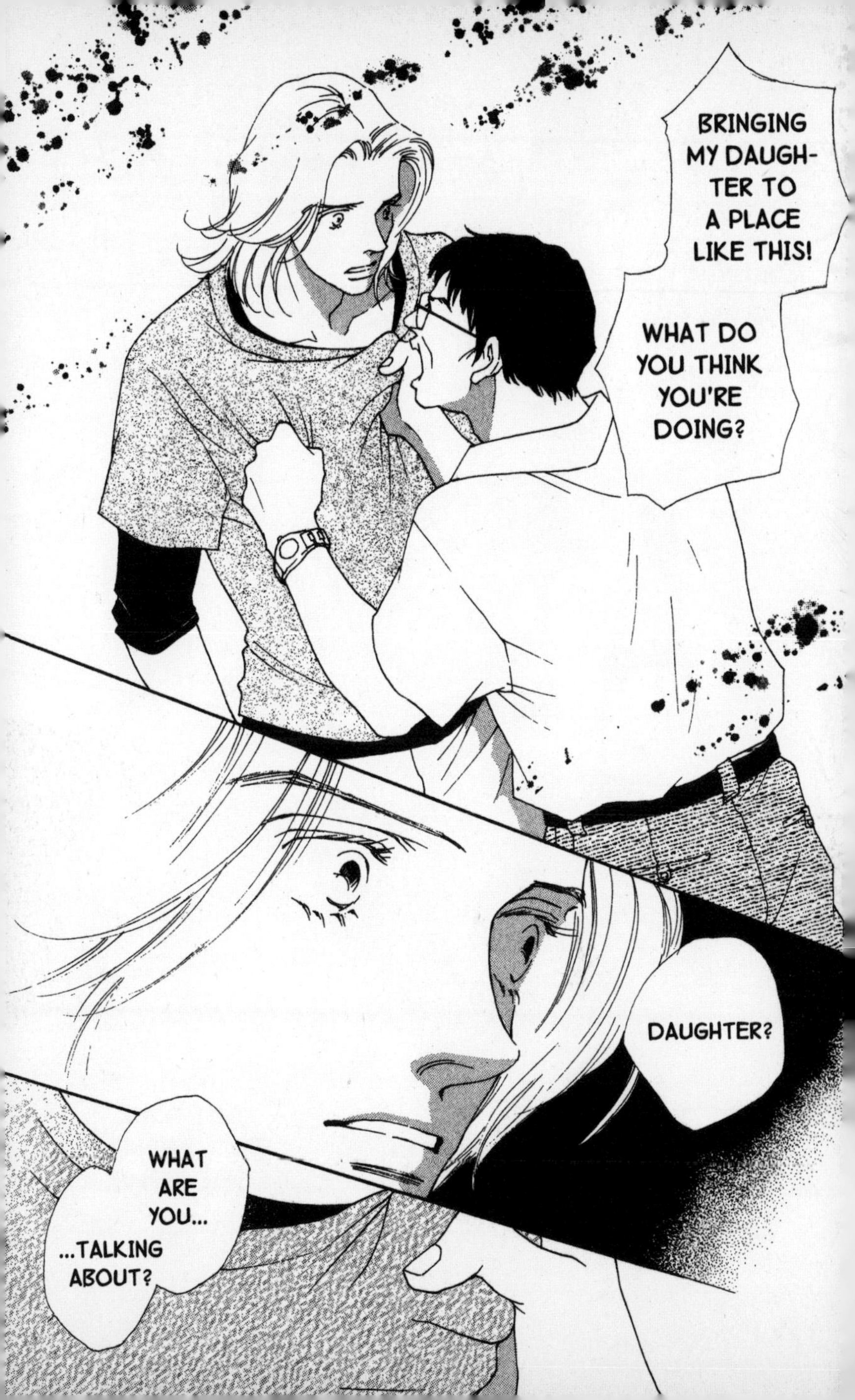
BRINGING MY DAUGHTER TO A PLACE LIKE THIS!
WHAT DO YOU THINK YOU'RE DOING?
DAUGHTER?
WHAT ARE YOU...
...TALKING ABOUT?

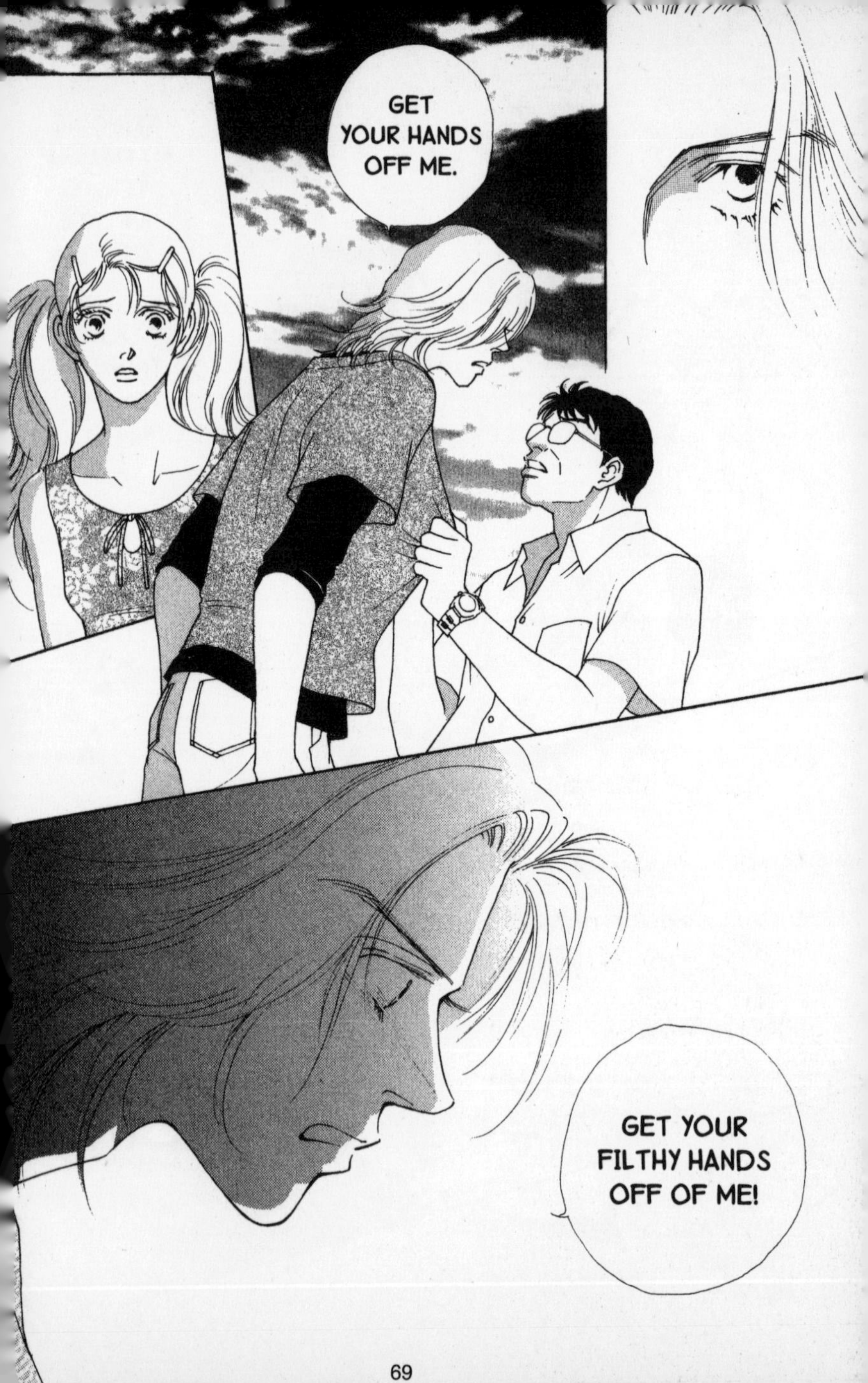
GET YOUR HANDS OFF ME.
GET YOUR FILTHY HANDS OFF OF ME!

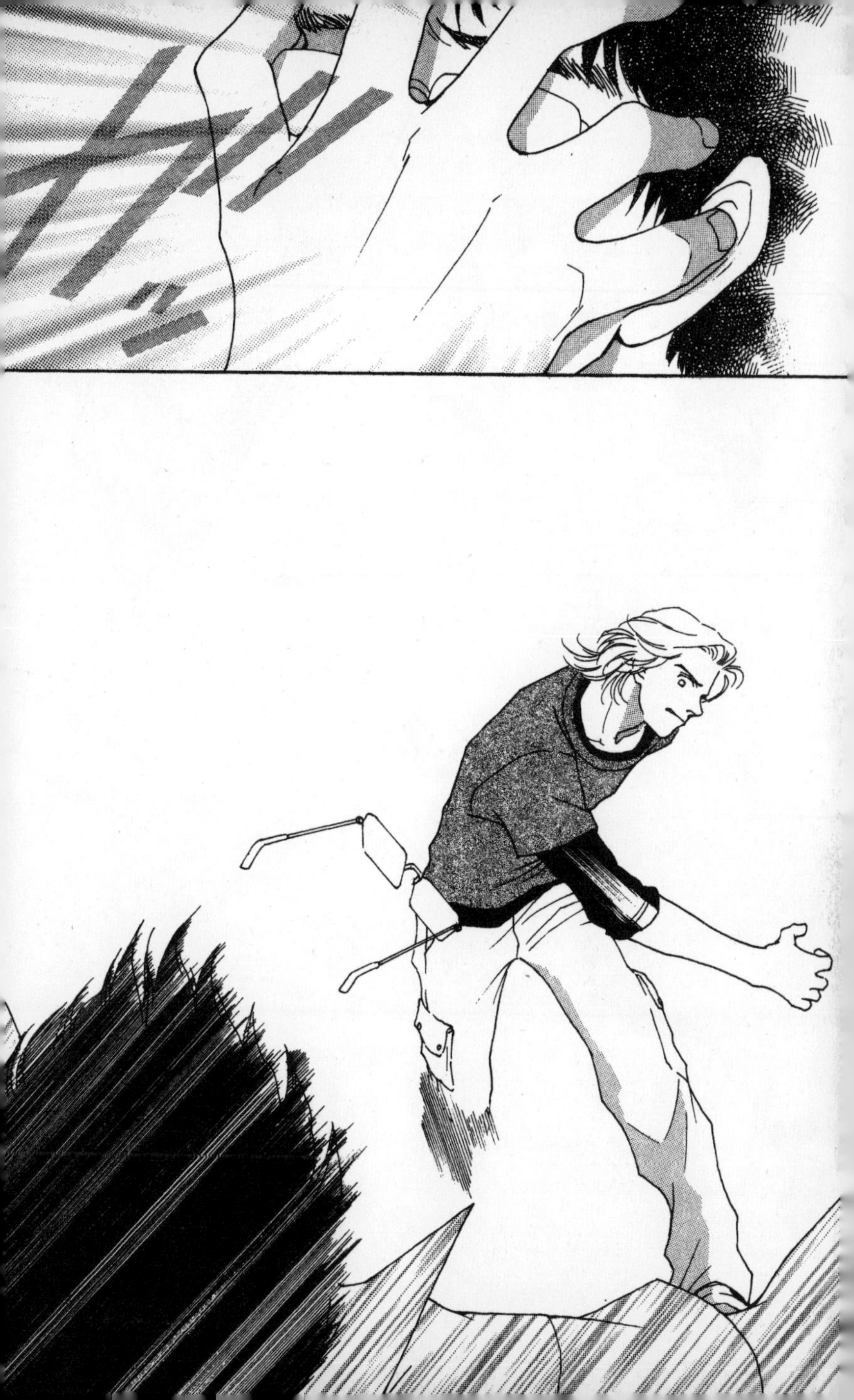

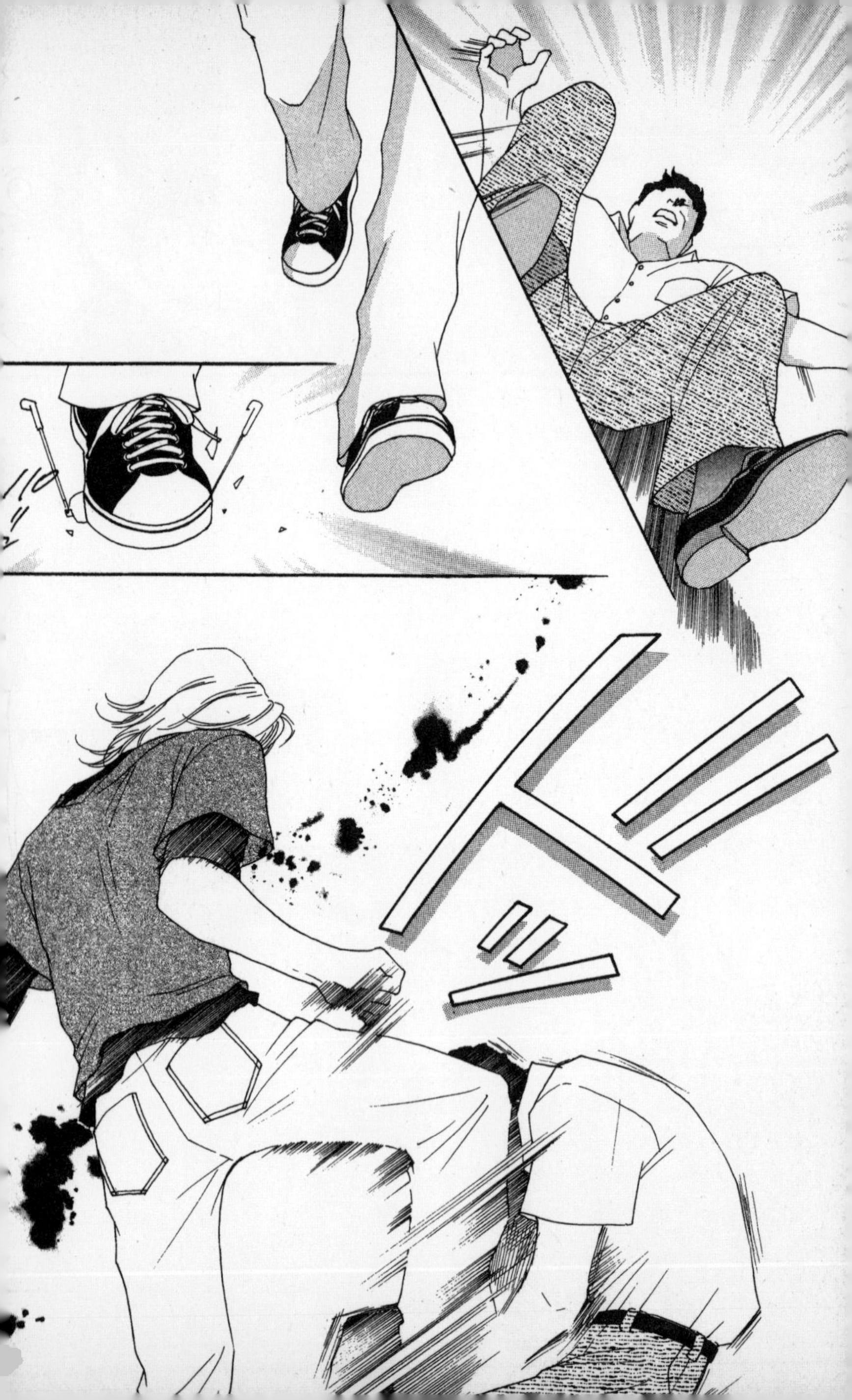
ドッ

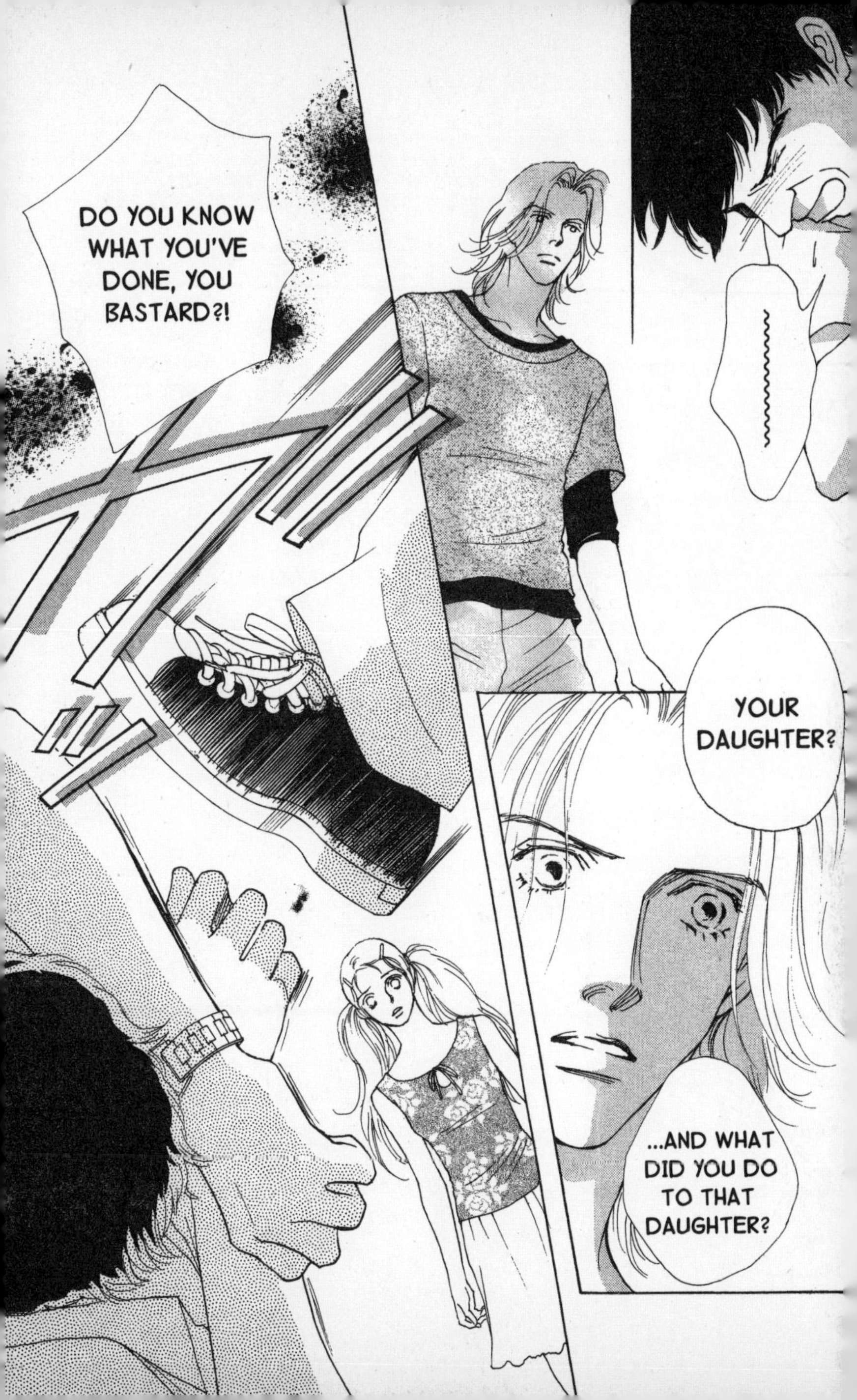
DO YOU KNOW WHAT YOU'VE DONE, YOU BASTARD?!
YOUR DAUGHTER?
...AND WHAT DID YOU DO TO THAT DAUGHTER?

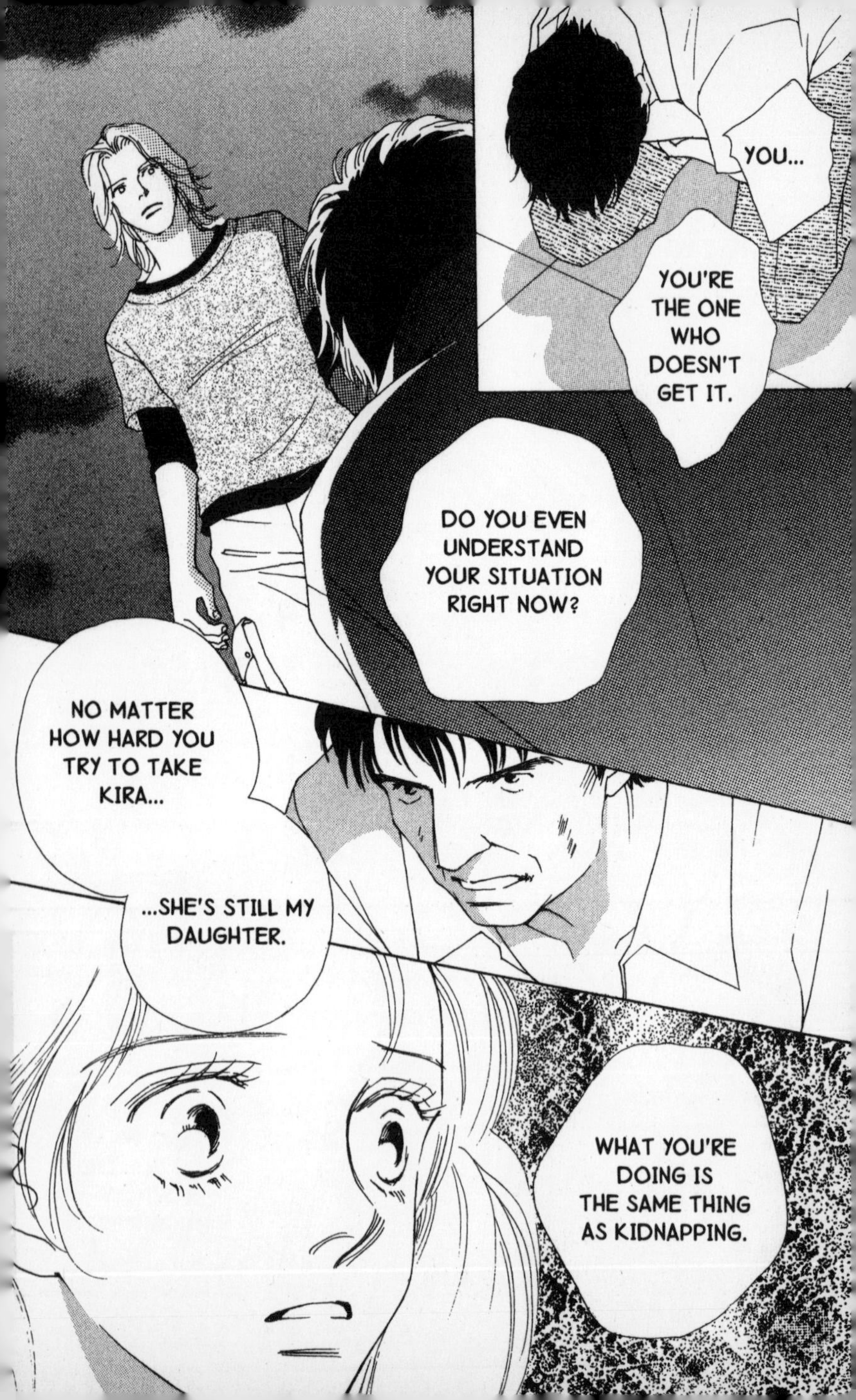
YOU...
YOU'RE THE ONE WHO DOESN'T GET IT.
DO YOU EVEN UNDERSTAND YOUR SITUATION RIGHT NOW?
NO MATTER HOW HARD YOU TRY TO TAKE KIRA...
...SHE'S STILL MY DAUGHTER.
WHAT YOU'RE DOING IS THE SAME THING AS KIDNAPPING.

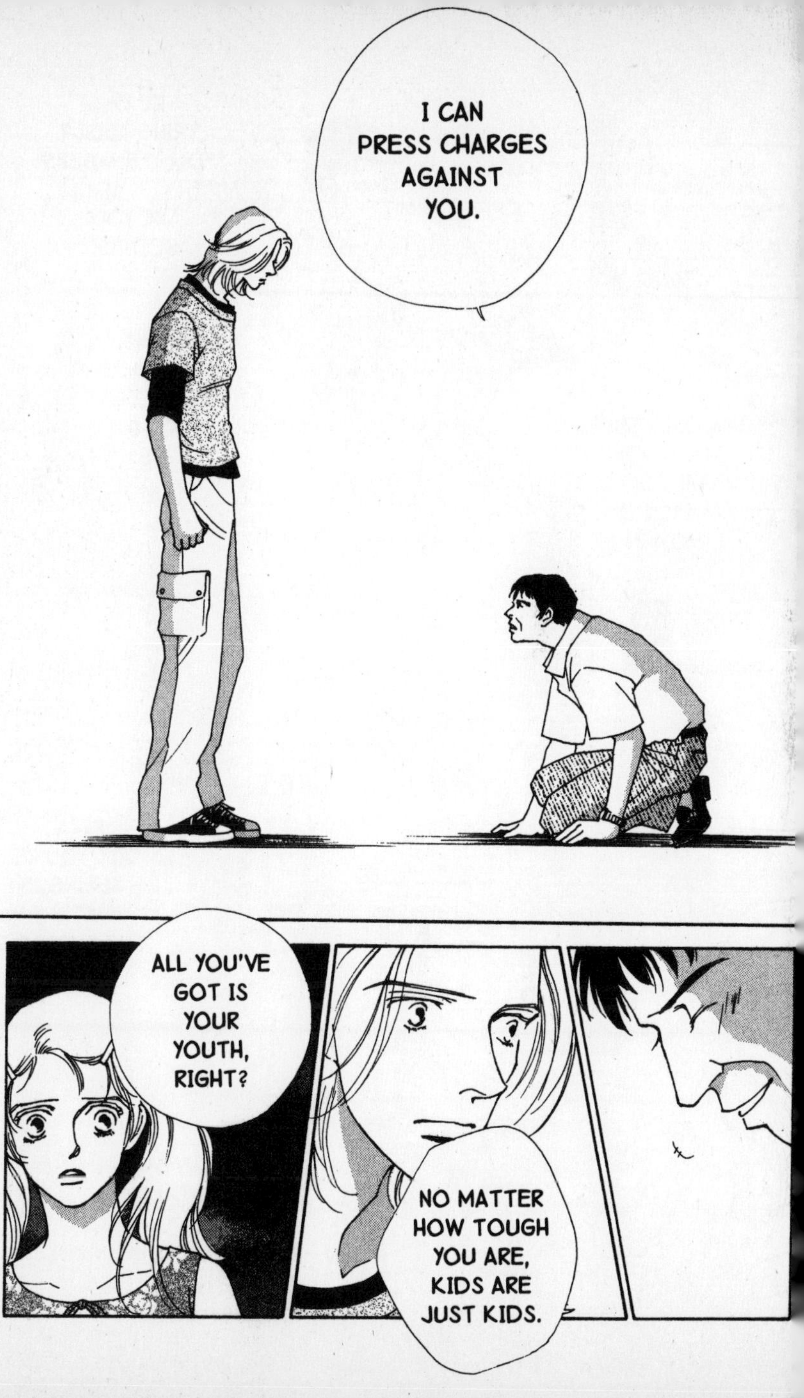
I CAN PRESS CHARGES AGAINST YOU.
ALL YOU'VE GOT IS YOUR YOUTH, RIGHT?
NO MATTER HOW TOUGH YOU ARE, KIDS ARE JUST KIDS.

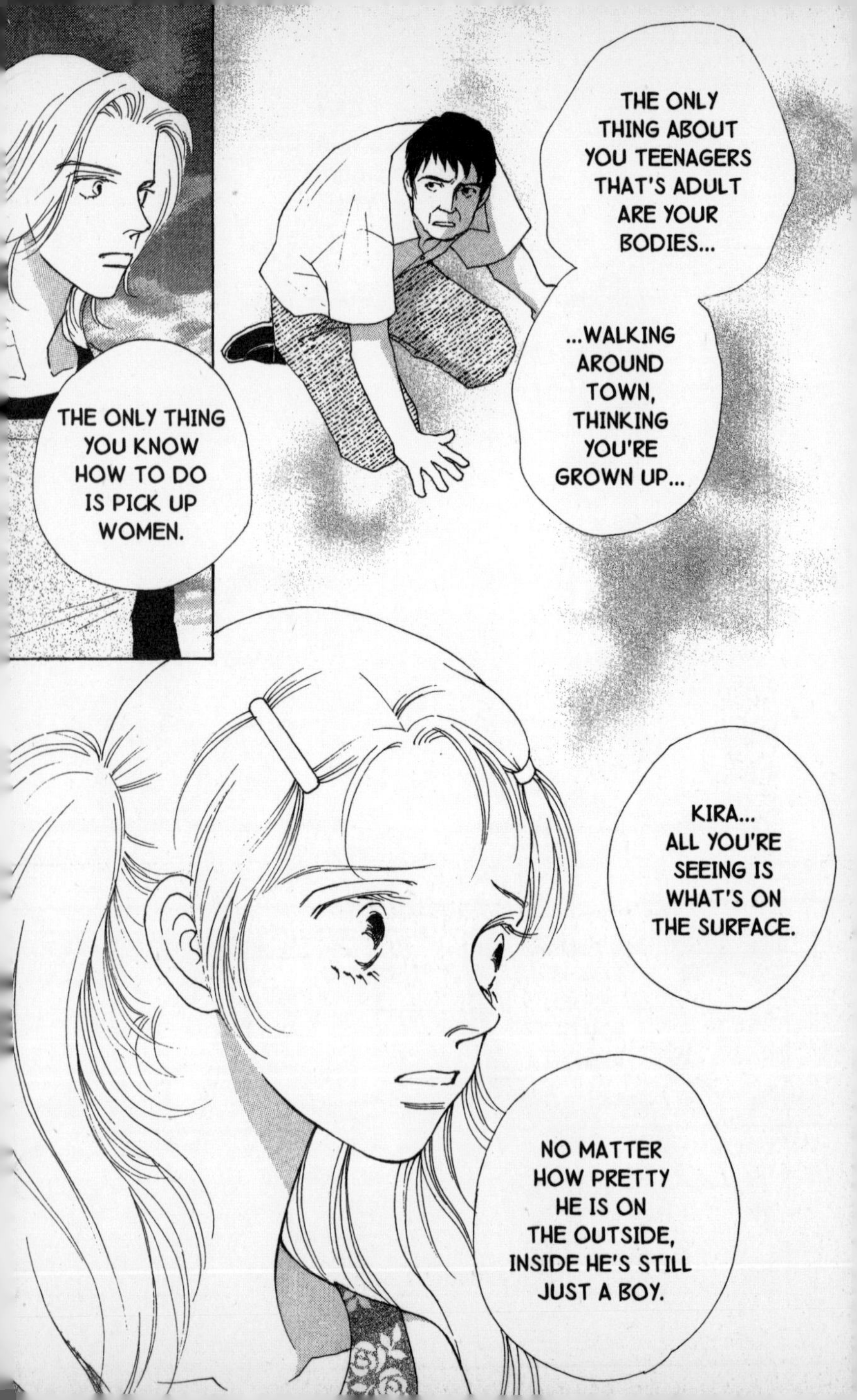
THE ONLY THING ABOUT YOU TEENAGERS THAT'S ADULT ARE YOUR BODIES...
...WALKING AROUND TOWN, THINKING YOU'RE GROWN UP...
THE ONLY THING YOU KNOW HOW TO DO IS PICK UP WOMEN.
KIRA... ALL YOU'RE SEEING IS WHAT'S ON THE SURFACE.
NO MATTER HOW PRETTY HE IS ON THE OUTSIDE, INSIDE HE'S STILL JUST A BOY.

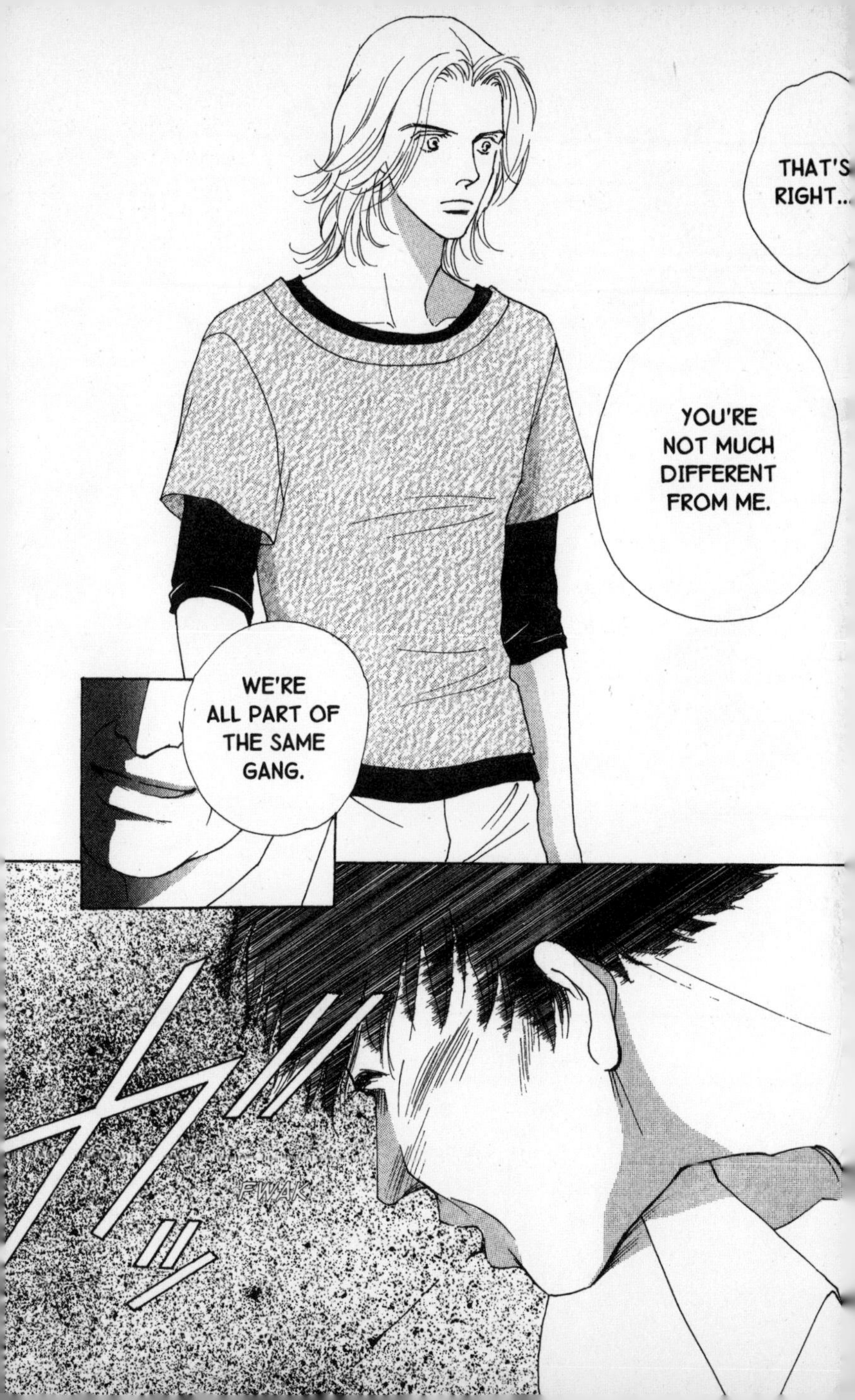
THAT'S RIGHT...
YOU'RE NOT MUCH DIFFERENT FROM ME.
WE'RE ALL PART OF THE SAME GANG.
FWAK

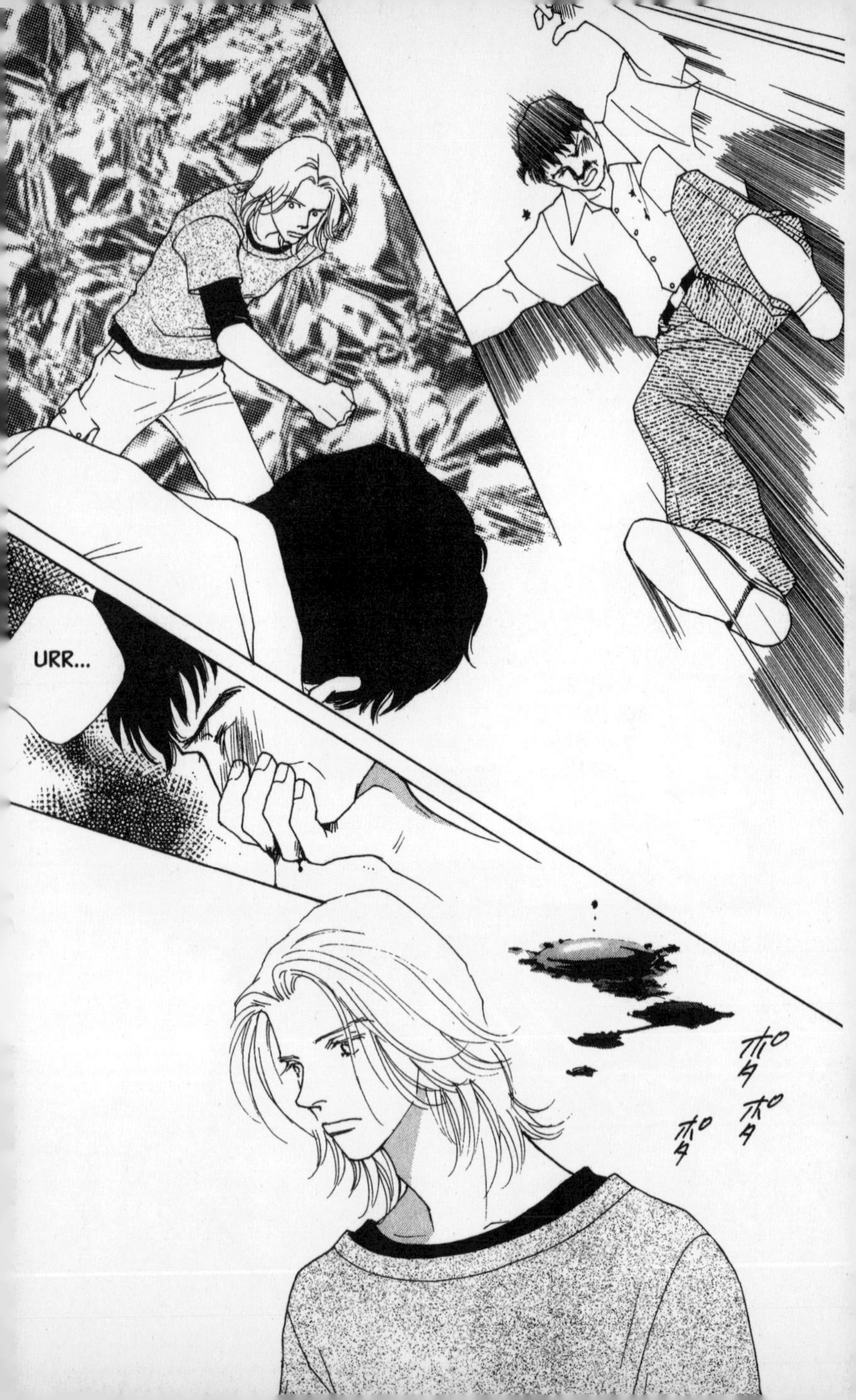
URR...
ポタ ポタ ポタ

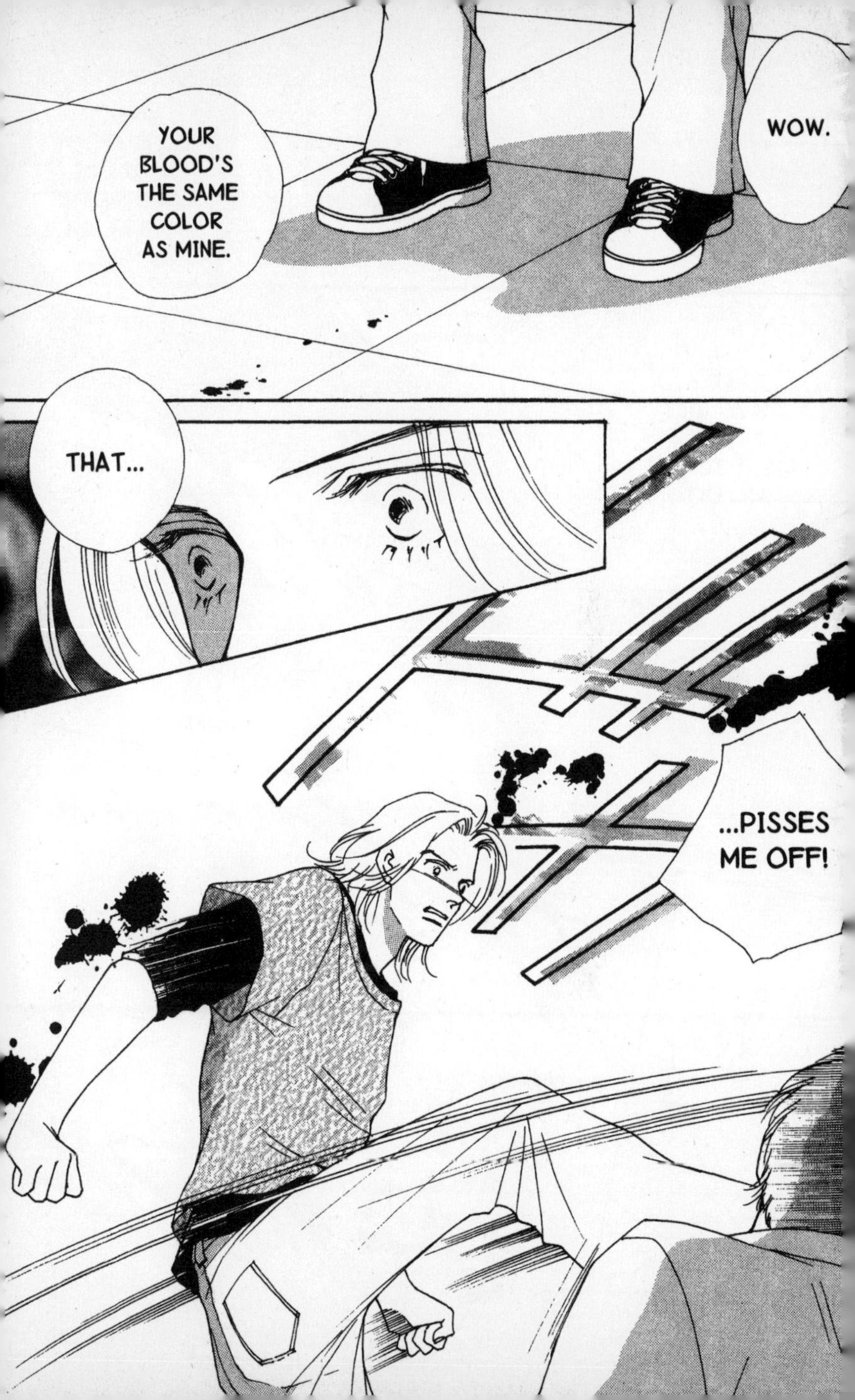
WOW.
YOUR BLOOD'S THE SAME COLOR AS MINE.
THAT...
...PISSES ME OFF!

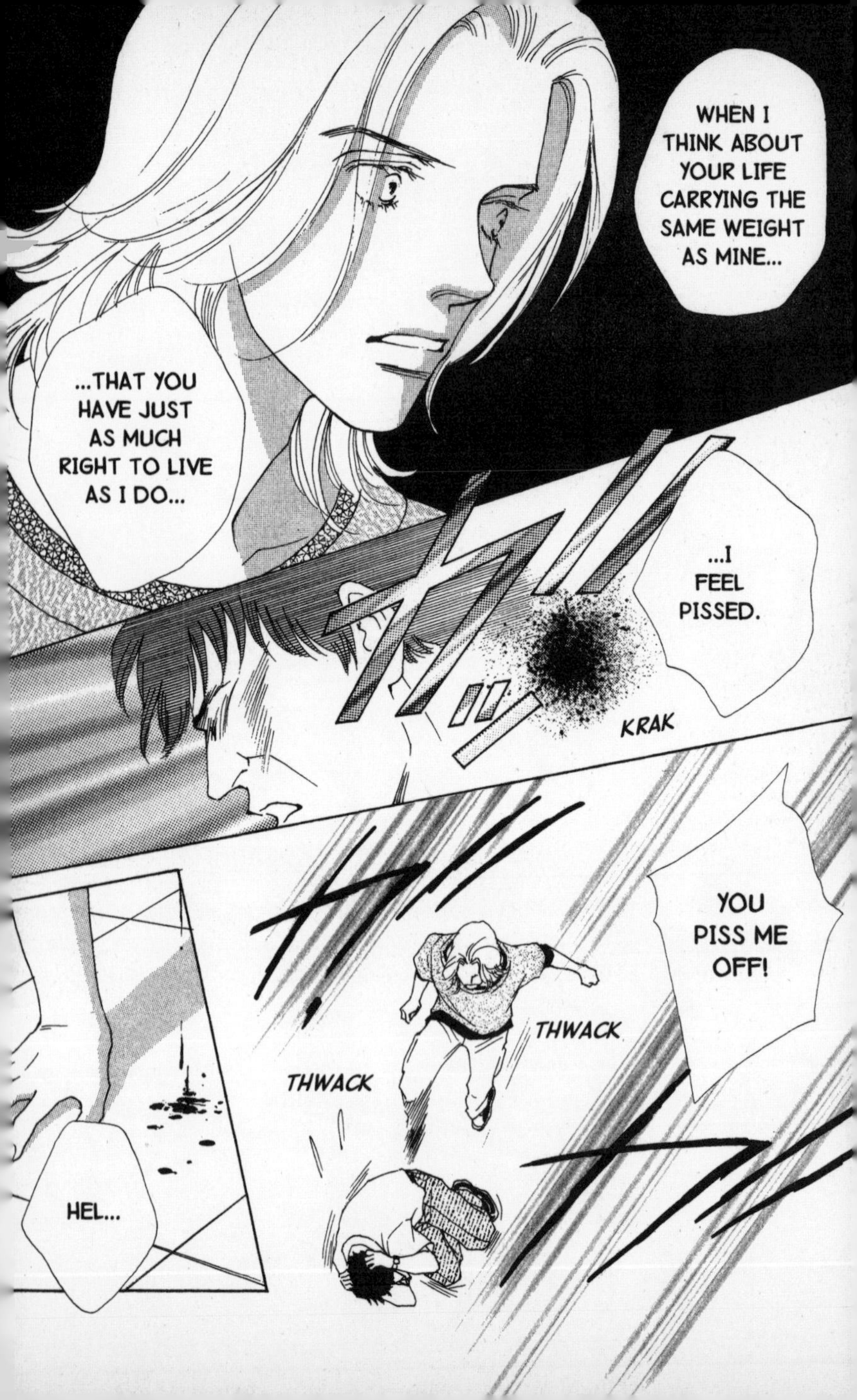
WHEN I THINK ABOUT YOUR LIFE CARRYING THE SAME WEIGHT AS MINE...
...THAT YOU HAVE JUST AS MUCH RIGHT TO LIVE AS I DO...
...I FEEL PISSED.
KRAK
YOU PISS ME OFF!
THWACK
THWACK
HEL...

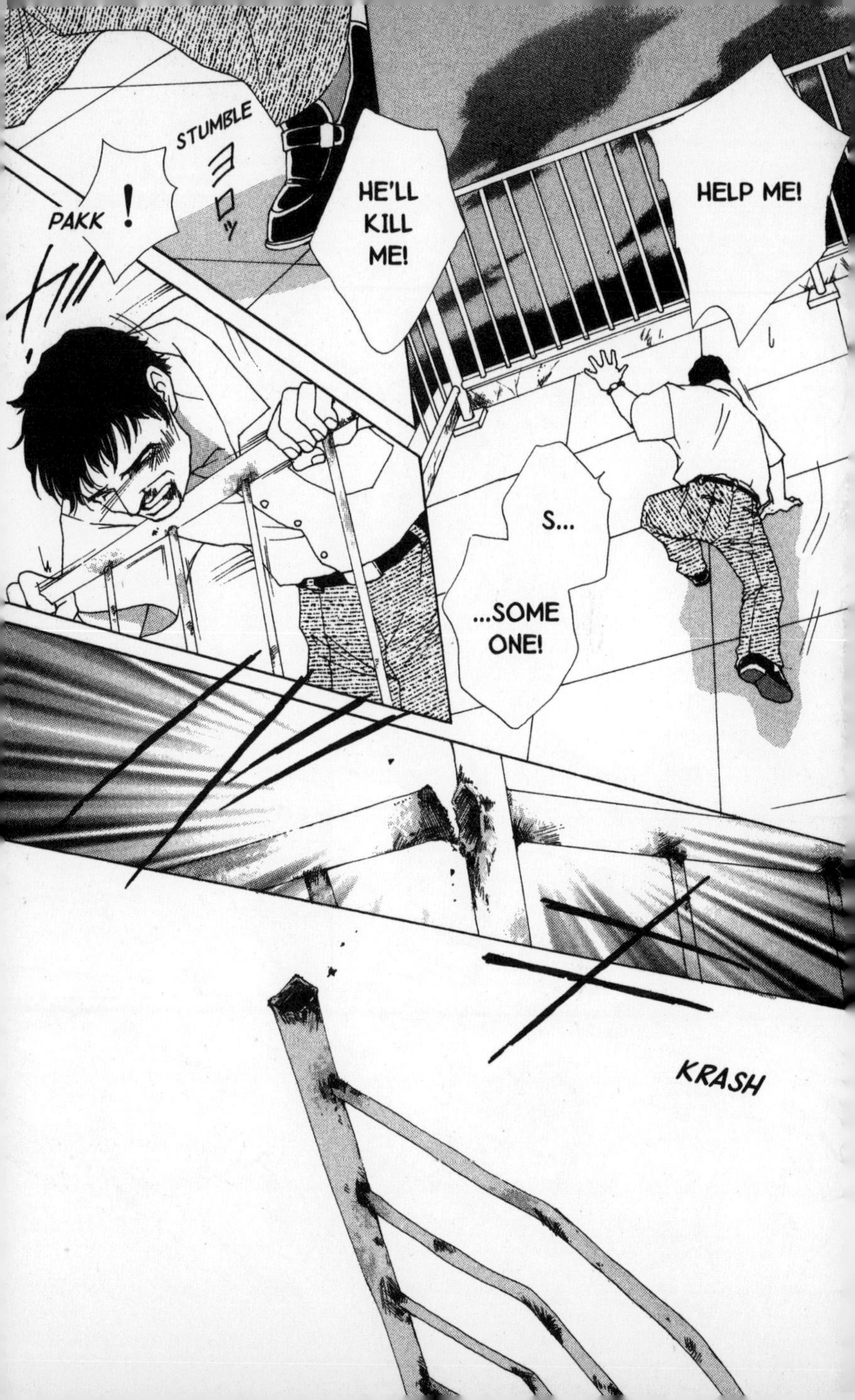
HELP ME!
HE'LL KILL ME!
STUMBLE
ヨロッ
!
PAKK
S...
...SOME ONE!
KRASH

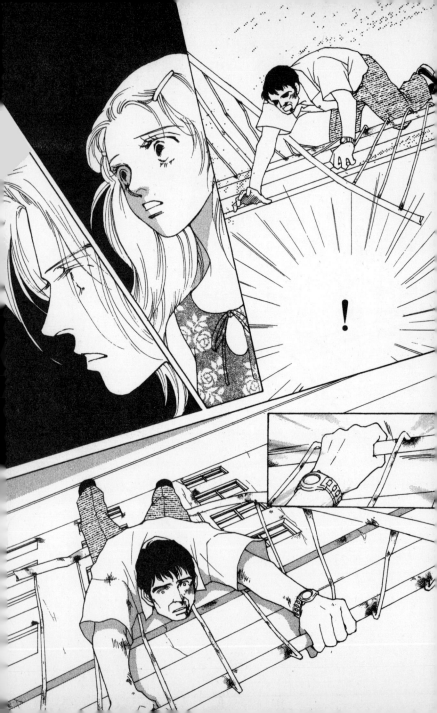

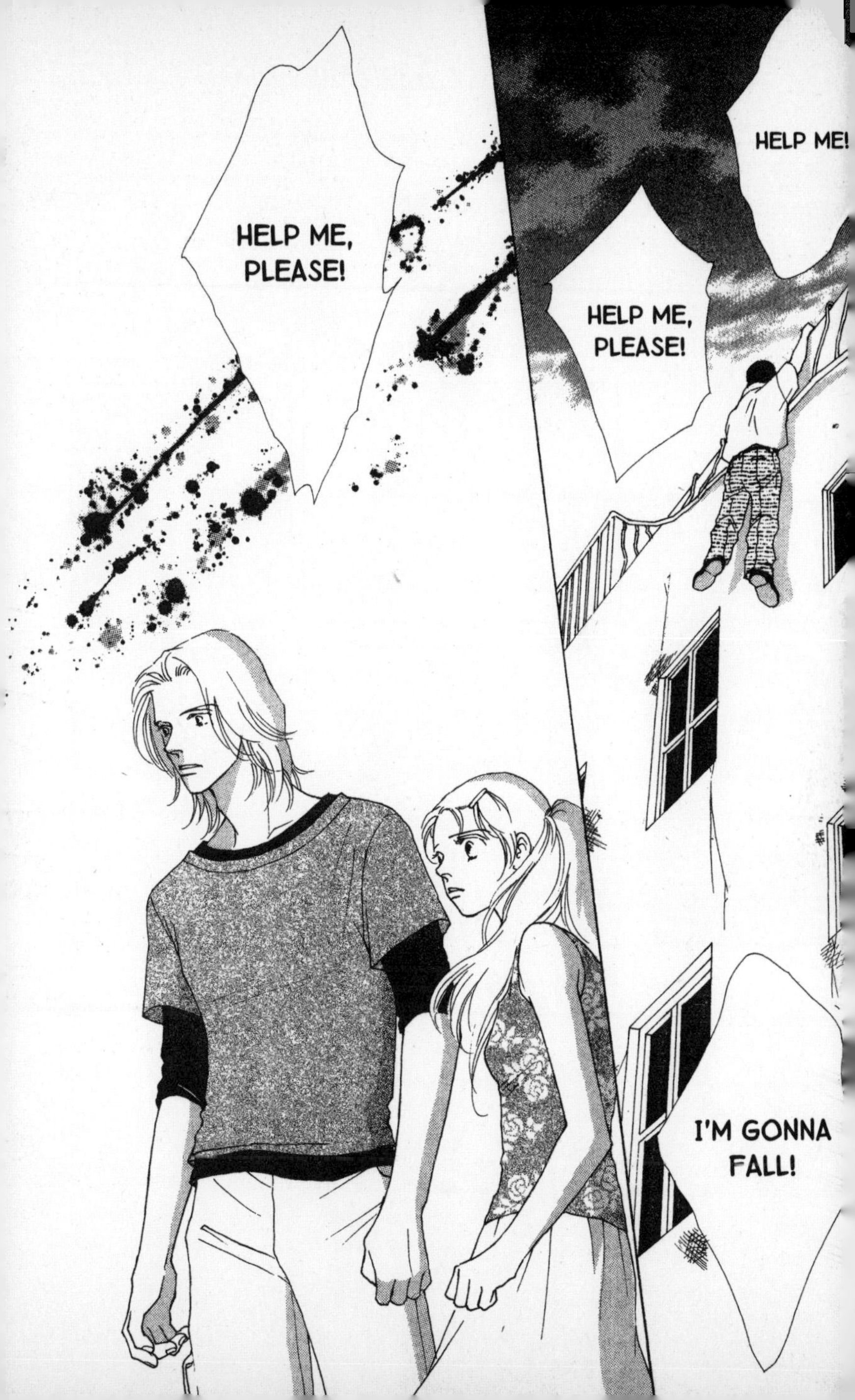
HELP ME!
HELP ME, PLEASE!
I'M GONNA FALL!
HELP ME, PLEASE!

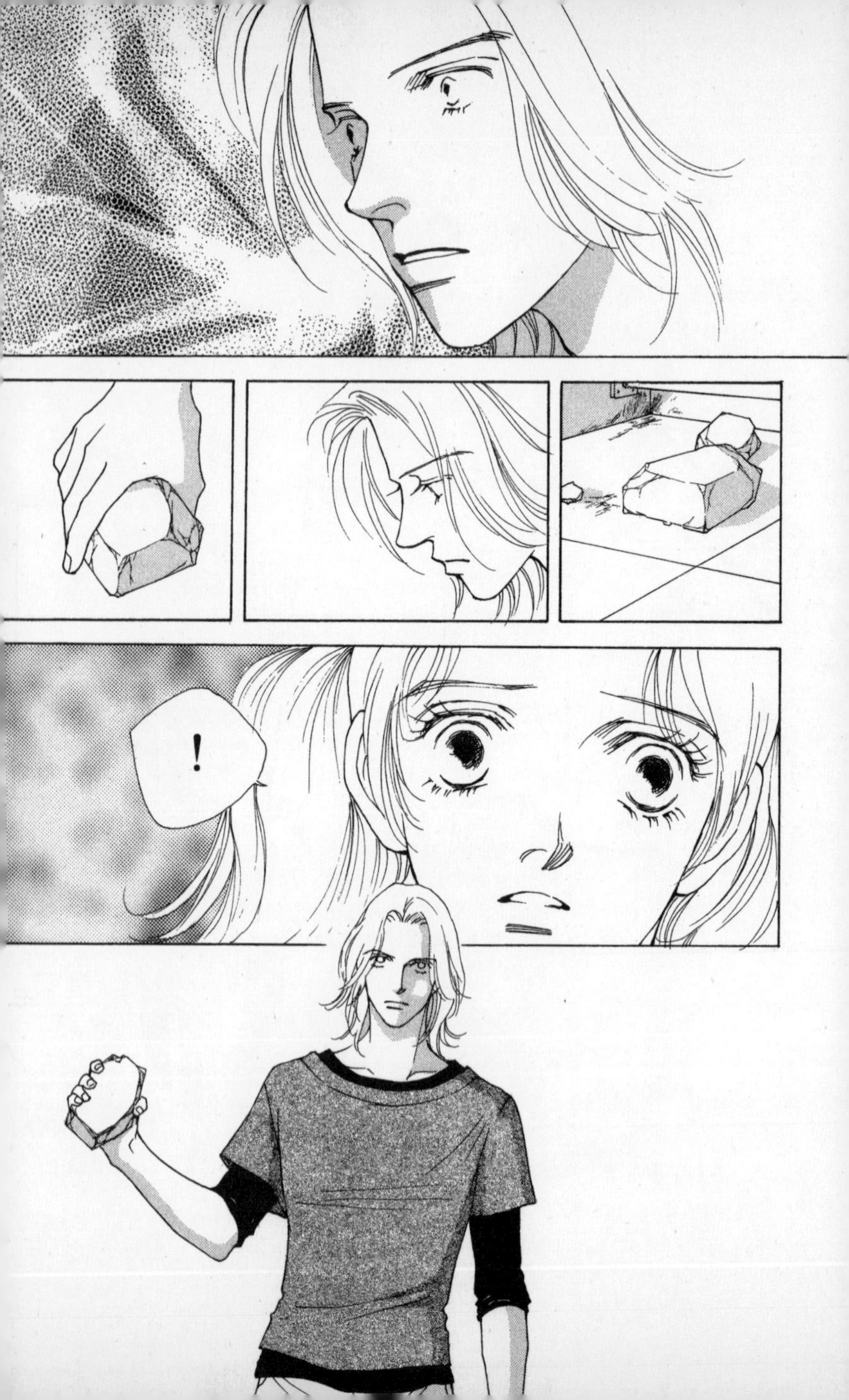
!

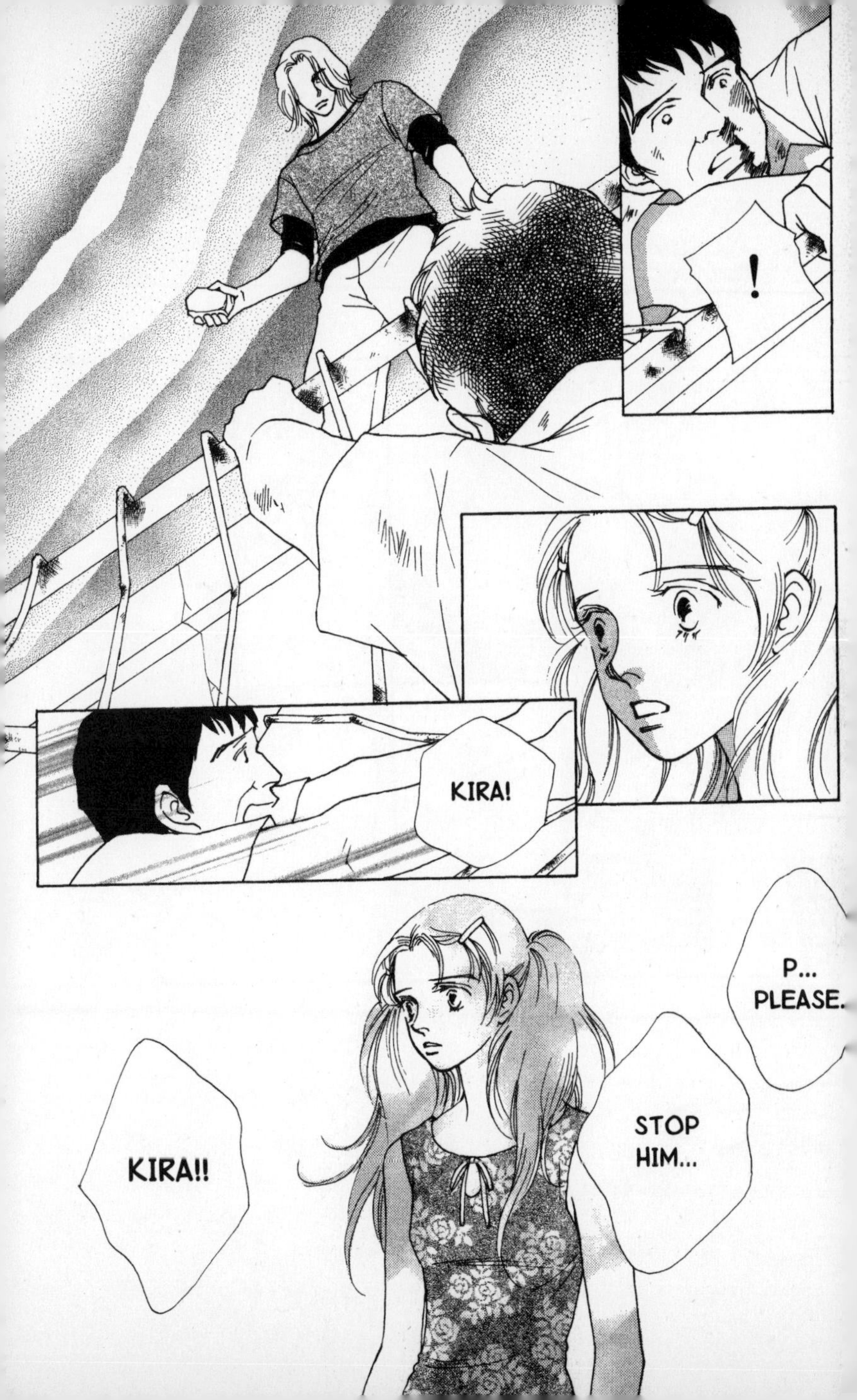
!
KIRA!
P... PLEASE.
STOP HIM...
KIRA!!

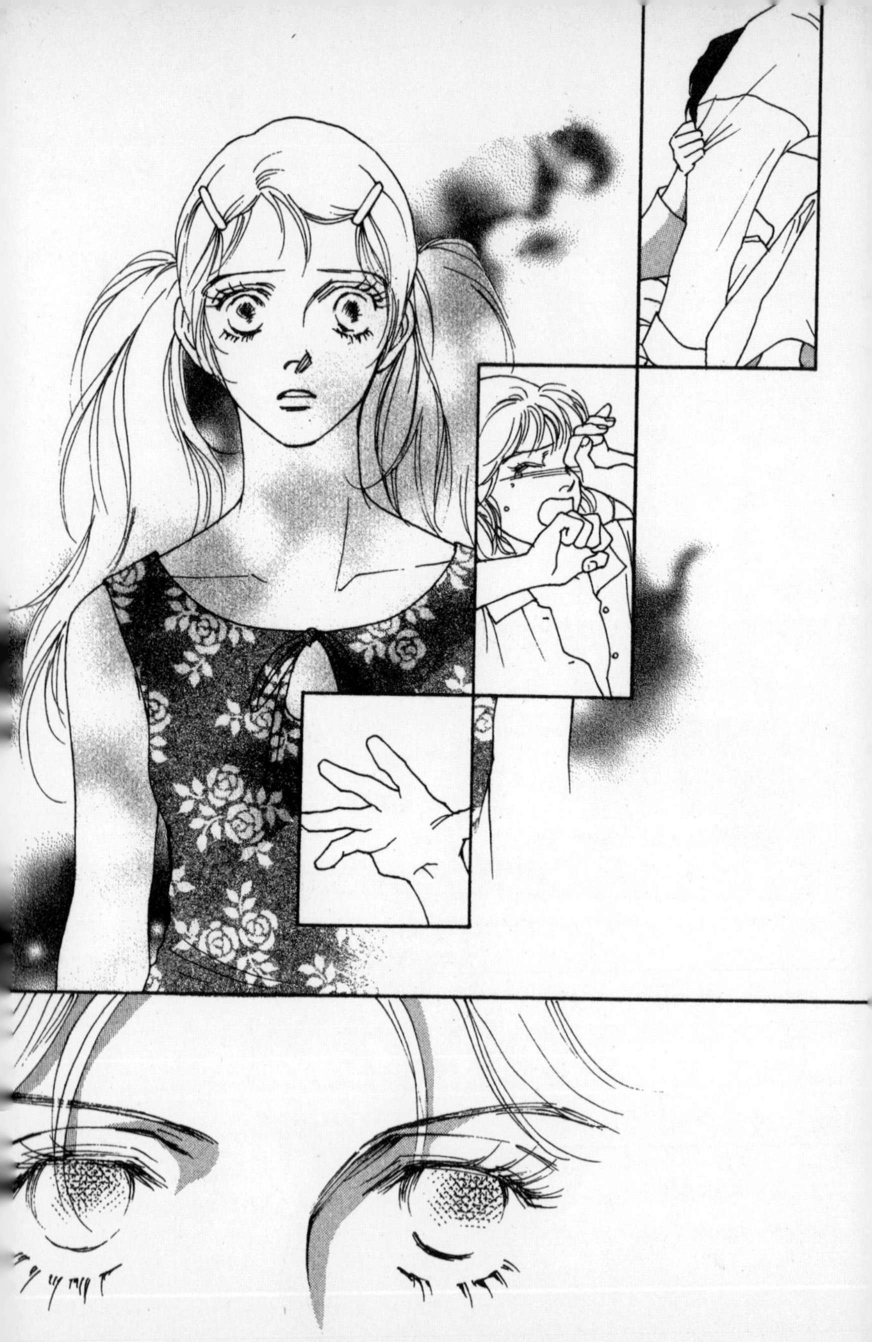

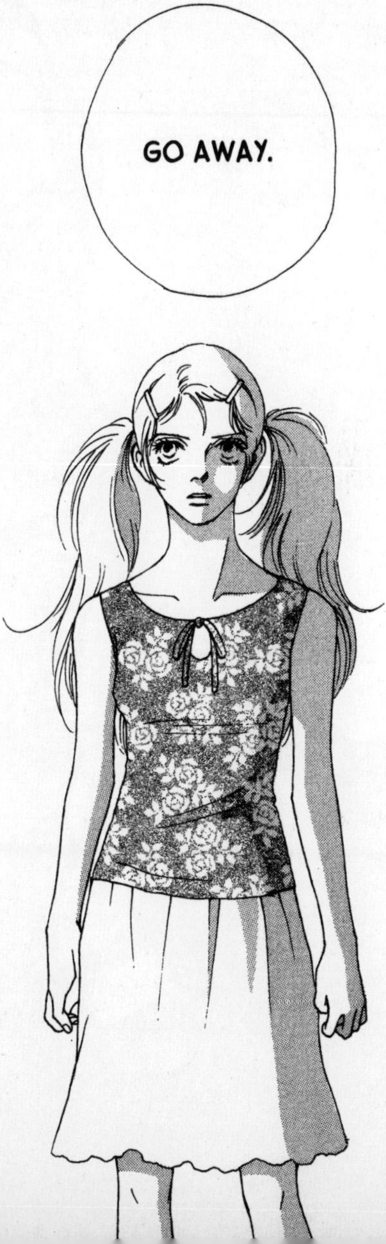
GO AWAY.

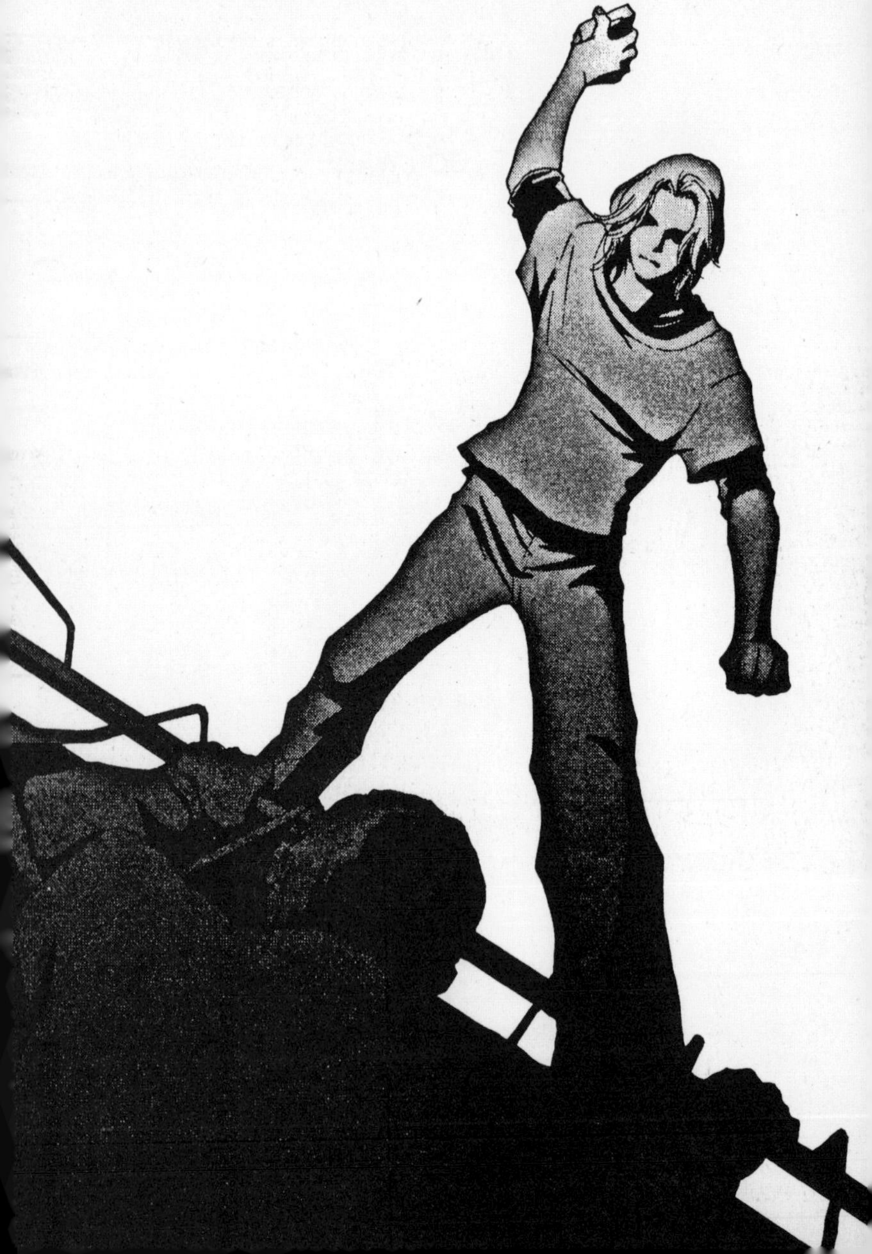

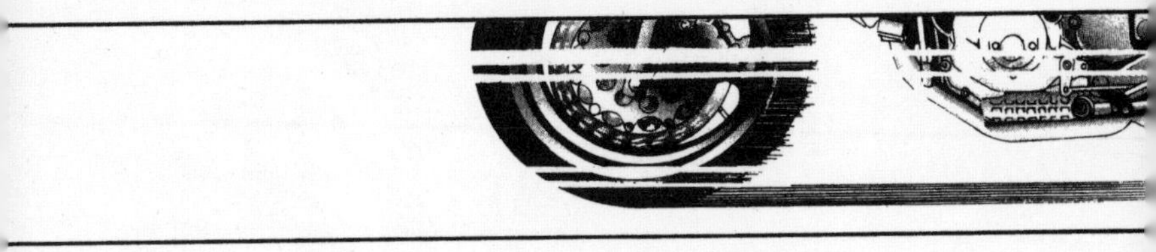

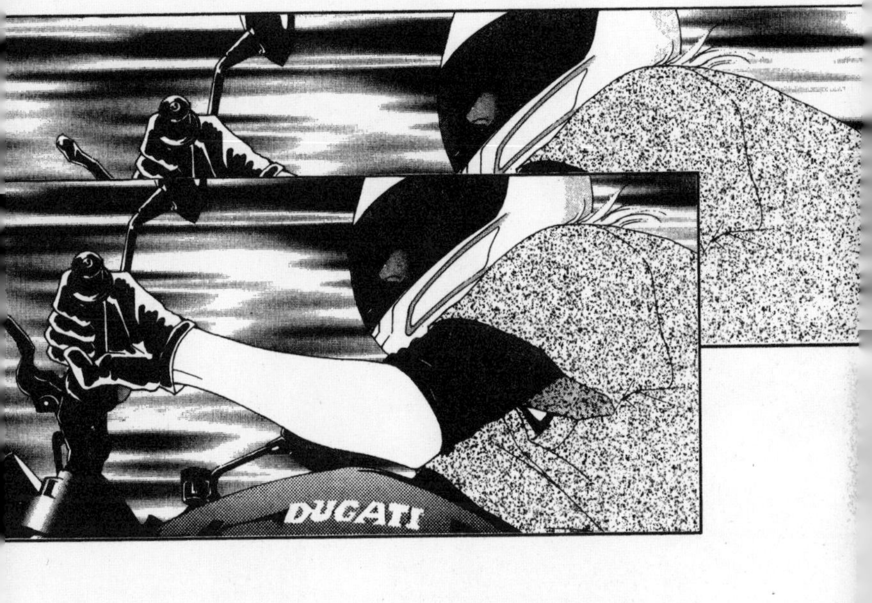
DUCATI

MARS

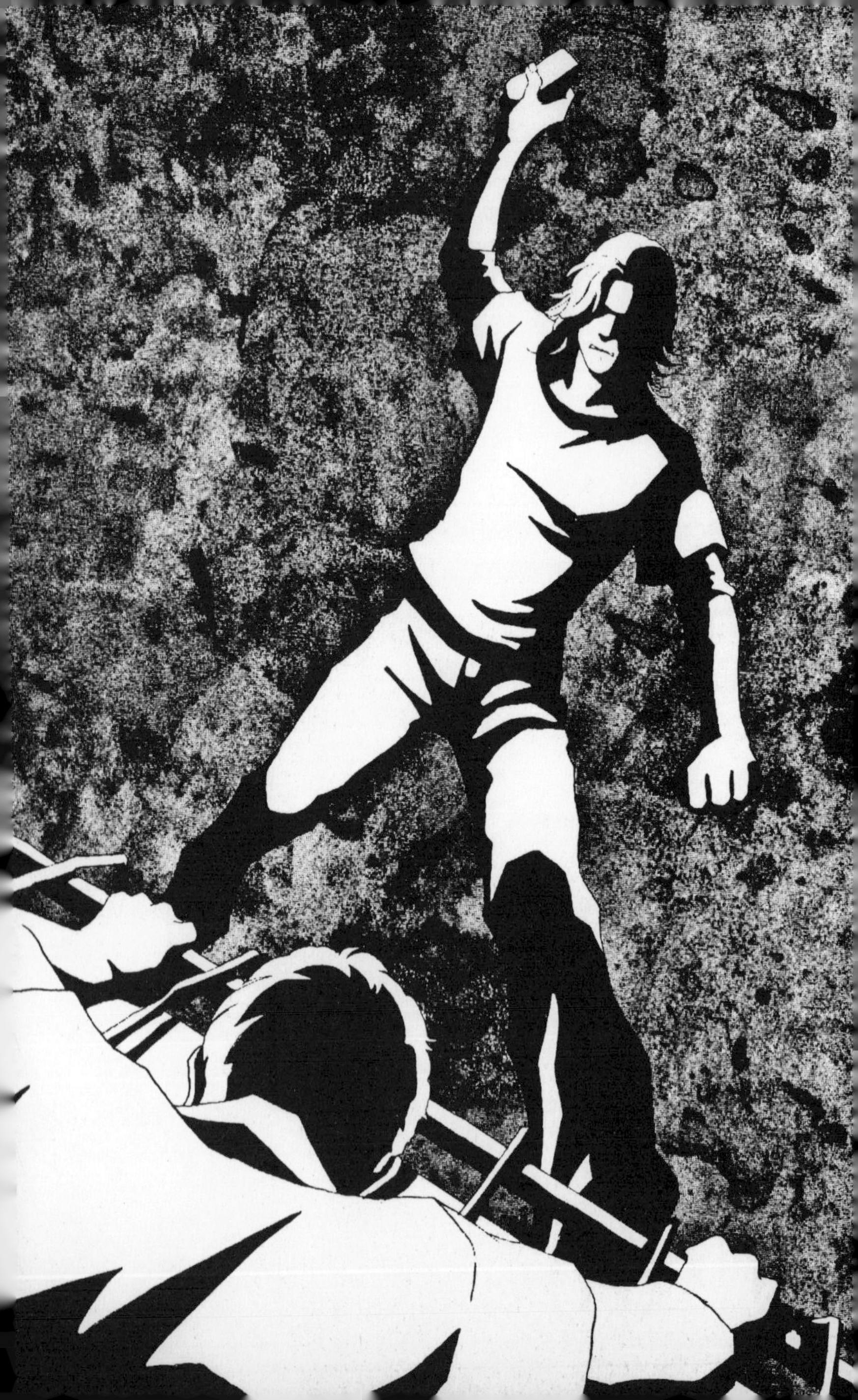

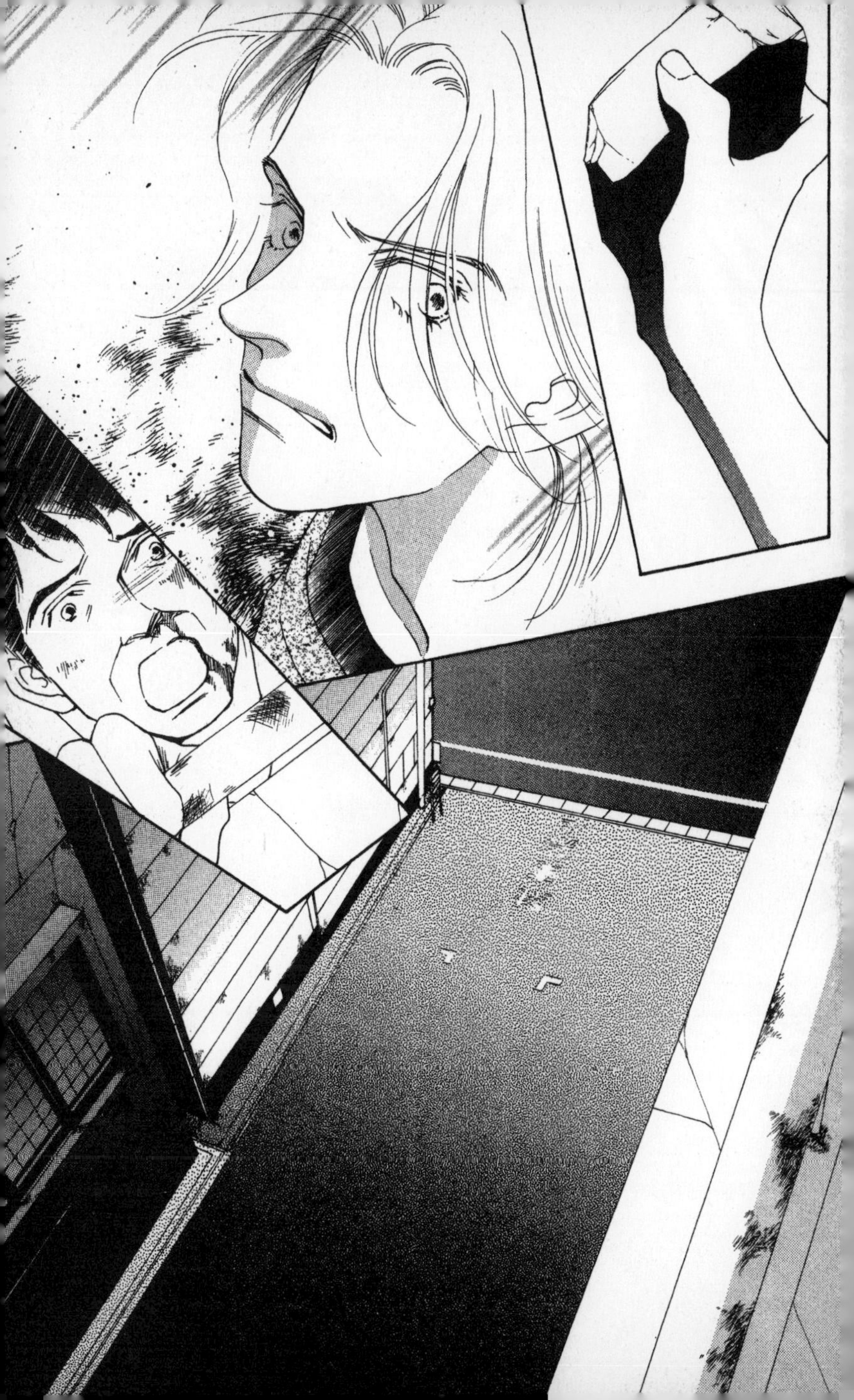

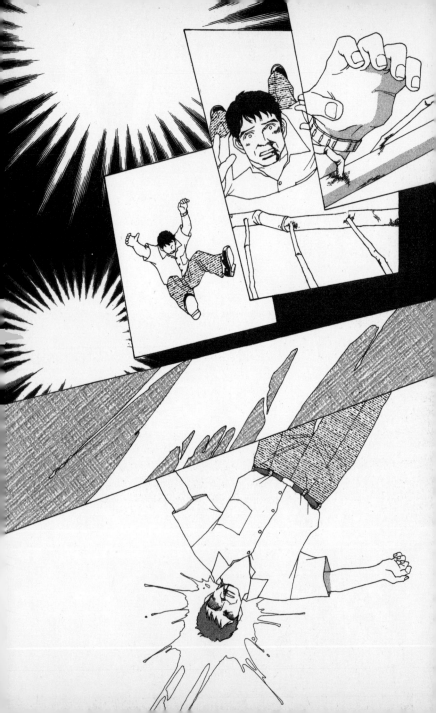

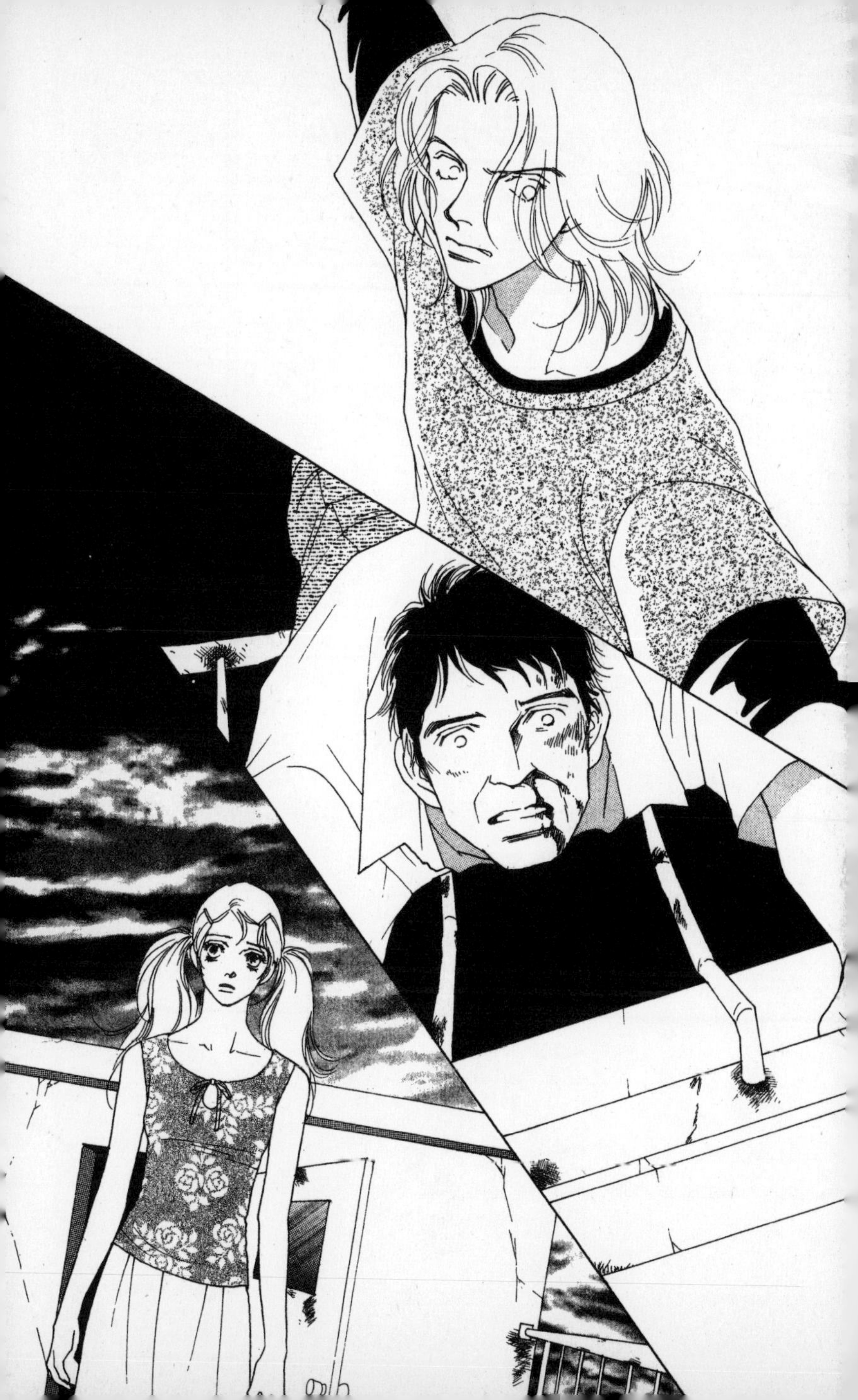

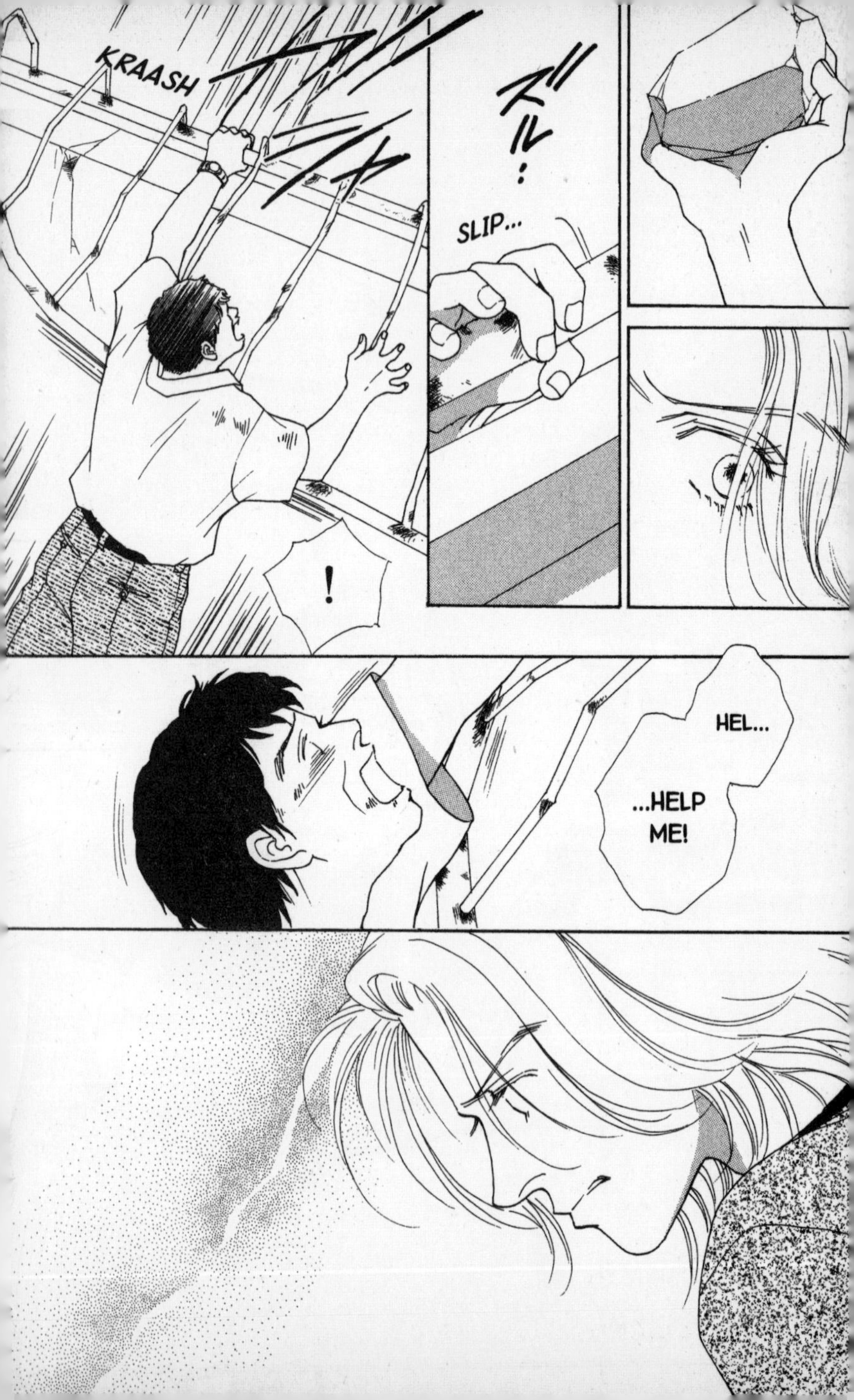
ズル!!
SLIP...
KRAASH
!
HEL...
...HELP ME!

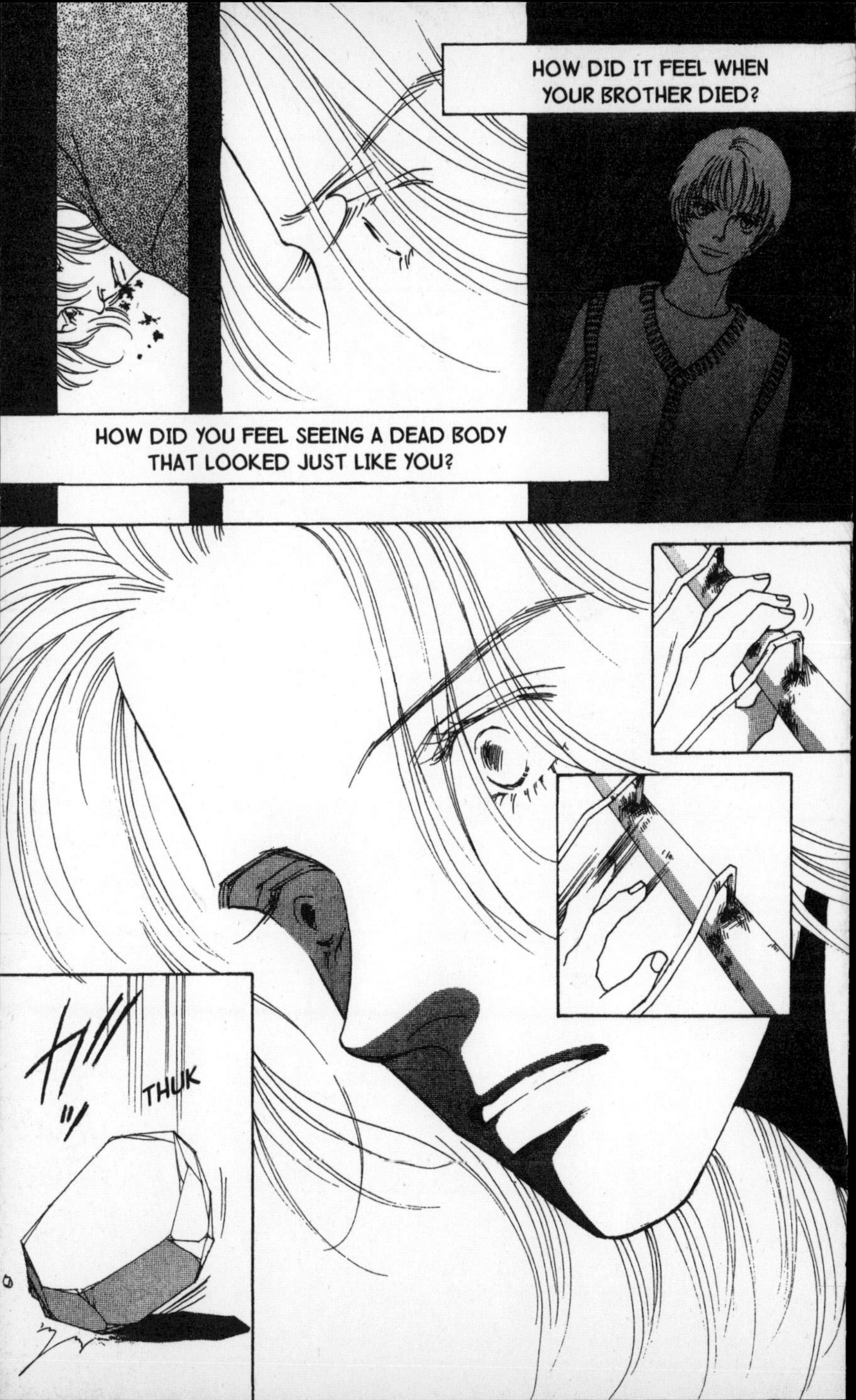
HOW DID IT FEEL WHEN YOUR BROTHER DIED?
HOW DID YOU FEEL SEEING A DEAD BODY THAT LOOKED JUST LIKE YOU?
THUK

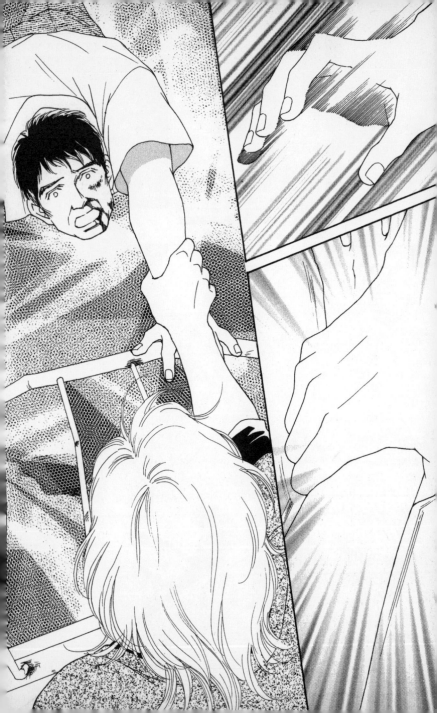

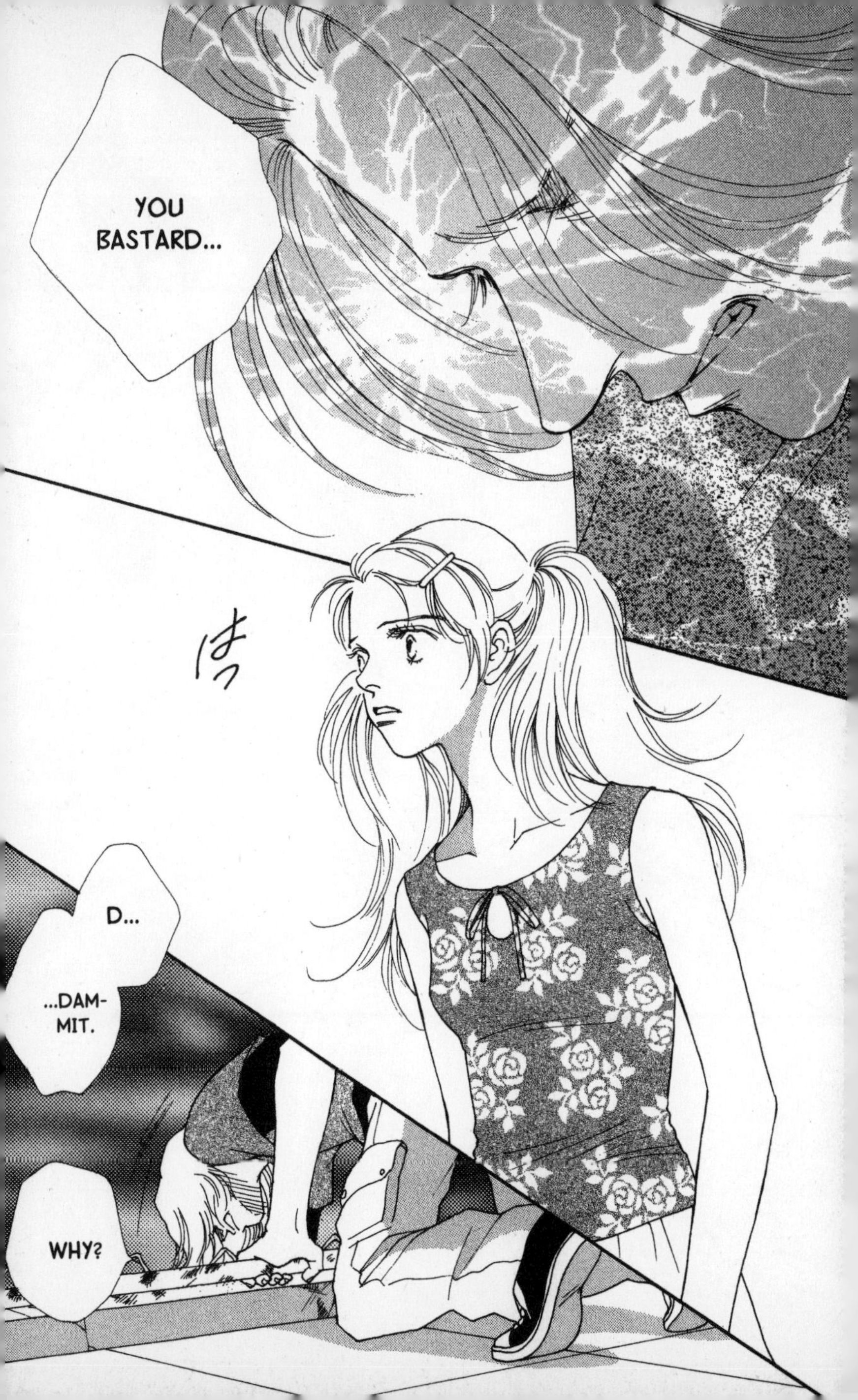
YOU BASTARD...
はっ
D...
...DAM-MIT.
WHY?

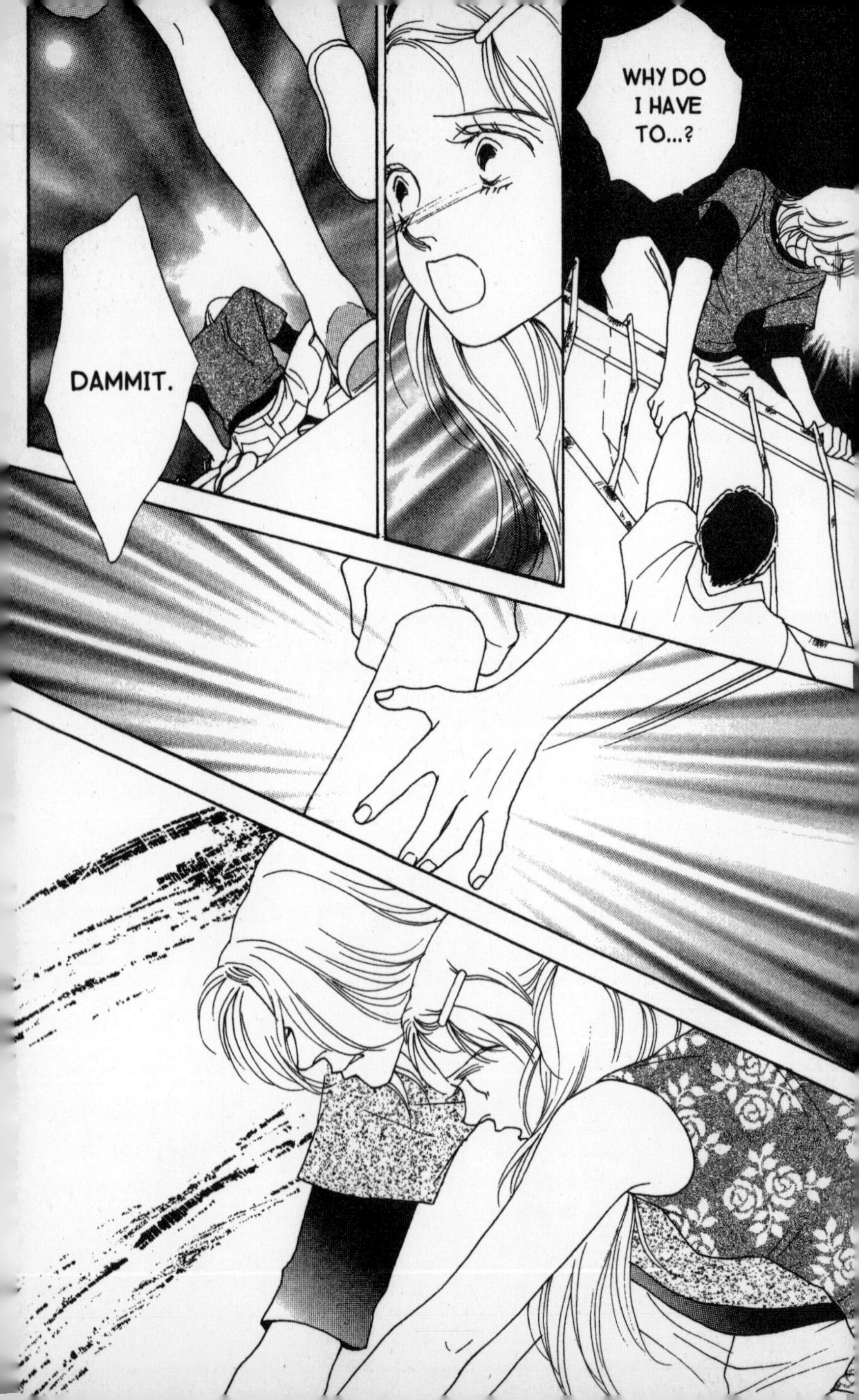
WHY DO I HAVE TO...?
DAMMIT.

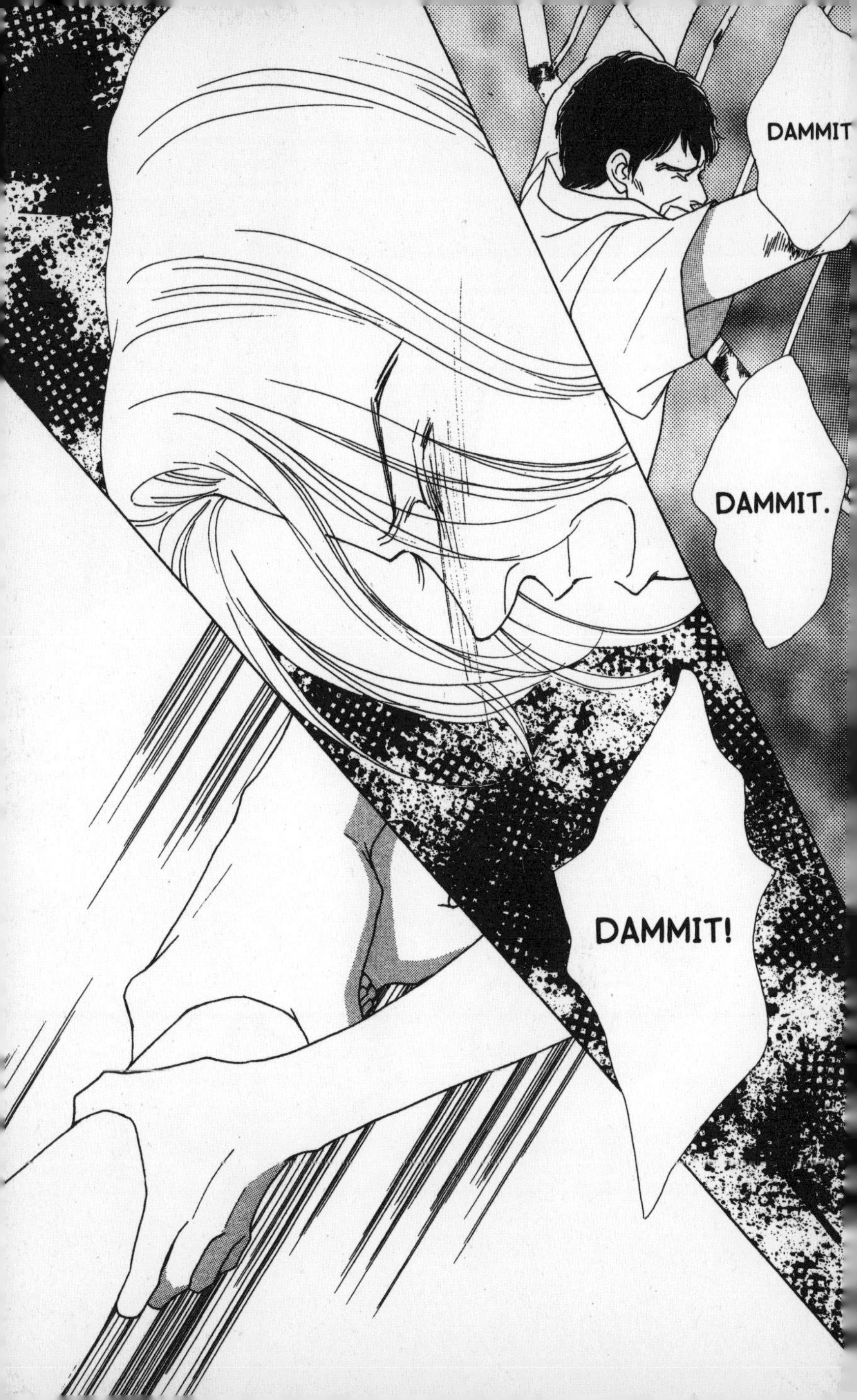
DAMMIT
DAMMIT.
DAMMIT!

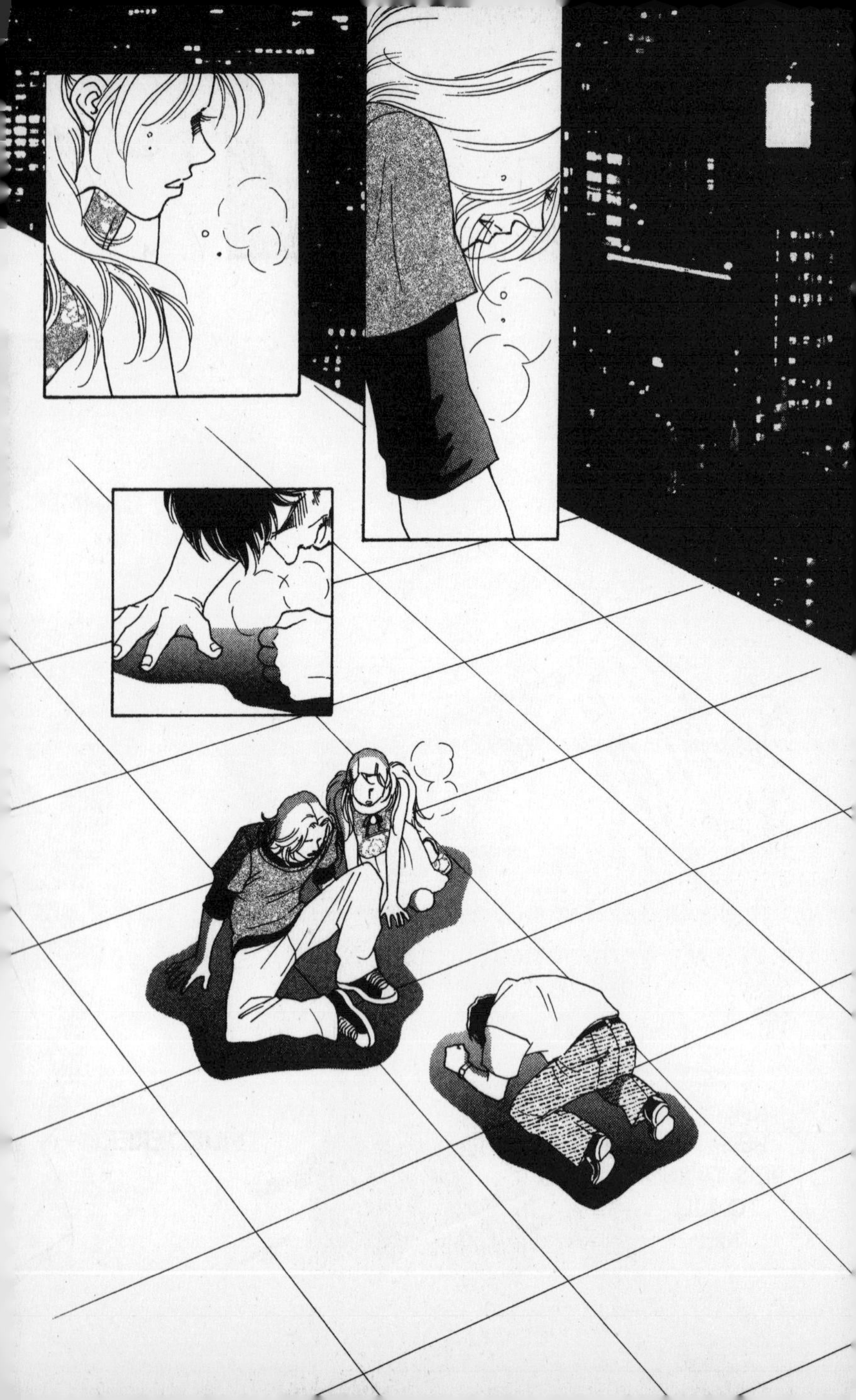

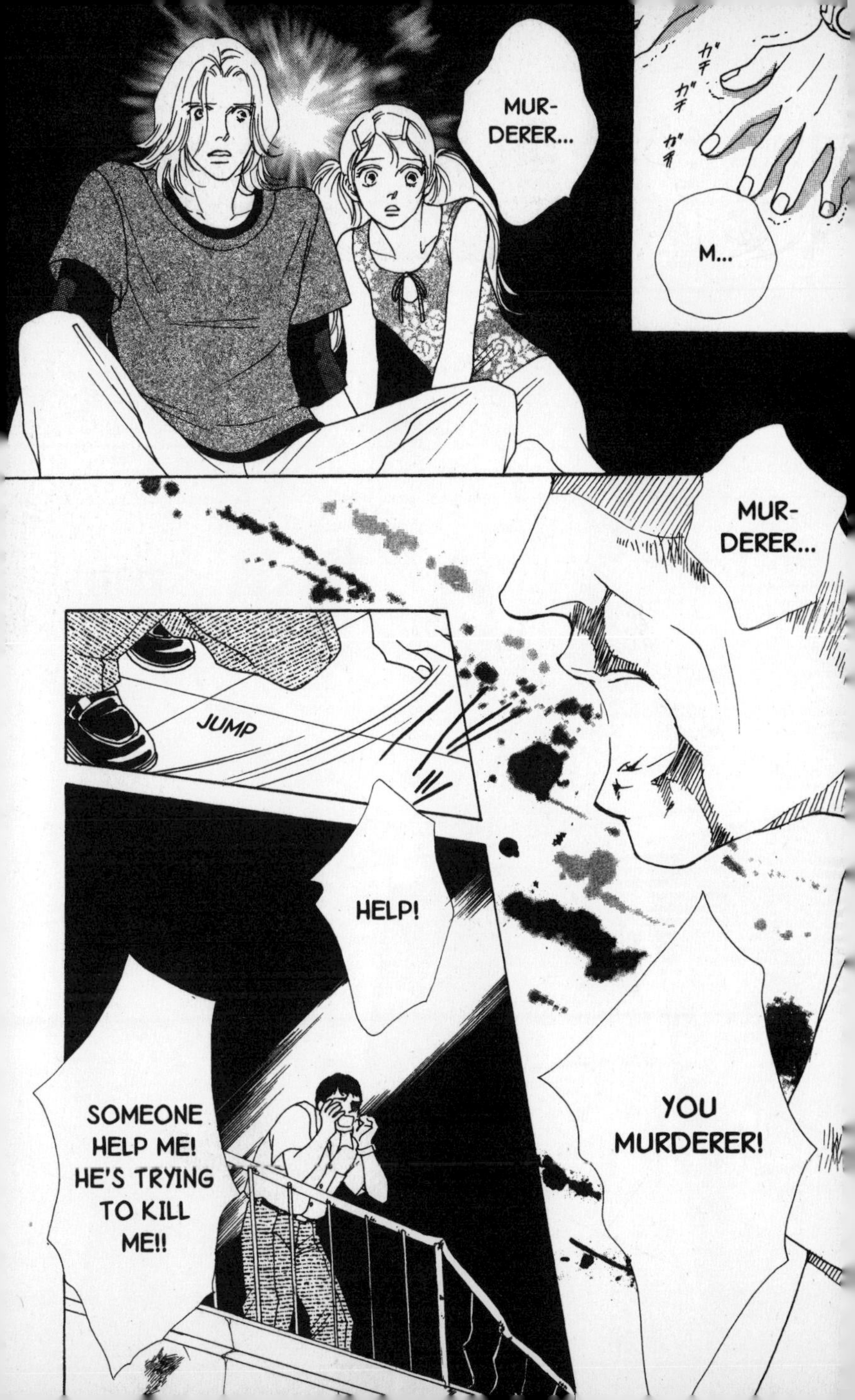
ガチ
ガチ
ガチ
M...
MUR-DERER...
MUR-DERER...
YOU MURDERER!
JUMP
HELP!
SOMEONE HELP ME! HE'S TRYING TO KILL ME!!

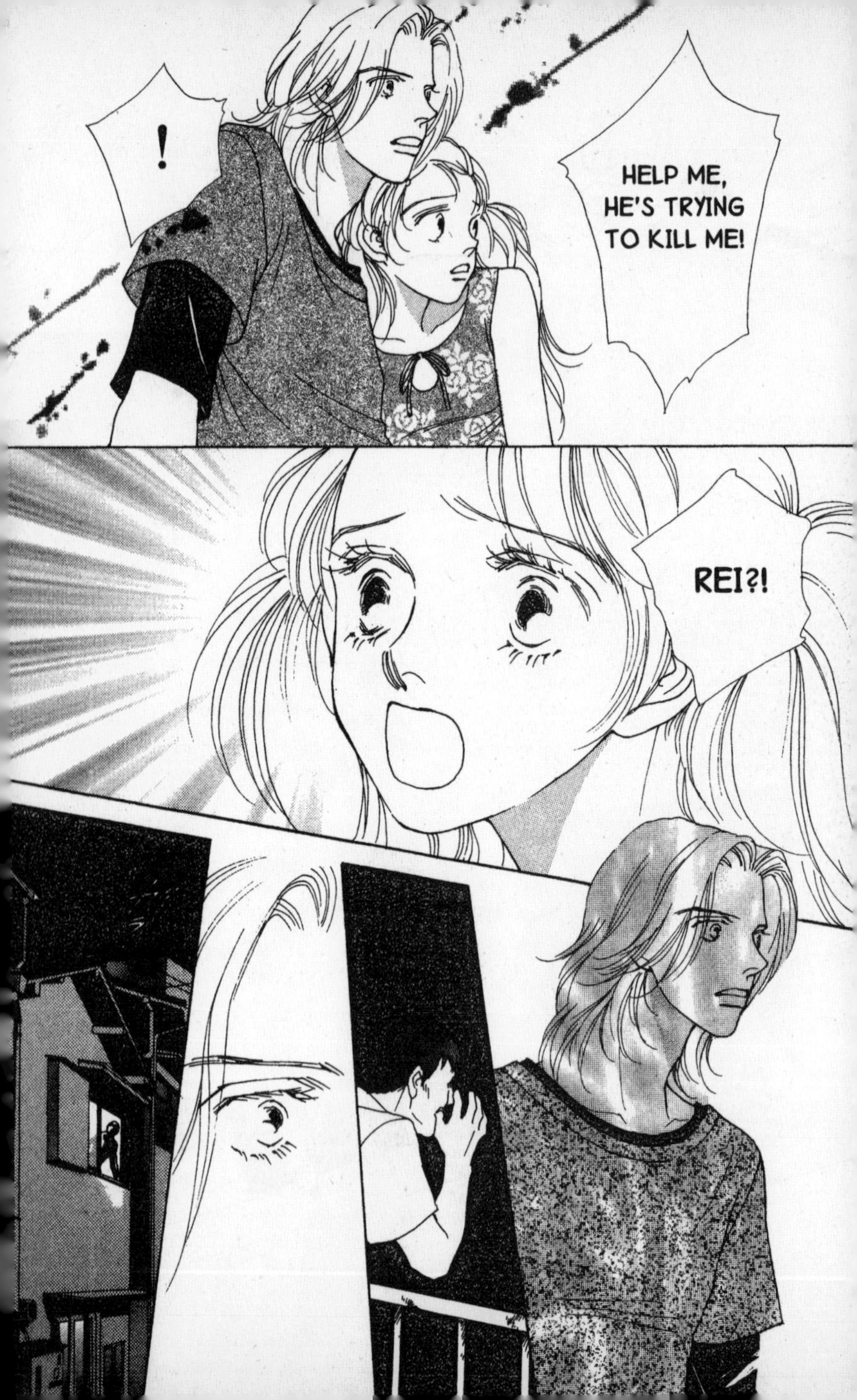
HELP ME, HE'S TRYING TO KILL ME!
!
REI?!

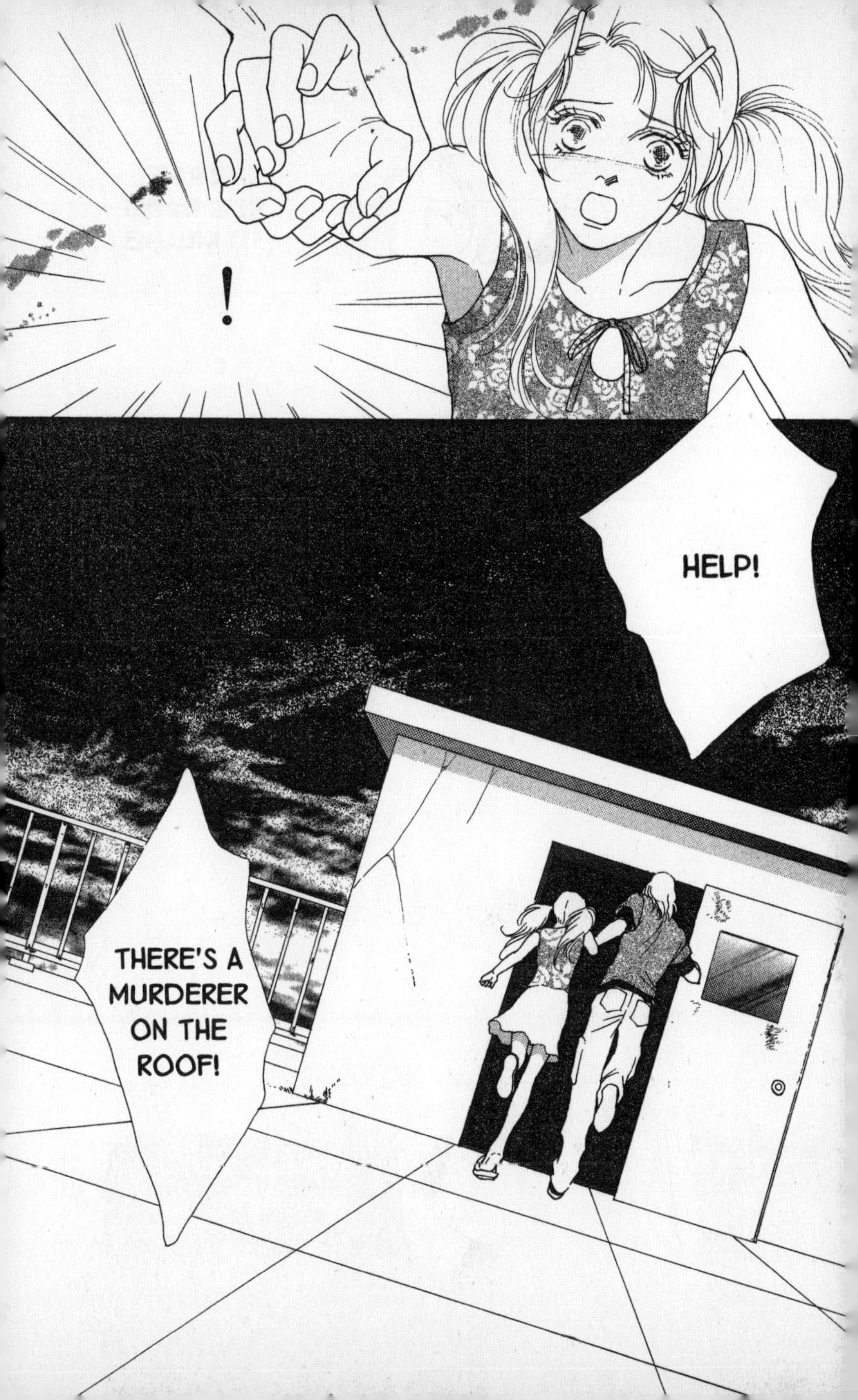
!
HELP!
THERE'S A MURDERER ON THE ROOF!

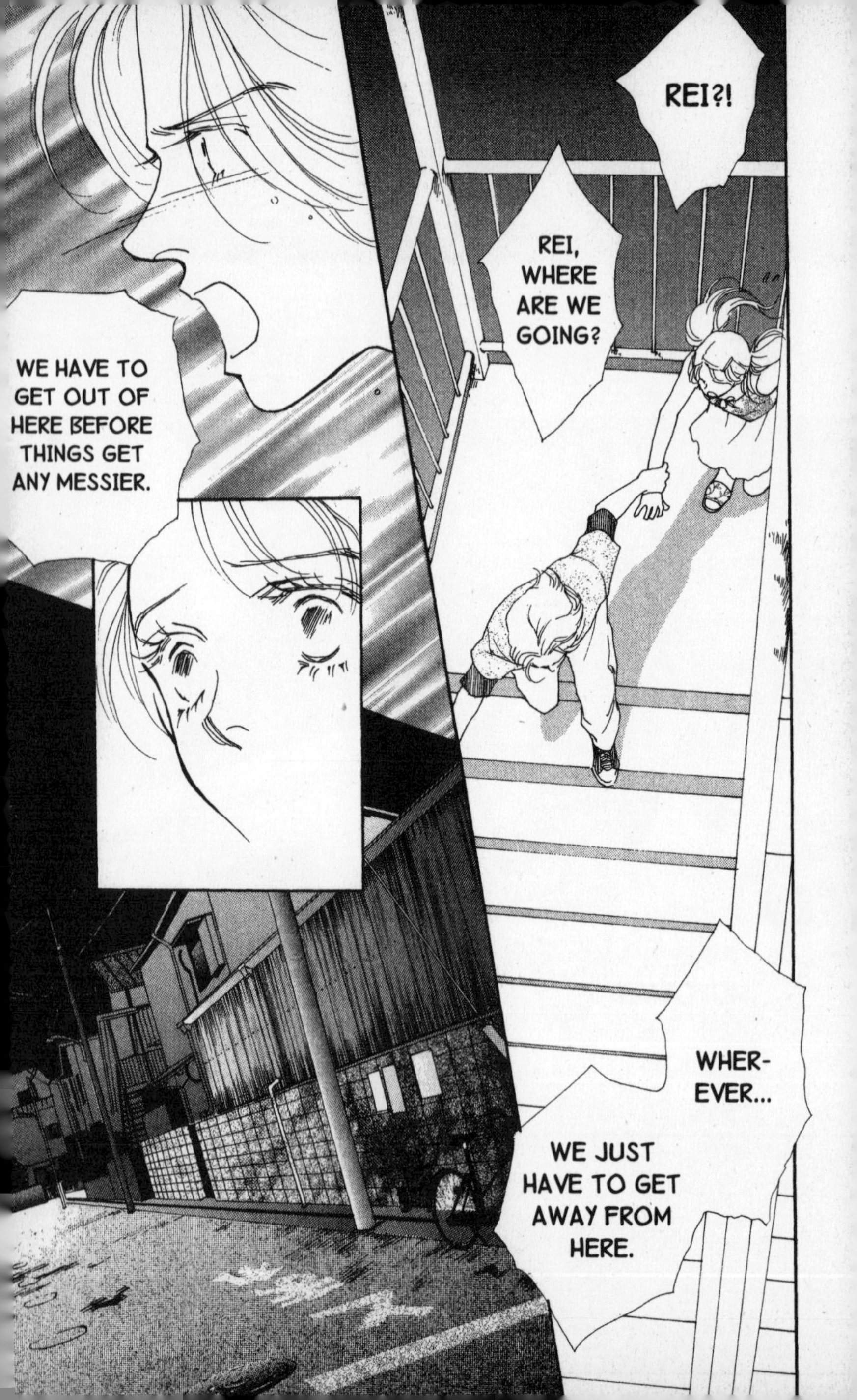
REI?!
REI, WHERE ARE WE GOING?
WHER- EVER...
WE JUST HAVE TO GET AWAY FROM HERE.
WE HAVE TO GET OUT OF HERE BEFORE THINGS GET ANY MESSIER.

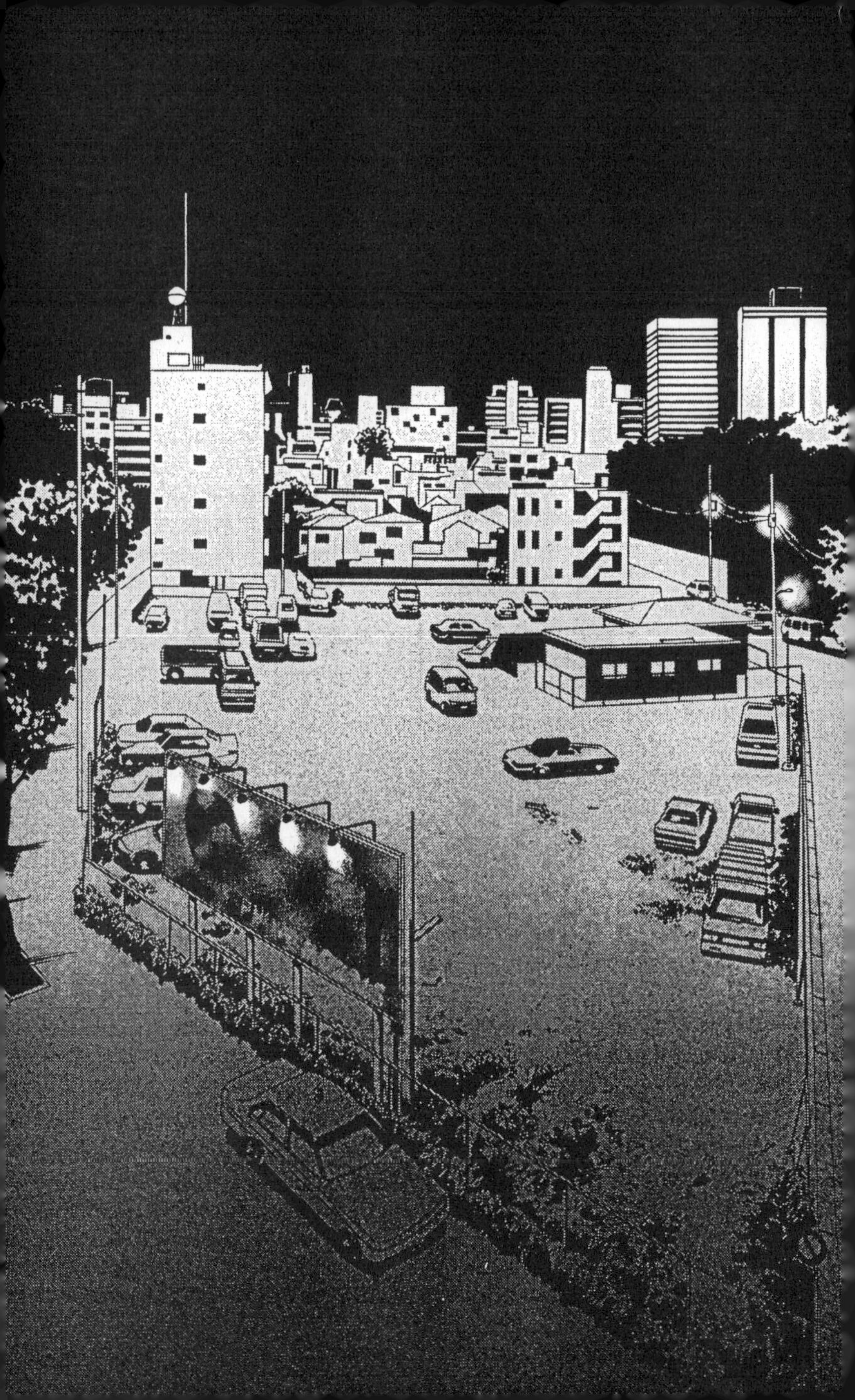

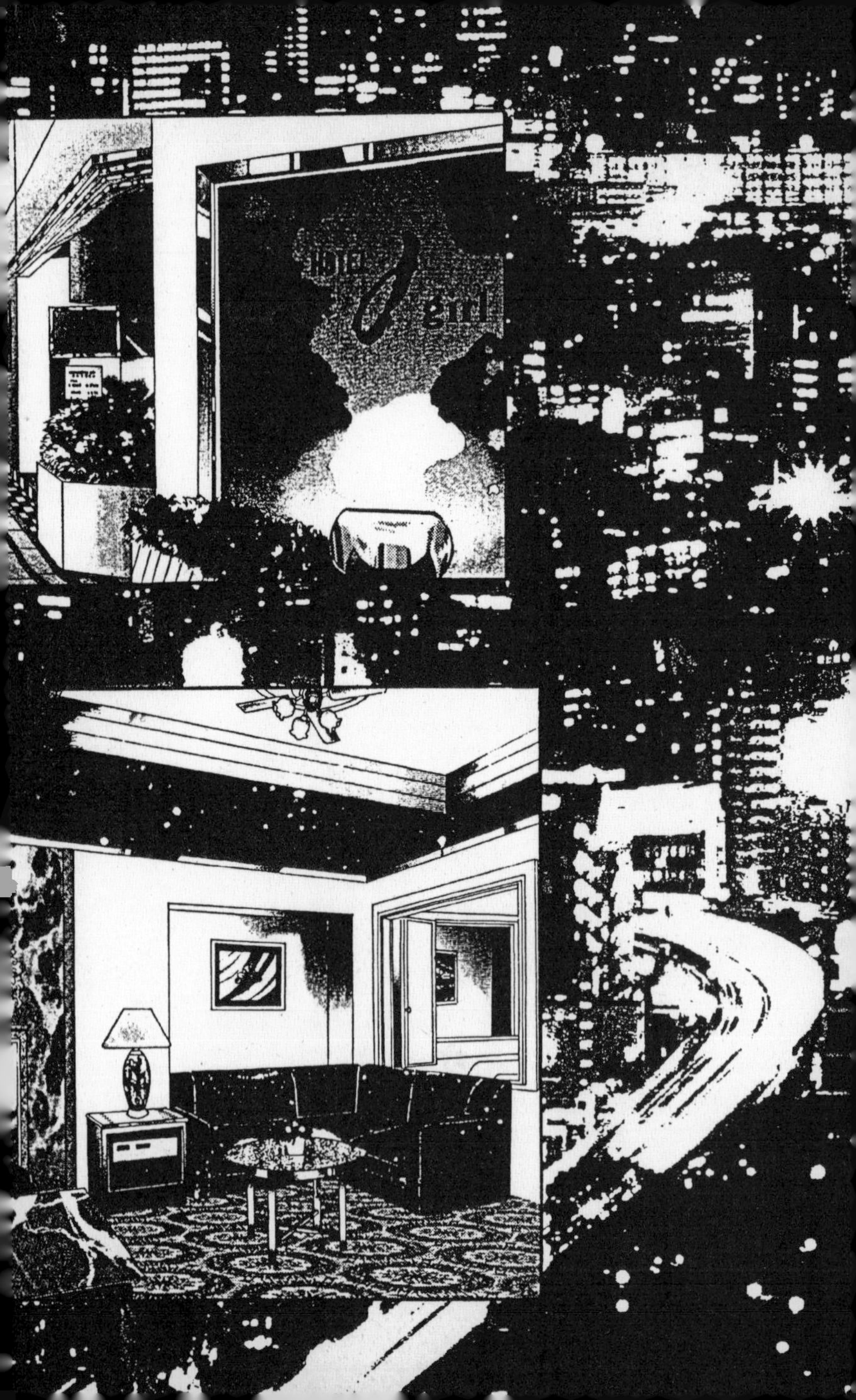

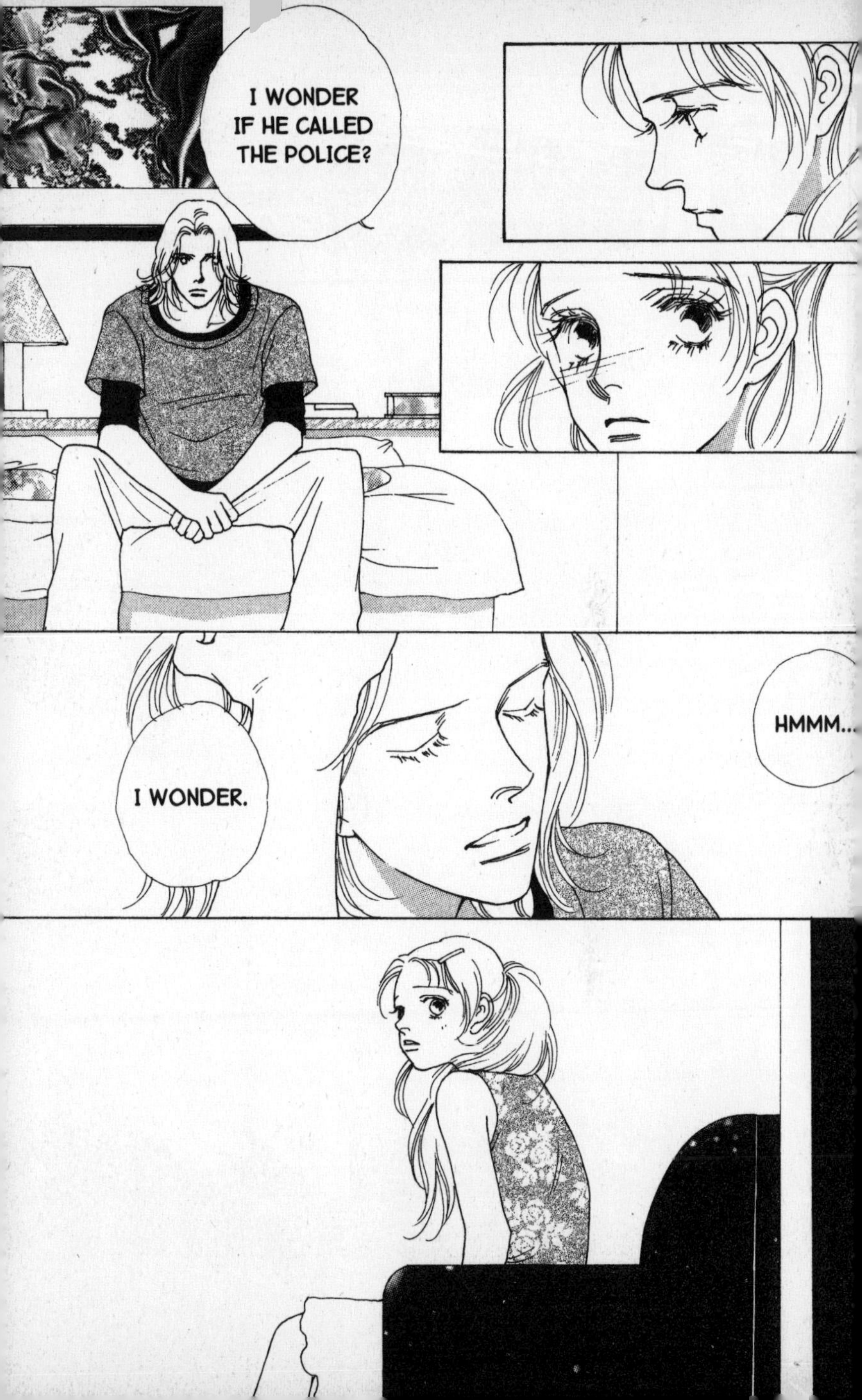
I WONDER IF HE CALLED THE POLICE?
HMMM...
I WONDER.

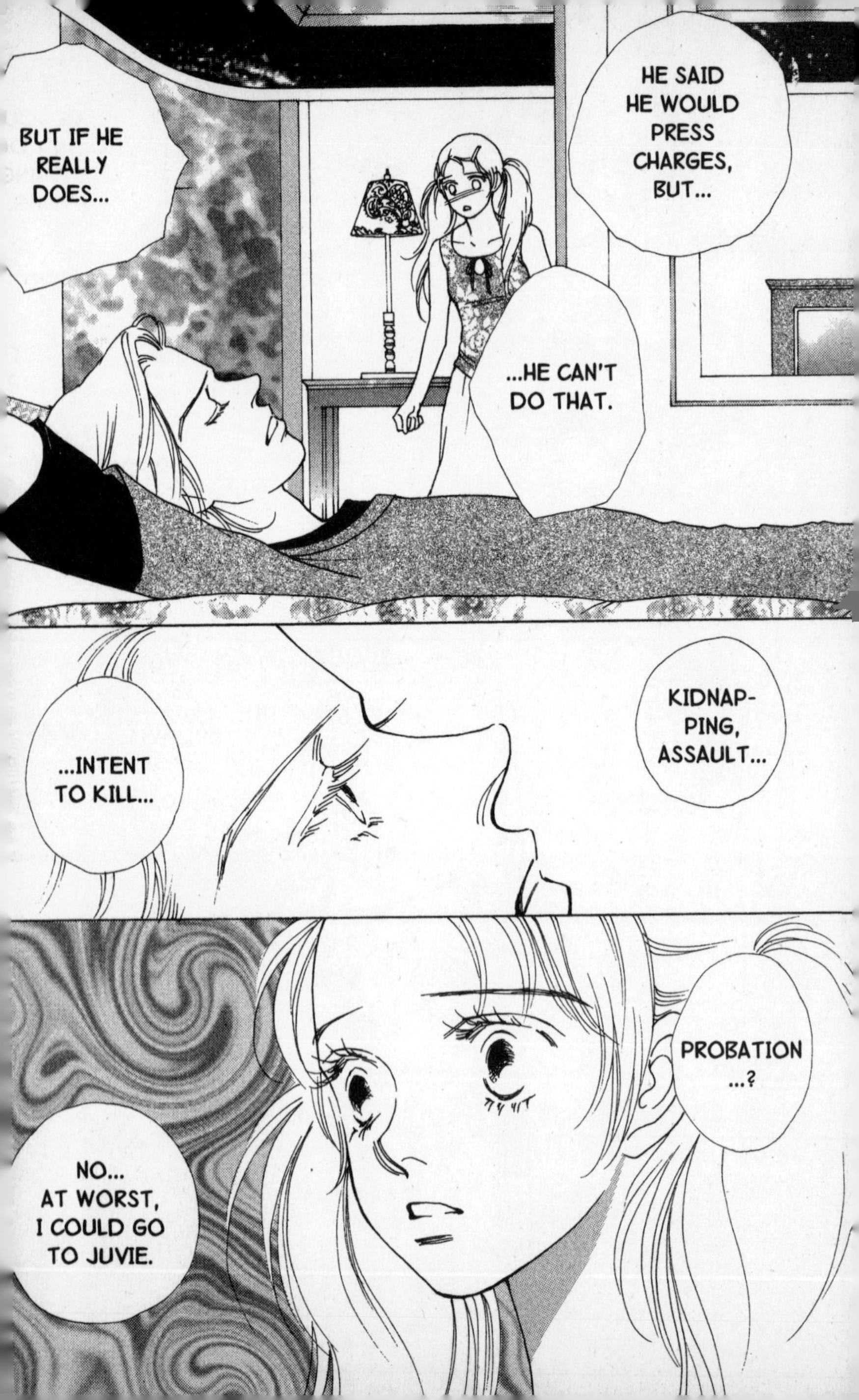
HE SAID HE WOULD PRESS CHARGES, BUT...
...HE CAN'T DO THAT.
BUT IF HE REALLY DOES...
KIDNAP-PING, ASSAULT...
...INTENT TO KILL...
PROBATION ...?
NO... AT WORST, I COULD GO TO JUVIE.

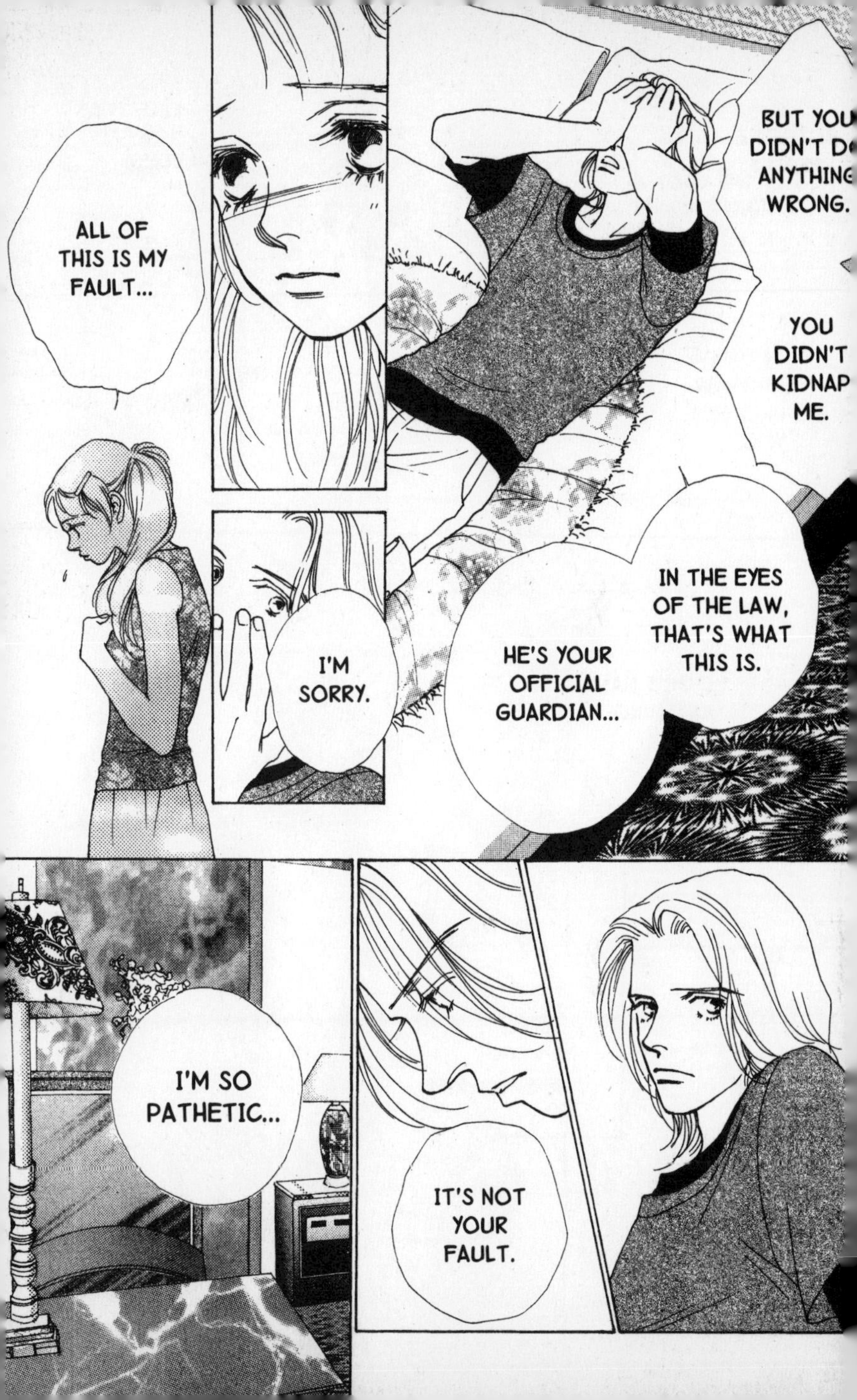

BUT YOU DIDN'T DO ANYTHING WRONG.
YOU DIDN'T KIDNAP ME.
IN THE EYES OF THE LAW, THAT'S WHAT THIS IS.
HE'S YOUR OFFICIAL GUARDIAN...
I'M SORRY.
ALL OF THIS IS MY FAULT...
IT'S NOT YOUR FAULT.
I'M SO PATHETIC...

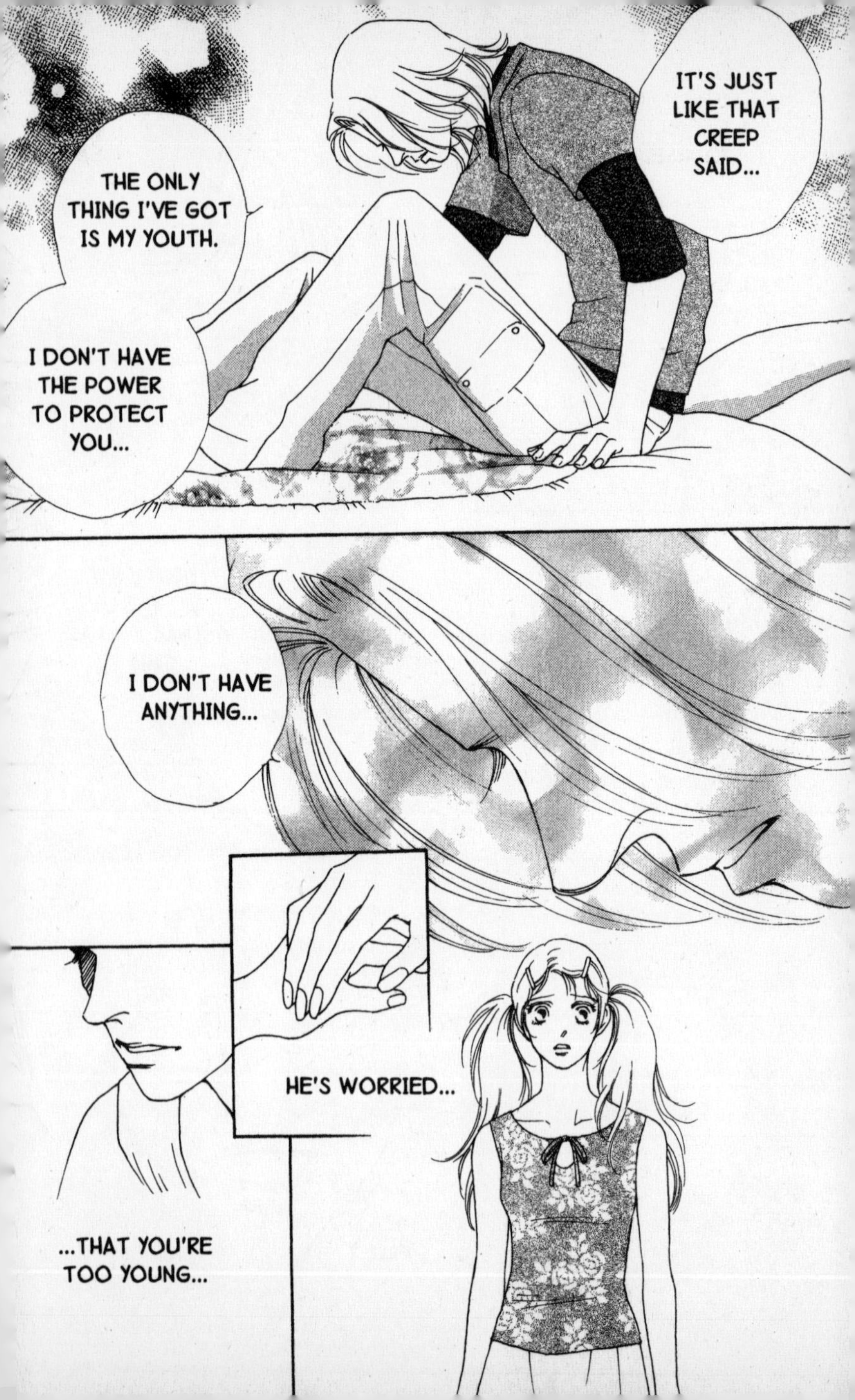

IT'S JUST LIKE THAT CREEP SAID...
THE ONLY THING I'VE GOT IS MY YOUTH.
I DON'T HAVE THE POWER TO PROTECT YOU...
I DON'T HAVE ANYTHING...
HE'S WORRIED...
...THAT YOU'RE TOO YOUNG...

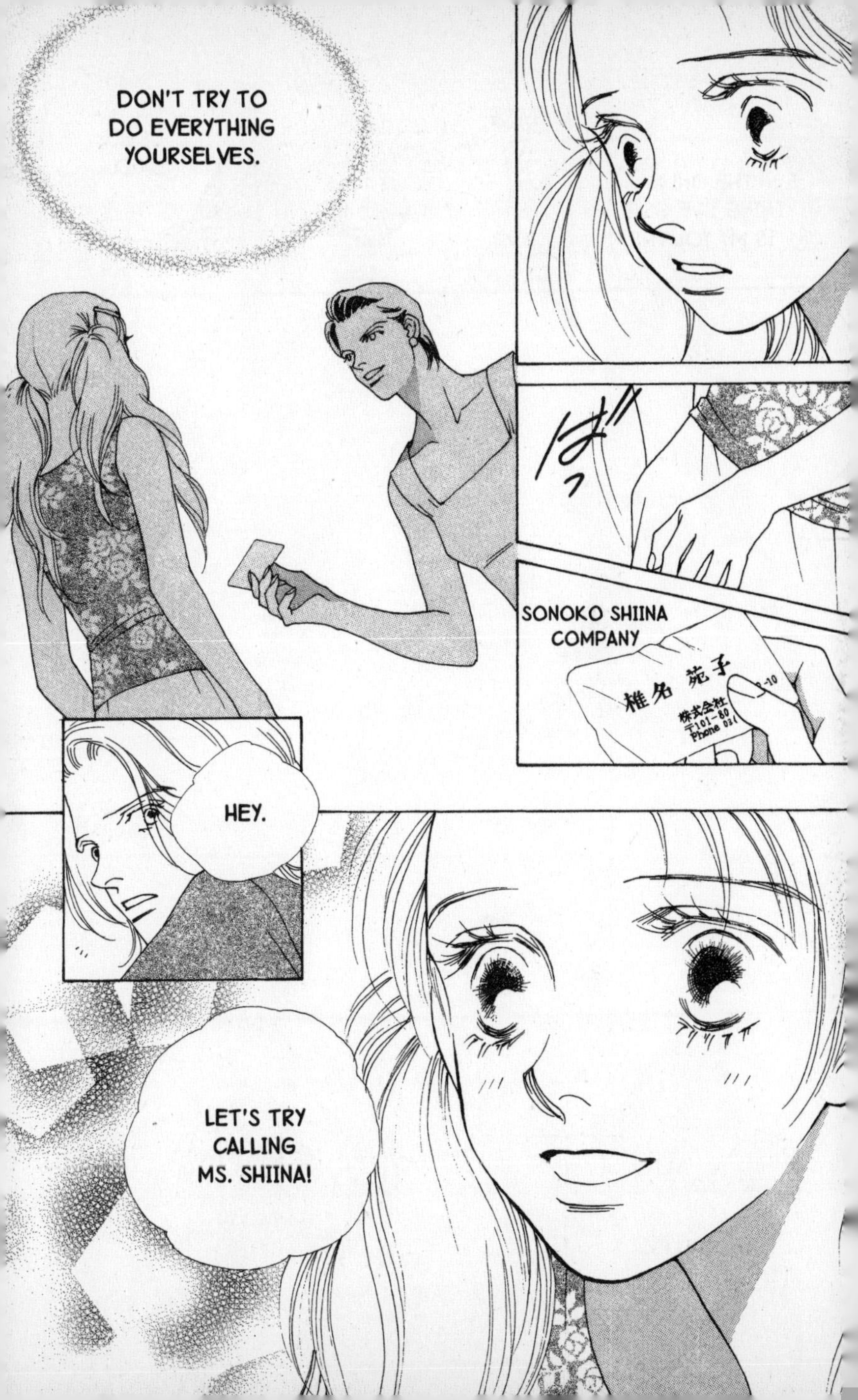
ぱっ
SONOKO SHIINA COMPANY
椎名 苑子
株式会社
DON'T TRY TO DO EVERYTHING YOURSELVES.
HEY.
LET'S TRY CALLING MS. SHIINA!

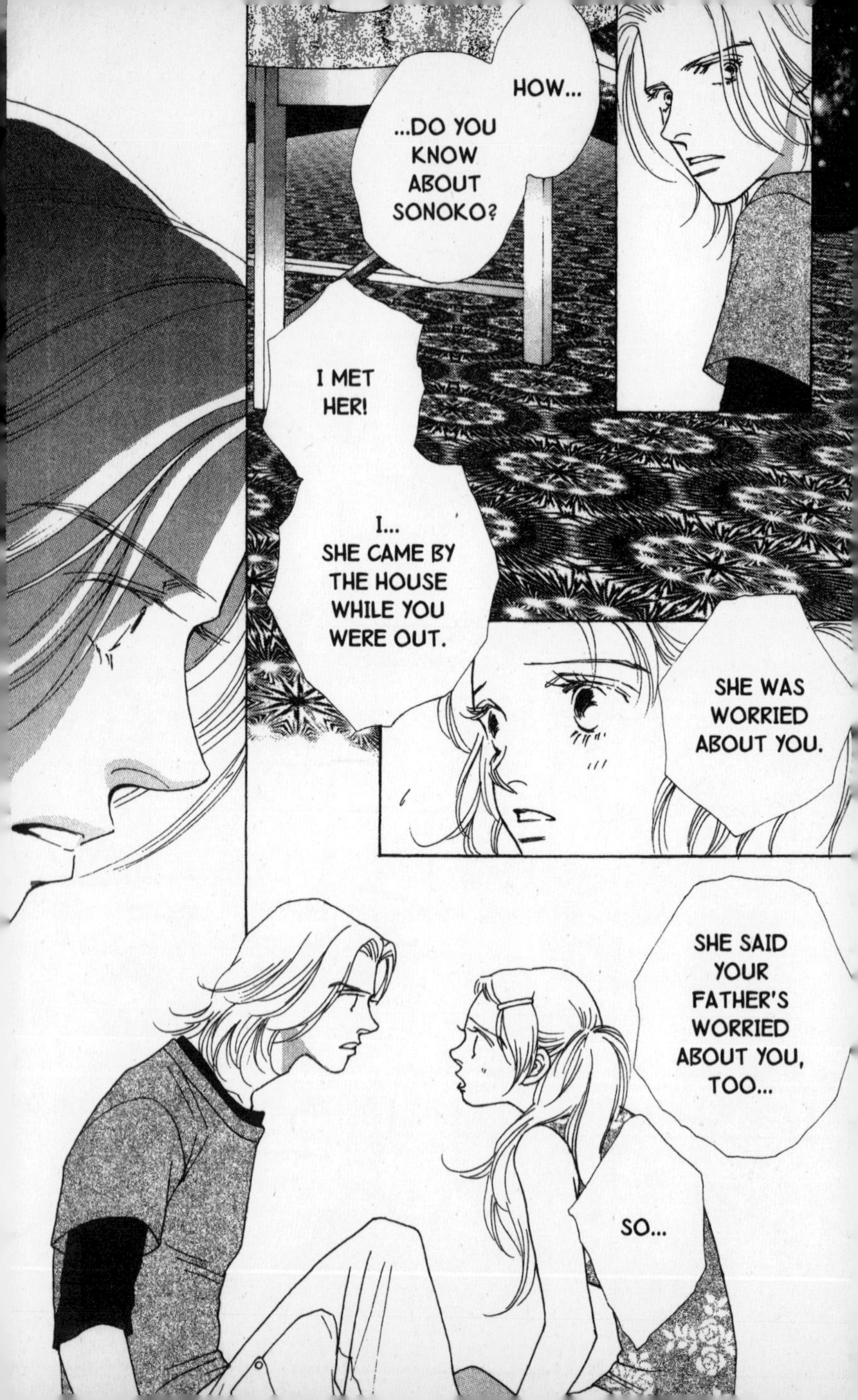
HOW...
...DO YOU KNOW ABOUT SONOKO?
I MET HER!
I... SHE CAME BY THE HOUSE WHILE YOU WERE OUT.
SHE WAS WORRIED ABOUT YOU.
SHE SAID YOUR FATHER'S WORRIED ABOUT YOU, TOO...
SO...

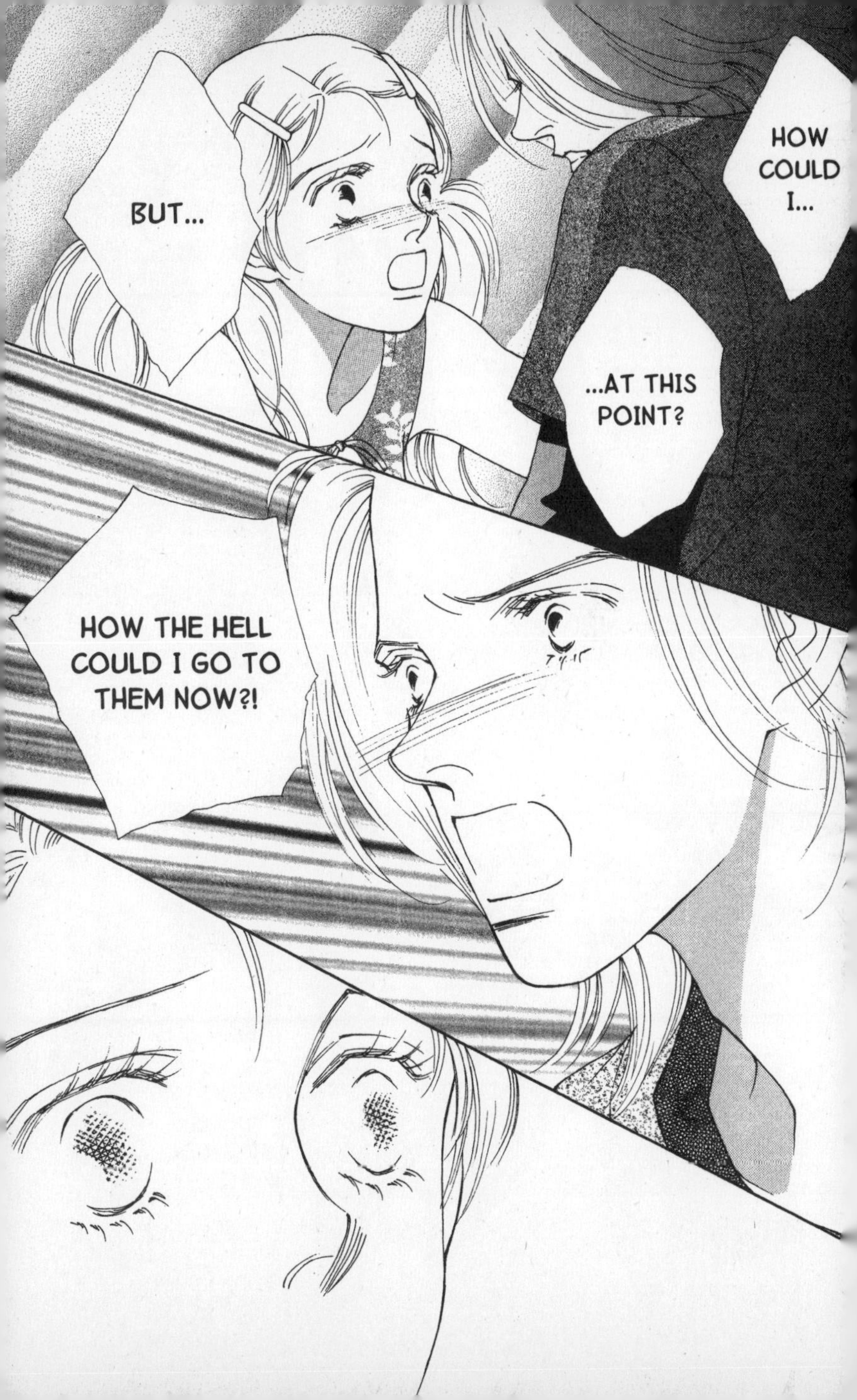
HOW COULD I...
...AT THIS POINT?
BUT...
HOW THE HELL COULD I GO TO THEM NOW?!

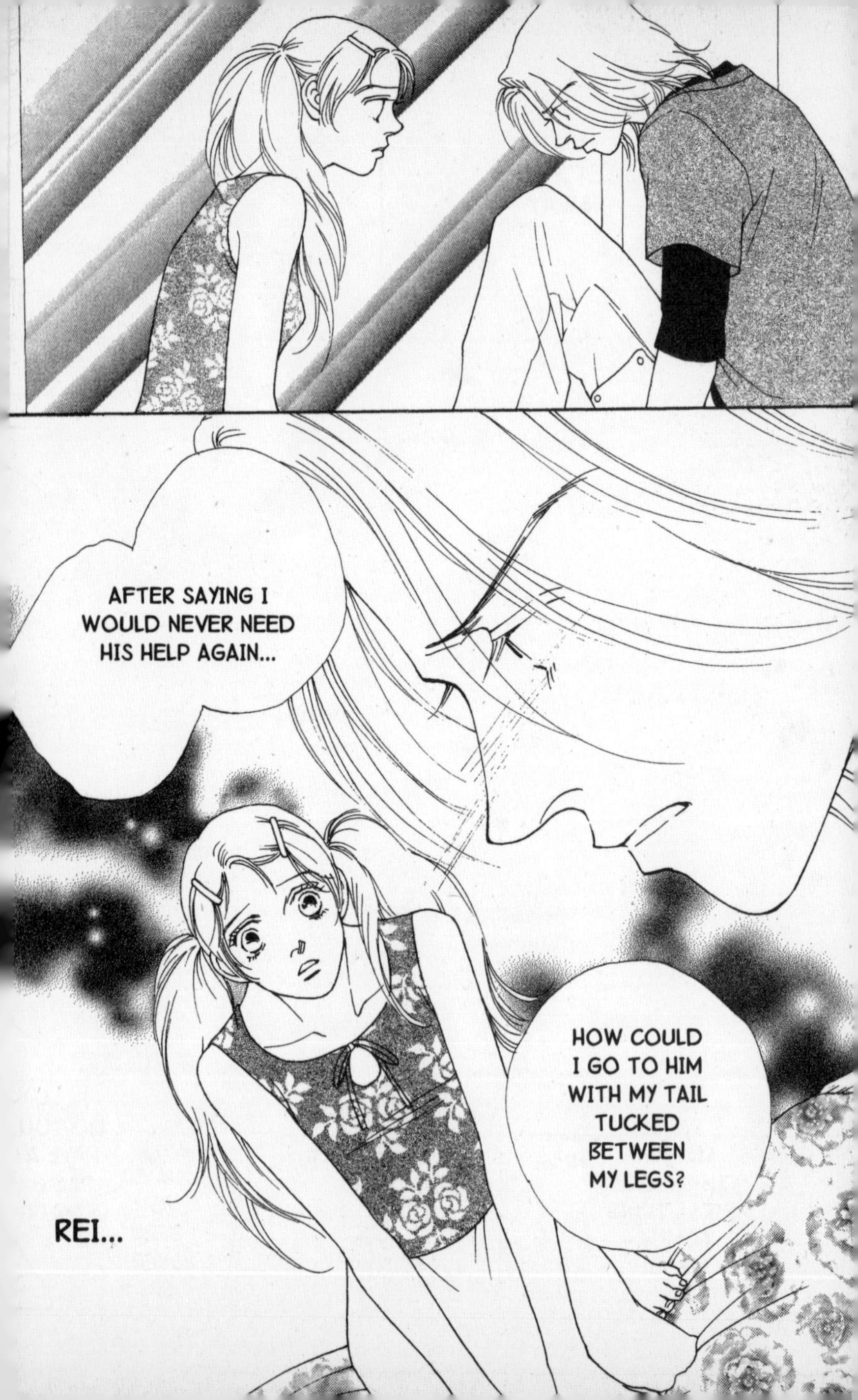
AFTER SAYING I WOULD NEVER NEED HIS HELP AGAIN...
HOW COULD I GO TO HIM WITH MY TAIL TUCKED BETWEEN MY LEGS?
REI...

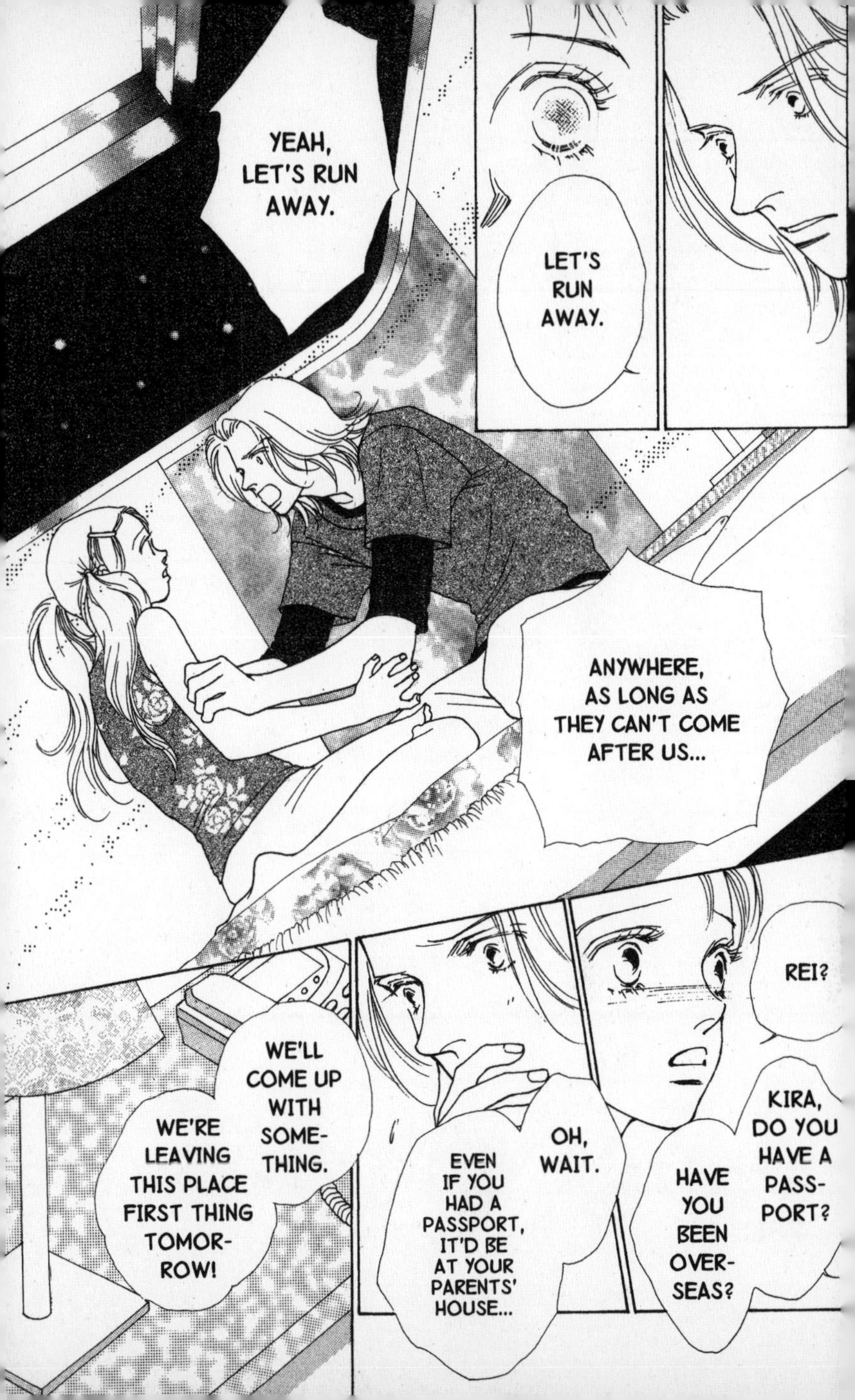
LET'S RUN AWAY.
YEAH, LET'S RUN AWAY.
ANYWHERE, AS LONG AS THEY CAN'T COME AFTER US...
REI?
KIRA, DO YOU HAVE A PASSPORT?
HAVE YOU BEEN OVERSEAS?
OH, WAIT.
EVEN IF YOU HAD A PASSPORT, IT'D BE AT YOUR PARENTS' HOUSE...
WE'LL COME UP WITH SOMETHING.
WE'RE LEAVING THIS PLACE FIRST THING TOMORROW!

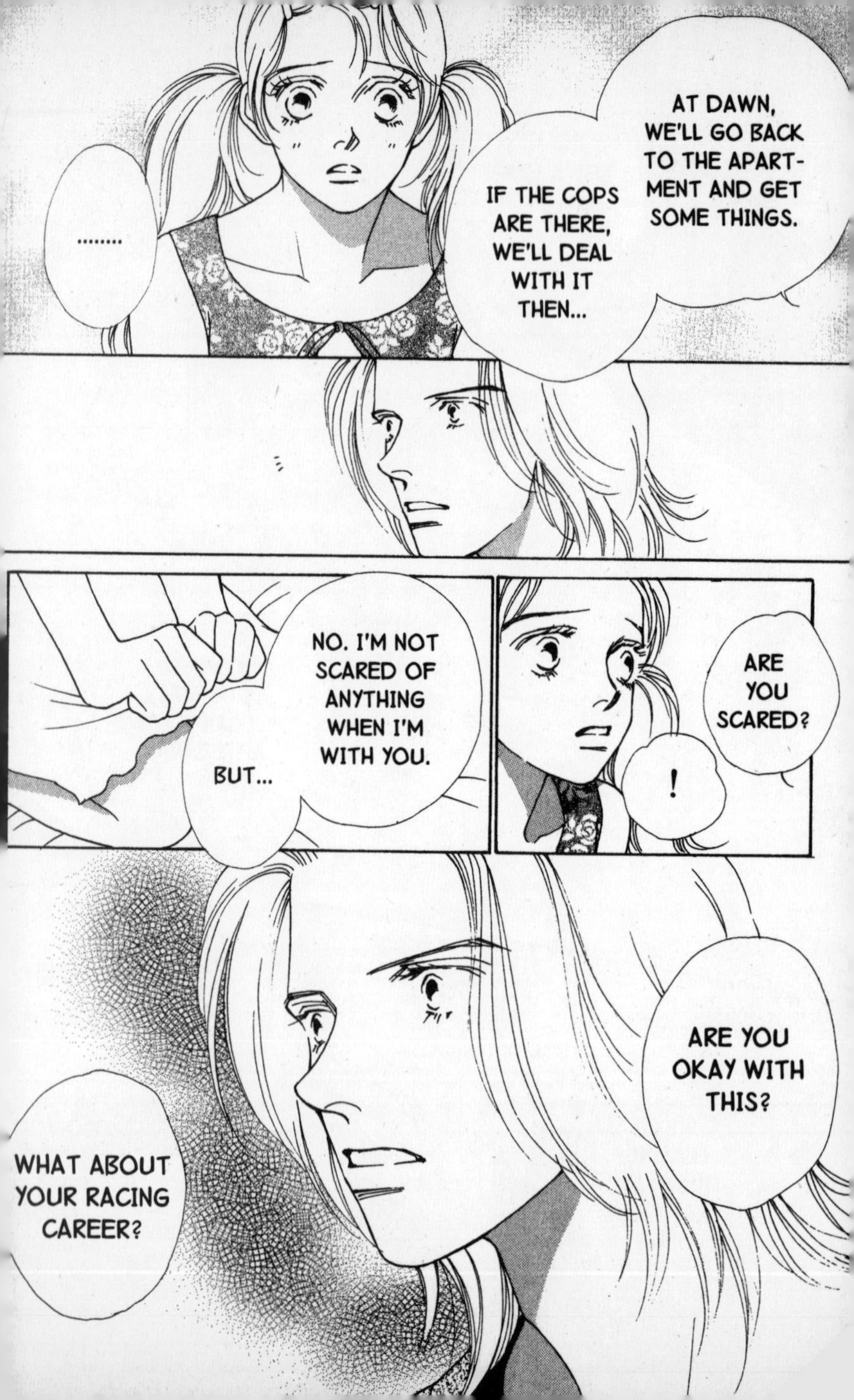
AT DAWN, WE'LL GO BACK TO THE APART-MENT AND GET SOME THINGS.
IF THE COPS ARE THERE, WE'LL DEAL WITH IT THEN...
....
ARE YOU SCARED?
!
NO. I'M NOT SCARED OF ANYTHING WHEN I'M WITH YOU.
BUT...
ARE YOU OKAY WITH THIS?
WHAT ABOUT YOUR RACING CAREER?

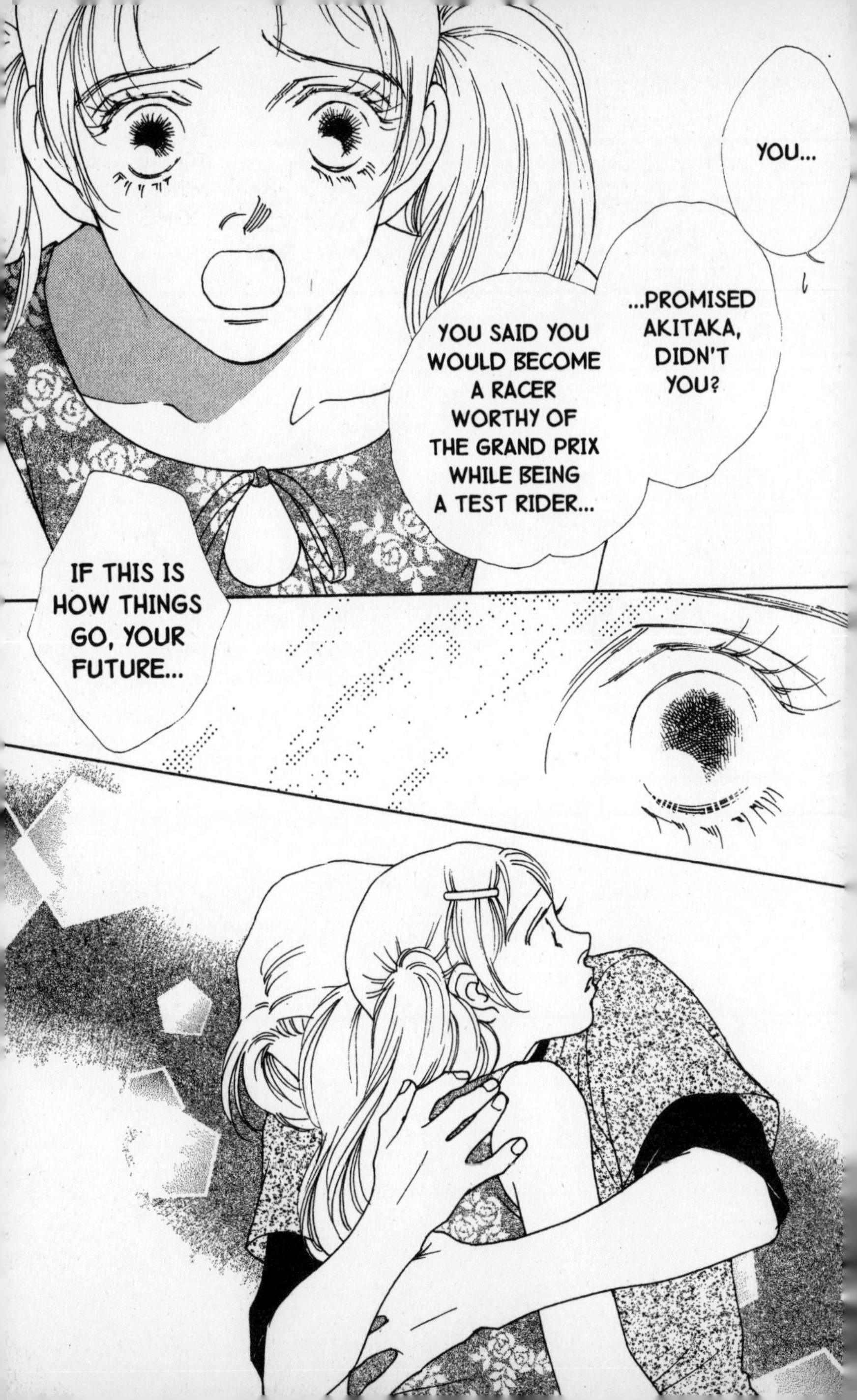
YOU...
...PROMISED AKITAKA, DIDN'T YOU?
YOU SAID YOU WOULD BECOME A RACER WORTHY OF THE GRAND PRIX WHILE BEING A TEST RIDER...
IF THIS IS HOW THINGS GO, YOUR FUTURE...

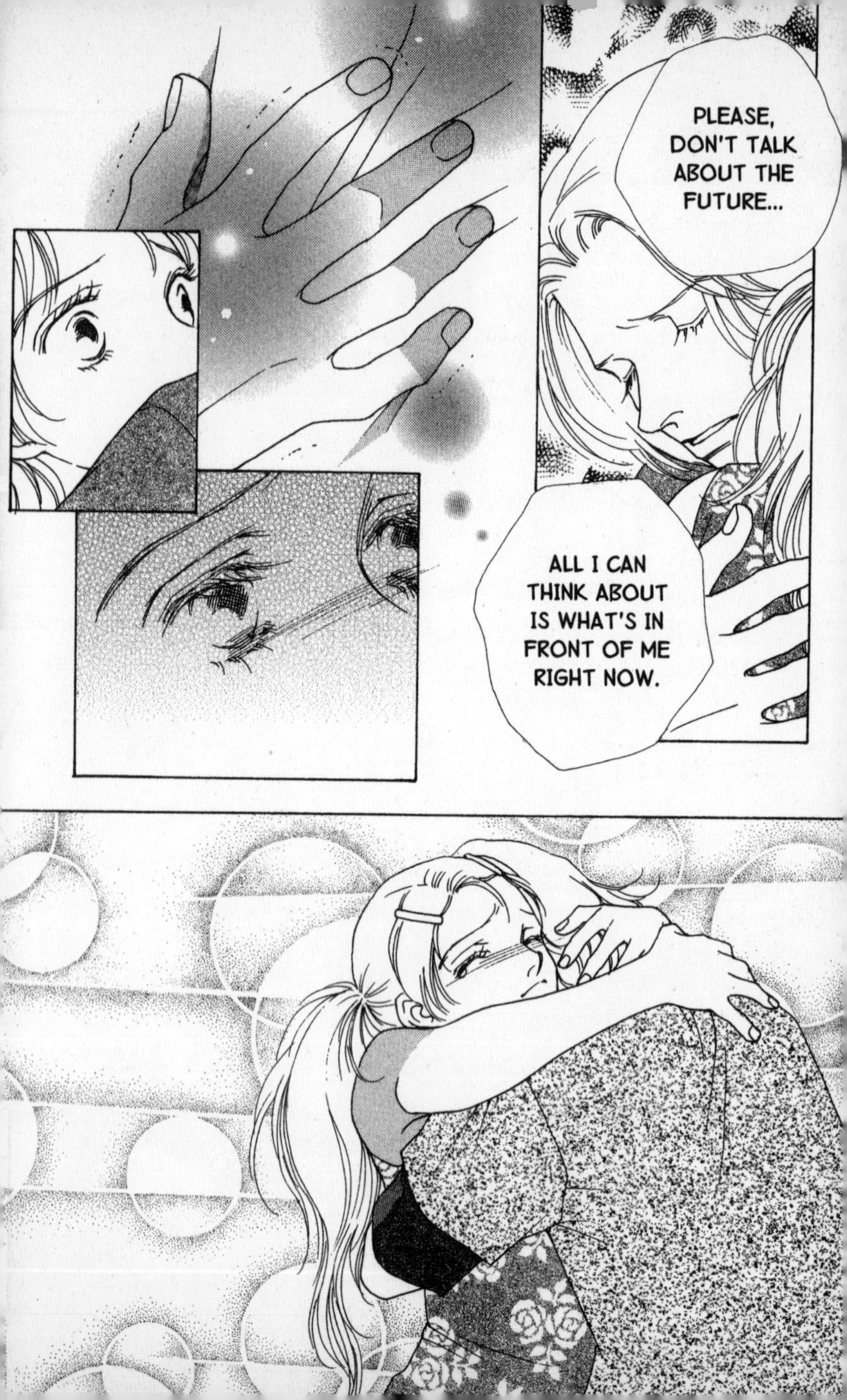
PLEASE, DON'T TALK ABOUT THE FUTURE...
ALL I CAN THINK ABOUT IS WHAT'S IN FRONT OF ME RIGHT NOW.

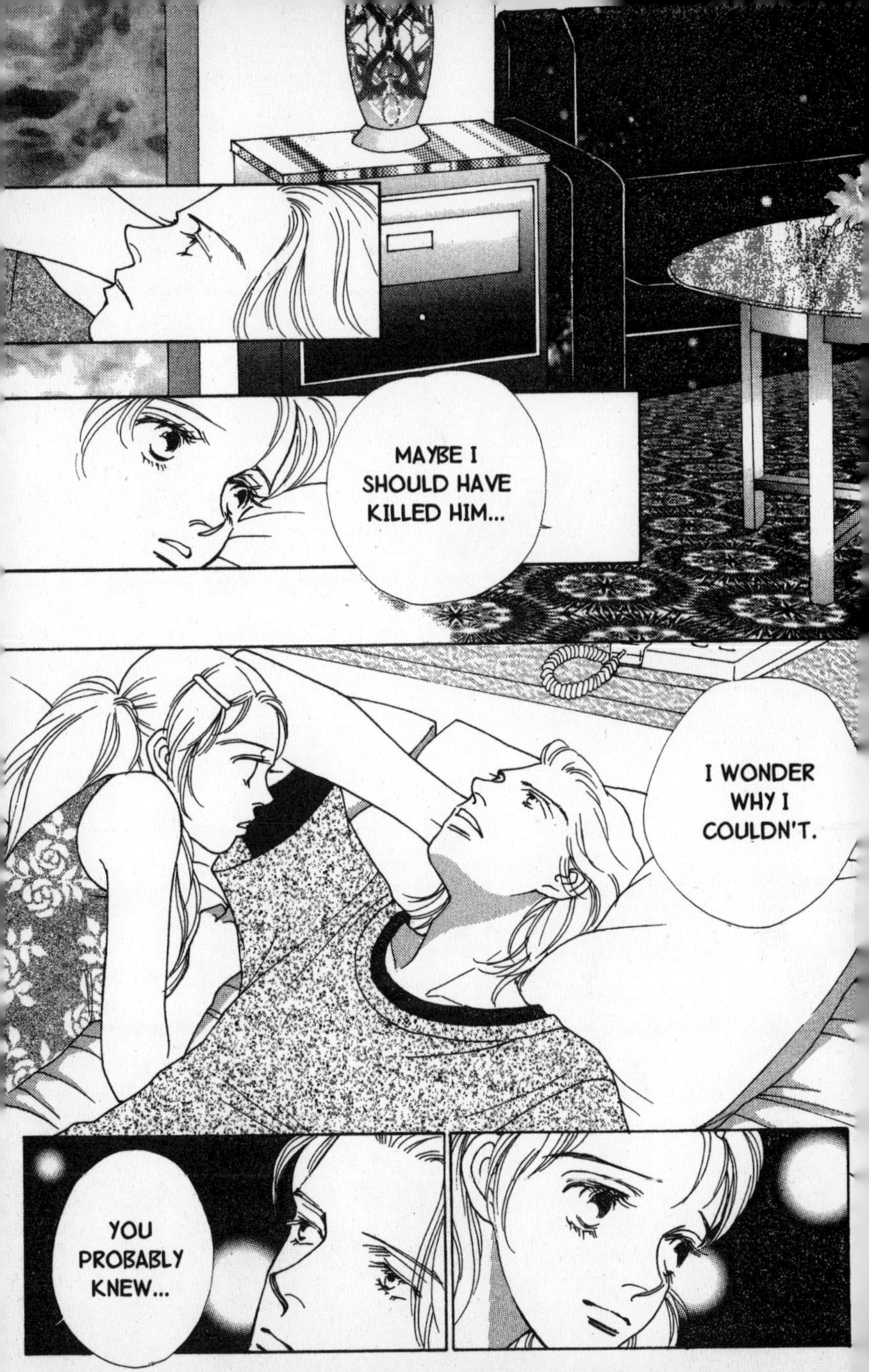
MAYBE I SHOULD HAVE KILLED HIM...
I WONDER WHY I COULDN'T.
YOU PROBABLY KNEW...

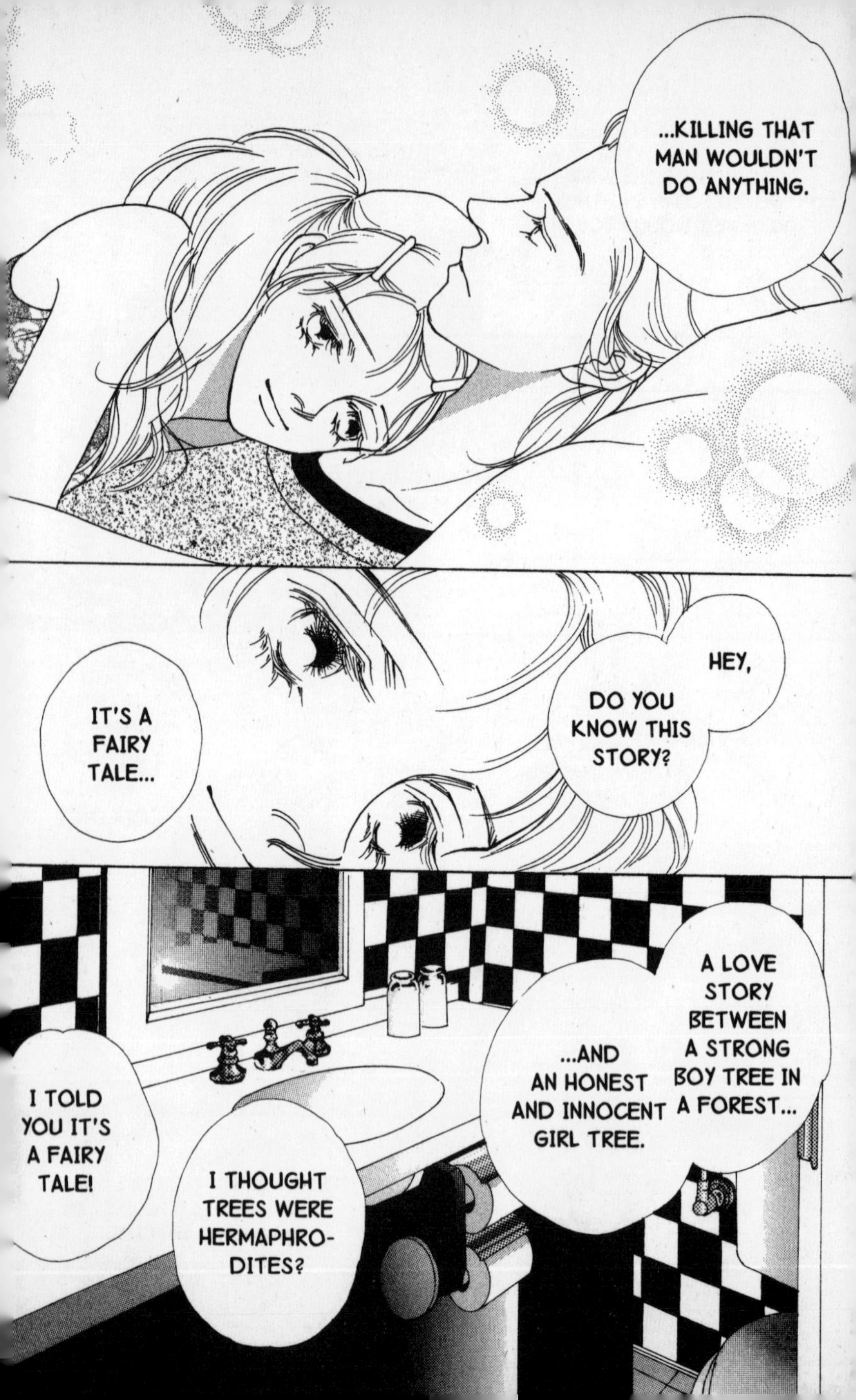
...KILLING THAT MAN WOULDN'T DO ANYTHING.
HEY,
DO YOU KNOW THIS STORY?
IT'S A FAIRY TALE...
A LOVE STORY BETWEEN A STRONG BOY TREE IN A FOREST...
...AND AN HONEST AND INNOCENT GIRL TREE.
I THOUGHT TREES WERE HERMAPHRO-DITES?
I TOLD YOU IT'S A FAIRY TALE!

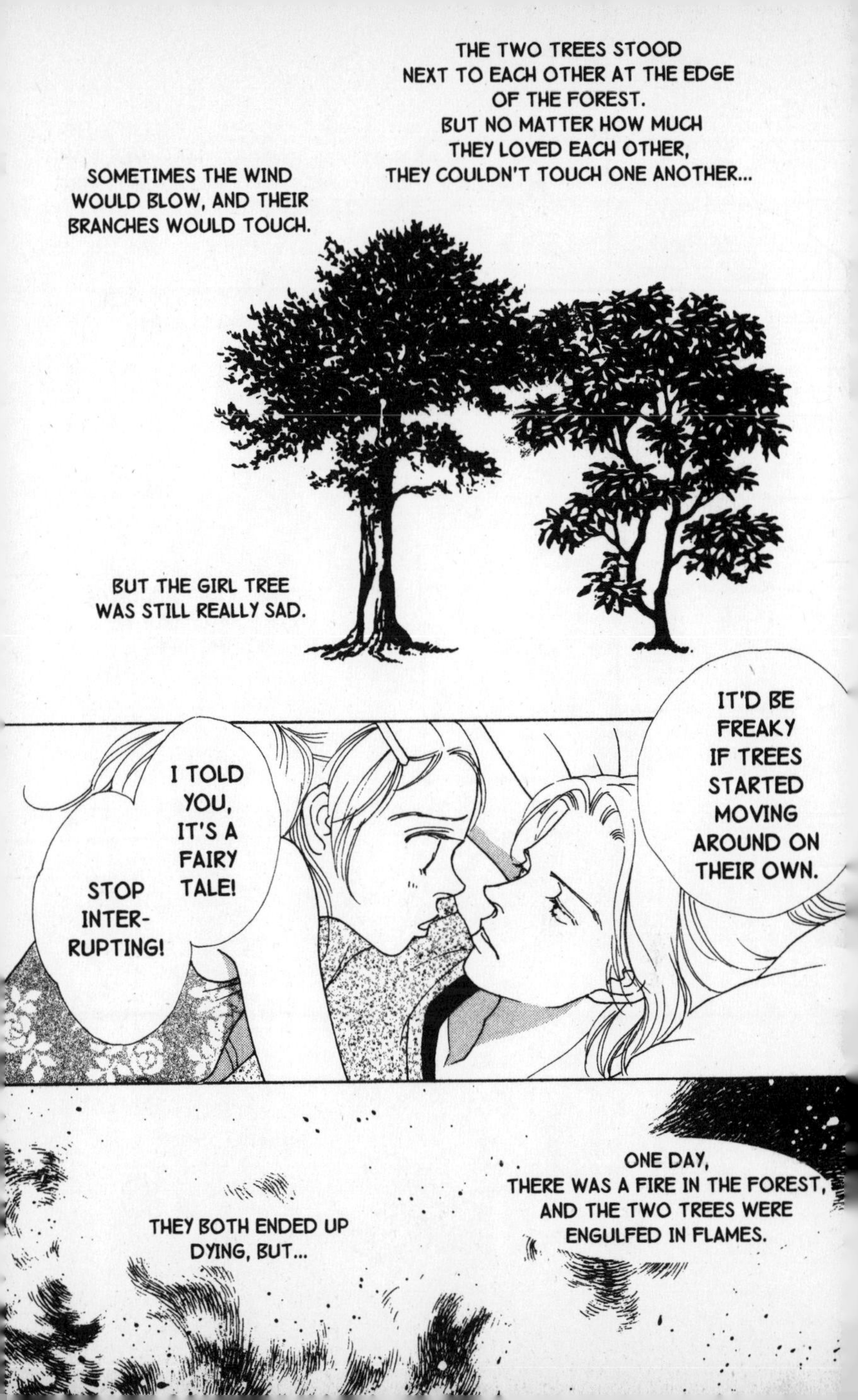
THE TWO TREES STOOD NEXT TO EACH OTHER AT THE EDGE OF THE FOREST. BUT NO MATTER HOW MUCH THEY LOVED EACH OTHER, THEY COULDN'T TOUCH ONE ANOTHER...
SOMETIMES THE WIND WOULD BLOW, AND THEIR BRANCHES WOULD TOUCH.
BUT THE GIRL TREE WAS STILL REALLY SAD.
IT'D BE FREAKY IF TREES STARTED MOVING AROUND ON THEIR OWN.
I TOLD YOU, IT'S A FAIRY TALE!
STOP INTER-RUPTING!
ONE DAY, THERE WAS A FIRE IN THE FOREST, AND THE TWO TREES WERE ENGULFED IN FLAMES.
THEY BOTH ENDED UP DYING, BUT...

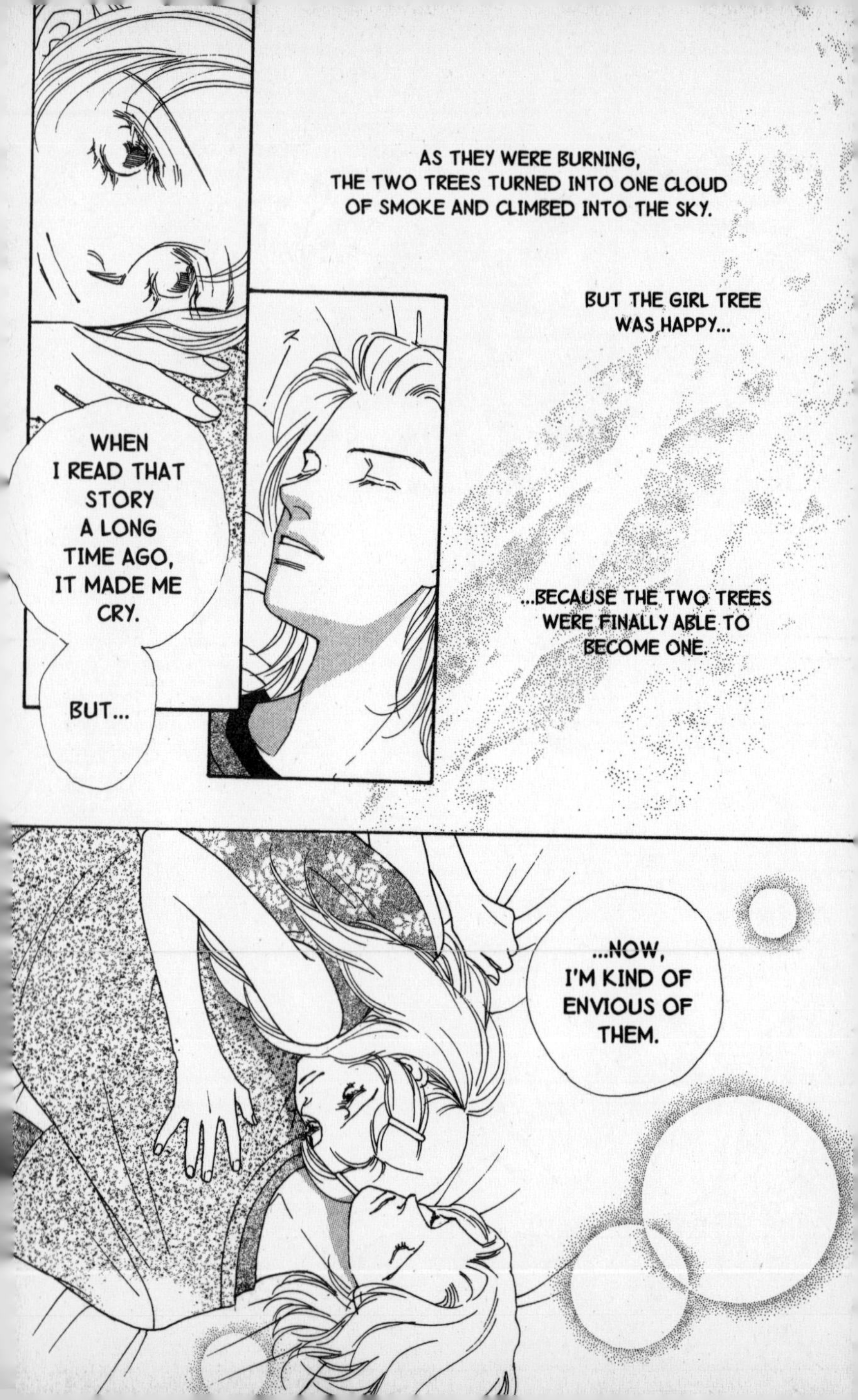
AS THEY WERE BURNING, THE TWO TREES TURNED INTO ONE CLOUD OF SMOKE AND CLIMBED INTO THE SKY.
BUT THE GIRL TREE WAS HAPPY...
...BECAUSE THE TWO TREES WERE FINALLY ABLE TO BECOME ONE.
WHEN I READ THAT STORY A LONG TIME AGO, IT MADE ME CRY.
BUT...
...NOW, I'M KIND OF ENVIOUS OF THEM.

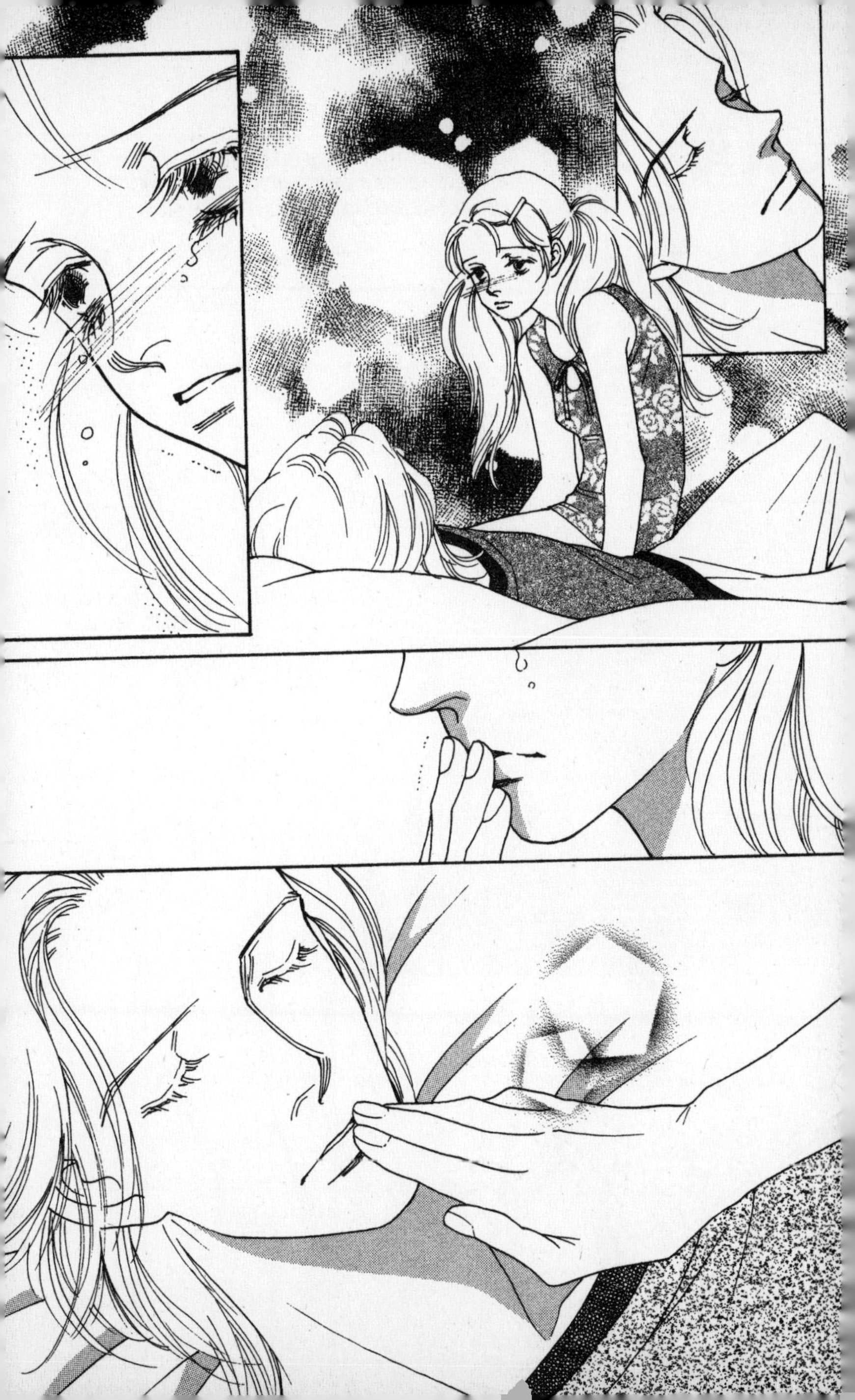

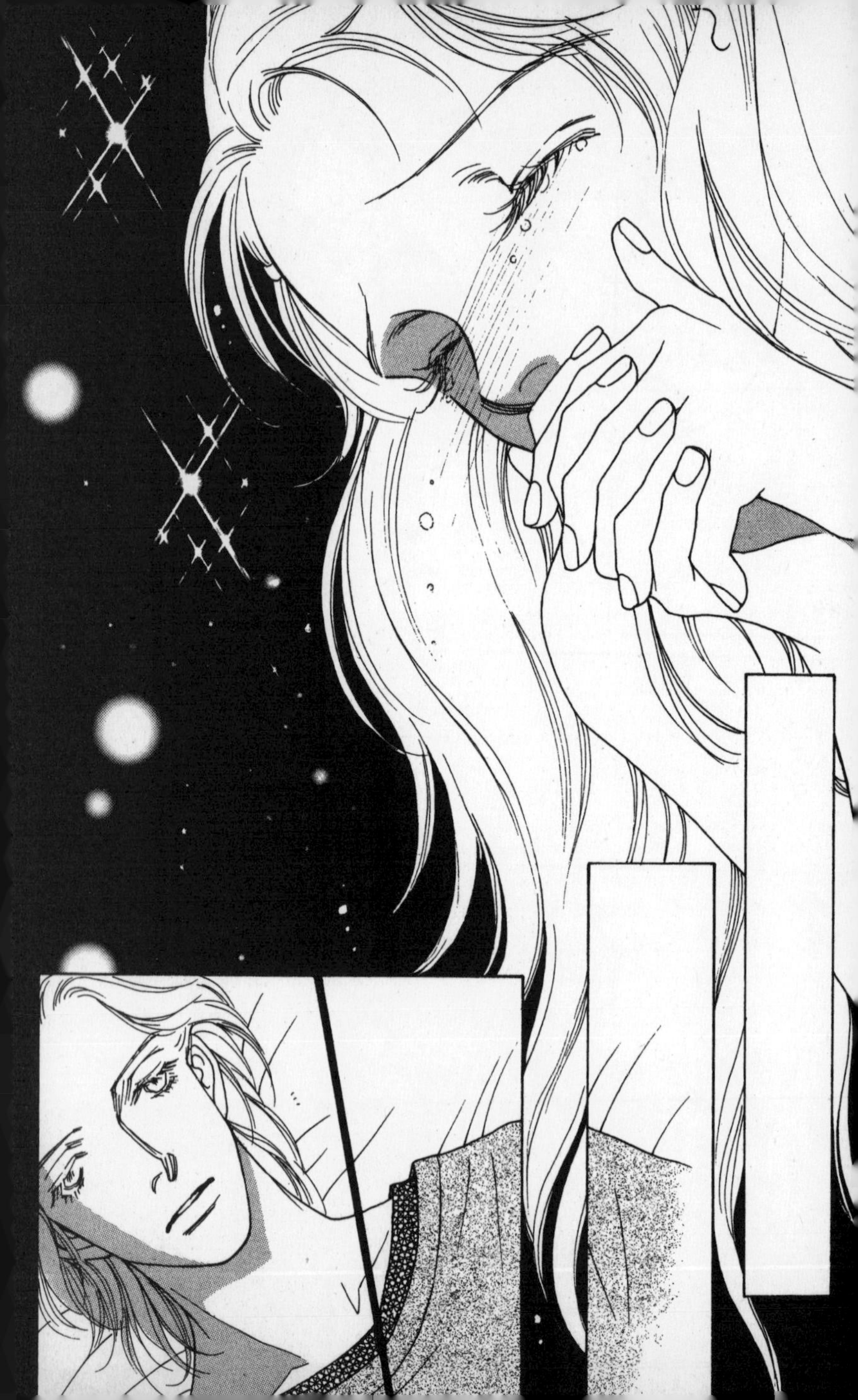

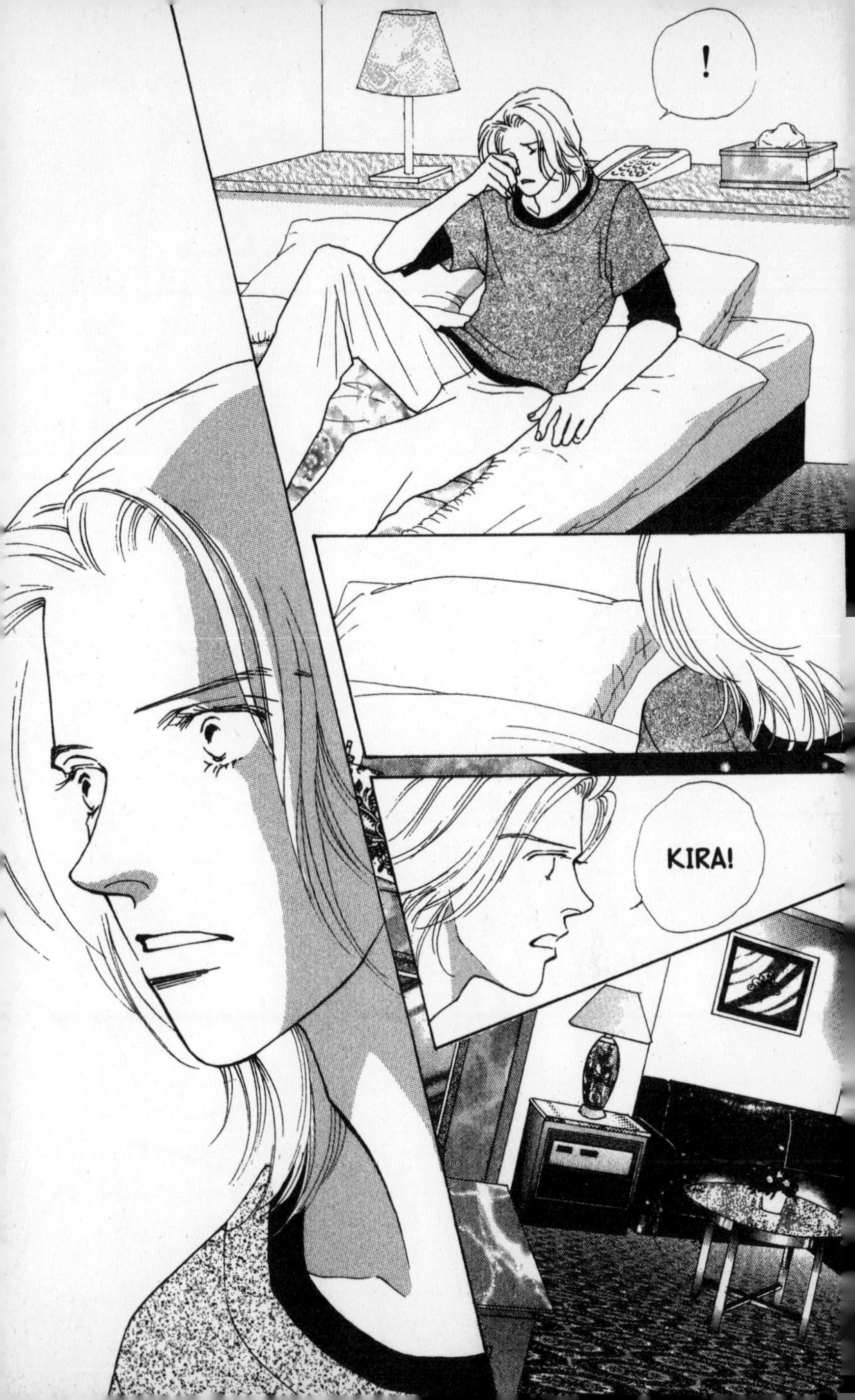
!
KIRA!

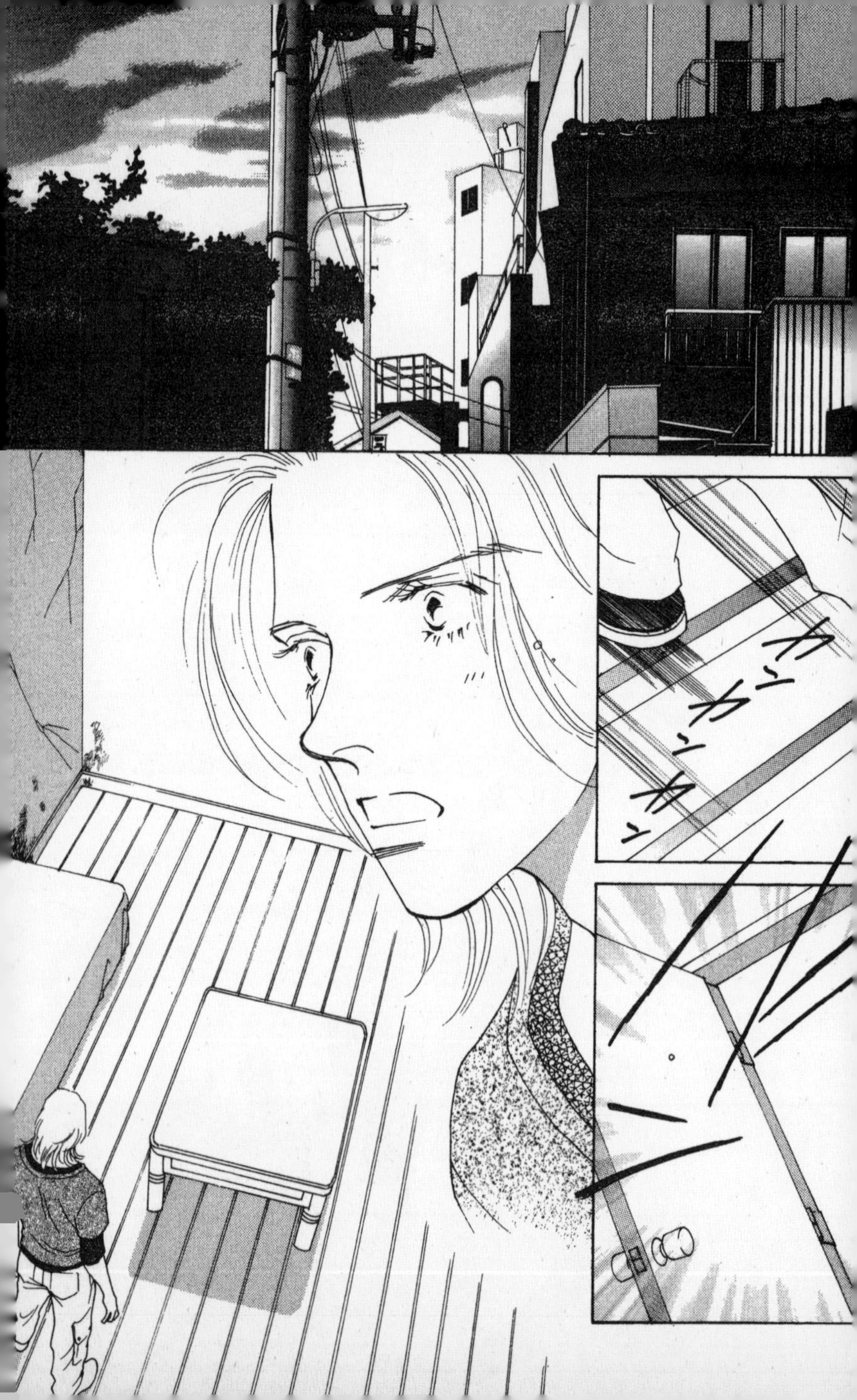
カンカンカン

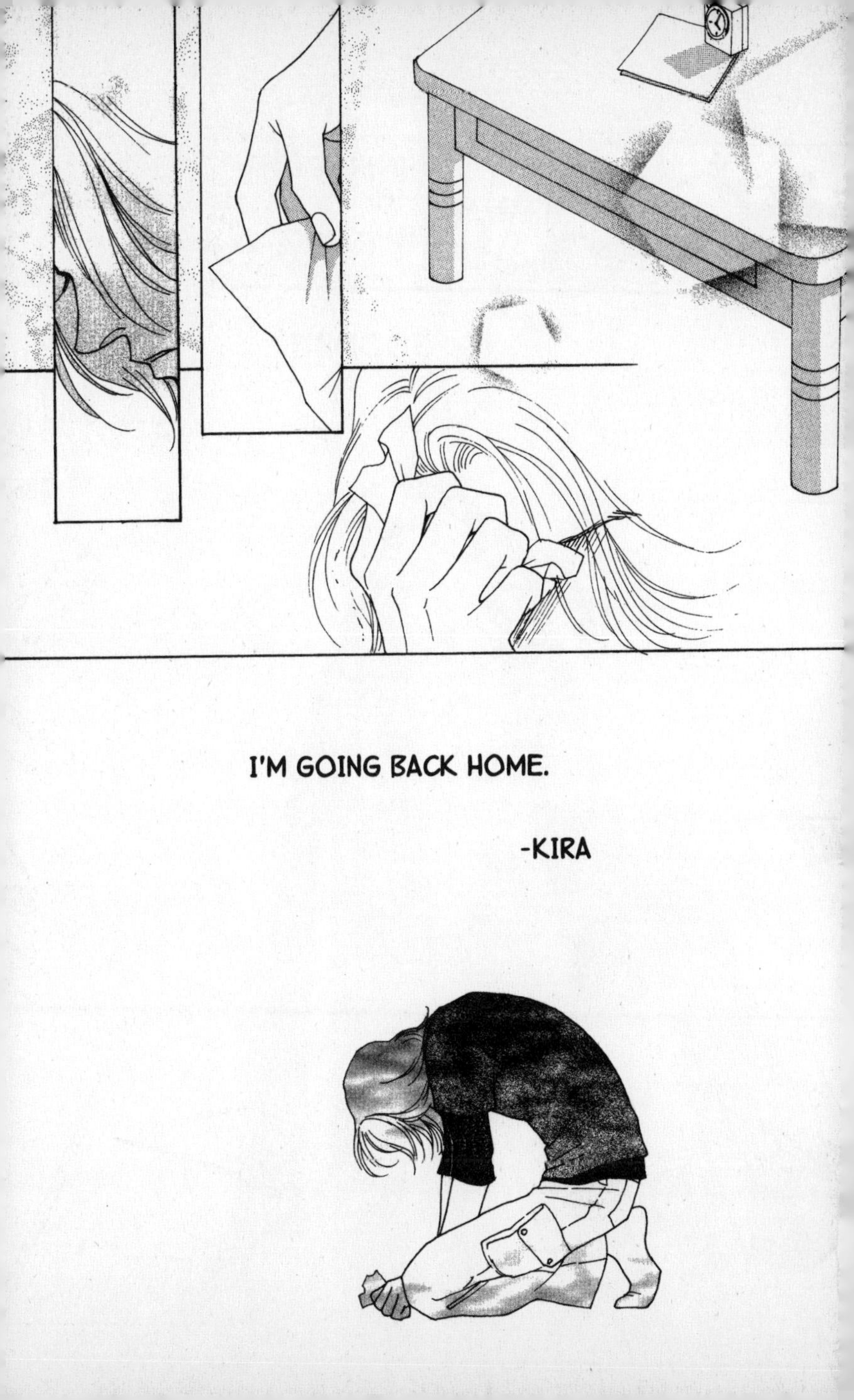
I'M GOING BACK HOME.
-KIRA

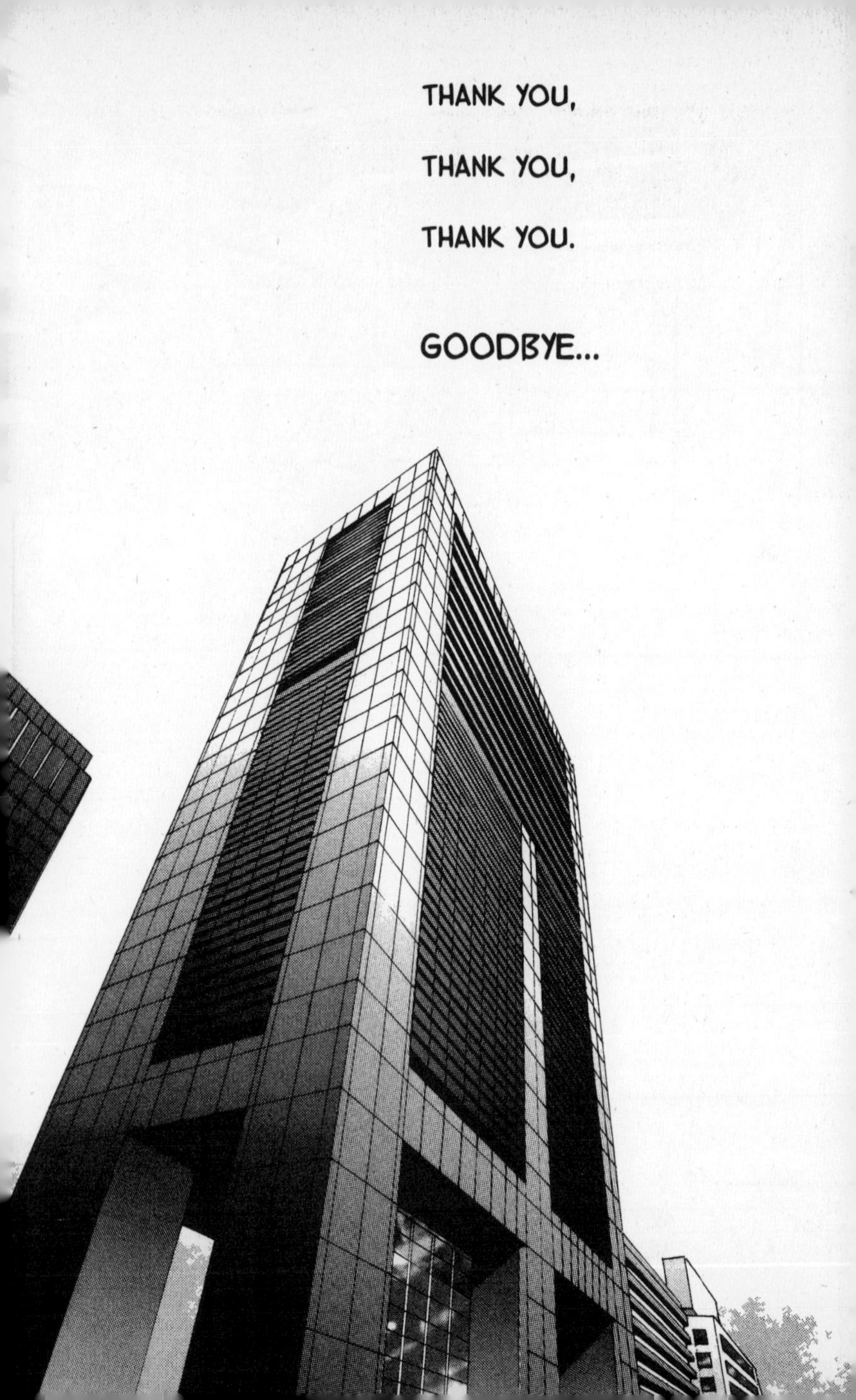
THANK YOU,
THANK YOU,
THANK YOU.
GOODBYE...

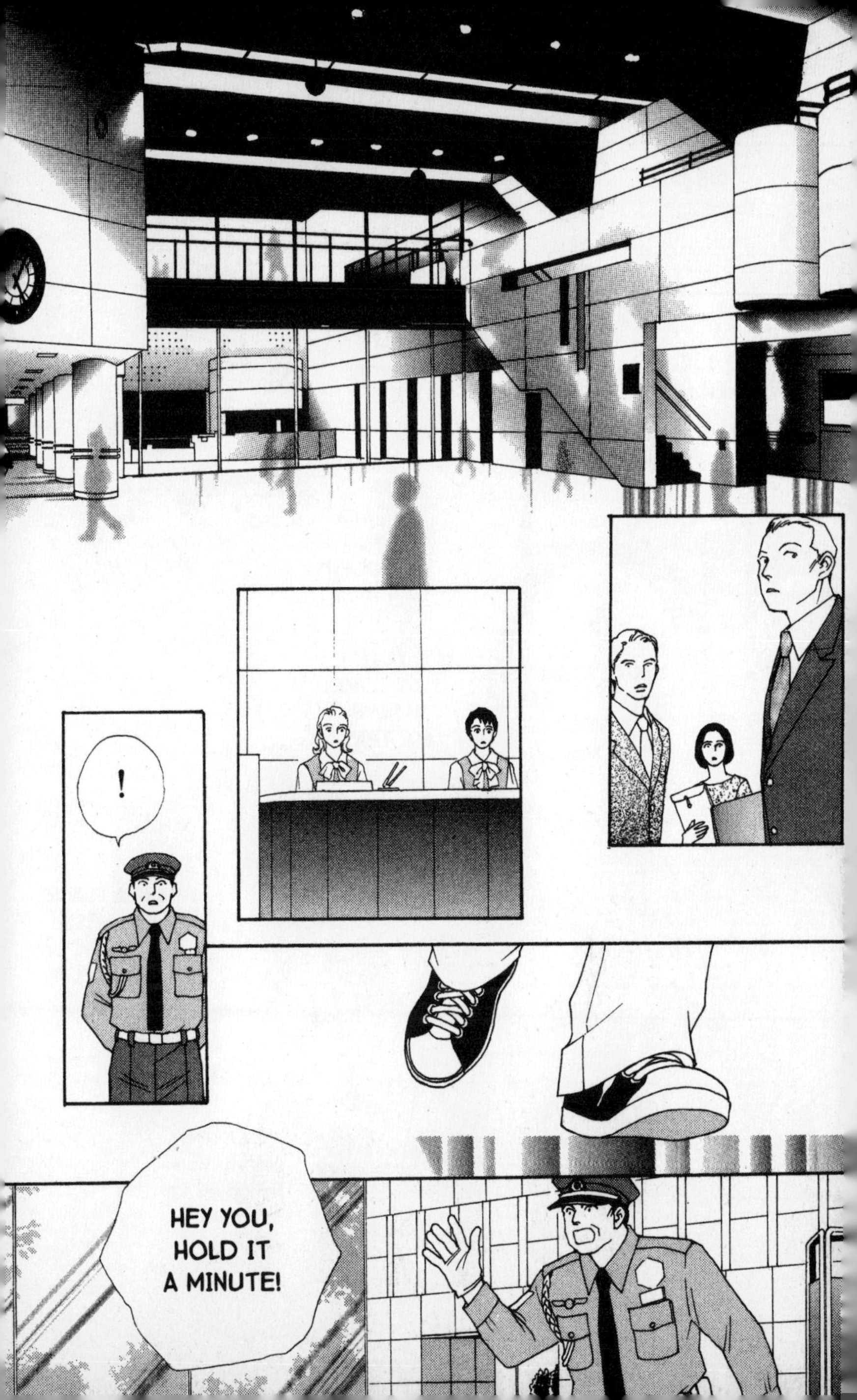
!
HEY YOU, HOLD IT A MINUTE!

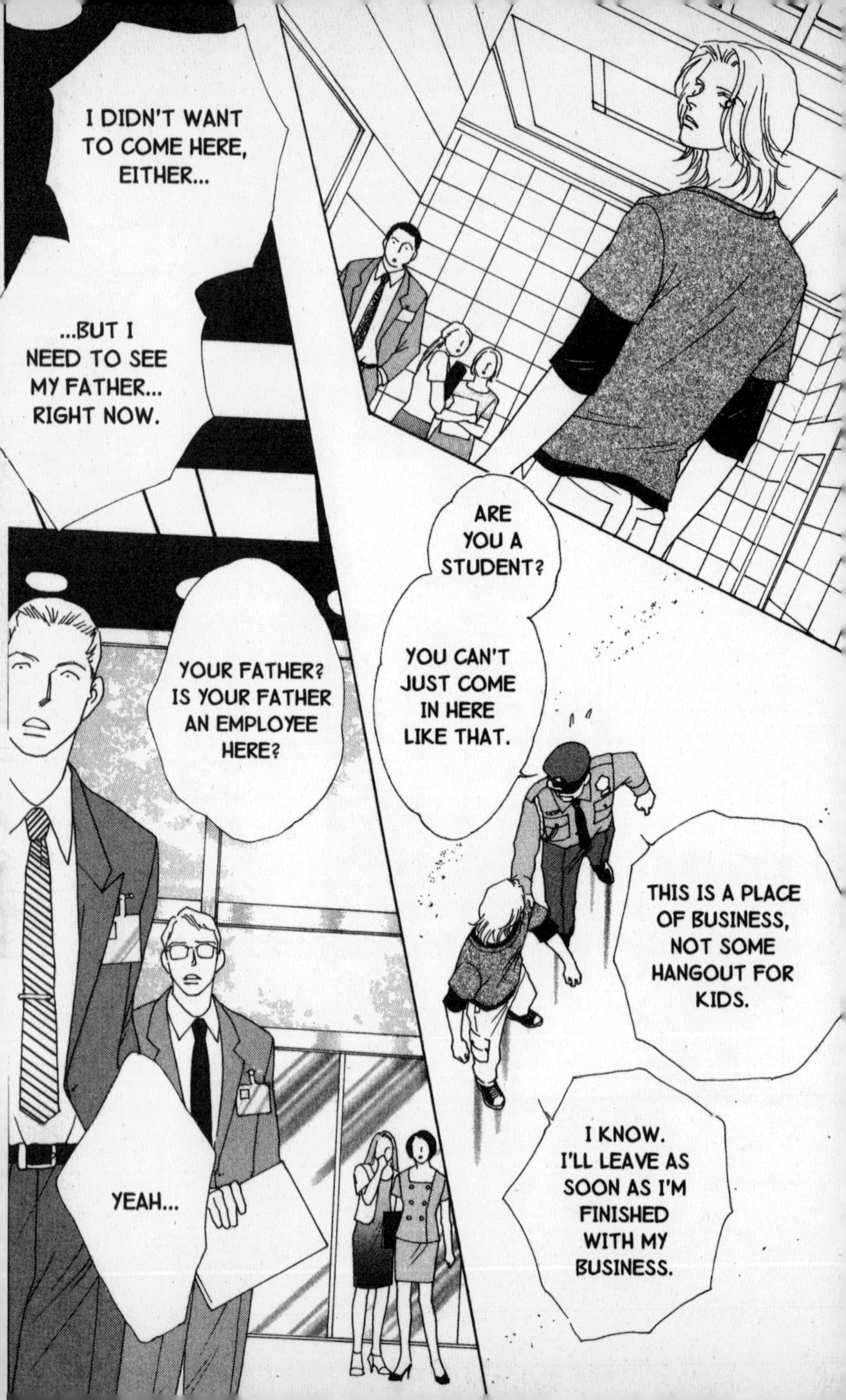
ARE YOU A STUDENT?
YOU CAN'T JUST COME IN HERE LIKE THAT.
THIS IS A PLACE OF BUSINESS, NOT SOME HANGOUT FOR KIDS.
I KNOW. I'LL LEAVE AS SOON AS I'M FINISHED WITH MY BUSINESS.
I DIDN'T WANT TO COME HERE, EITHER...
...BUT I NEED TO SEE MY FATHER... RIGHT NOW.
YOUR FATHER? IS YOUR FATHER AN EMPLOYEE HERE?
YEAH...

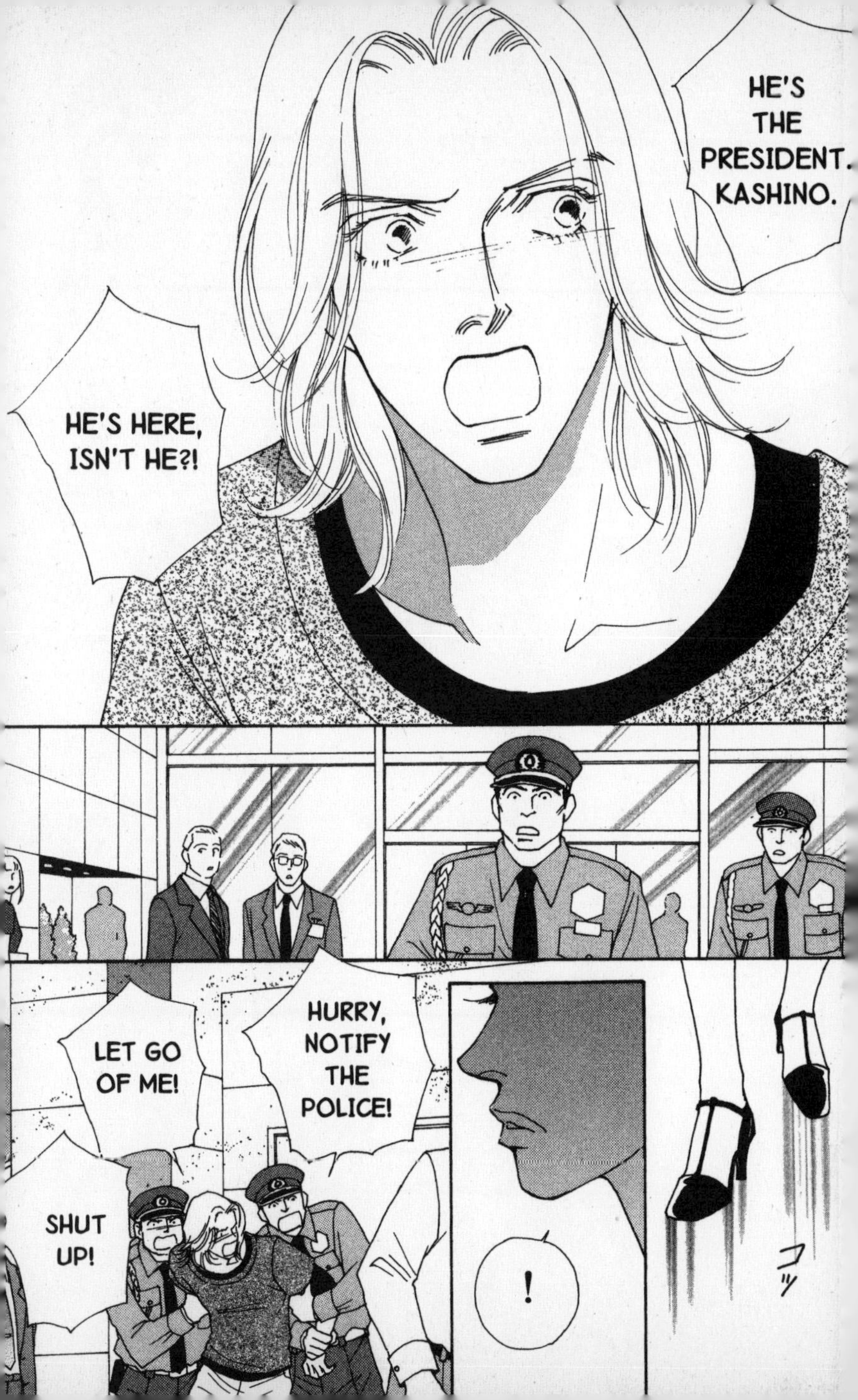
HE'S THE PRESIDENT. KASHINO.
HE'S HERE, ISN'T HE?!
コッ
!
HURRY, NOTIFY THE POLICE!
LET GO OF ME!
SHUT UP!

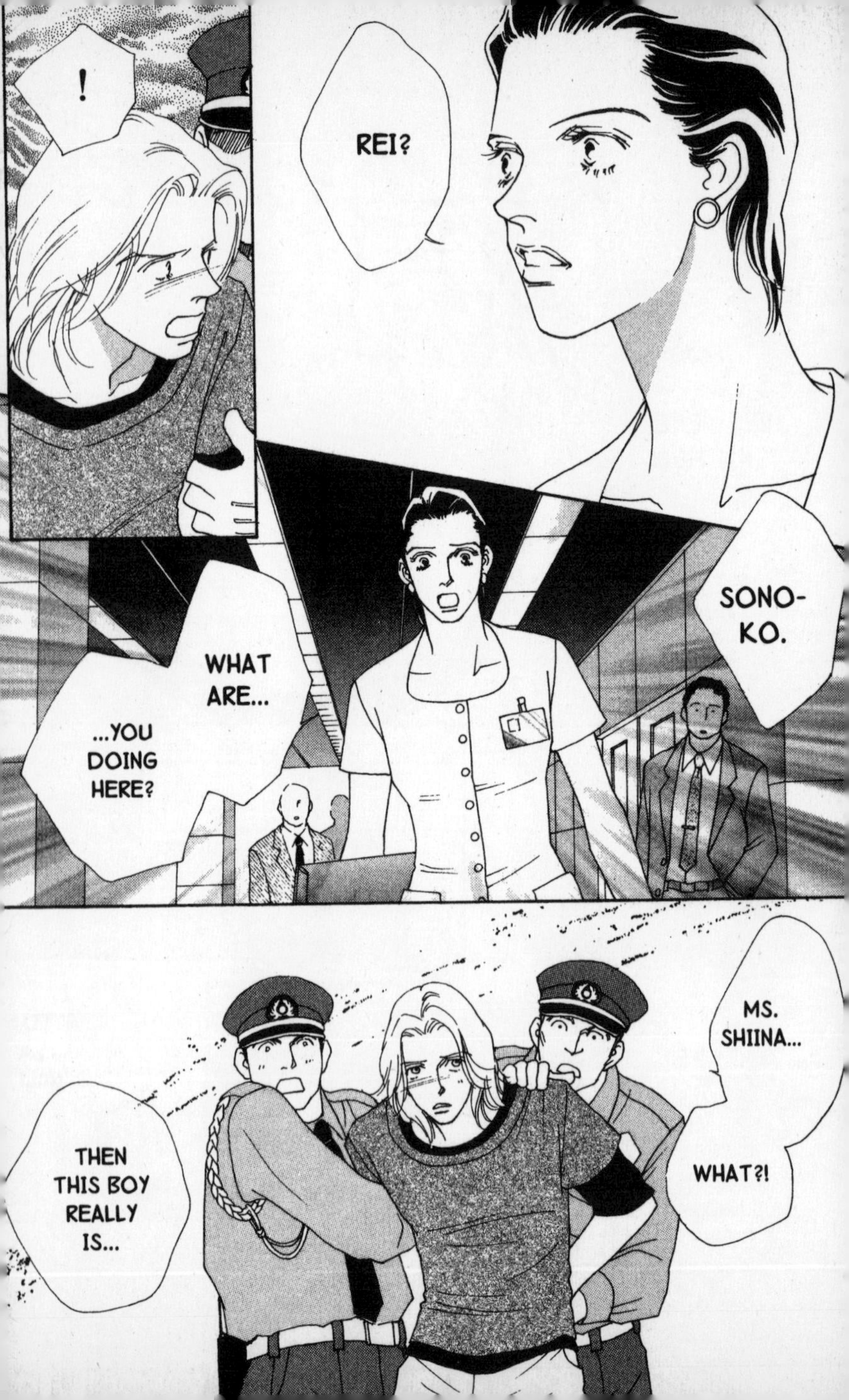
REI?
!
SONO-KO.
WHAT ARE...
...YOU DOING HERE?
MS. SHIINA...
WHAT?!
THEN THIS BOY REALLY IS...

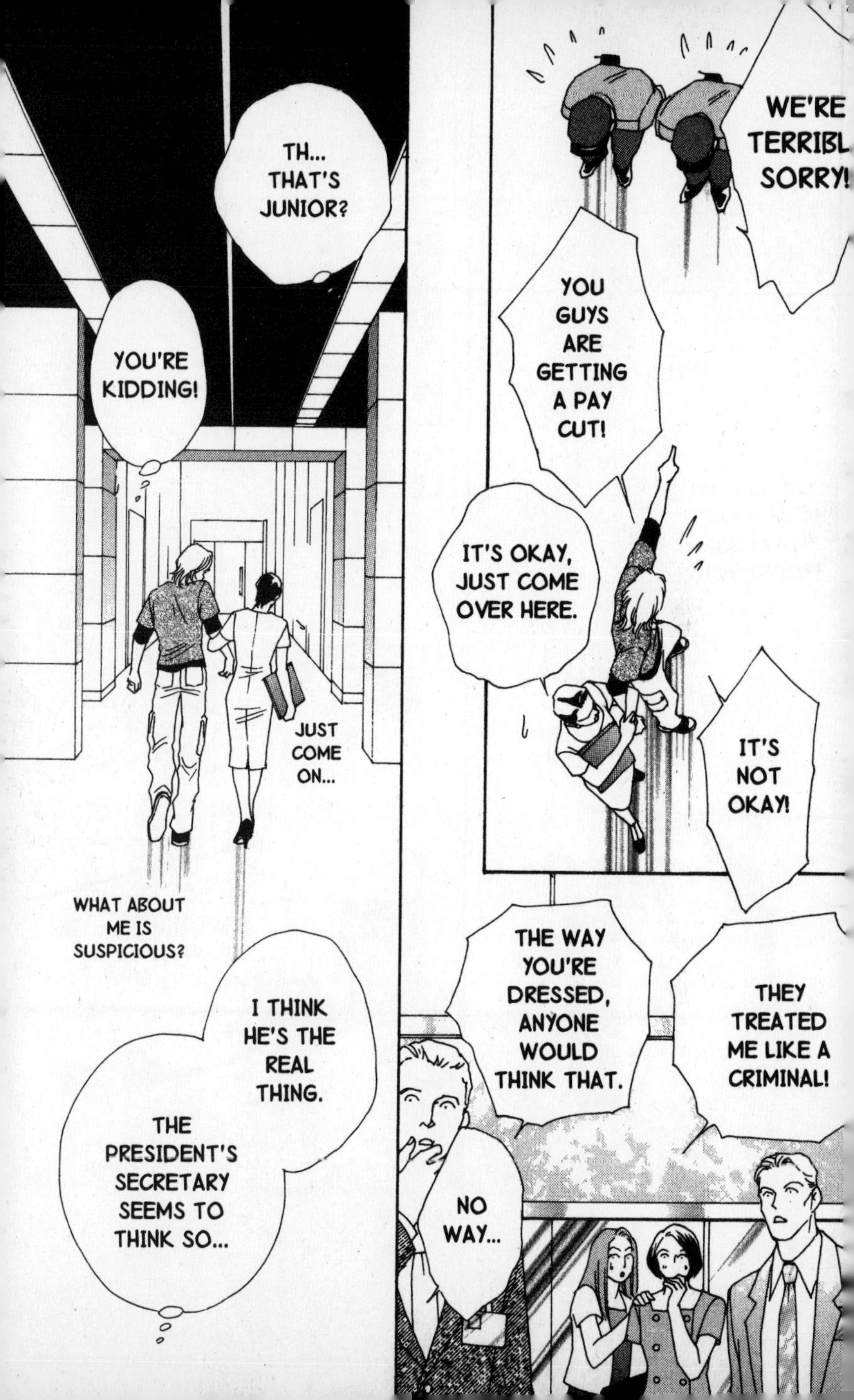
WE'RE TERRIBL SORRY!
YOU GUYS ARE GETTING A PAY CUT!
IT'S OKAY, JUST COME OVER HERE.
IT'S NOT OKAY!
THEY TREATED ME LIKE A CRIMINAL!
THE WAY YOU'RE DRESSED, ANYONE WOULD THINK THAT.
NO WAY...
TH... THAT'S JUNIOR?
YOU'RE KIDDING!
JUST COME ON...
WHAT ABOUT ME IS SUSPICIOUS?
I THINK HE'S THE REAL THING.
THE PRESIDENT'S SECRETARY SEEMS TO THINK SO...

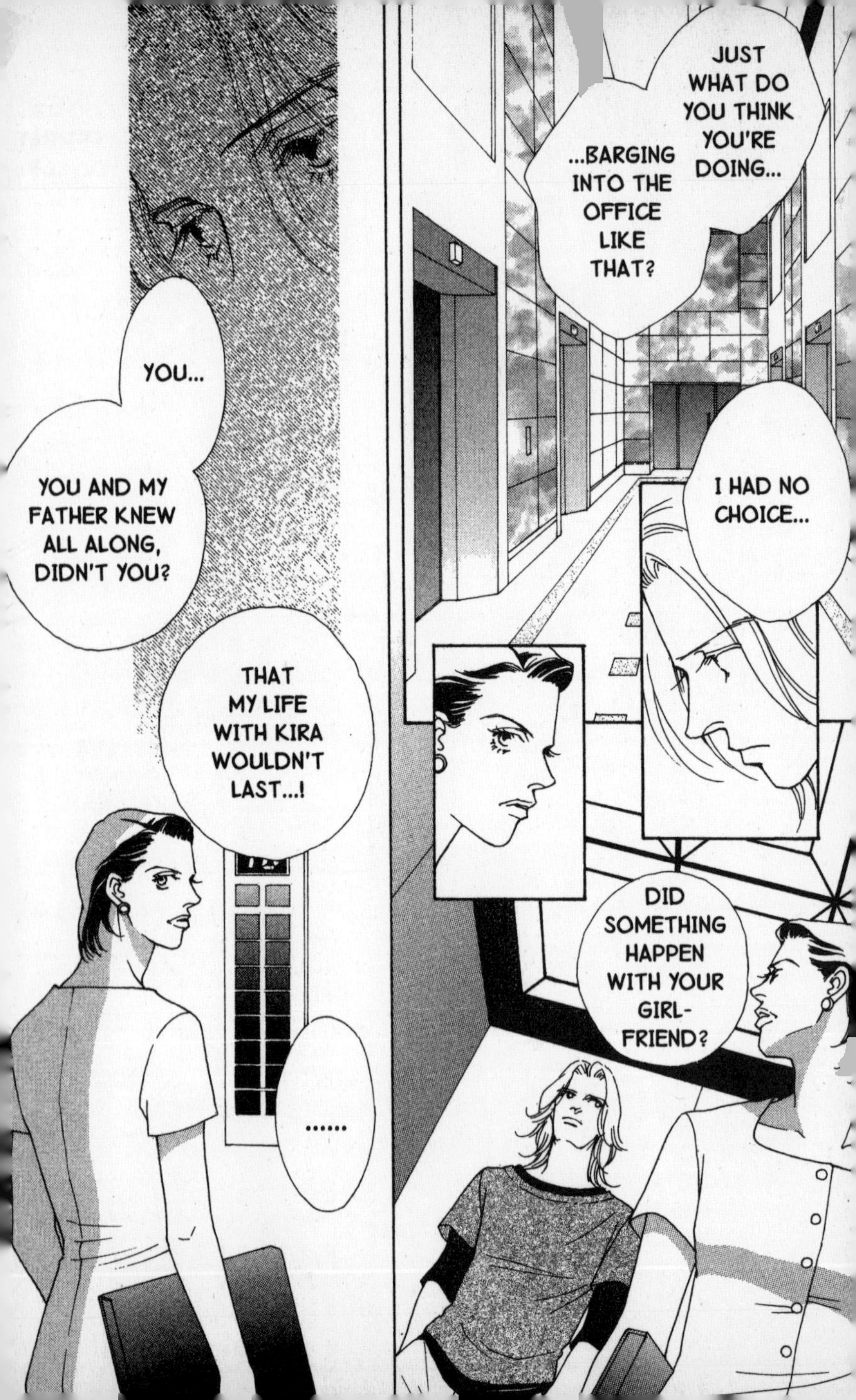
JUST WHAT DO YOU THINK YOU'RE DOING...
...BARGING INTO THE OFFICE LIKE THAT?
I HAD NO CHOICE...
DID SOMETHING HAPPEN WITH YOUR GIRL-FRIEND?
YOU...
YOU AND MY FATHER KNEW ALL ALONG, DIDN'T YOU?
THAT MY LIFE WITH KIRA WOULDN'T LAST...!
......

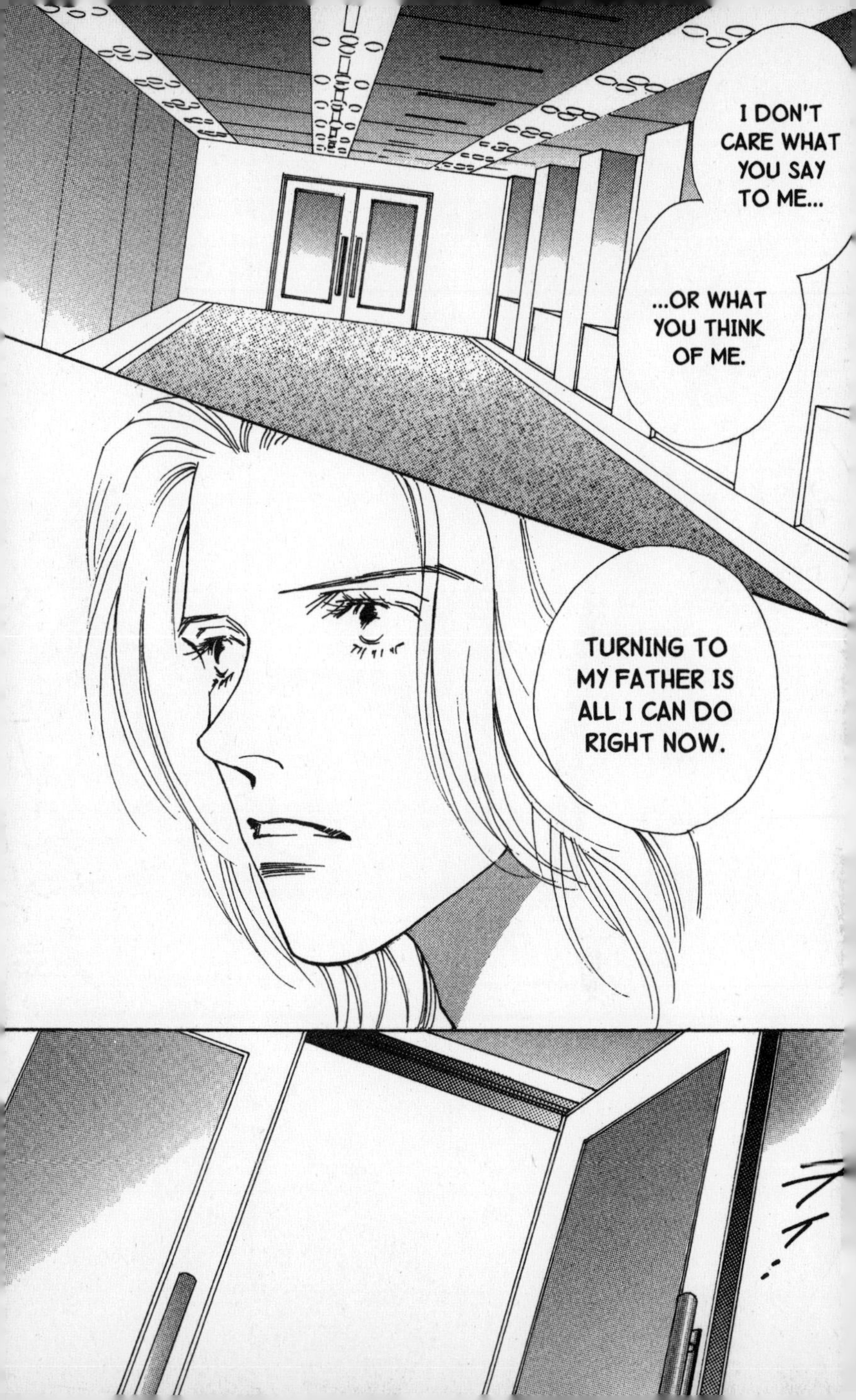
I DON'T CARE WHAT YOU SAY TO ME...
...OR WHAT YOU THINK OF ME.
TURNING TO MY FATHER IS ALL I CAN DO RIGHT NOW.

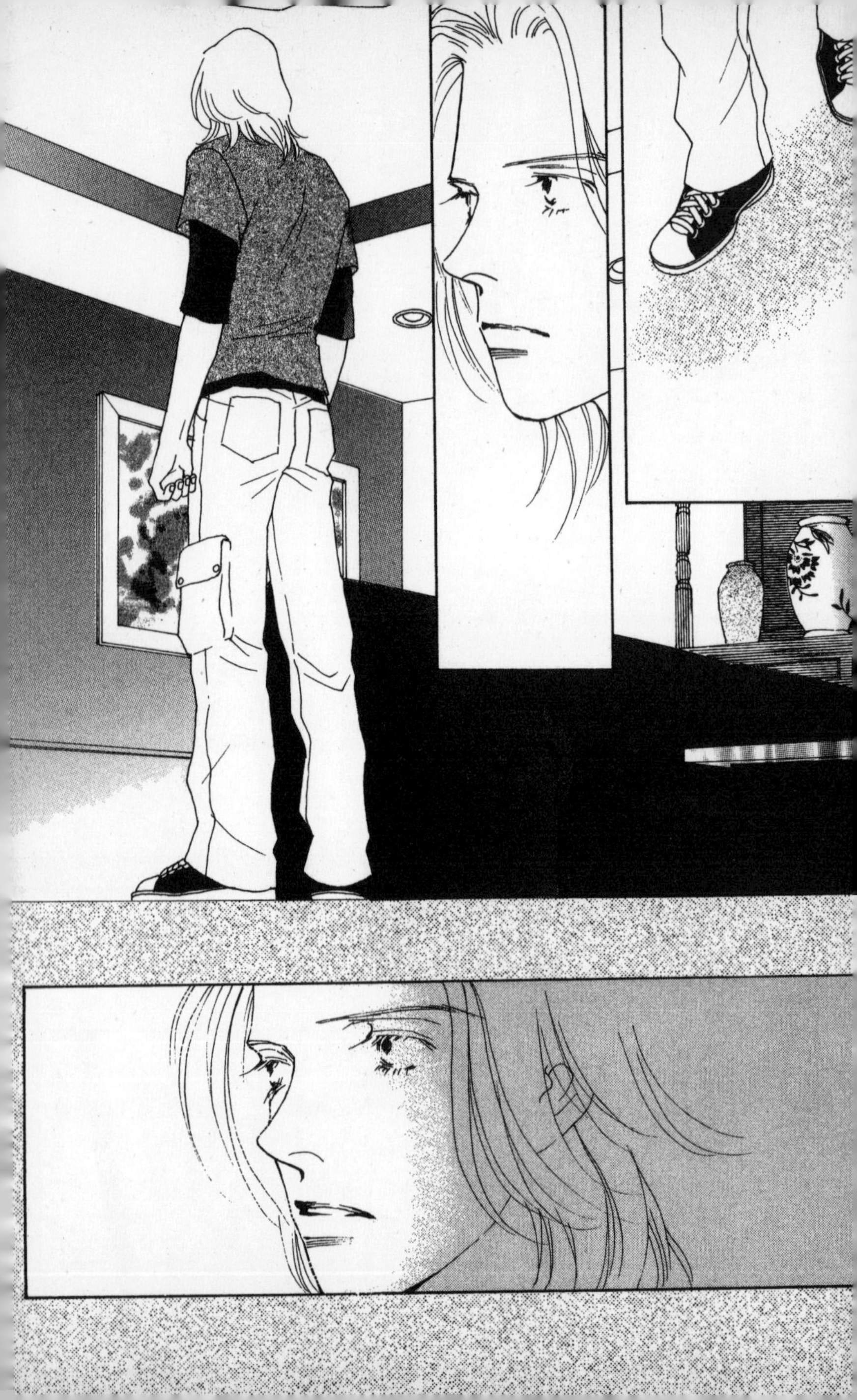

QUITE AN
ENTRANCE
YOU MADE.

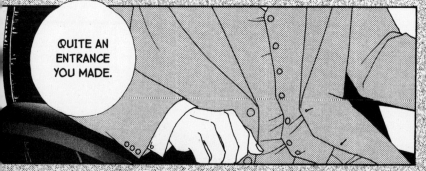

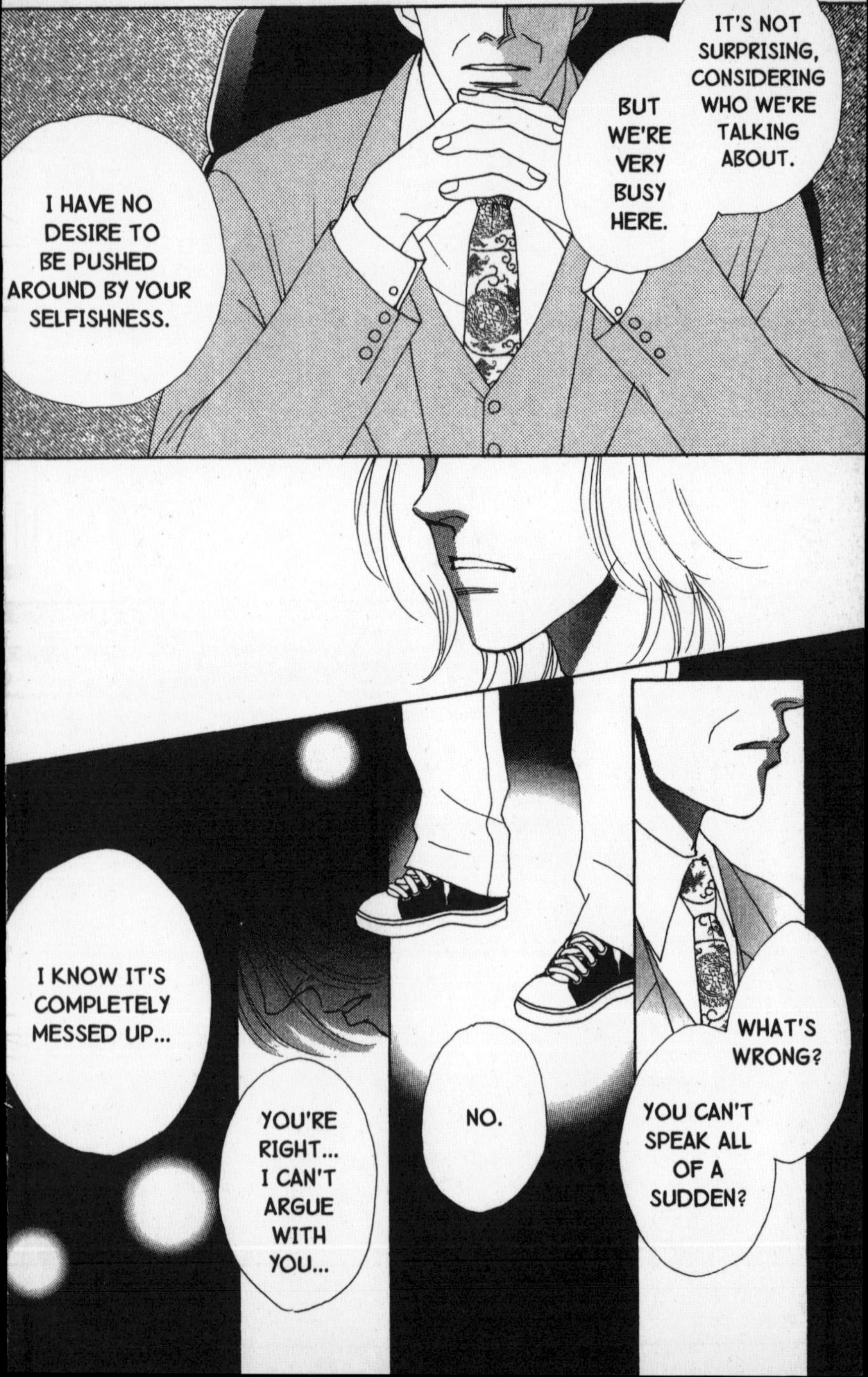
IT'S NOT SURPRISING, CONSIDERING WHO WE'RE TALKING ABOUT.
BUT WE'RE VERY BUSY HERE.
I HAVE NO DESIRE TO BE PUSHED AROUND BY YOUR SELFISHNESS.
WHAT'S WRONG?
YOU CAN'T SPEAK ALL OF A SUDDEN?
NO.
YOU'RE RIGHT... I CAN'T ARGUE WITH YOU...
I KNOW IT'S COMPLETELY MESSED UP...

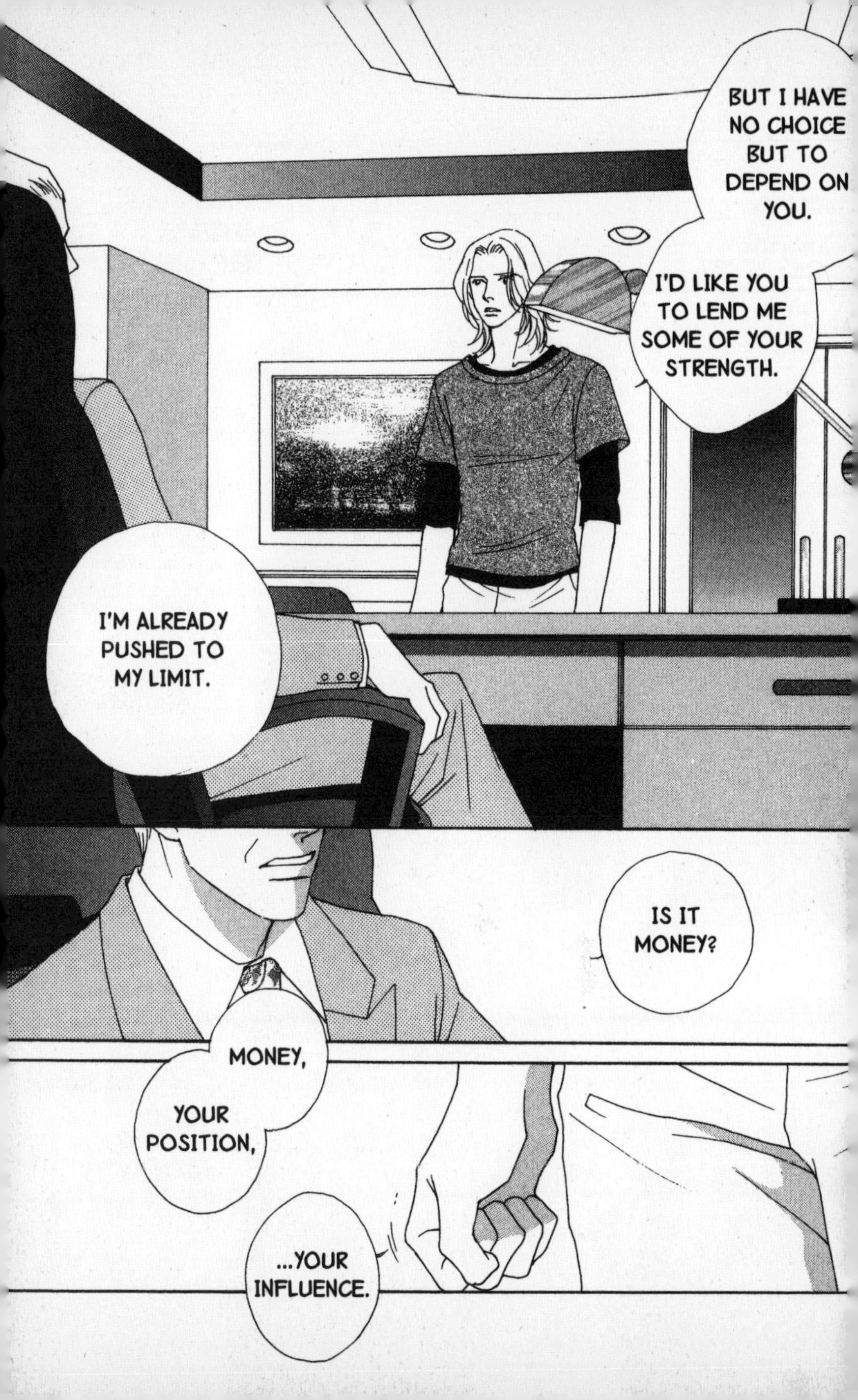
BUT I HAVE NO CHOICE BUT TO DEPEND ON YOU.
I'D LIKE YOU TO LEND ME SOME OF YOUR STRENGTH.
I'M ALREADY PUSHED TO MY LIMIT.
IS IT MONEY?
MONEY,
YOUR POSITION,
...YOUR INFLUENCE.

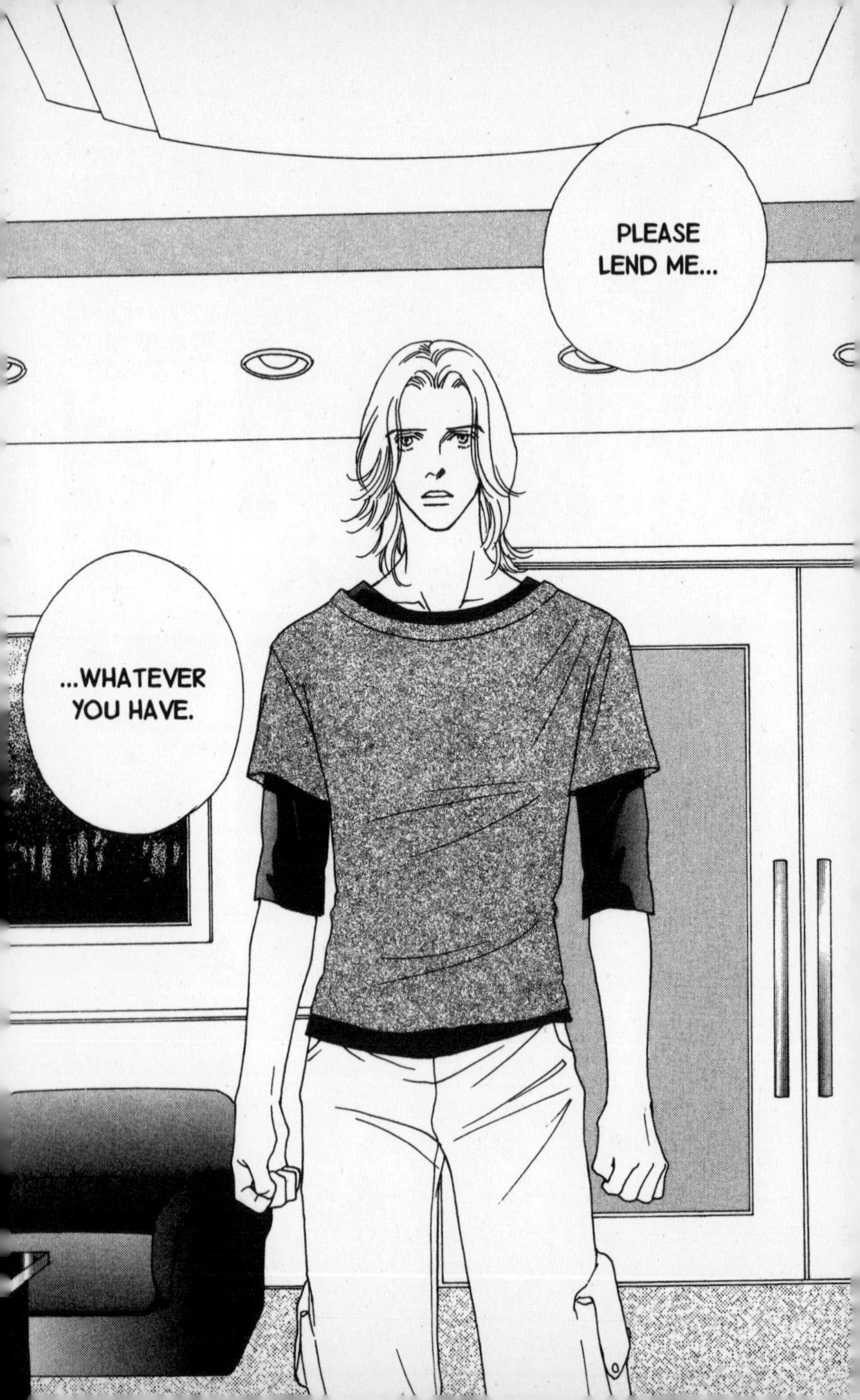
PLEASE LEND ME...
...WHATEVER YOU HAVE.

MARS

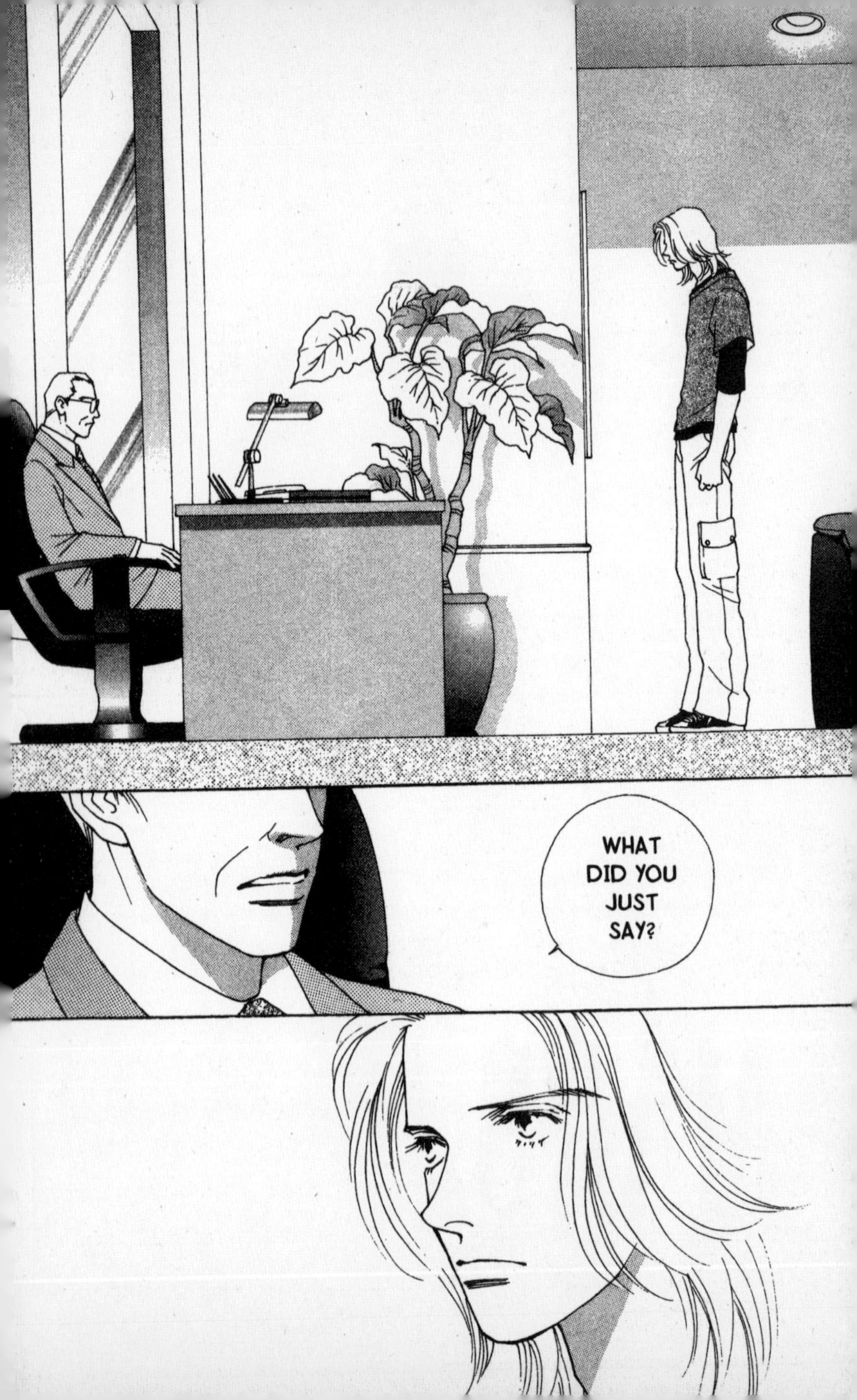
WHAT DID YOU JUST SAY?

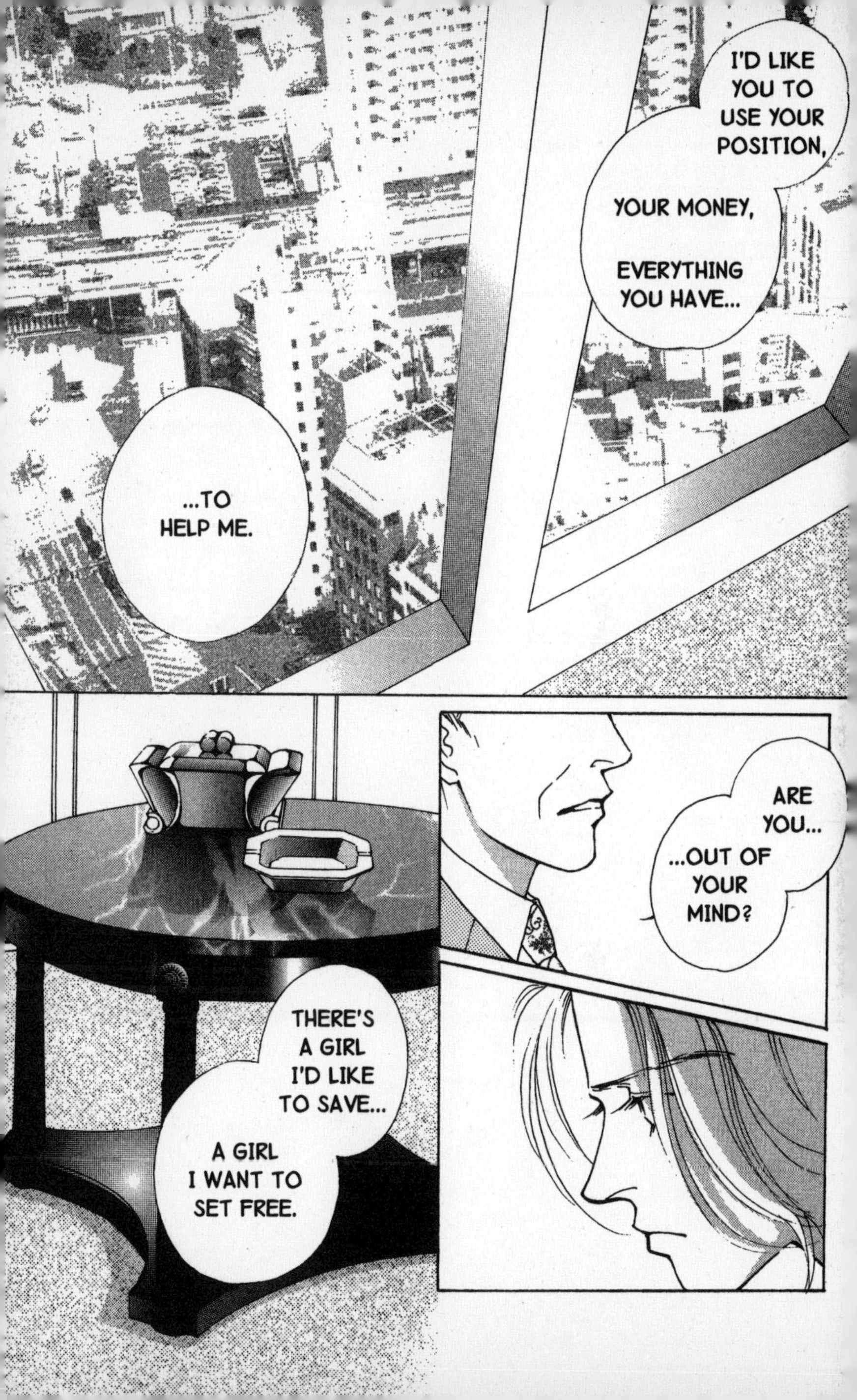
I'D LIKE YOU TO USE YOUR POSITION,
YOUR MONEY,
EVERYTHING YOU HAVE...
...TO HELP ME.
ARE YOU...
...OUT OF YOUR MIND?
THERE'S A GIRL I'D LIKE TO SAVE...
A GIRL I WANT TO SET FREE.

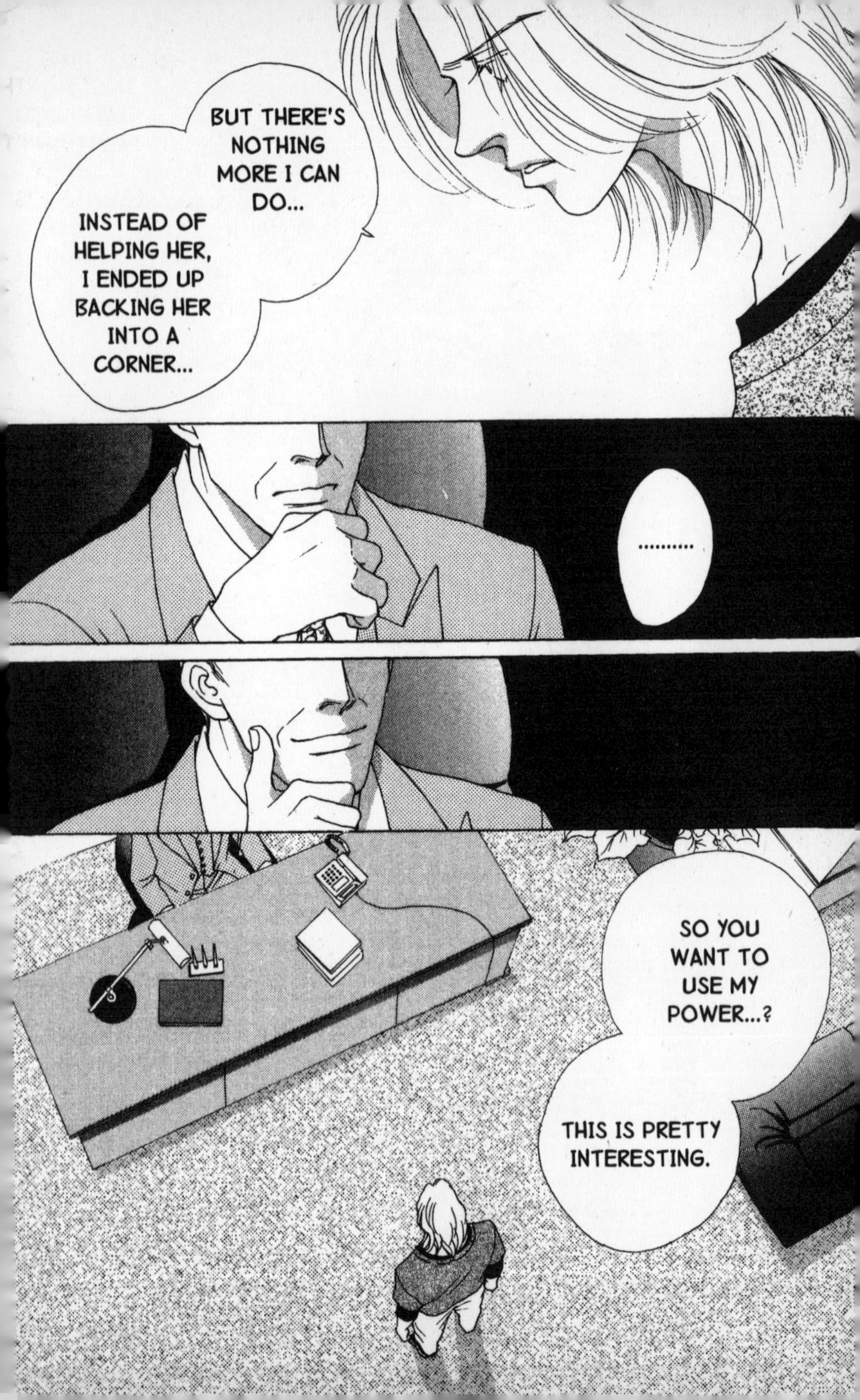
BUT THERE'S NOTHING MORE I CAN DO...
INSTEAD OF HELPING HER, I ENDED UP BACKING HER INTO A CORNER...
....
SO YOU WANT TO USE MY POWER...?
THIS IS PRETTY INTERESTING.

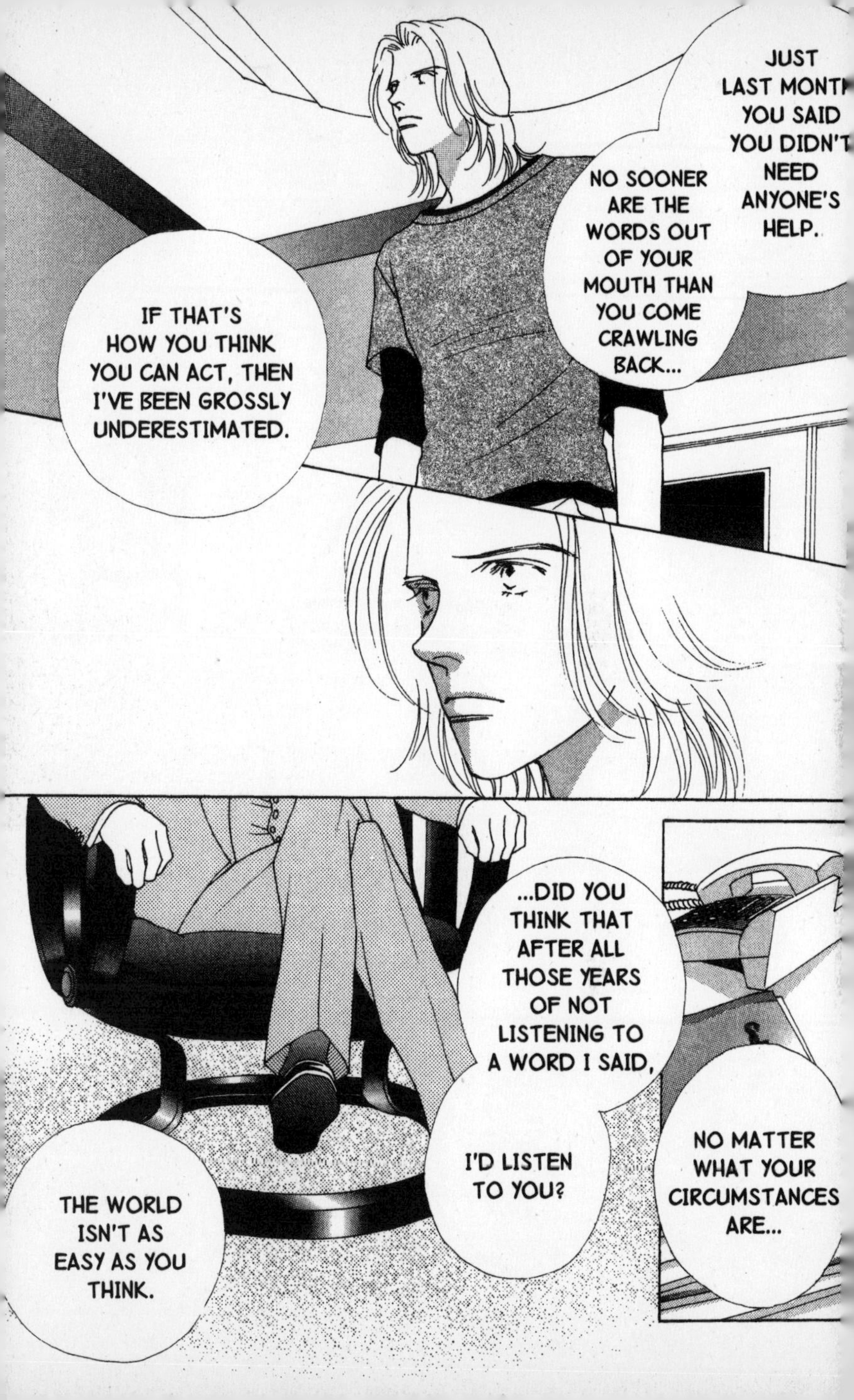
JUST LAST MONTH YOU SAID YOU DIDN'T NEED ANYONE'S HELP.
NO SOONER ARE THE WORDS OUT OF YOUR MOUTH THAN YOU COME CRAWLING BACK...
IF THAT'S HOW YOU THINK YOU CAN ACT, THEN I'VE BEEN GROSSLY UNDERESTIMATED.
NO MATTER WHAT YOUR CIRCUMSTANCES ARE...
...DID YOU THINK THAT AFTER ALL THOSE YEARS OF NOT LISTENING TO A WORD I SAID,
I'D LISTEN TO YOU?
THE WORLD ISN'T AS EASY AS YOU THINK.

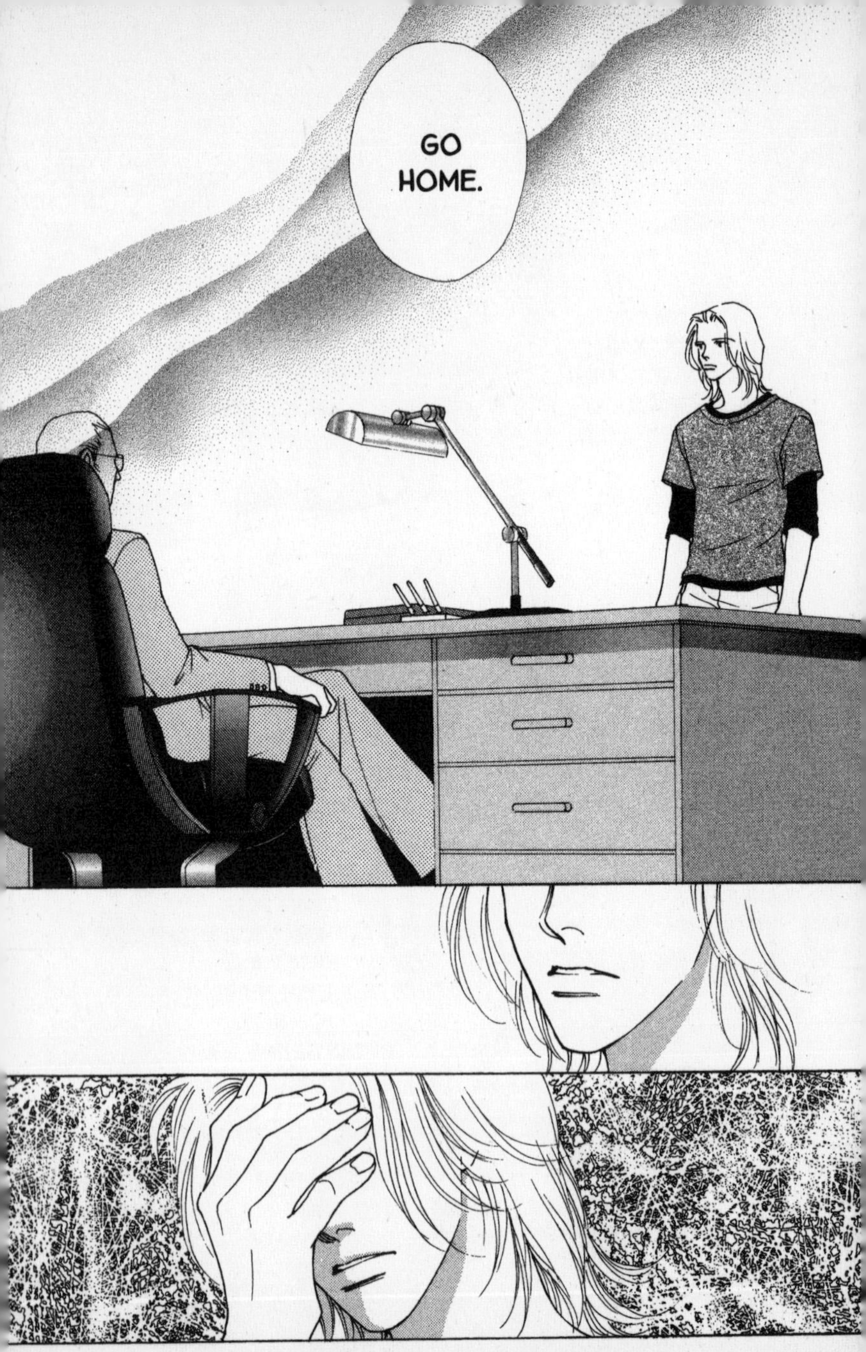
GO HOME.

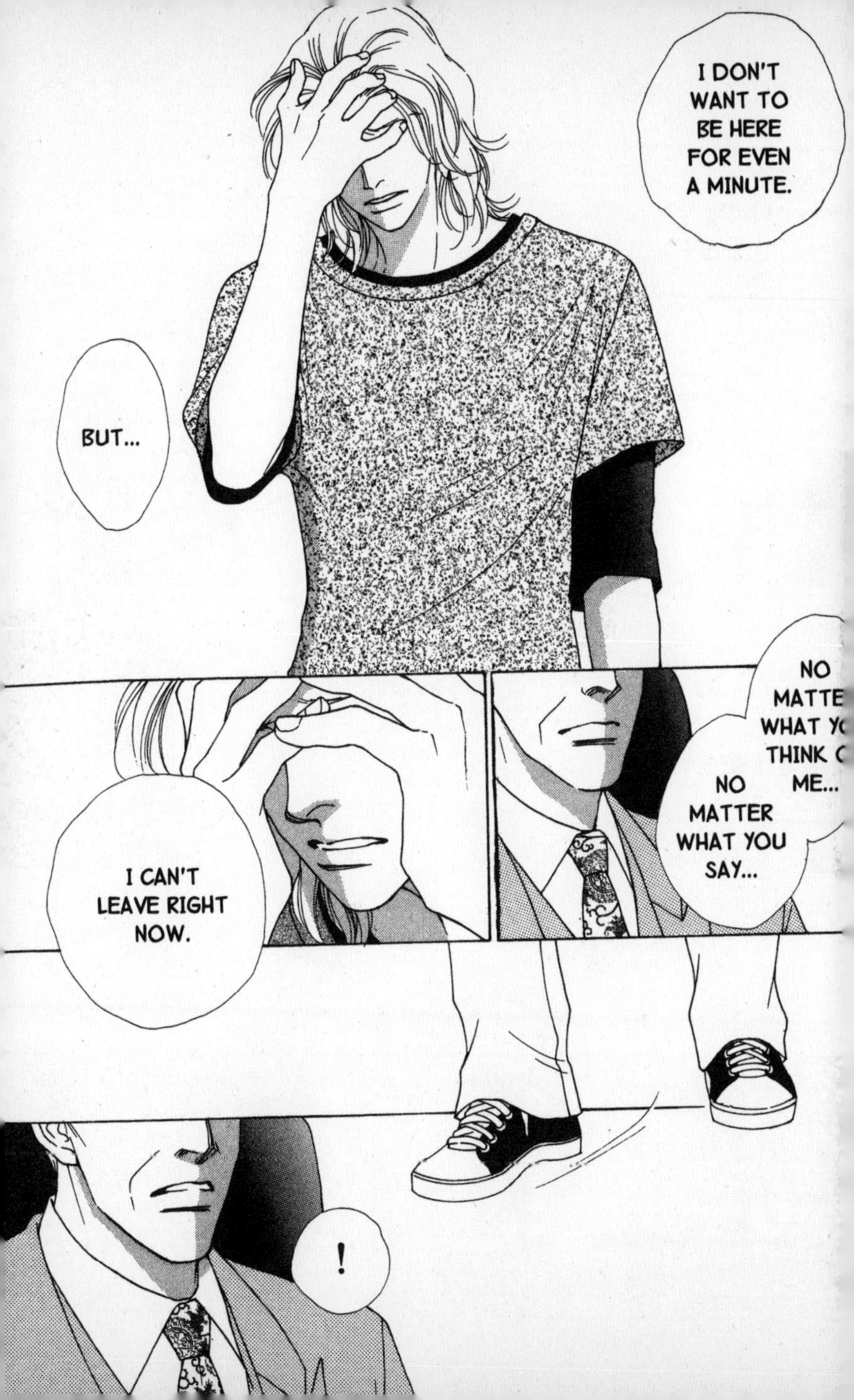

I DON'T WANT TO BE HERE FOR EVEN A MINUTE.
BUT...
NO MATTE WHAT Y THINK ME...
NO MATTER WHAT YOU SAY...
I CAN'T LEAVE RIGHT NOW.
!

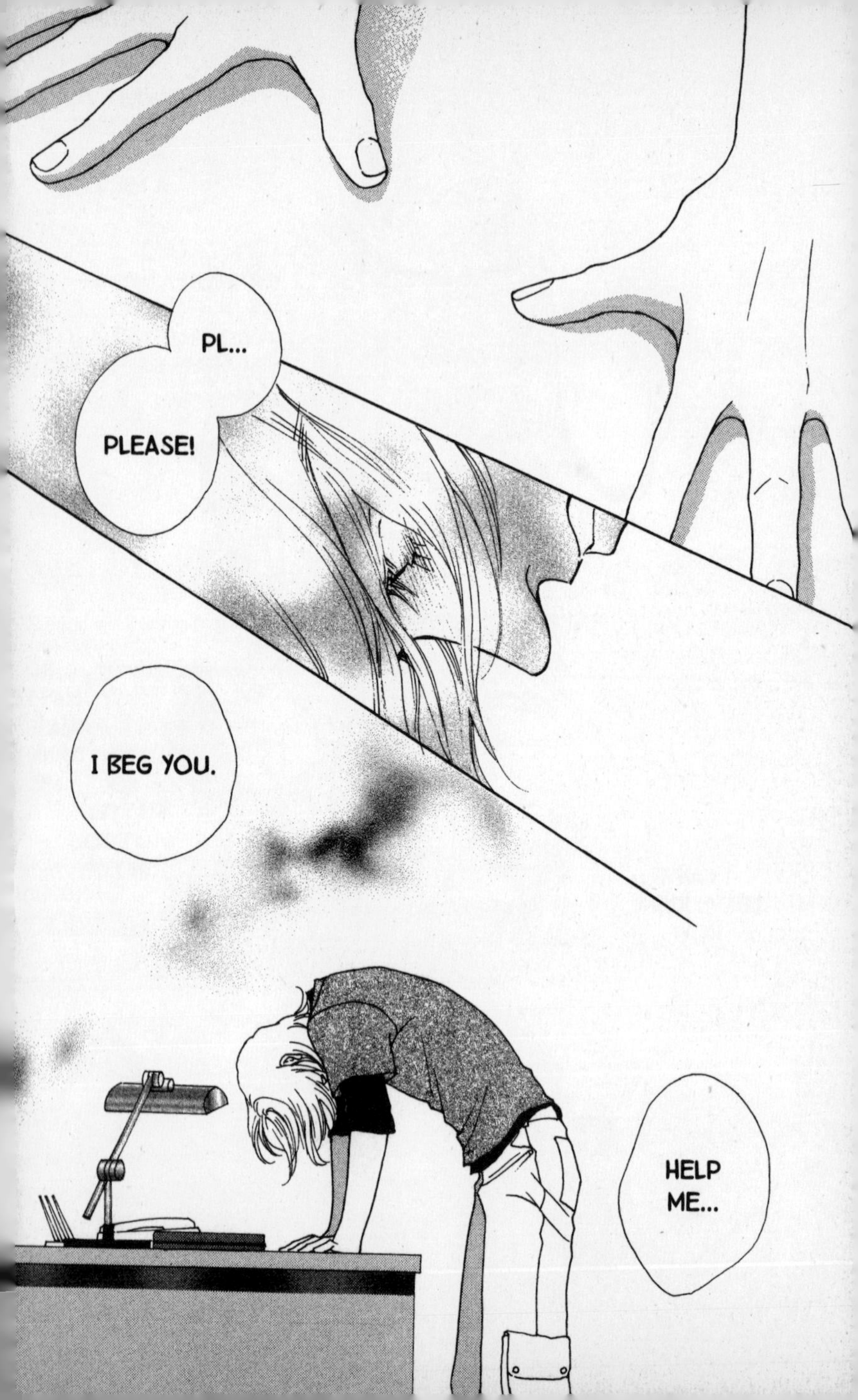
PL...
PLEASE!
I BEG YOU.
HELP ME...

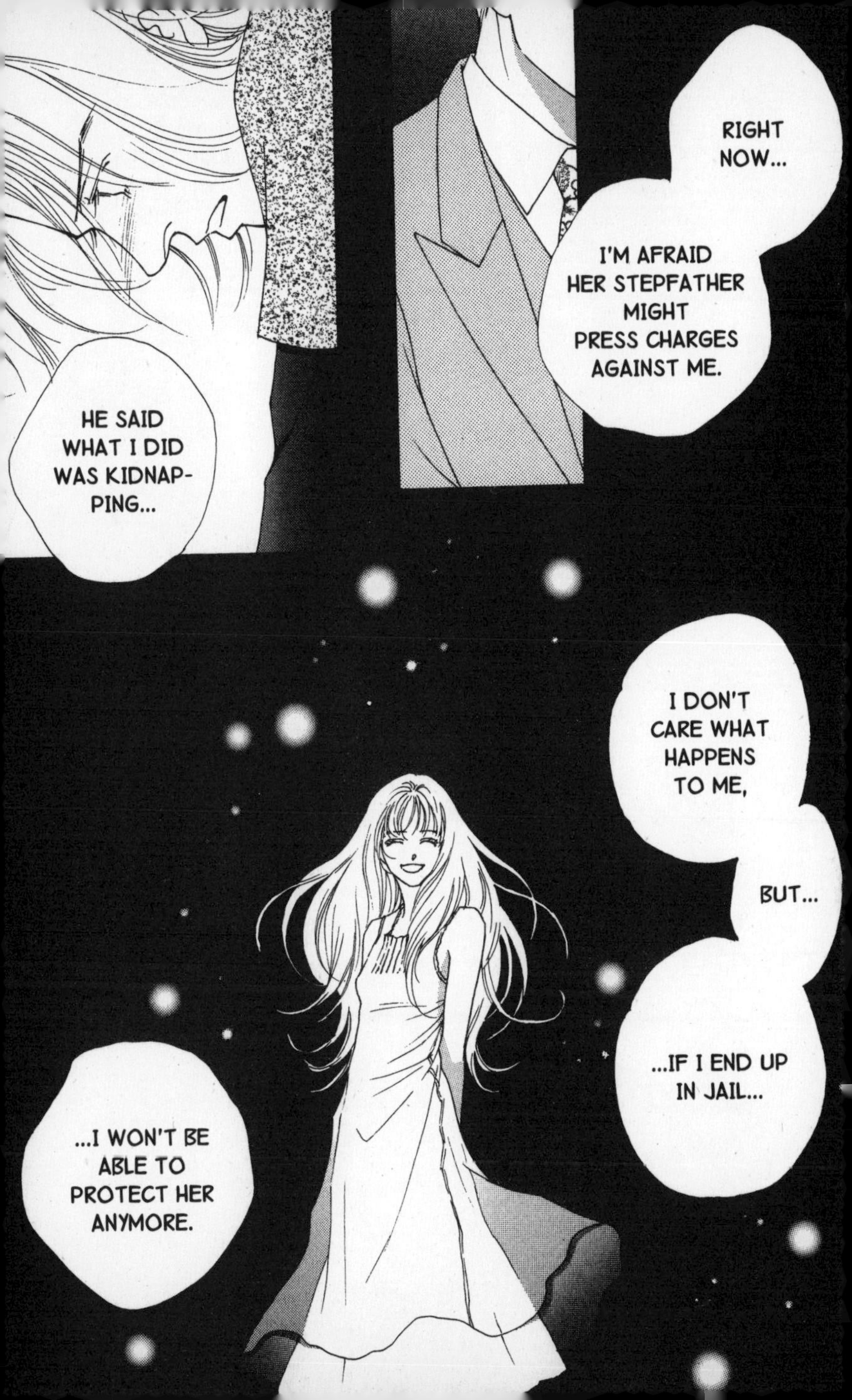
RIGHT NOW...
I'M AFRAID HER STEPFATHER MIGHT PRESS CHARGES AGAINST ME.
HE SAID WHAT I DID WAS KIDNAP-PING...
I DON'T CARE WHAT HAPPENS TO ME,
BUT...
...IF I END UP IN JAIL...
...I WON'T BE ABLE TO PROTECT HER ANYMORE.

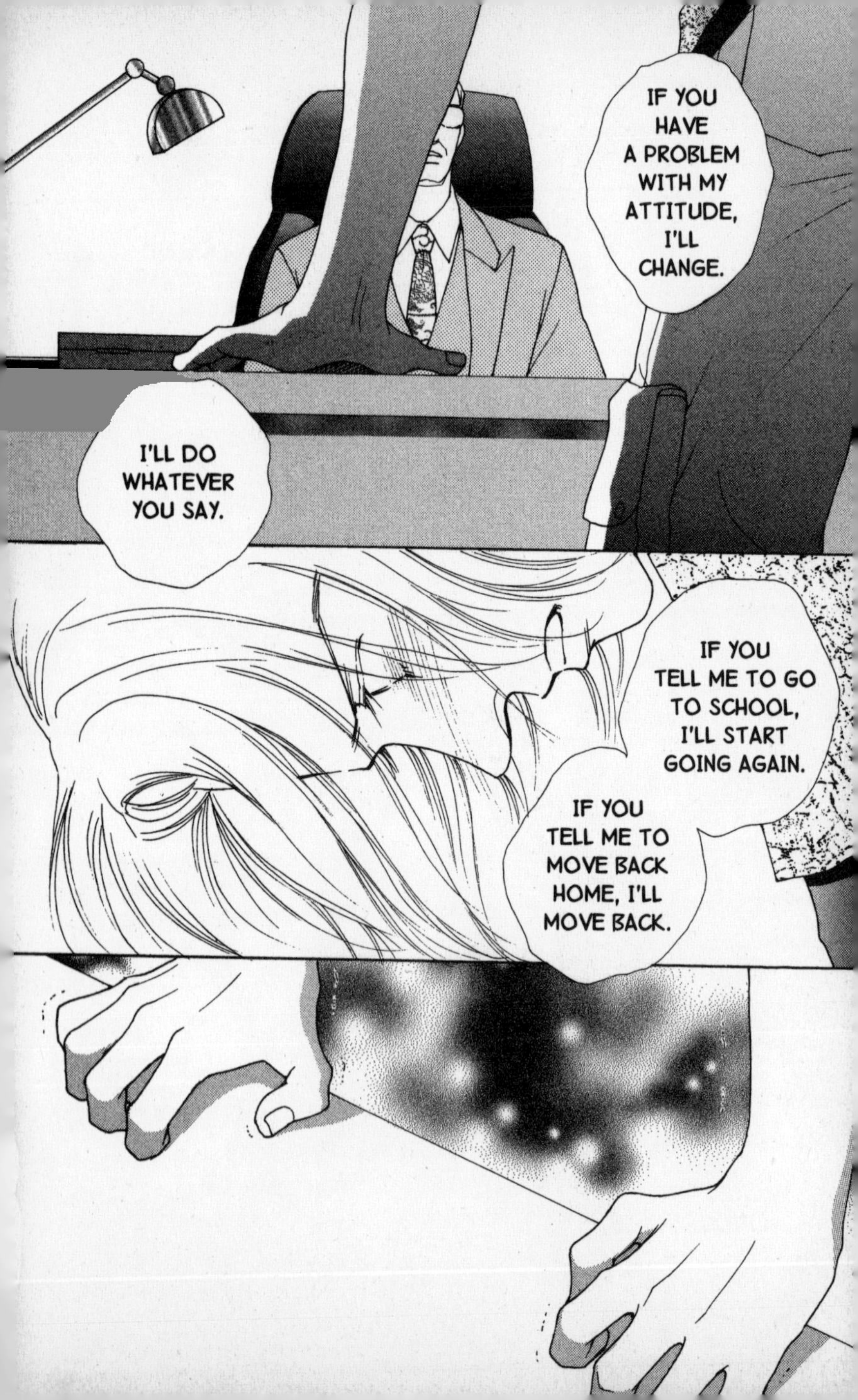
IF YOU HAVE A PROBLEM WITH MY ATTITUDE, I'LL CHANGE.
I'LL DO WHATEVER YOU SAY.
IF YOU TELL ME TO GO TO SCHOOL, I'LL START GOING AGAIN.
IF YOU TELL ME TO MOVE BACK HOME, I'LL MOVE BACK.

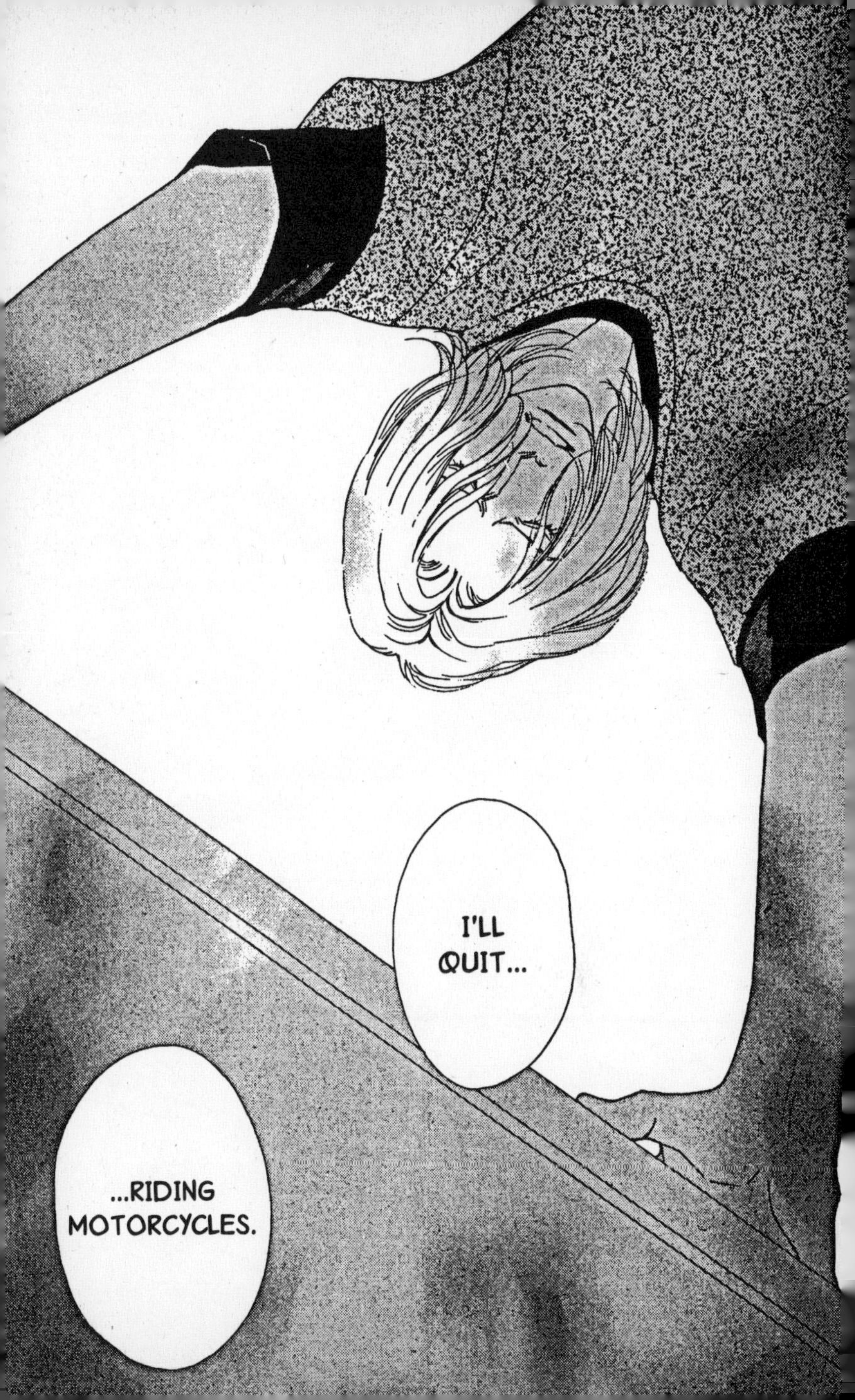
I'LL QUIT...
...RIDING MOTORCYCLES.

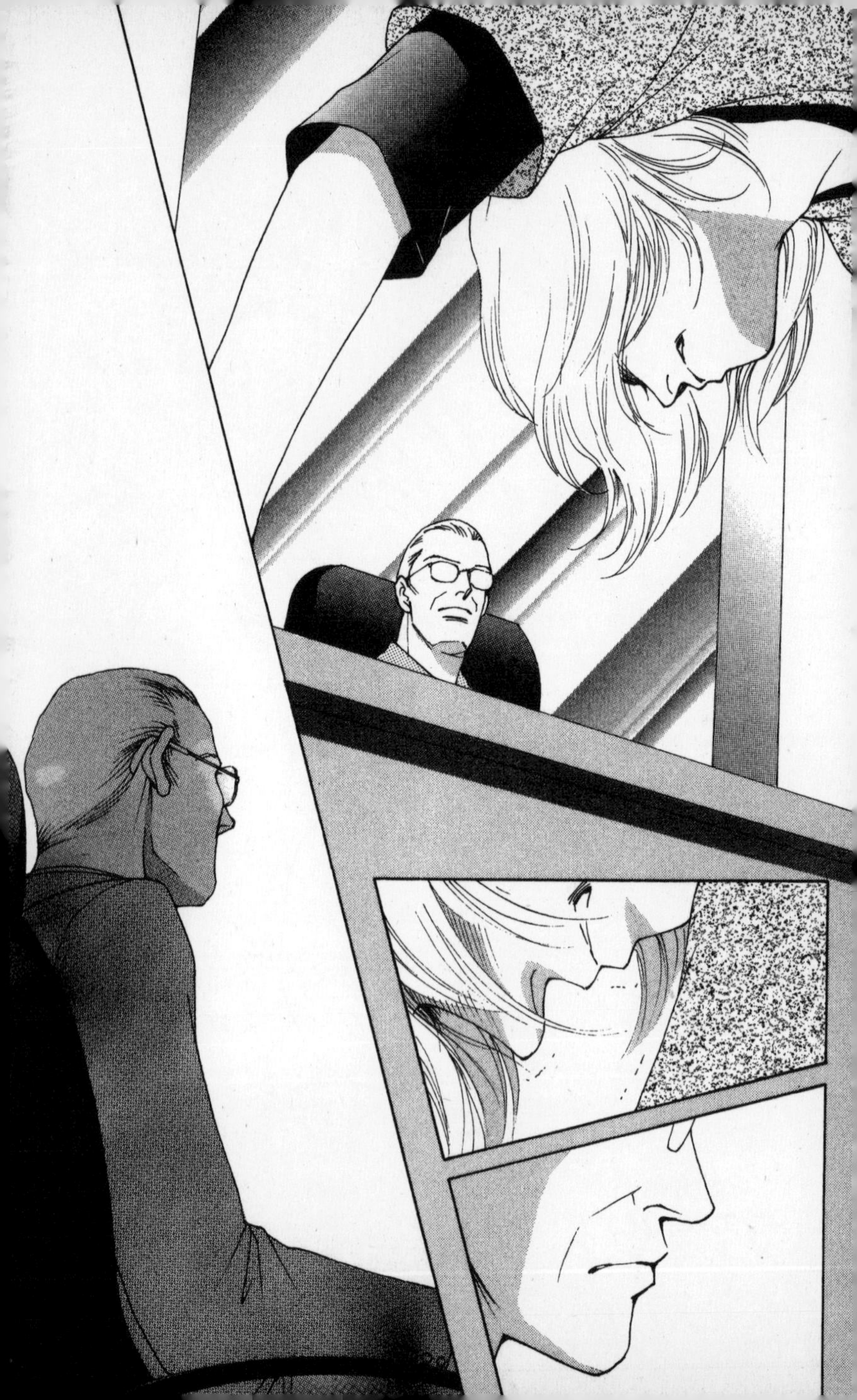

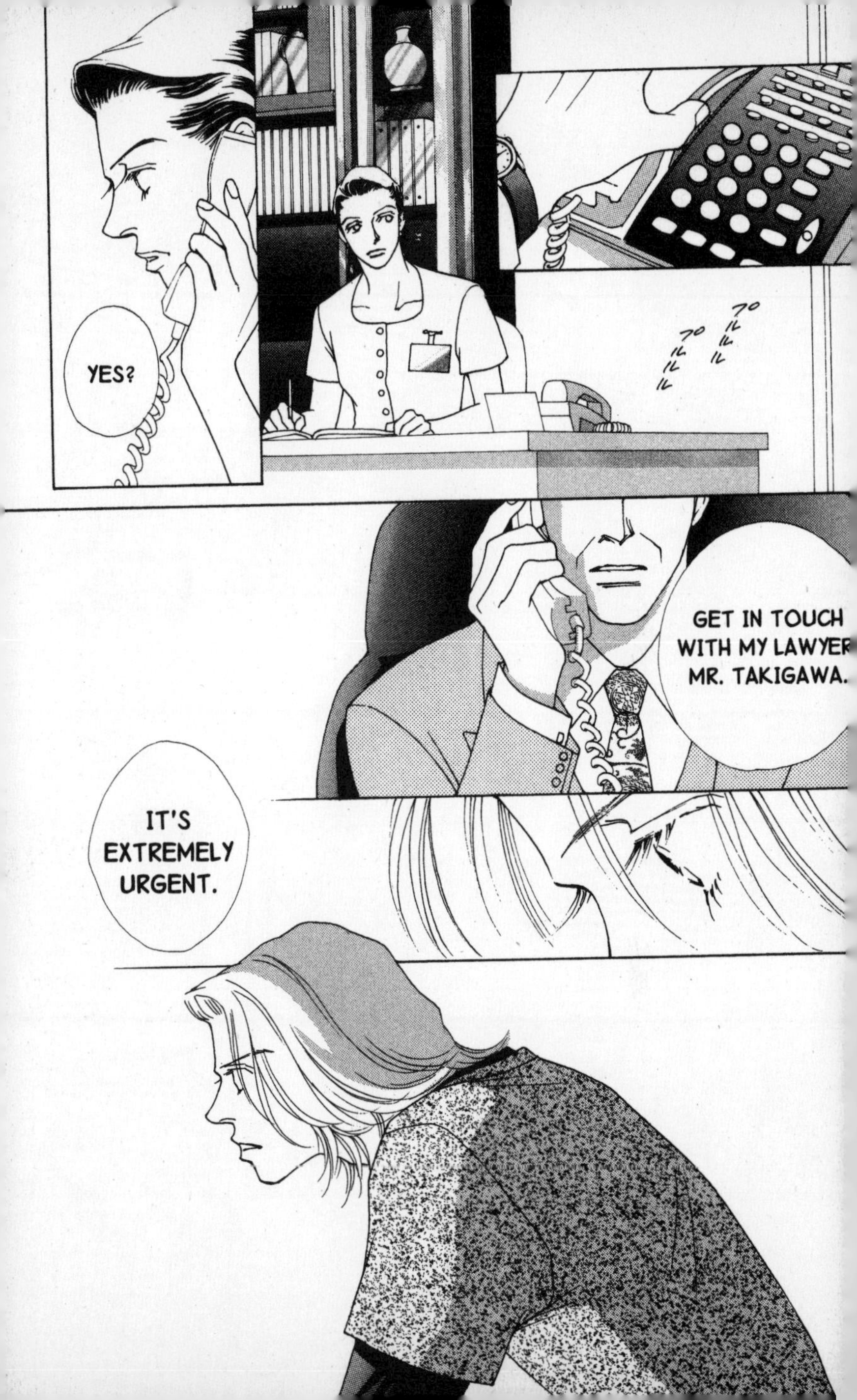

プルル
プルル
YES?
GET IN TOUCH WITH MY LAWYER MR. TAKIGAWA.
IT'S EXTREMELY URGENT.

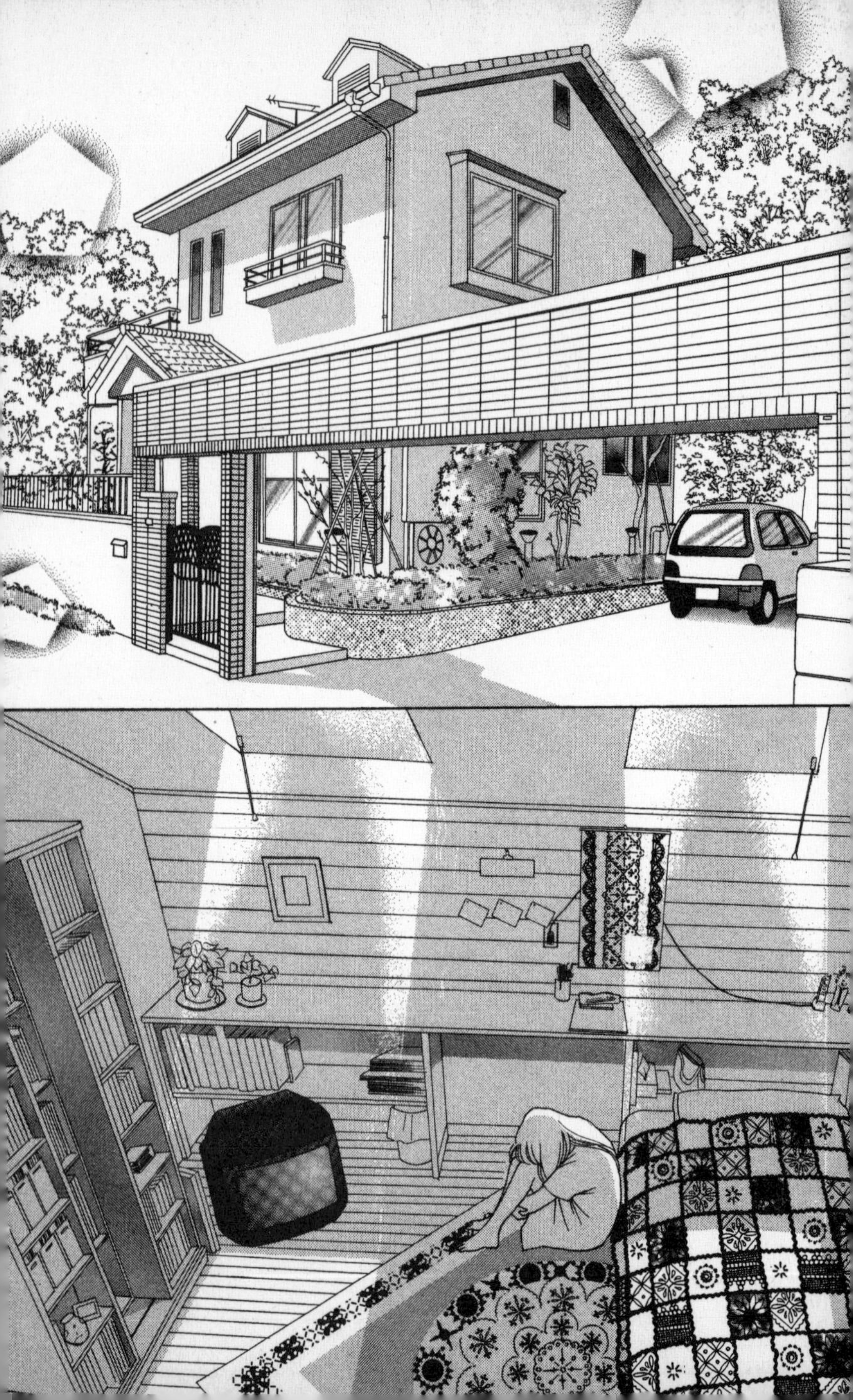

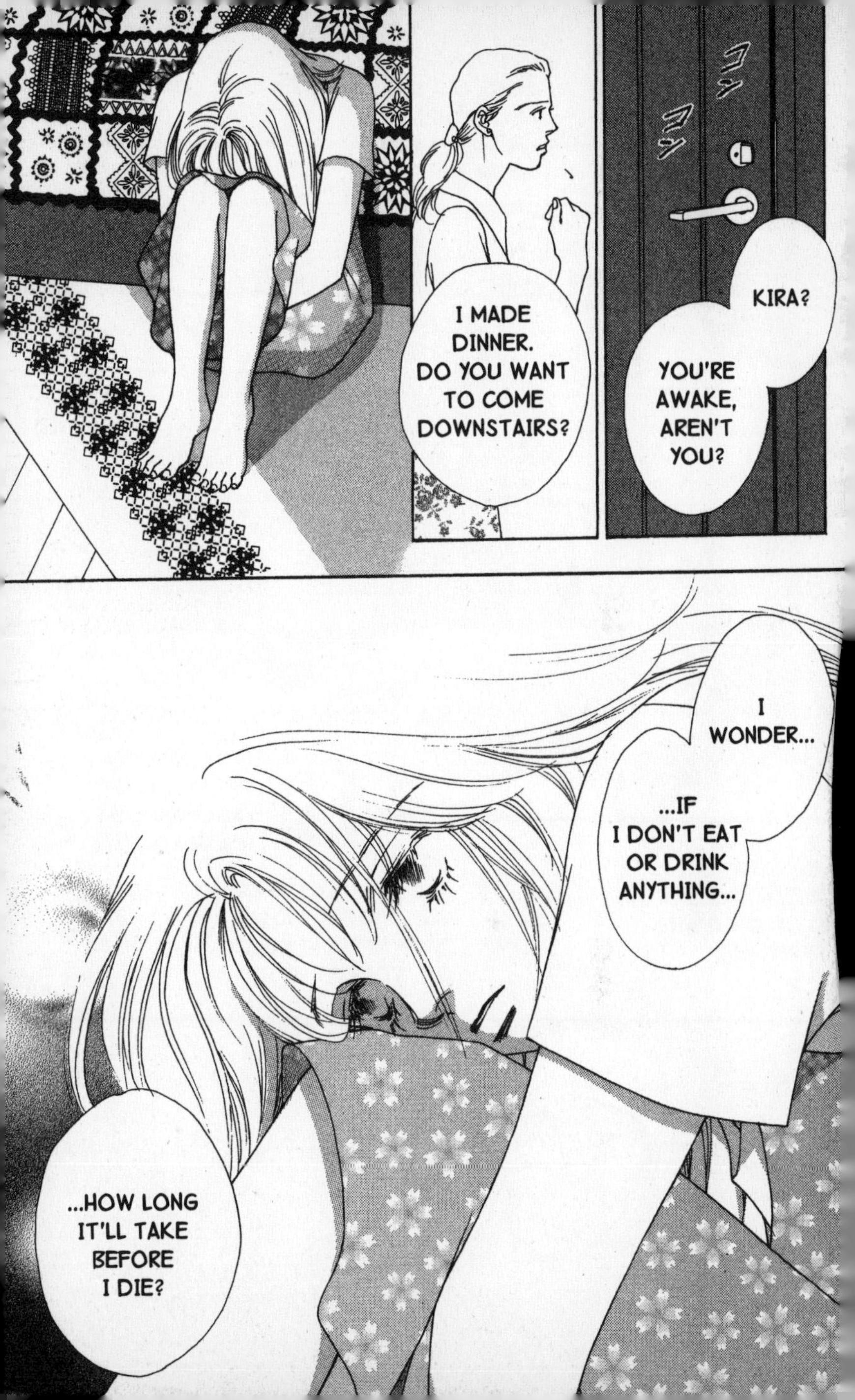
コン
コン
KIRA?
YOU'RE AWAKE, AREN'T YOU?
I MADE DINNER. DO YOU WANT TO COME DOWNSTAIRS?
I WONDER...
...IF I DON'T EAT OR DRINK ANYTHING...
...HOW LONG IT'LL TAKE BEFORE I DIE?

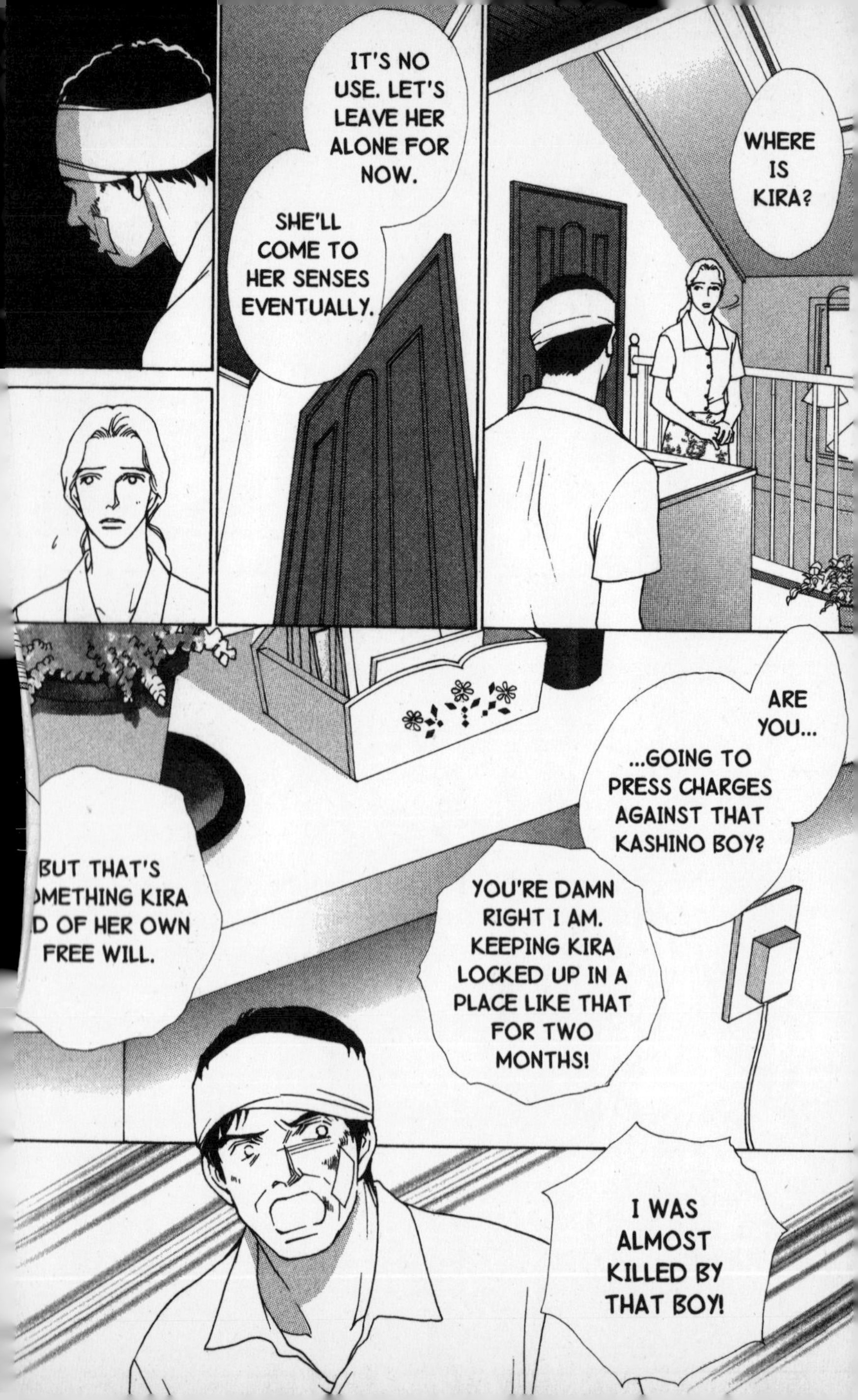
WHERE IS KIRA?
IT'S NO USE. LET'S LEAVE HER ALONE FOR NOW.
SHE'LL COME TO HER SENSES EVENTUALLY.
ARE YOU...
...GOING TO PRESS CHARGES AGAINST THAT KASHINO BOY?
YOU'RE DAMN RIGHT I AM. KEEPING KIRA LOCKED UP IN A PLACE LIKE THAT FOR TWO MONTHS!
BUT THAT'S
OMETHING KIRA
D OF HER OWN
FREE WILL.
I WAS ALMOST KILLED BY THAT BOY!

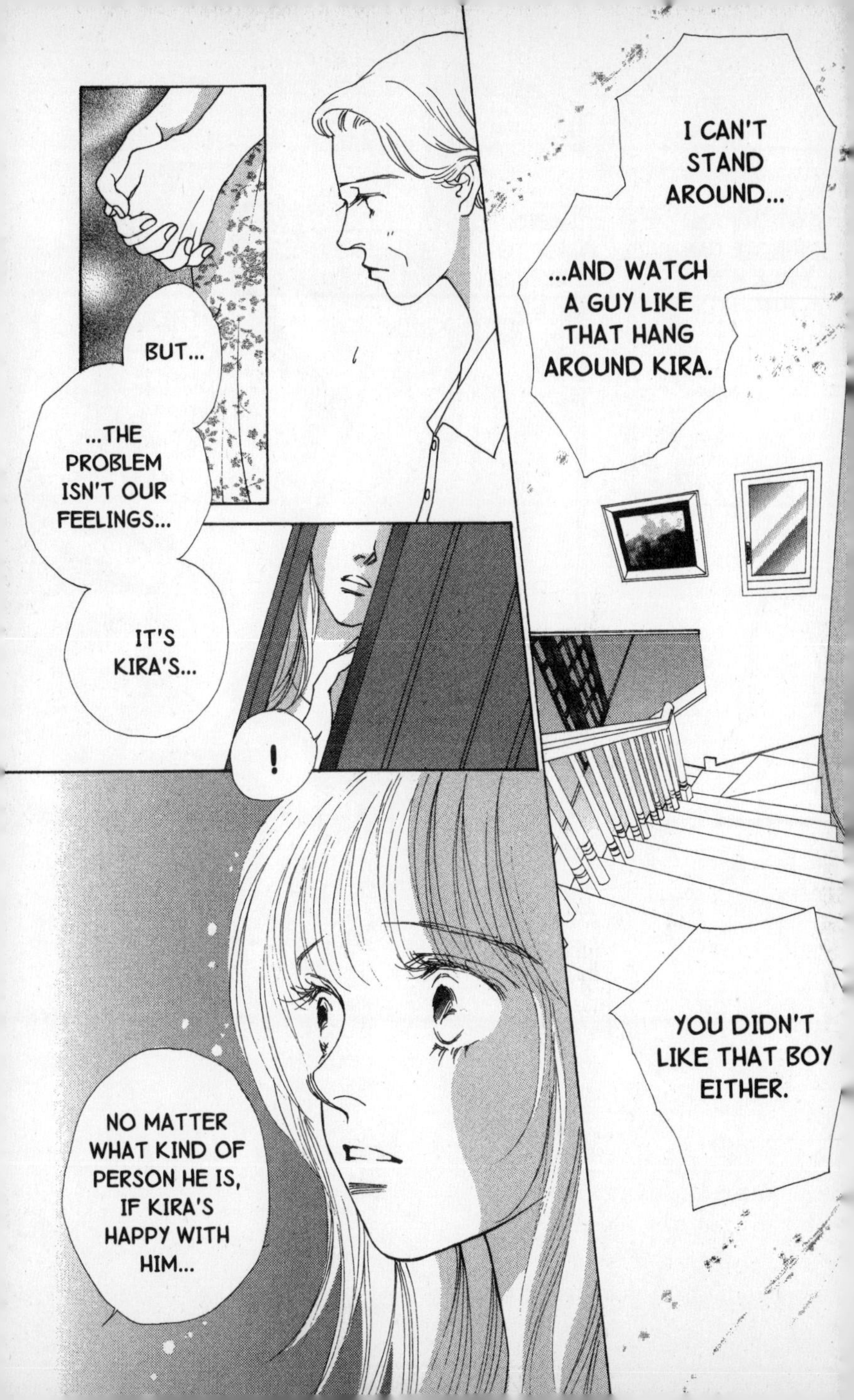
I CAN'T STAND AROUND...
...AND WATCH A GUY LIKE THAT HANG AROUND KIRA.
YOU DIDN'T LIKE THAT BOY EITHER.
BUT...
...THE PROBLEM ISN'T OUR FEELINGS...
IT'S KIRA'S...
!
NO MATTER WHAT KIND OF PERSON HE IS, IF KIRA'S HAPPY WITH HIM...

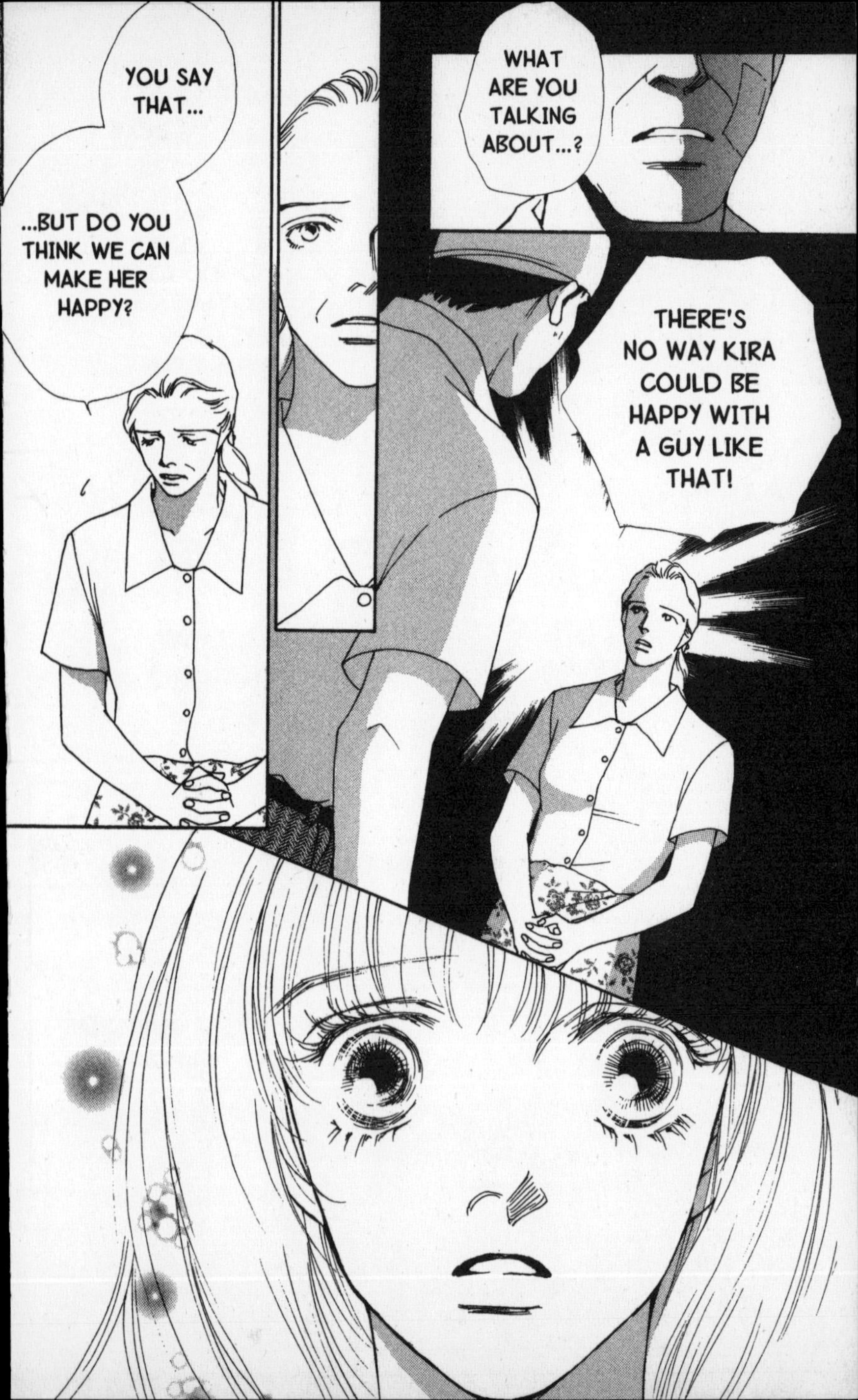
WHAT ARE YOU TALKING ABOUT...?
THERE'S NO WAY KIRA COULD BE HAPPY WITH A GUY LIKE THAT!
YOU SAY THAT...
...BUT DO YOU THINK WE CAN MAKE HER HAPPY?

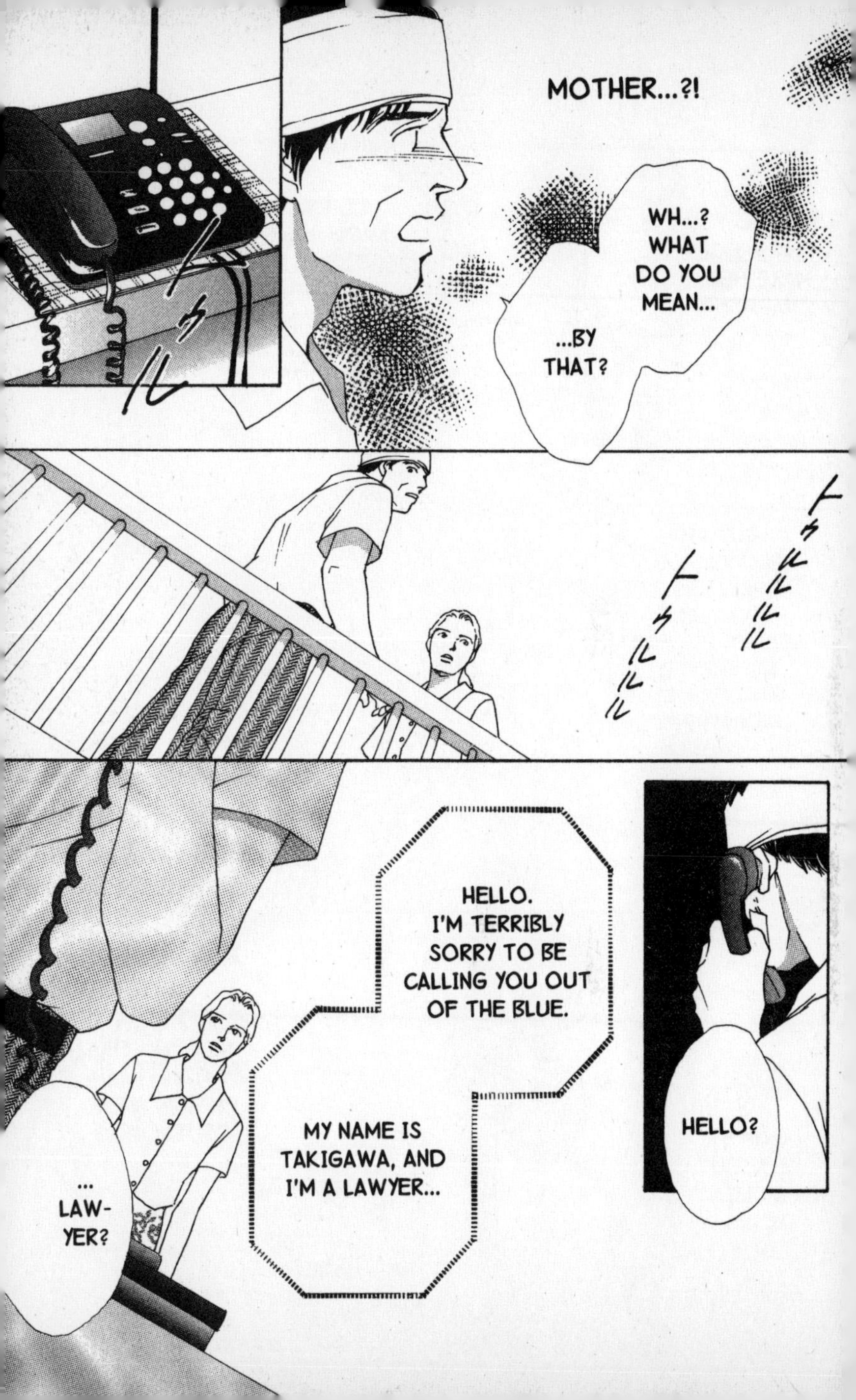
MOTHER...?!
WH...? WHAT DO YOU MEAN...
...BY THAT?
トゥルルル
トゥルルル
HELLO?
HELLO. I'M TERRIBLY SORRY TO BE CALLING YOU OUT OF THE BLUE.
MY NAME IS TAKIGAWA, AND I'M A LAWYER...
... LAWYER?

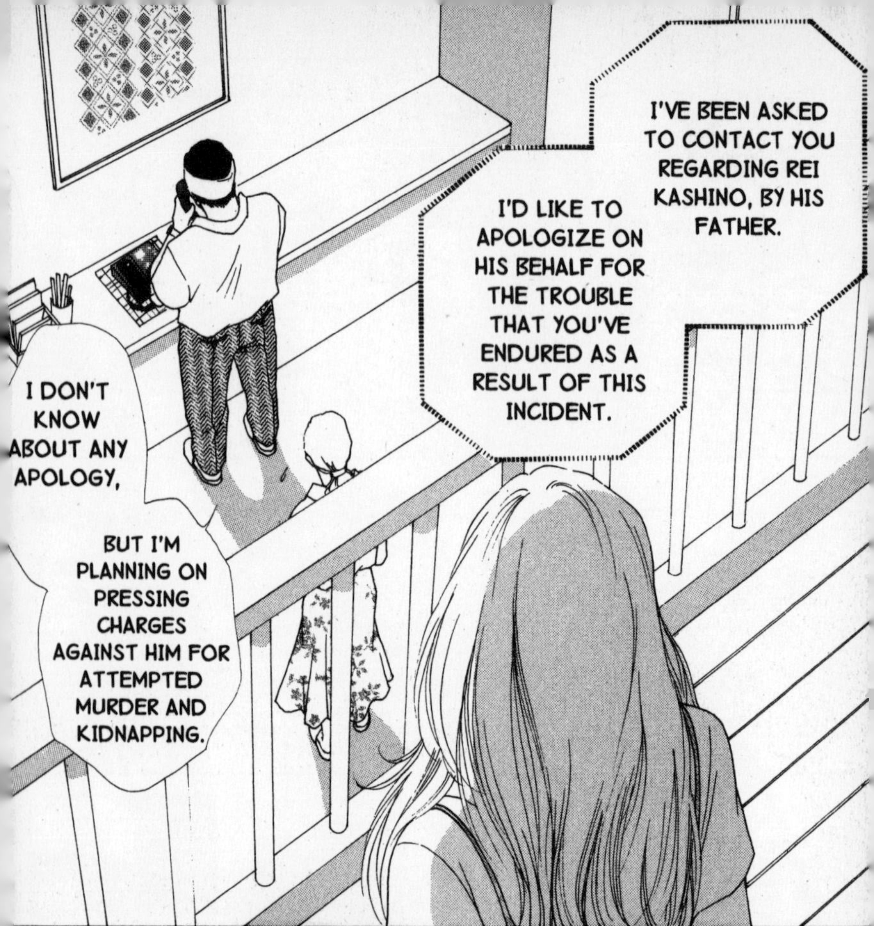
I'VE BEEN ASKED TO CONTACT YOU REGARDING REI KASHINO, BY HIS FATHER.
I'D LIKE TO APOLOGIZE ON HIS BEHALF FOR THE TROUBLE THAT YOU'VE ENDURED AS A RESULT OF THIS INCIDENT.
I DON'T KNOW ABOUT ANY APOLOGY,
BUT I'M PLANNING ON PRESSING CHARGES AGAINST HIM FOR ATTEMPTED MURDER AND KIDNAPPING.
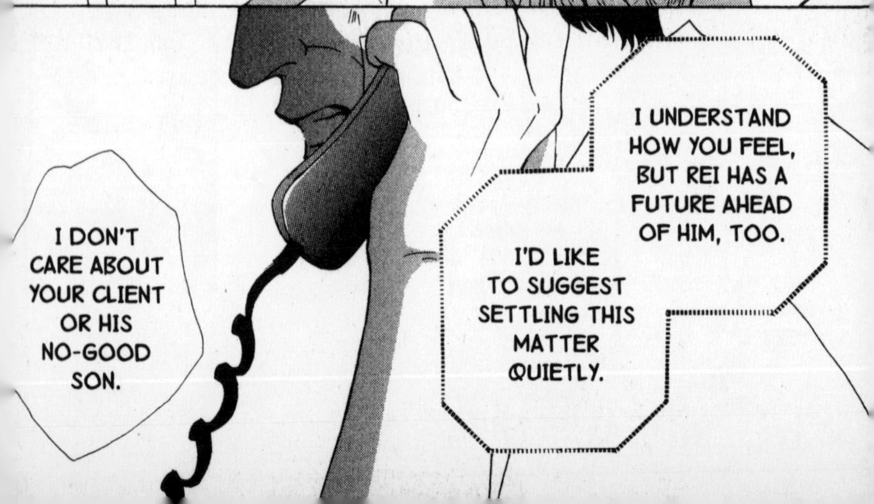
I UNDERSTAND HOW YOU FEEL, BUT REI HAS A FUTURE AHEAD OF HIM, TOO.
I'D LIKE TO SUGGEST SETTLING THIS MATTER QUIETLY.
I DON'T CARE ABOUT YOUR CLIENT OR HIS NO-GOOD SON.

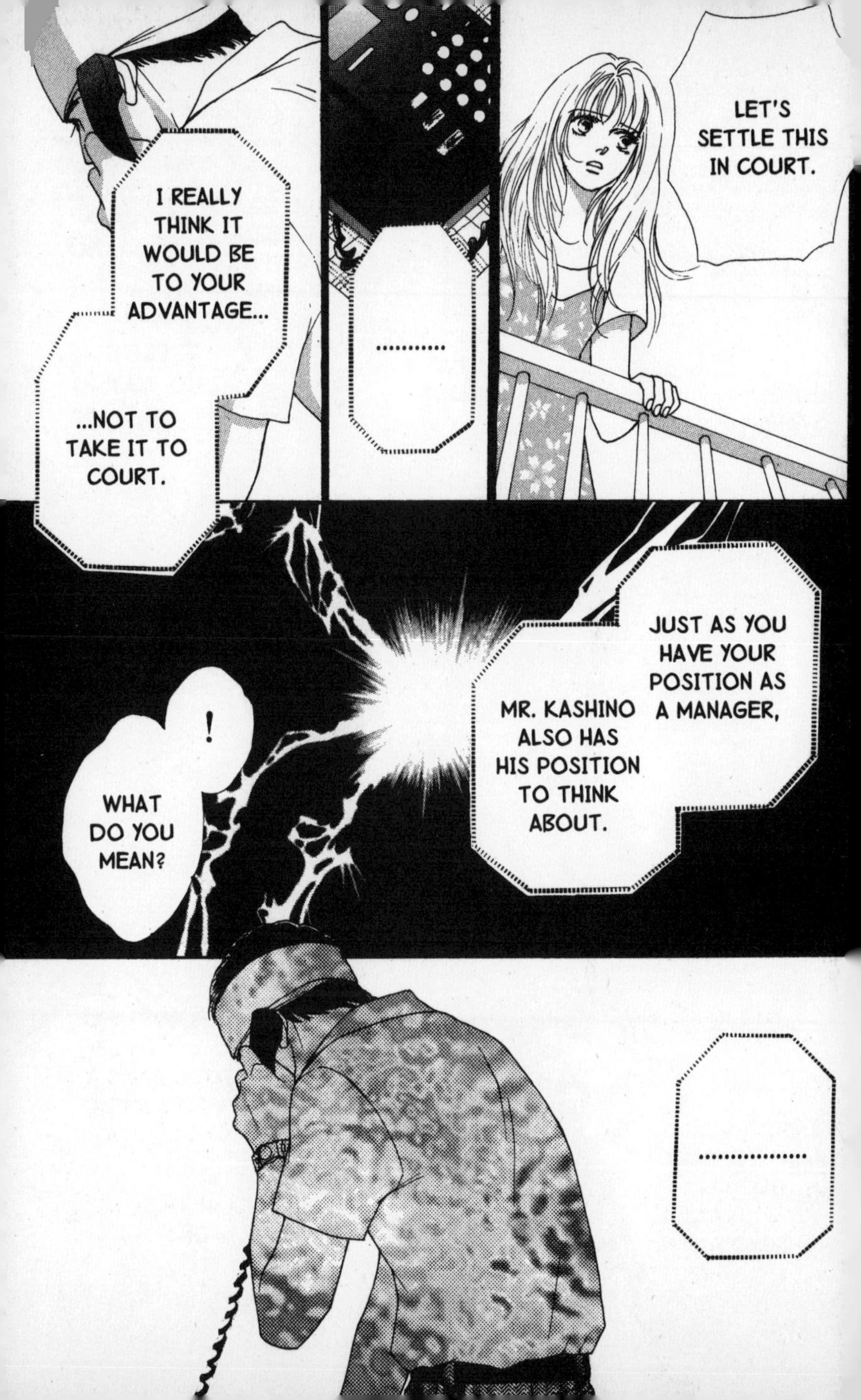
LET'S SETTLE THIS IN COURT.
....
I REALLY THINK IT WOULD BE TO YOUR ADVANTAGE...
...NOT TO TAKE IT TO COURT.
JUST AS YOU HAVE YOUR POSITION AS A MANAGER,
MR. KASHINO ALSO HAS HIS POSITION TO THINK ABOUT.
!
WHAT DO YOU MEAN?
....

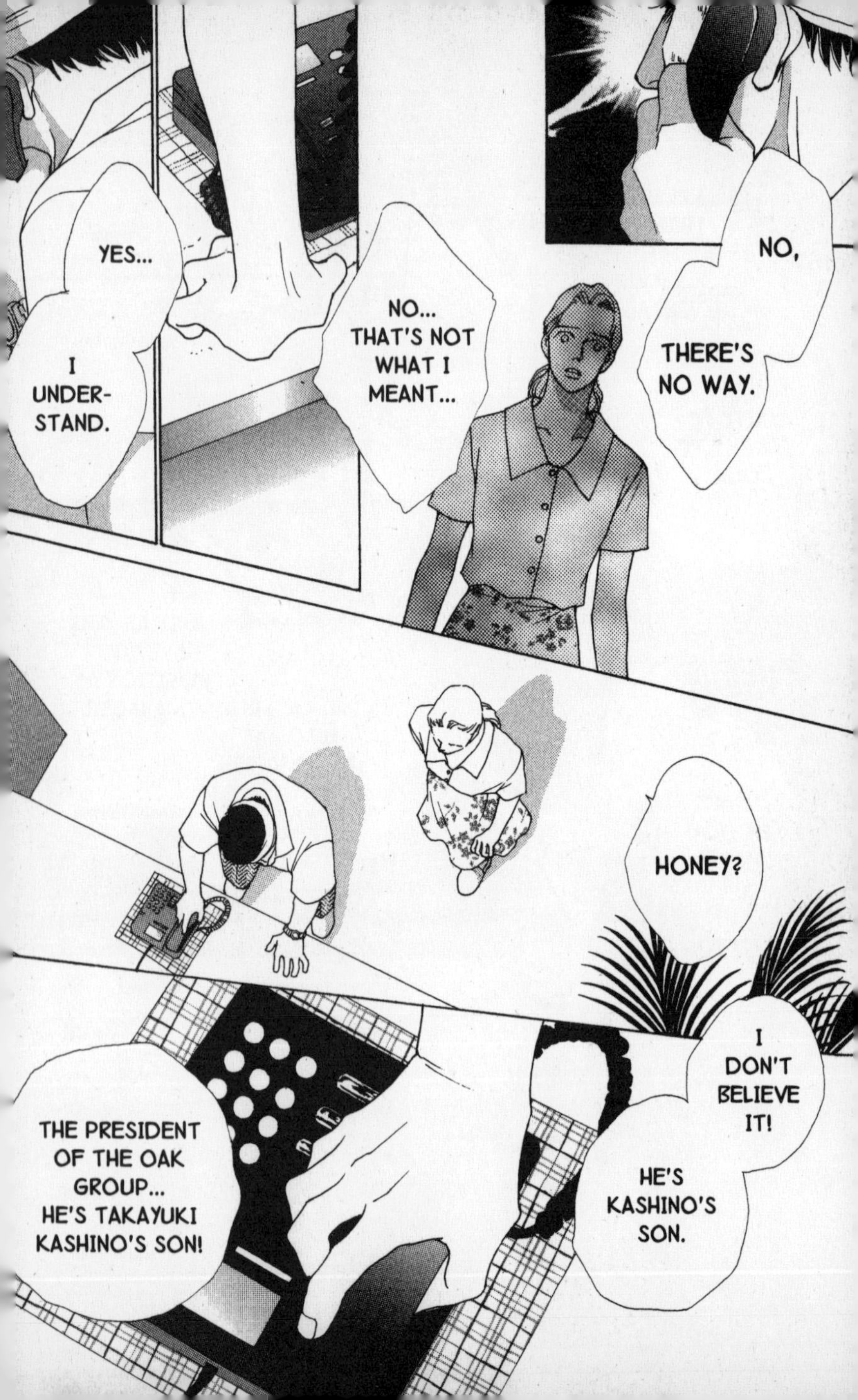
NO, THERE'S NO WAY.
NO... THAT'S NOT WHAT I MEANT...
YES... I UNDERSTAND.
HONEY?
I DON'T BELIEVE IT!
HE'S KASHINO'S SON.
THE PRESIDENT OF THE OAK GROUP... HE'S TAKAYUKI KASHINO'S SON!

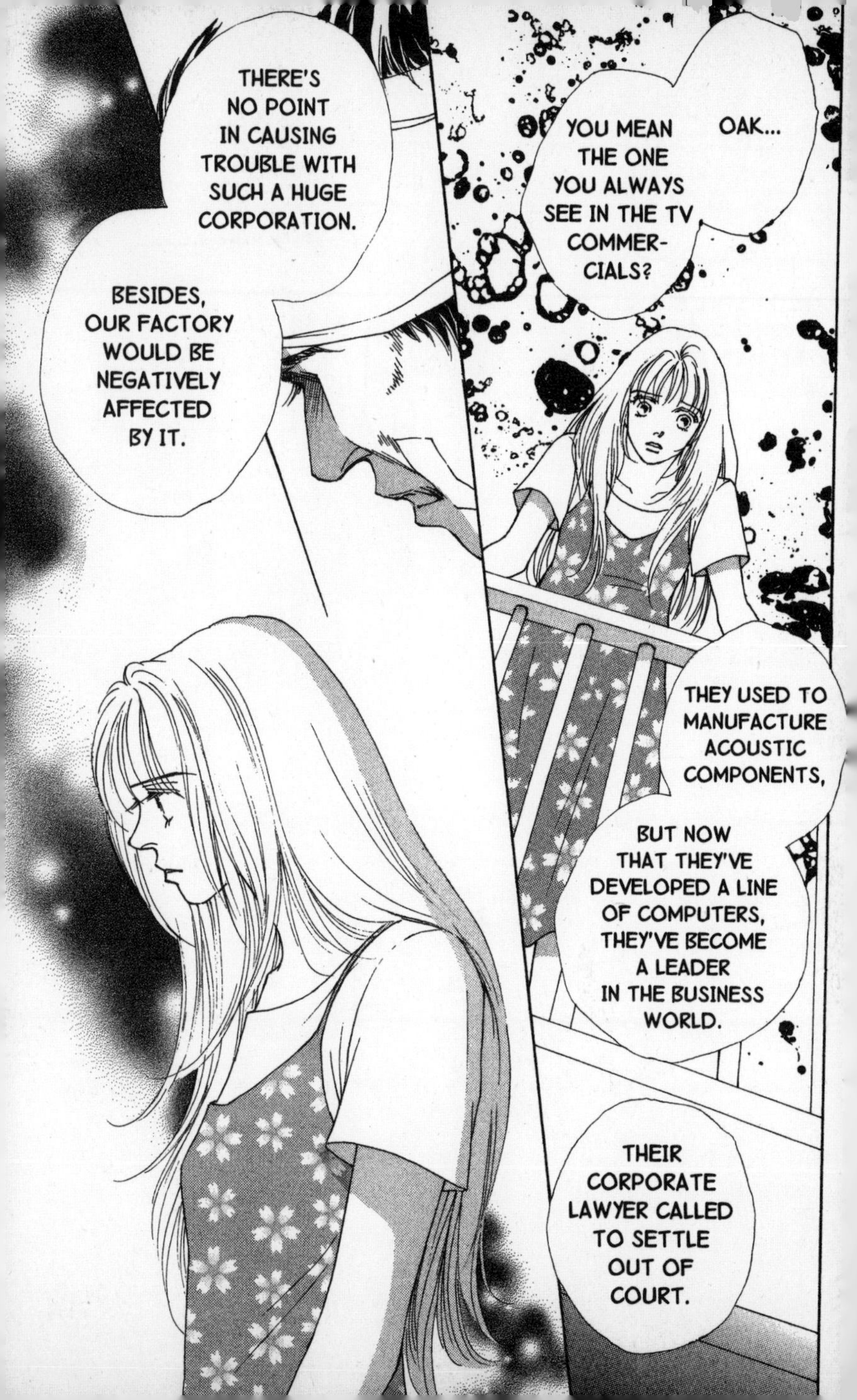
OAK...
YOU MEAN THE ONE YOU ALWAYS SEE IN THE TV COMMER-CIALS?
THEY USED TO MANUFACTURE ACOUSTIC COMPONENTS,
BUT NOW THAT THEY'VE DEVELOPED A LINE OF COMPUTERS, THEY'VE BECOME A LEADER IN THE BUSINESS WORLD.
THEIR CORPORATE LAWYER CALLED TO SETTLE OUT OF COURT.
THERE'S NO POINT IN CAUSING TROUBLE WITH SUCH A HUGE CORPORATION.
BESIDES, OUR FACTORY WOULD BE NEGATIVELY AFFECTED BY IT.

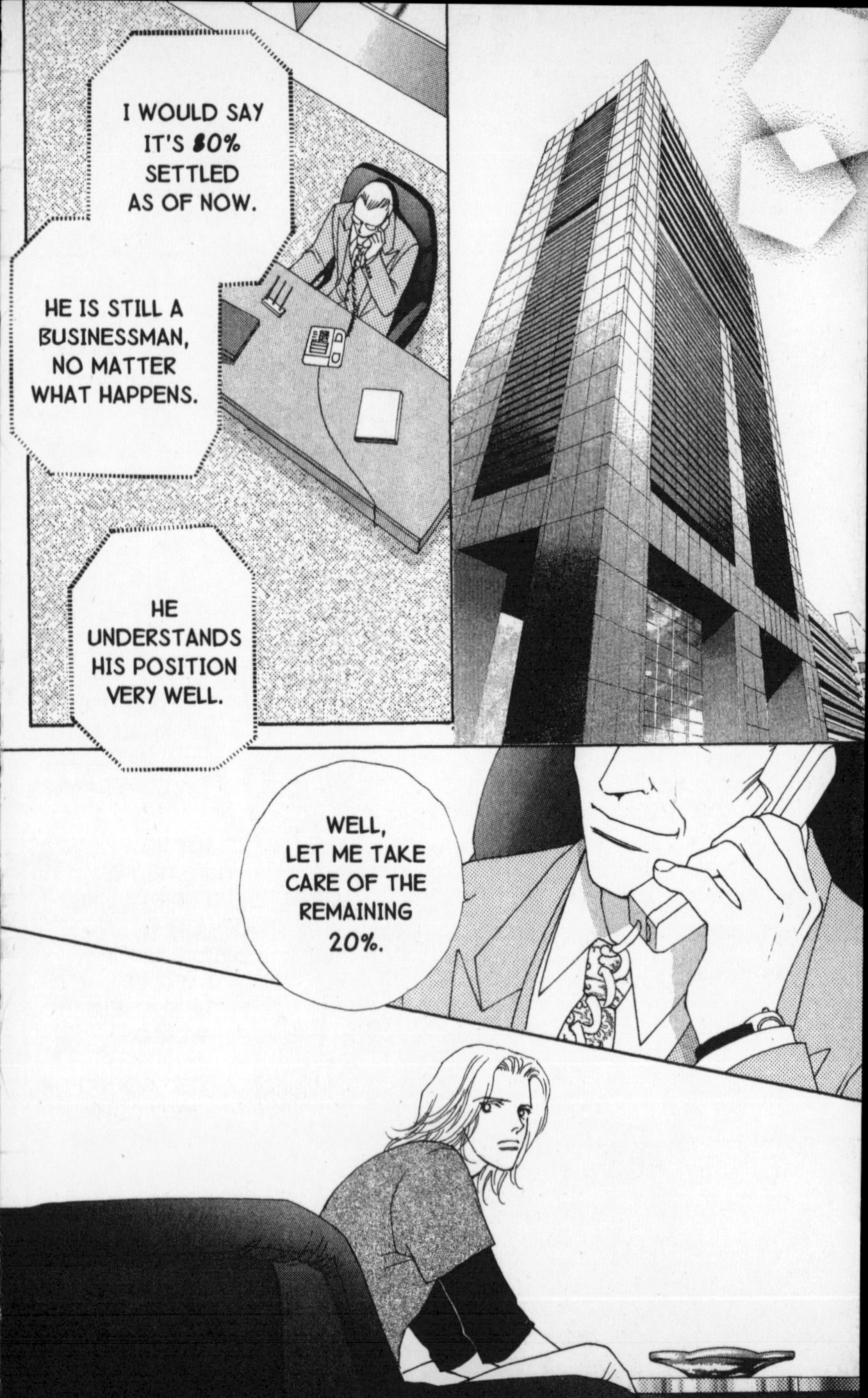
I WOULD SAY IT'S 80% SETTLED AS OF NOW.
HE IS STILL A BUSINESSMAN, NO MATTER WHAT HAPPENS.
HE UNDERSTANDS HIS POSITION VERY WELL.
WELL, LET ME TAKE CARE OF THE REMAINING 20%.

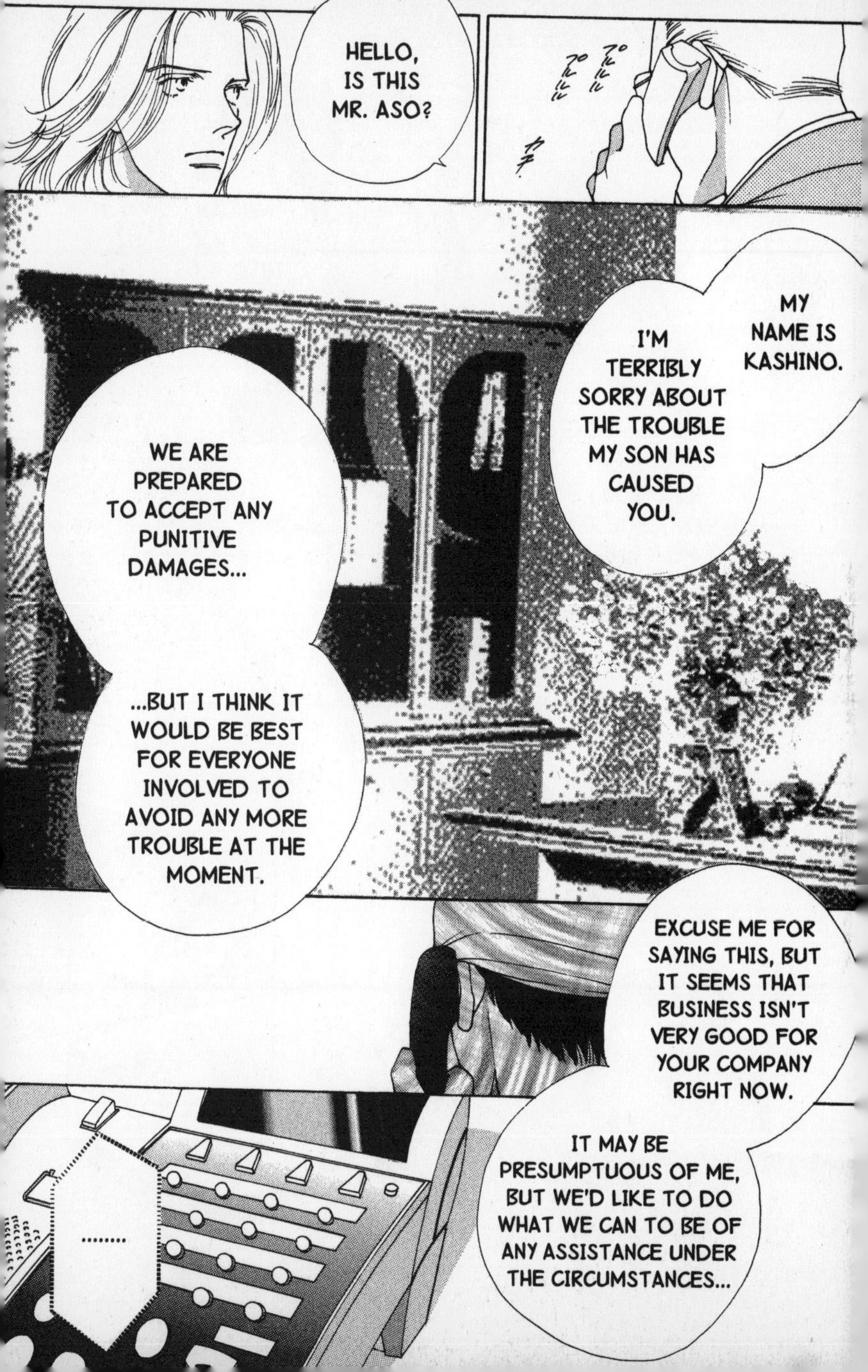
HELLO, IS THIS MR. ASO?
MY NAME IS KASHINO.
I'M TERRIBLY SORRY ABOUT THE TROUBLE MY SON HAS CAUSED YOU.
WE ARE PREPARED TO ACCEPT ANY PUNITIVE DAMAGES...
...BUT I THINK IT WOULD BE BEST FOR EVERYONE INVOLVED TO AVOID ANY MORE TROUBLE AT THE MOMENT.
EXCUSE ME FOR SAYING THIS, BUT IT SEEMS THAT BUSINESS ISN'T VERY GOOD FOR YOUR COMPANY RIGHT NOW.
IT MAY BE PRESUMPTUOUS OF ME, BUT WE'D LIKE TO DO WHAT WE CAN TO BE OF ANY ASSISTANCE UNDER THE CIRCUMSTANCES...
....

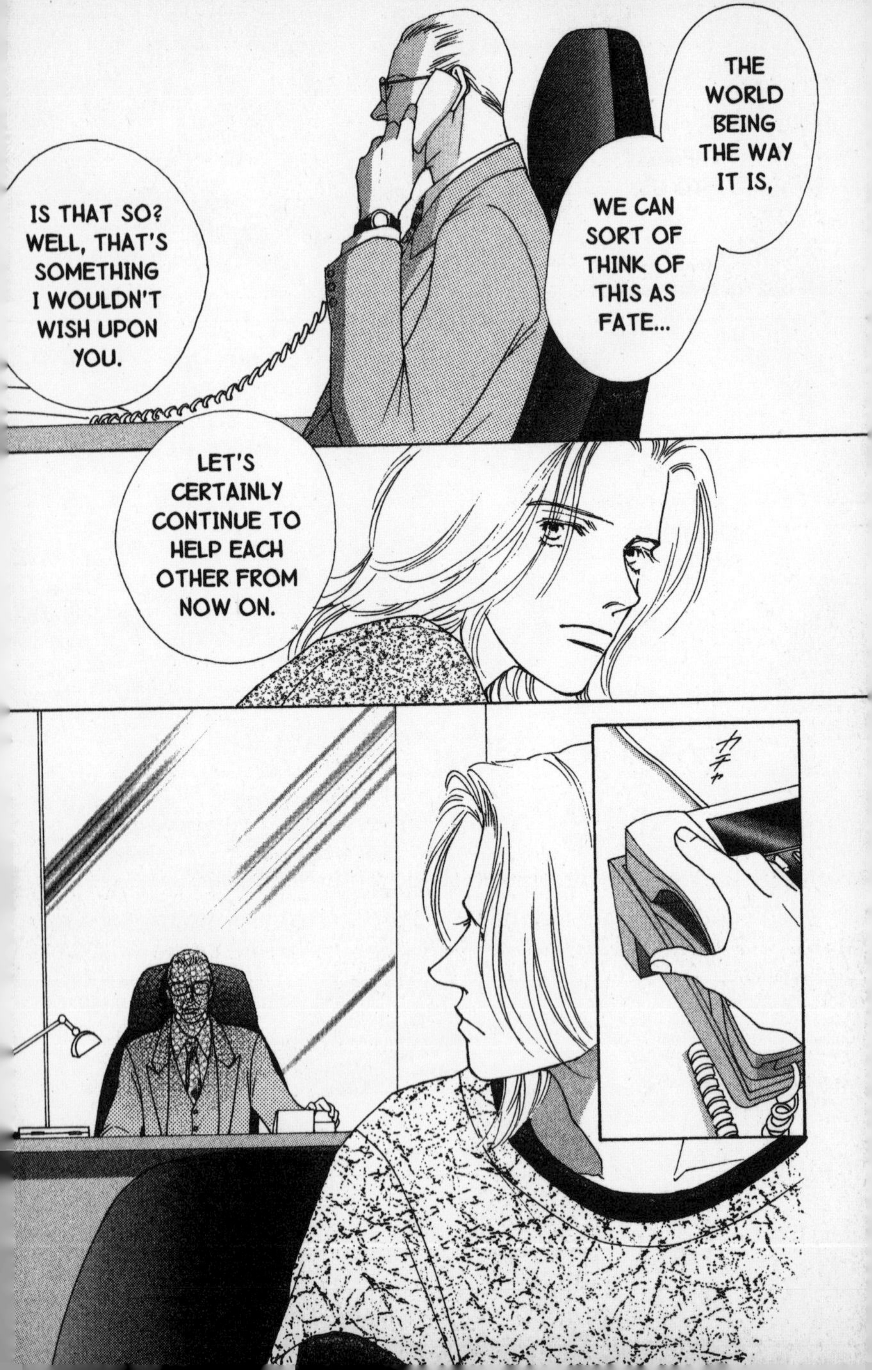
THE WORLD BEING THE WAY IT IS,
WE CAN SORT OF THINK OF THIS AS FATE...
IS THAT SO? WELL, THAT'S SOMETHING I WOULDN'T WISH UPON YOU.
LET'S CERTAINLY CONTINUE TO HELP EACH OTHER FROM NOW ON.
カチャ

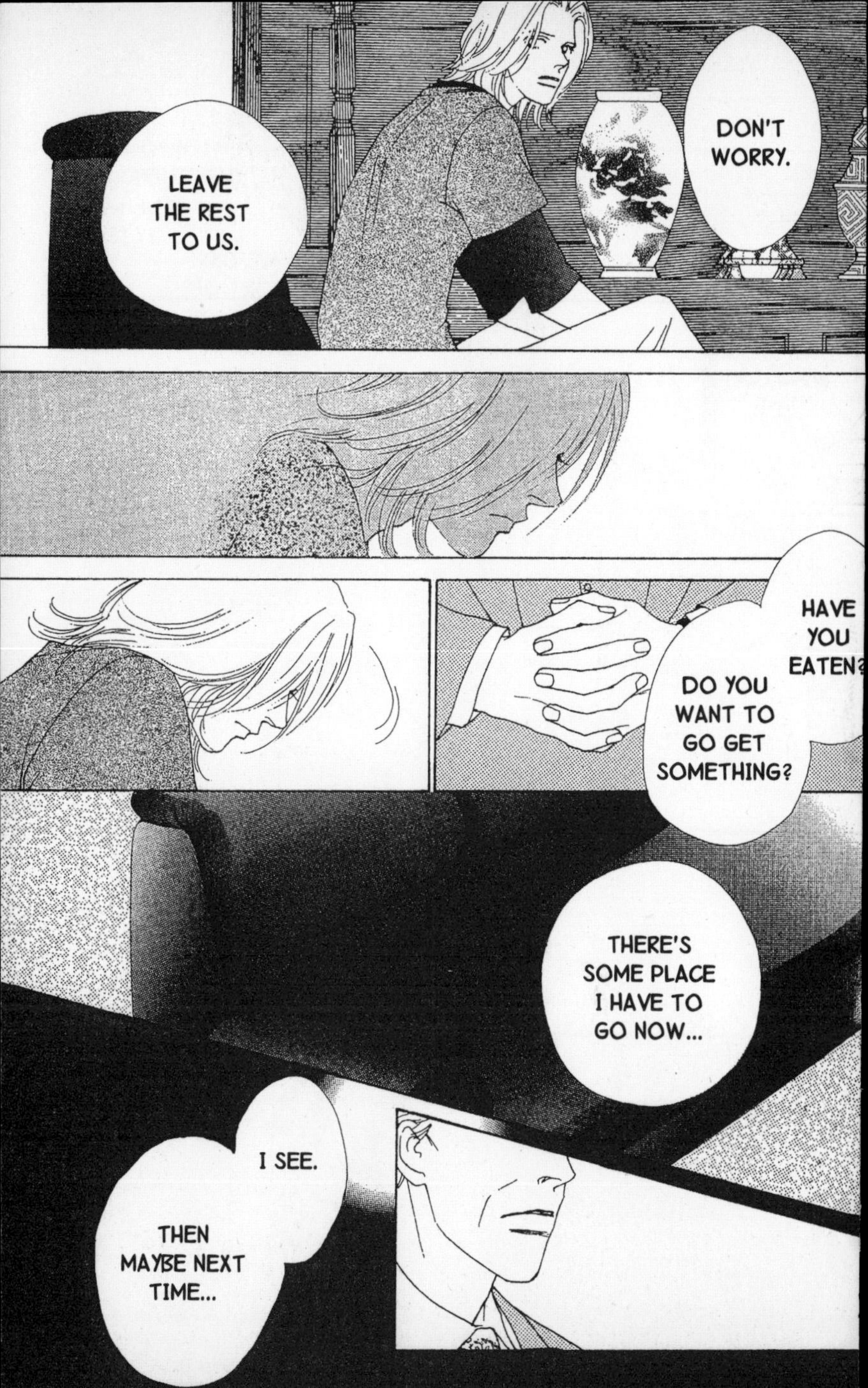
DON'T WORRY.
LEAVE THE REST TO US.
HAVE YOU EATEN?
DO YOU WANT TO GO GET SOMETHING?
THERE'S SOME PLACE I HAVE TO GO NOW...
I SEE.
THEN MAYBE NEXT TIME...

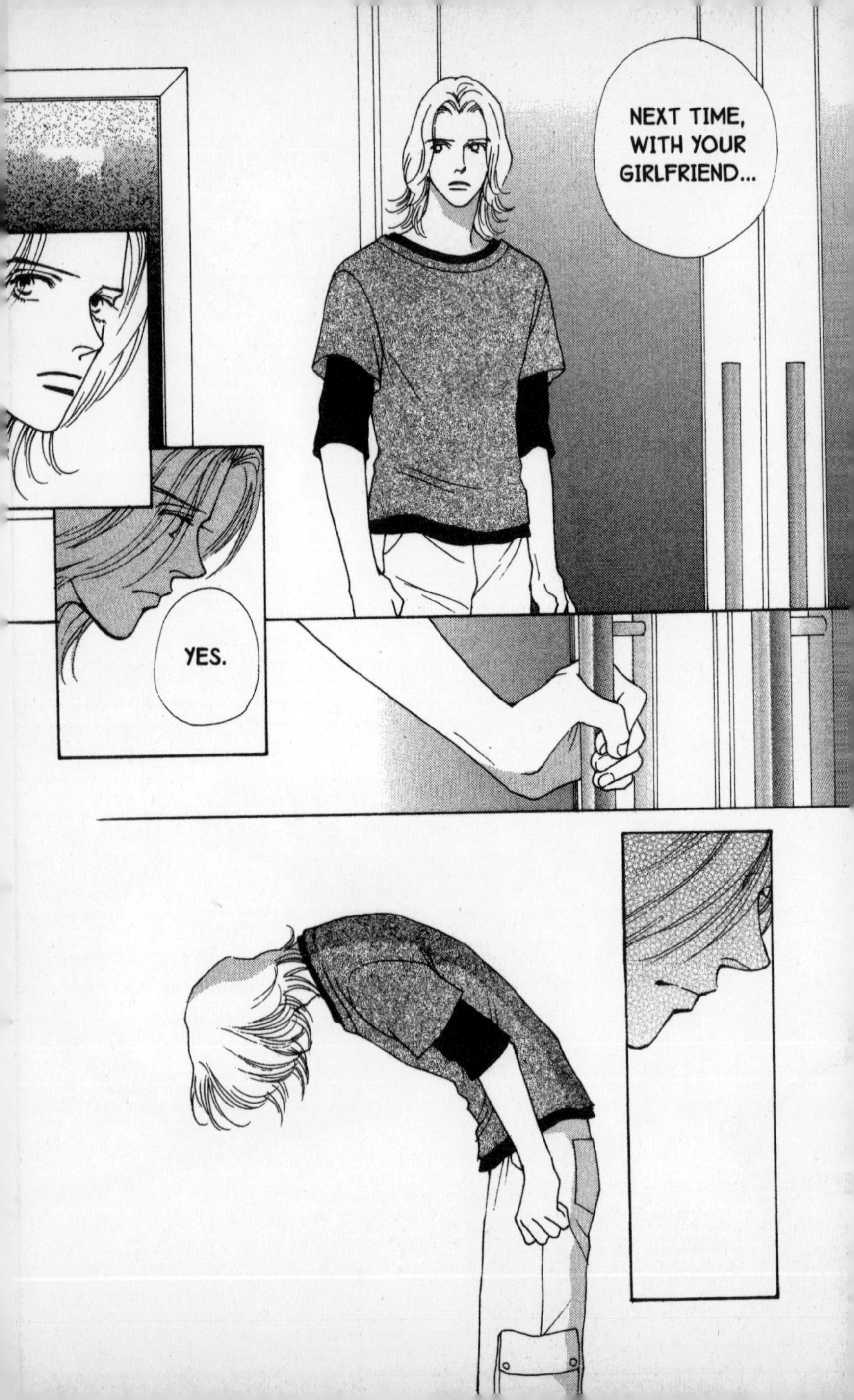
NEXT TIME, WITH YOUR GIRLFRIEND...
YES.

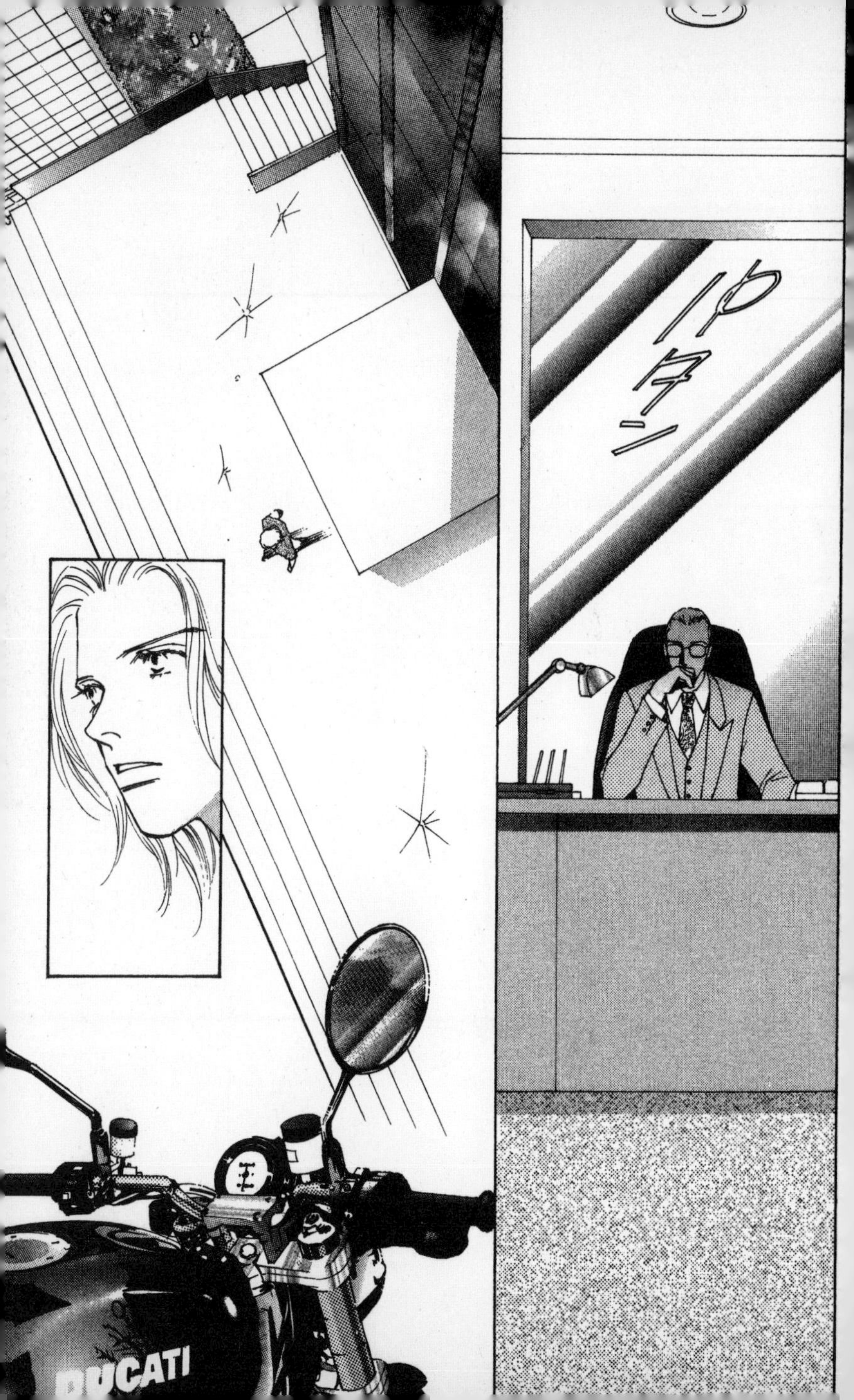
パタン
DUCATI

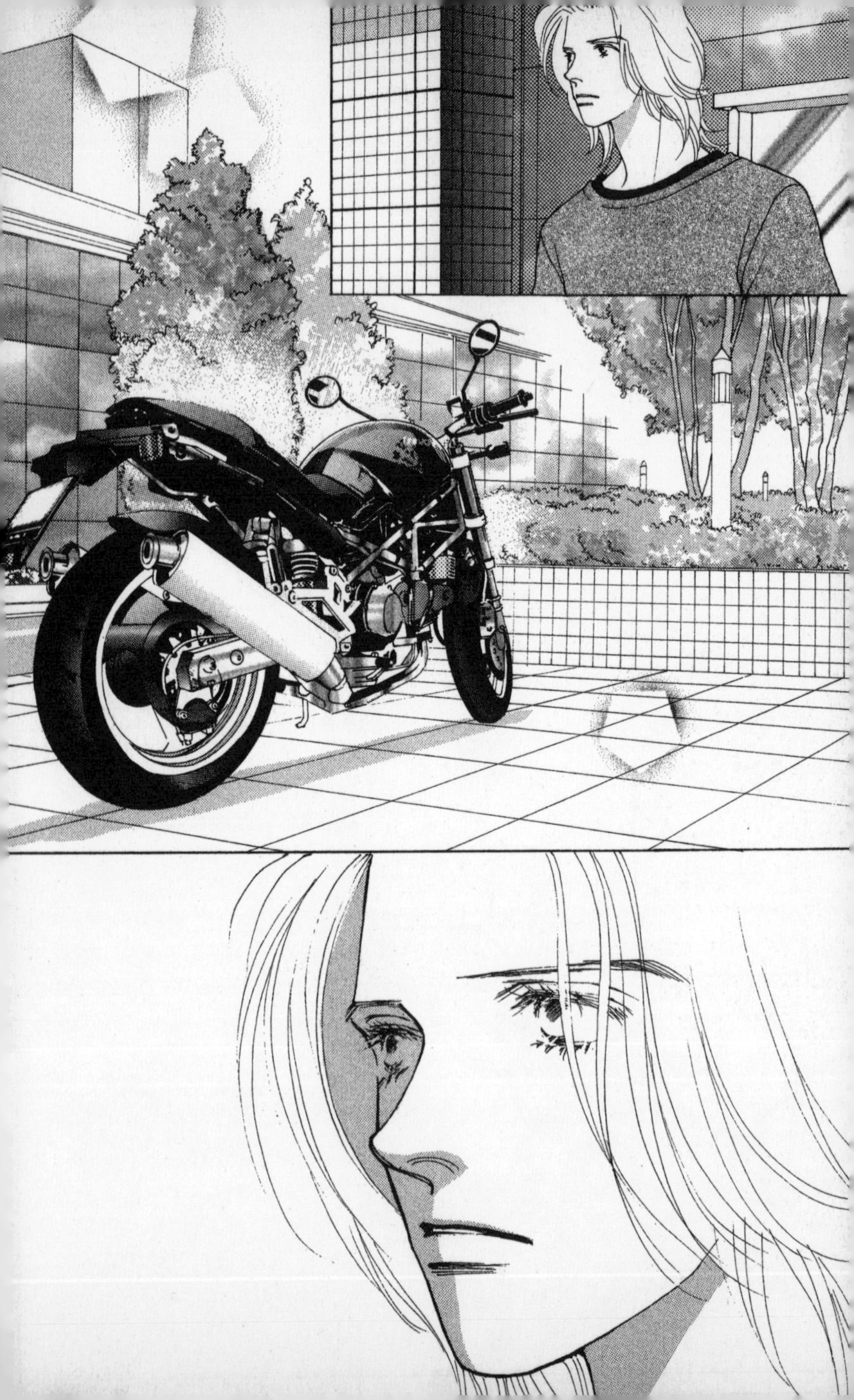

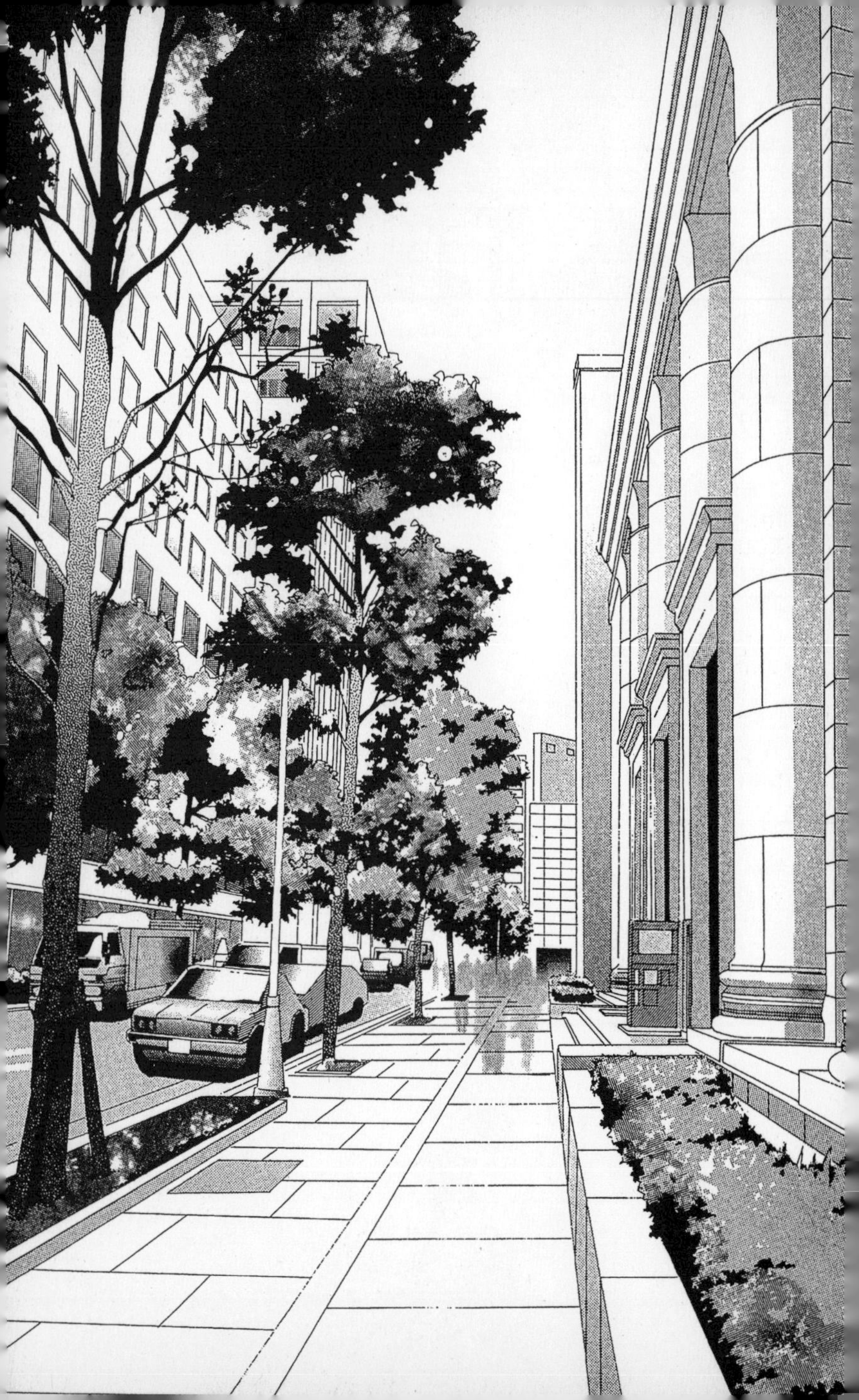

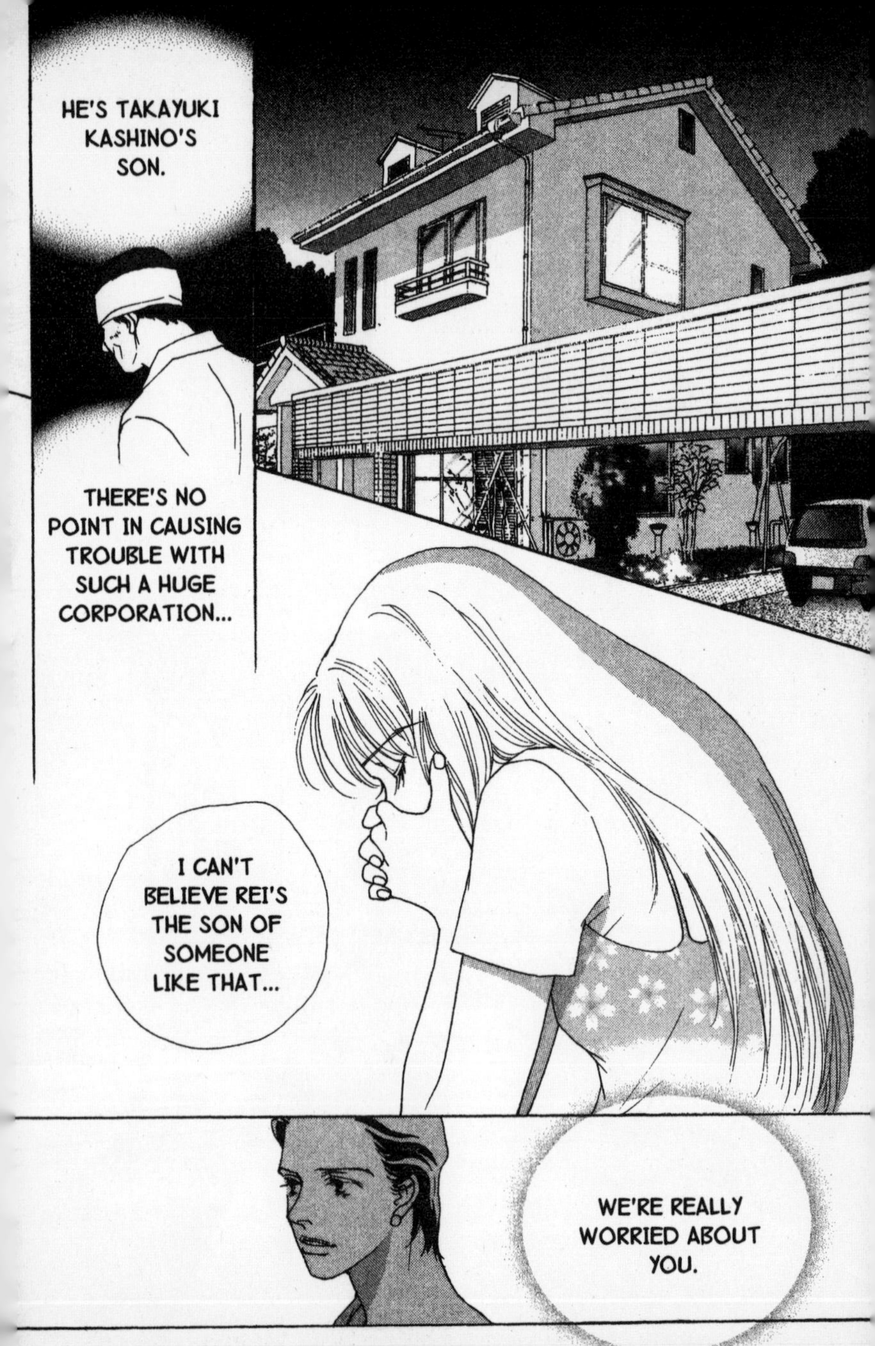
HE'S TAKAYUKI KASHINO'S SON.
THERE'S NO POINT IN CAUSING TROUBLE WITH SUCH A HUGE CORPORATION...
I CAN'T BELIEVE REI'S THE SON OF SOMEONE LIKE THAT...
WE'RE REALLY WORRIED ABOUT YOU.

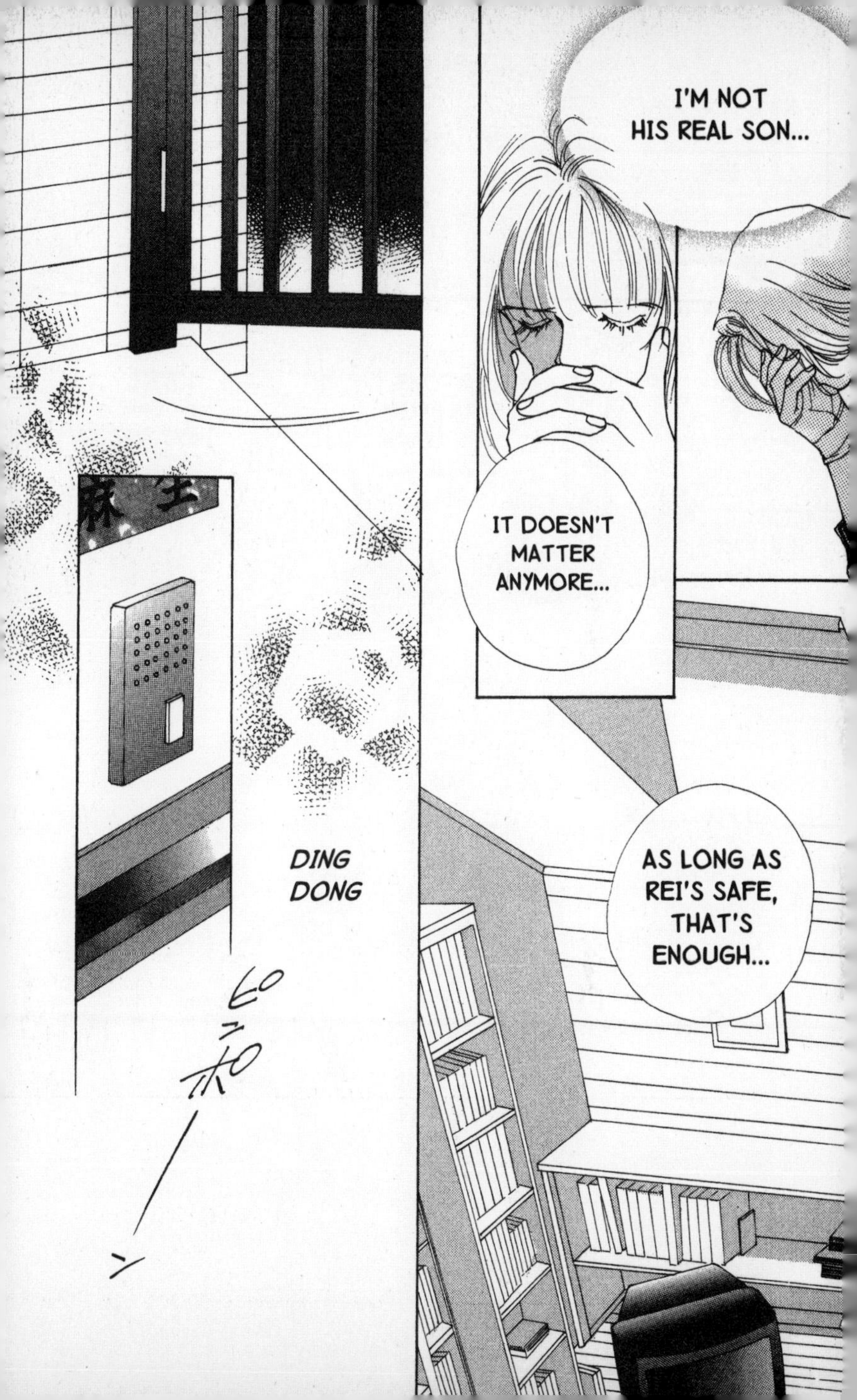
I'M NOT HIS REAL SON...
IT DOESN'T MATTER ANYMORE...
AS LONG AS REI'S SAFE, THAT'S ENOUGH...
麻生
DING DONG
ピンポーン

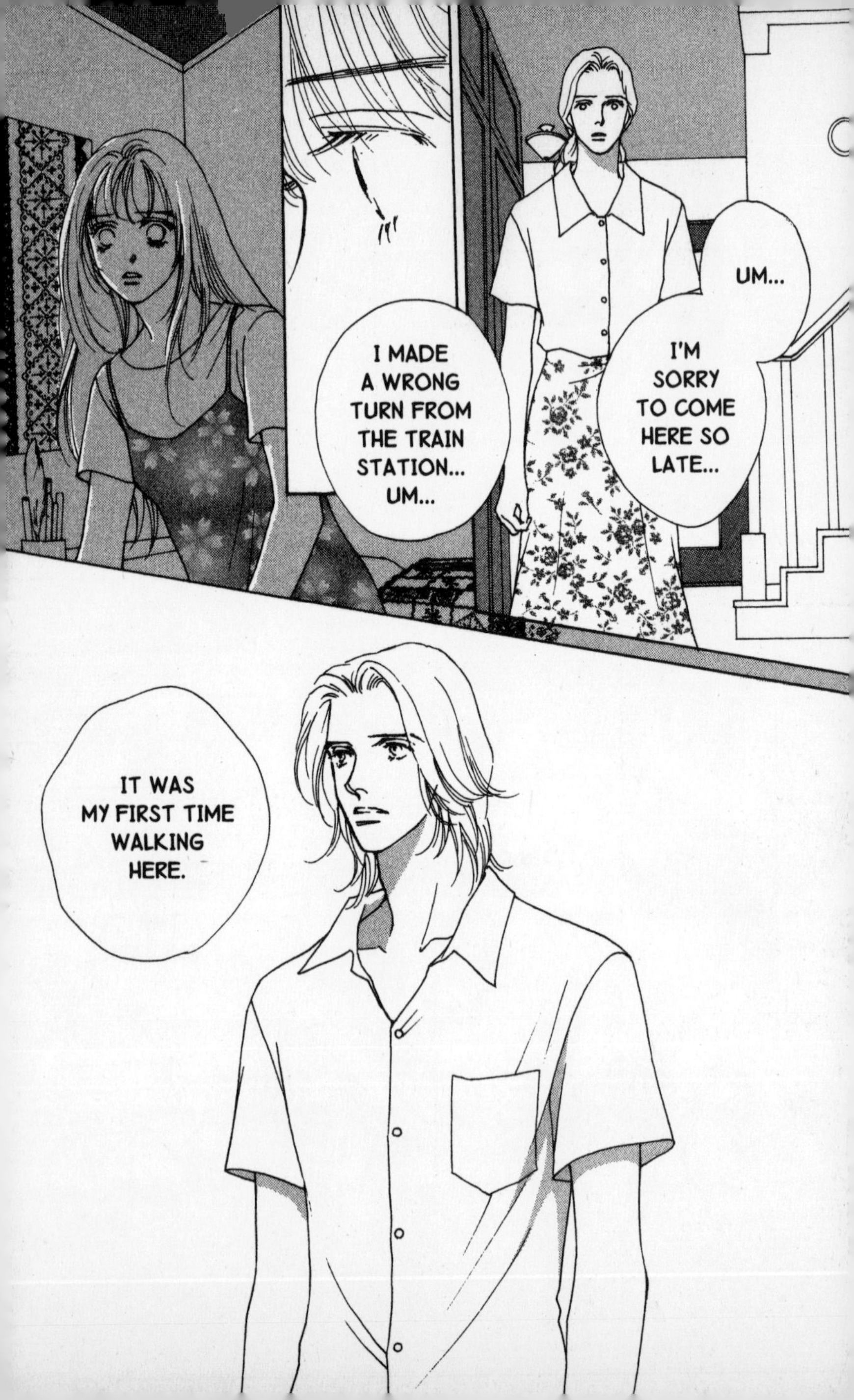
UM...
I'M SORRY TO COME HERE SO LATE...
I MADE A WRONG TURN FROM THE TRAIN STATION... UM...
IT WAS MY FIRST TIME WALKING HERE.

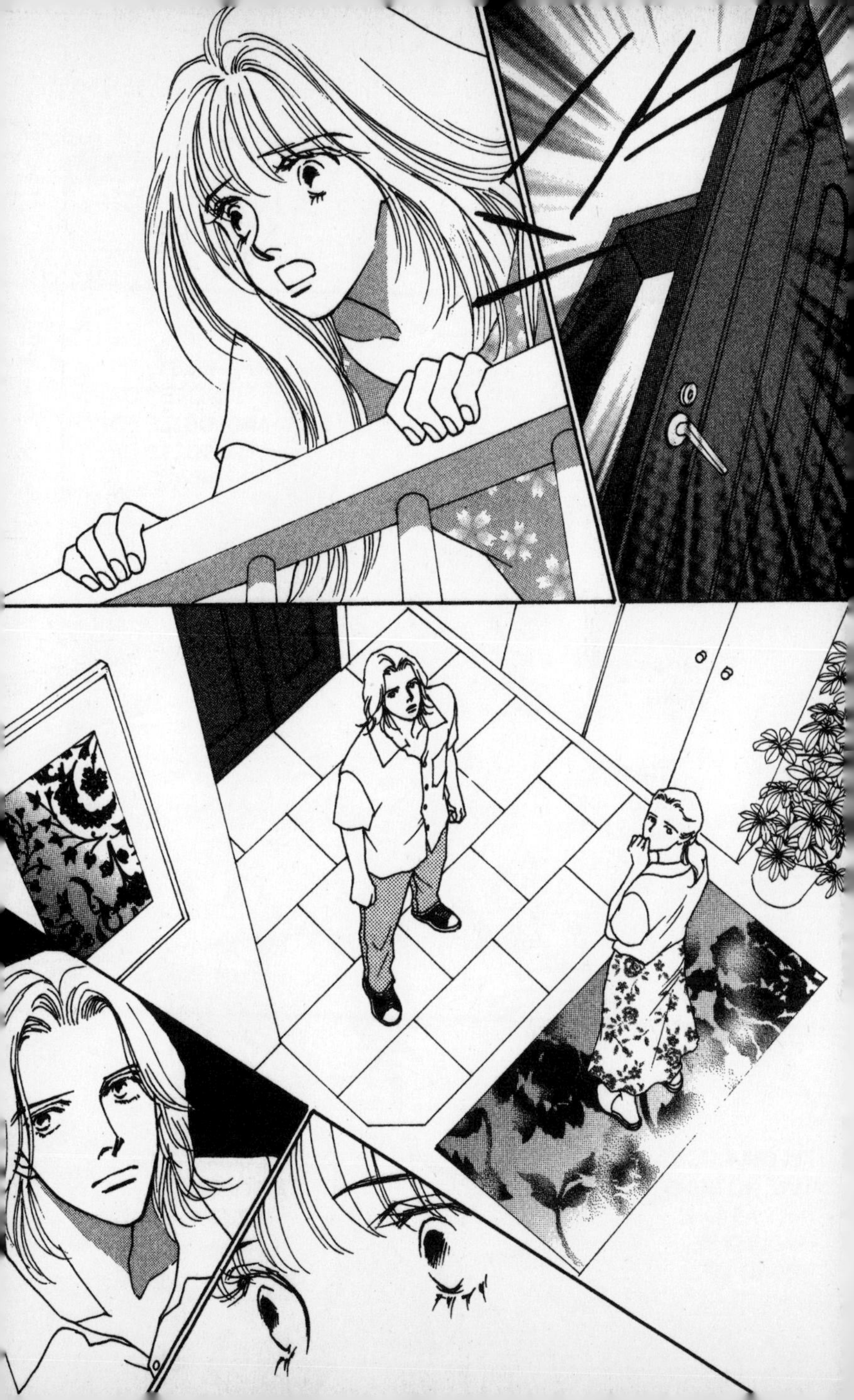

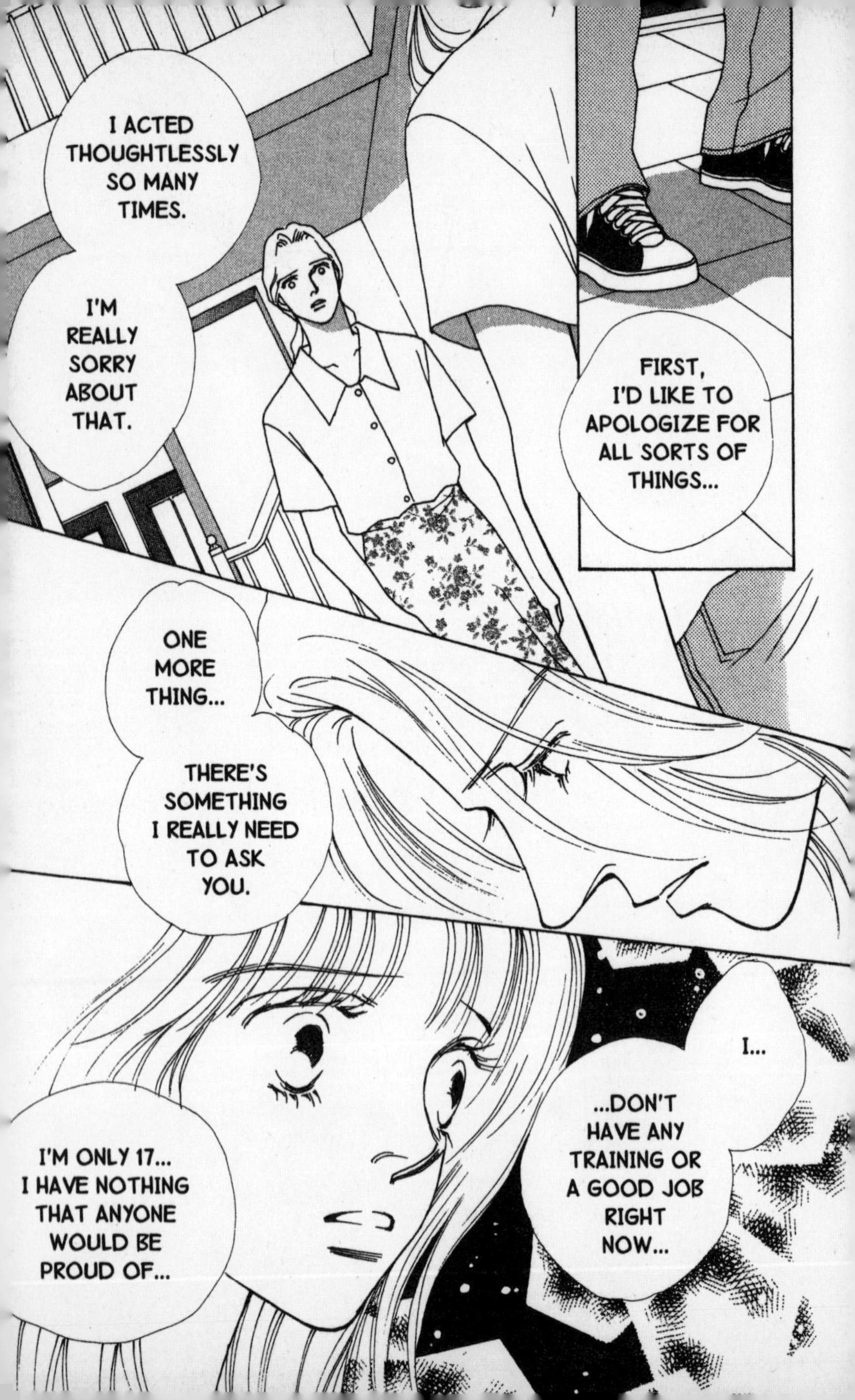
FIRST, I'D LIKE TO APOLOGIZE FOR ALL SORTS OF THINGS...
I ACTED THOUGHTLESSLY SO MANY TIMES.
I'M REALLY SORRY ABOUT THAT.
ONE MORE THING...
THERE'S SOMETHING I REALLY NEED TO ASK YOU.
I...
...DON'T HAVE ANY TRAINING OR A GOOD JOB RIGHT NOW...
I'M ONLY 17... I HAVE NOTHING THAT ANYONE WOULD BE PROUD OF...

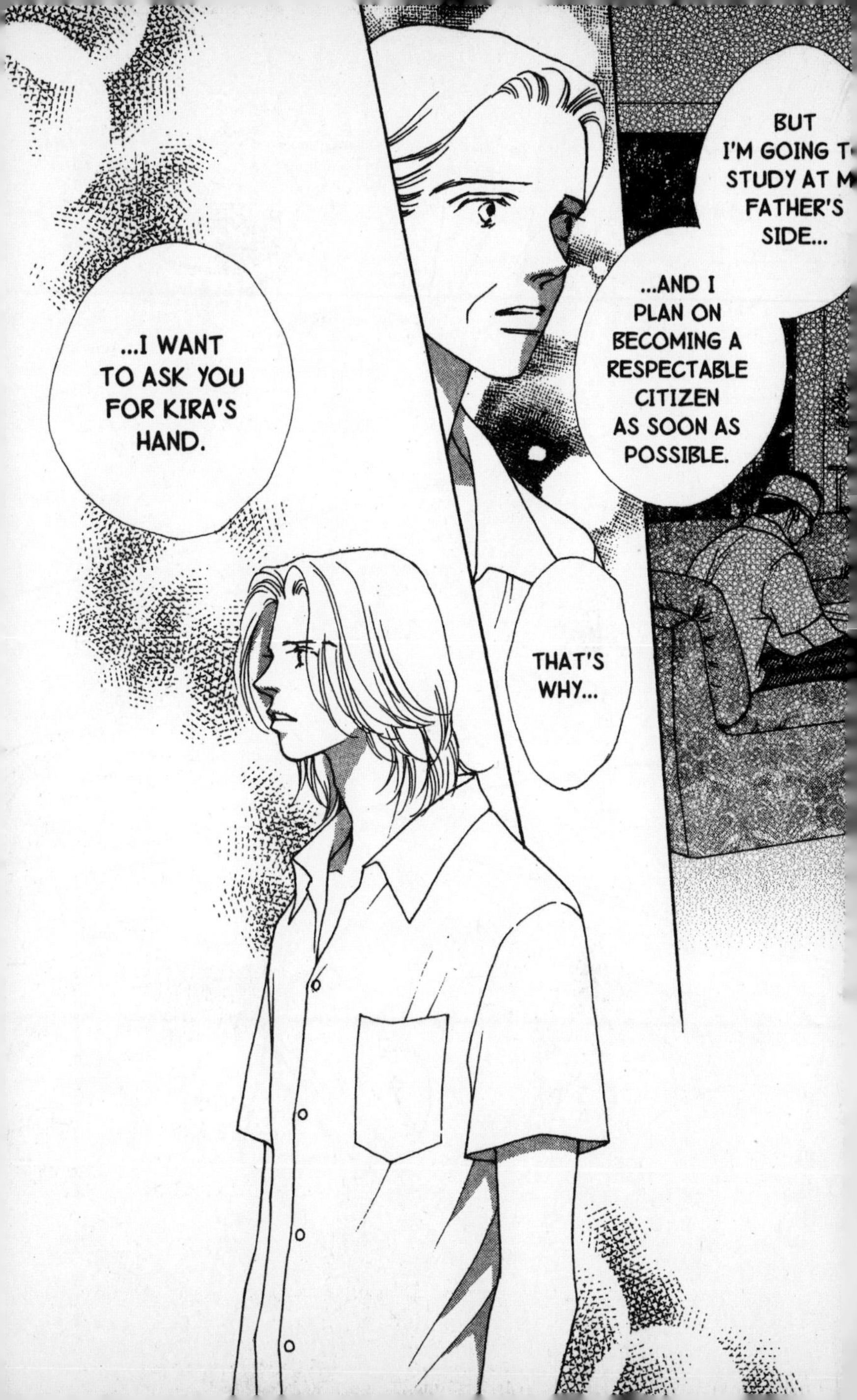
BUT I'M GOING T STUDY AT M FATHER'S SIDE...
...AND I PLAN ON BECOMING A RESPECTABLE CITIZEN AS SOON AS POSSIBLE.
THAT'S WHY...
...I WANT TO ASK YOU FOR KIRA'S HAND.

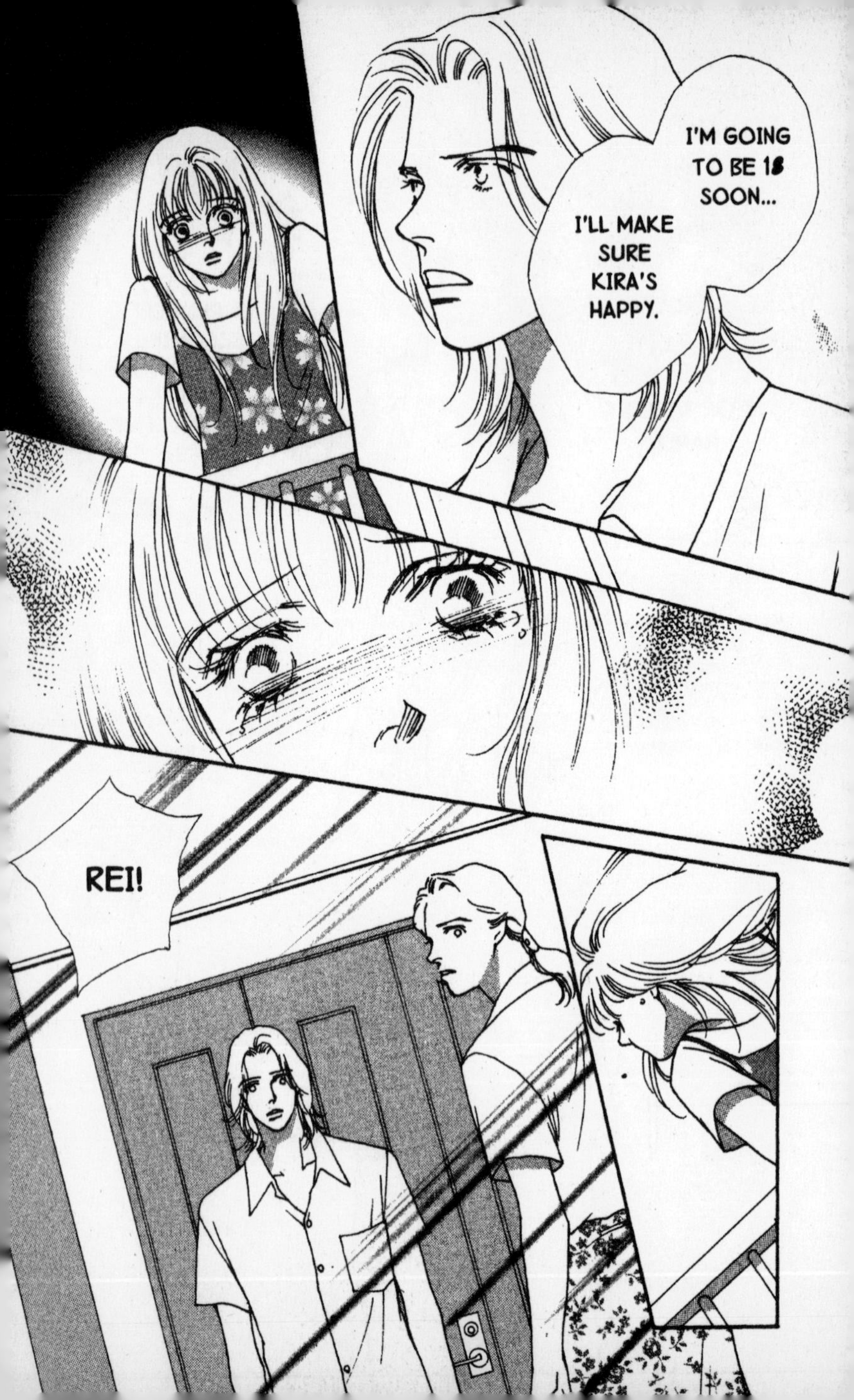
I'M GOING TO BE 18 SOON...
I'LL MAKE SURE KIRA'S HAPPY.
REI!

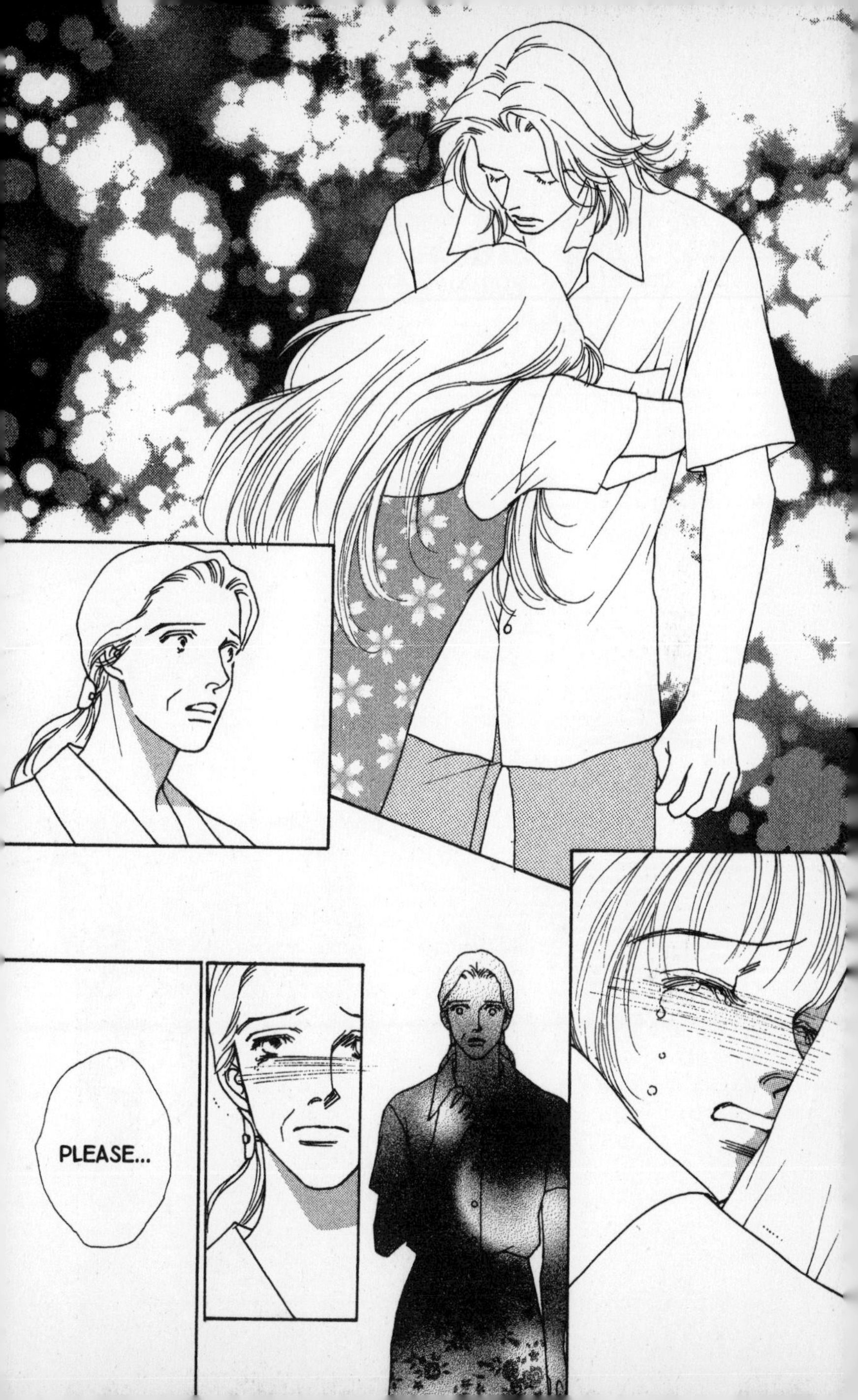
PLEASE...

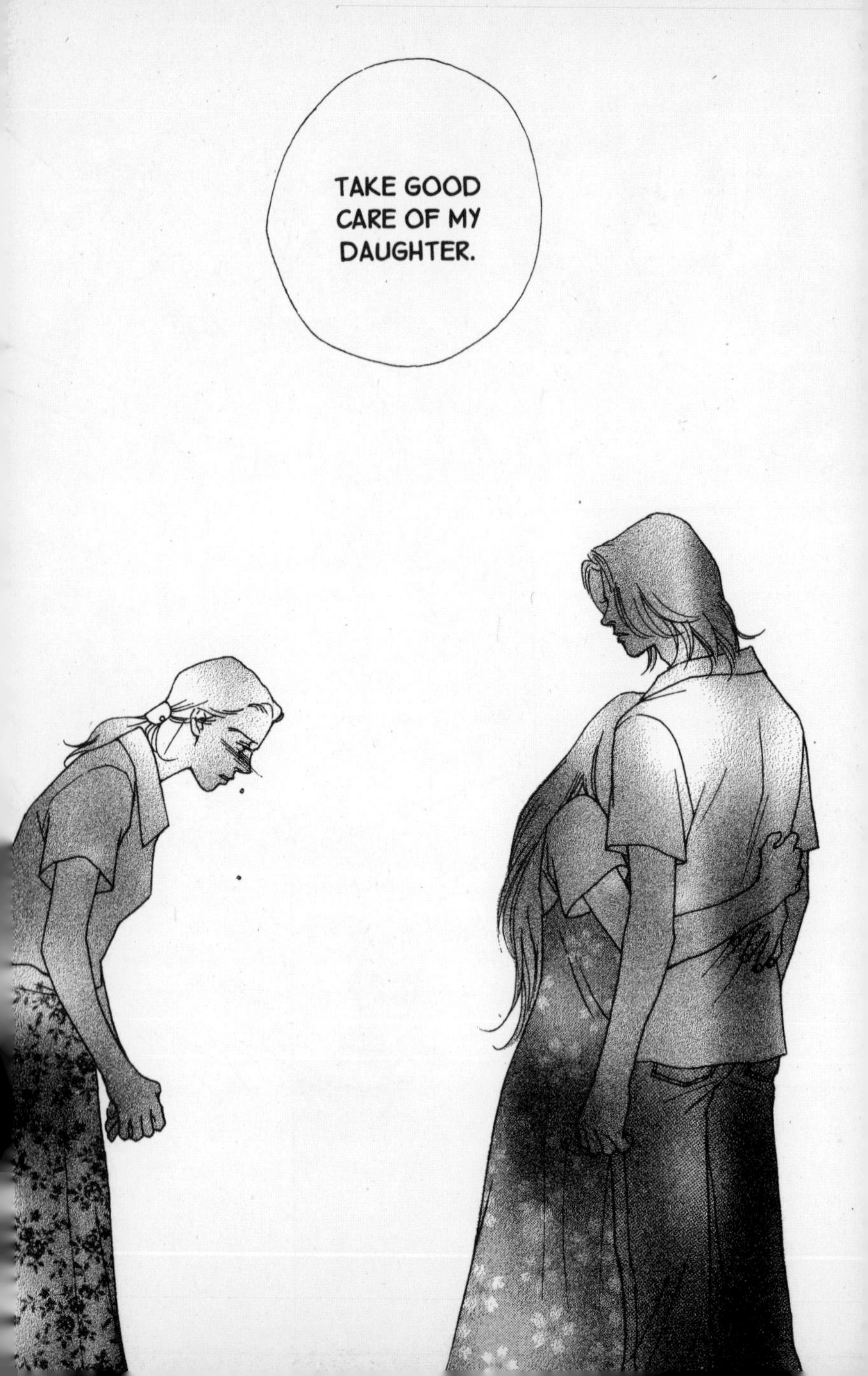
TAKE GOOD CARE OF MY DAUGHTER.

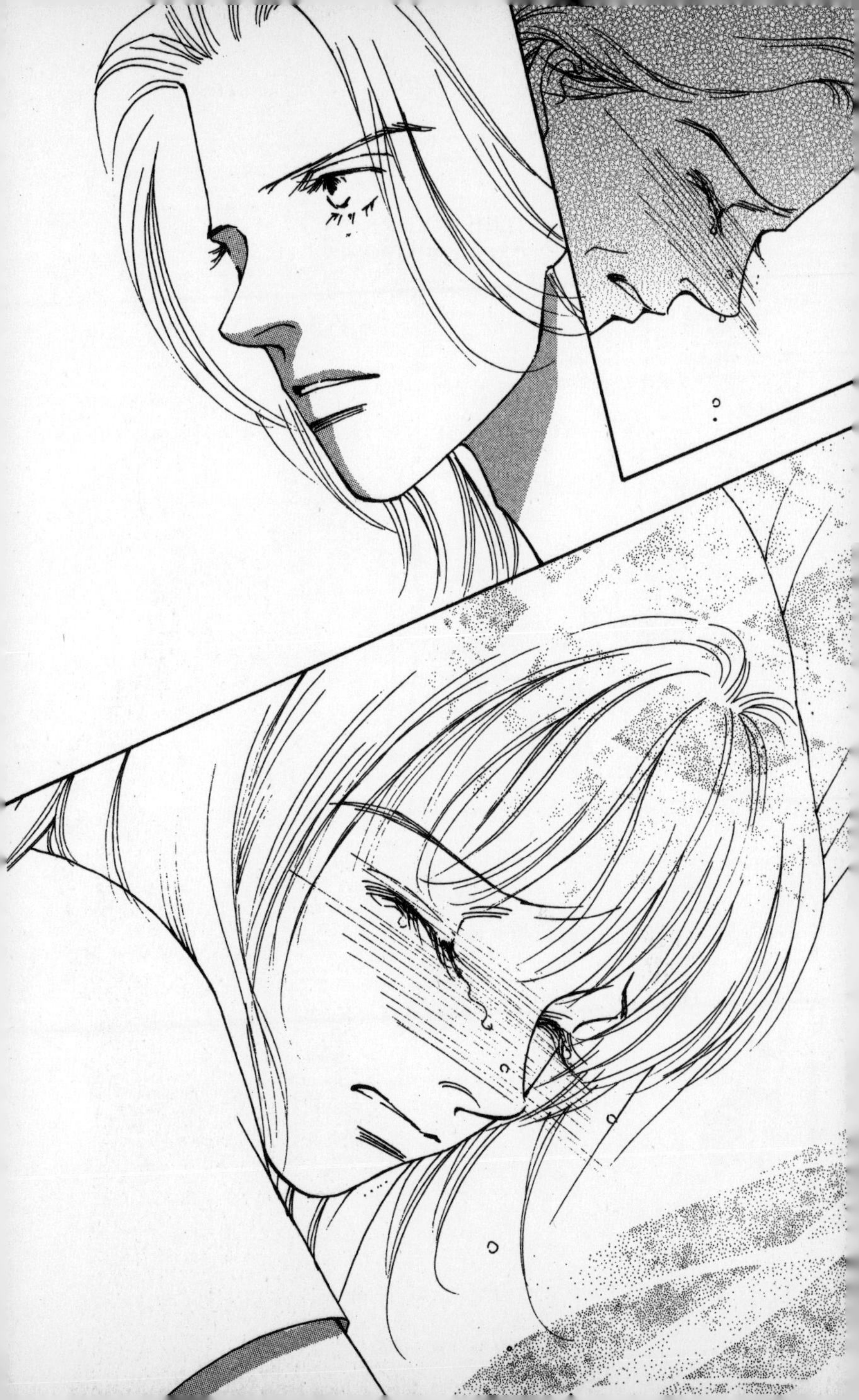

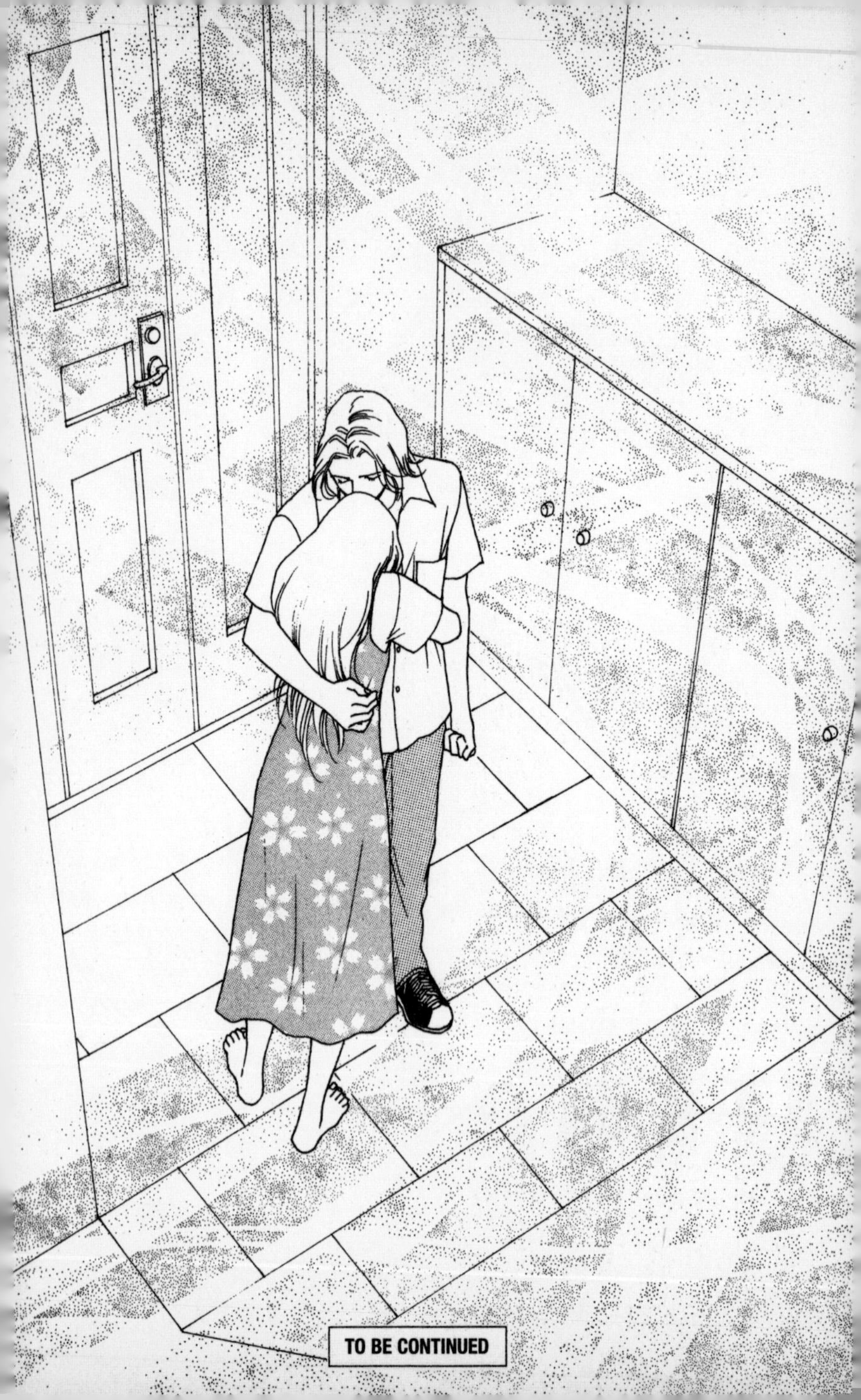
TO BE CONTINUED

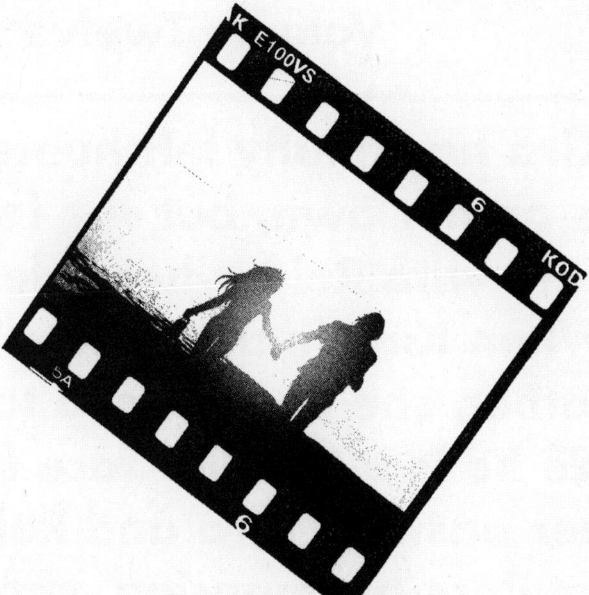
K E100VS
6
KOD
5A
6

MARS

Coming Soon...

MARS

Volume Twelve

Kira has finally left home and is on her own, but she feels safe with Rei by her side. When Kira finally meets Rei's father, she is surprised to realize he is a familiar face from her past. As Kira and Rei explore his mansion, shocking family secrets are revealed. As Rei grapples to cope with the unearthed memories of his past, Rei leans on Kira for some much-needed support.

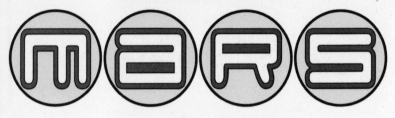

★★ SANA'S STAGE
KODOCHA

Sana Kurata:
part student, part TV star
and always on center-stage!

Take one popular, young actress used to getting her way.
Add a handful of ruthless bullies, some humorous twists,
and a plastic toy hammer, and you've got the recipe for
one crazy story.

Graphic Novels
In Stores Now.

TOKYOPOP

STOP!

This is the back of the book.
You wouldn't want to spoil a great ending!

This book is printed "manga-style," in the authentic Japanese right-to-left format. Since none of the artwork has been flipped or altered, readers get to experience the story just as the creator intended. You've been asking for it, so TOKYOPOP® delivered: authentic, hot-off-the-press, and far more fun!

DIRECTIONS

If this is your first time reading manga-style, here's a quick guide to help you understand how it works.

It's easy... just start in the top right panel and follow the numbers. Have fun, and look for more 100% authentic manga from TOKYOPOP®!